TOWNS, REGIONS AND INDUSTRIES

MANCHESTER
1824

Manchester University Press

Towns, regions and industries

Urban and industrial change in the Midlands,
c. 1700–1840

EDITED BY
JON STOBART AND NEIL RAVEN

MANCHESTER UNIVERSITY PRESS
Manchester and New York

distributed exclusively in the USA by Palgrave

Published by Manchester University Press
Oxford Road, Manchester M13 9NR, UK
and Room 400, 175 Fifth Avenue, New York, NY 10010, USA
www.manchesteruniversitypress.co.uk

Distributed exclusively in the USA by
Palgrave, 175 Fifth Avenue, New York, NY 10010, USA

Distributed exclusively in Canada by
UBC Press, University of British Columbia, 2029 West Mall,
Vancouver, BC, Canada V6T 1Z2

British Library Cataloguing-in-Publication Data
A catalogue record for this book is available from the British Library

Library of Congress Cataloging-in-Publication Data applied for

ISBN   0 7190 7086 4 *hardback*
EAN   978 0 7190 7086 0

First published 2005

13 12 11 10 09 08 07 06 05   10 9 8 7 6 5 4 3 2 1

Typeset by Carnegie Publishing Ltd, Lancaster
Printed in Great Britain
by CPI, Bath

Contents

List of figures   *page* vii

List of tables   viii

List of contributors   x

Preface   xiii

List of abbreviations   xiv

 1 Introduction: industrialisation and urbanisation in a regional
    context *Jon Stobart and Neil Raven*   1

Part I The Midlands: an industrial region

 2 Industrial and urban change in the Midlands: a regional survey
    Neil Raven and Tristram Hooley   23

 3 Industrialisation and the service economy *Andrew Hann*   42

 4 Industry, investment and consumption: urban women in
    the Midlands *Christine Wiskin*   62

 5 Networks and hinterlands: transport in the Midlands
    Neil Raven and Jon Stobart   80

 6 Towns and industries: the changing character of manufacturing
    towns *Barrie Trinder*   102

Part II Industrialisation and Midlands towns

 7 New towns of the industrial coalfields: Burslem and
    West Bromwich *Jon Stobart and Barrie Trinder*   121

 8 Industrialisation and social change: Wolverhampton transformed,
    1700–1840 *John Smith*   134

9 Industrial and urban growth in Nottingham, 1680–1840
   Joyce Ellis   147

10 Elite networking and the formation of an industrial small town:
   Loughborough, 1700–1840 *Peter Clark*   161

11 On the margins of industrialisation: Lichfield *Leonard Schwarz* 176

Part III The wider world: regional development in comparative context

12 National and international trade and the Midlands economy
   Malcolm Wanklyn   193

13 The growth of urban industrial regions: Belgian developments in
   comparative perspective, 1750–1850 *Hilde Greefs, Bruno Blondé
   and Peter Clark*   210

14 Towns, industries and regions: a European perspective on
   theoretical and practical relationships *Steve King*   228

Bibliography   246

Index   267

Figures

2.1 The surveyed towns of the Midlands   *page* 25

2.2 The industrial towns of the Midlands, *c.* 1790   31

5.1 Pickford's canal and carrier network, 1834   88

5.2 Customers of John and Thomas Wedgwood of Burslem,
Stoke-on-Trent, 1755–77   97

11.1 Shop tax per capita, 1785: percentage of mean for Worcestershire,
Warwickshire and Staffordshire   184

11.2 Sex ratios by age (females per 100 males) in Staffordshire
and selected towns, 1841   185

11.3 Staffordshire turnpike trusts: income per mile, 1837–40   187

Tables

3.1 Population per service provider in Midlands towns,
1790s and 1840s   *page* 44

3.2 The composition of the service sector in Midlands towns,
1790s and 1840s   47

3.3 Number of assessed shops and population per shop in selected
Worcestershire and Warwickshire towns, 1785   50

3.4 Number of shops and population per shop in selected
Worcestershire and Warwickshire towns, 1797–99 and 1842 51

3.5 Proportions of towns containing each retail category,
1790s and 1840s   53

3.6 Changing balance between different retail categories,
1748–1840s   56

3.7 Variation in the retail profiles of different types of town,
1790s and 1840s   57

4.1 Female advertisers in Midlands towns, 1797–1842: businesswomen
advertisers as percentage of all business advertisers   65

4.2 Occupations of females in Midlands towns, 1790s and 1842 67

5.1 Carrier services from principal transport centres in the Midlands,
1835   84

5.2 Carrier services from Leicestershire, Nottinghamshire and Black
Country towns, 1835   85

5.3 Services from the principal coaching centres of the Midlands,
1835   90

5.4 Extra-regional towns served by the coaches operating from
Midlands towns, 1835   92

5.5 The main thoroughfare towns of the Midlands, 1835   93

7.1 Population totals for Burslem and West Bromwich, 1738–1901   124

9.1 Populations of the fastest-growing towns in Nottinghamshire,
      1660s–1841   157

10.1 Principal occupations in Loughborough, 1811   169

10.2 Occupations of Loughborough bridgemasters and feoffees,
      1780–1840   171

11.1 Coach and carrier connections per week from Lichfield, 1834
      (excluding mail)   179

11.2 Occupations of males in Lichfield, 1747–1851   181

11.3 Principal male manufacturing occupations in Lichfield,
      1747–1851   182

13.1 The populations of the ten most important urban centres
      in Belgium, 1784–1900   222

Contributors

Bruno Blondé is Research Professor at the University of Antwerp. His publications cover the social stratification of sixteenth-century towns, eighteenth-century urban networks and small towns, the history of consumption and material culture in the Southern Netherlands during the seventeenth and eighteenth centuries.

Peter Clark is Professor of European Urban History at the University of Helsinki. He has written and edited numerous books on British and European towns. Recent publications include, P. Clark, ed., *Cambridge Urban History of Britain, Volume 2: 1540–1840* (Cambridge University Press, 2000) and *British Clubs and Societies 1580–1800: The Origins of an Associational World* (Oxford University Press, 2000). He is currently writing a book on the European City for Oxford University Press.

Joyce Ellis is Senior Lecturer in History at the University of Nottingham. Her research has focused on a range of topics in urban and regional development in the long eighteenth century. Recent publications include, *The Georgian Town 1680–1840* (Palgrave, 2001); 'The "Black Indies": economic development of Newcastle c. 1700–1840', in R. Colls and B. Lancaster (eds), *Newcastle upon Tyne. A Modern History* (Phillimore, 2001); and 'Comparison, competition and civic identity in eighteenth-century England', *Urban History*, 30 (2003).

Hilde Greefs is Assistant in History at the University of Antwerp. She recently defended her thesis on the business elite in the port-city of Antwerp during the first decades of the nineteenth century, after the reopening of the river Scheldt to maritime trade. She has also worked and published on migration, retailing and social life in Antwerp.

Andrew Hann is Honorary Research Fellow at the Centre for Urban History, University of Leicester. His main research interests lie in the history of retailing and consumption, with particular emphasis on the geographies of shop provision. Recent publications include, 'Retail provision and the county town: a comparative study of Nottingham and Shrewsbury, 1785–1842', in

E. Lord (ed.) *The English County Town, 1780–1910* (University of Leicester, 2004) and, with Jon Stobart, 'Retailing revolution in the eighteenth century: a regional approach', *Business History*, 46 (2004).

Tristram Hooley is an educational developer specialising in e-learning at the University of Leicester. He has worked as a project worker in the East Midlands Oral History Archive and as a researcher at the Centre for Urban History. He has published on oral history, the culture and politics of Second World War Britain and contemporary social movements. He teaches and produces educational materials on cultural history, transferable skills and the pedagogic use of information technology.

Steve King is Head of the Department of History at Oxford Brookes University and Director of the Wellcome Trust Centre for Health, Medicine and Society. His research focuses mainly around the issues of eighteenth- and nineteenth-century industrialisation, poverty and welfare, historical demography and medical history. His most recent publications are *The Poor in England 1700–1850: An Economy of Makeshifts*, edited with A. Tomkins (Manchester University Press, 2003), and *Being Poor in Modern Europe: Historical Perspectives 1800–1950*, edited with A. Gestrich (Peter Lang, 2004).

Neil Raven is Honorary Visiting Fellow at the Centre for Urban History, University of Leicester, and Regional Co-ordinator for the Higher Education Summer School programme at the East Midlands Universities Association. His research interests are in the small towns and county capitals of the late eighteenth and nineteenth centuries. Recent publications include, 'The English county town during the Industrial Revolution: Chelmsford, c. 1790–1840', *Urban History*, 30 (2003) and *Work, Women and Wages in England 1600–1850*, edited with P. Lane and K. Snell (Boydell and Brewer, 2004).

Leonard Schwarz is Senior Lecturer in the Department of Modern History at Birmingham University. His published work is on English urban history in the long eighteenth century, most recently the employment of servants and the nature of 'leisure towns'. Recent publications include *Experiencing Wages. Social and Cultural Aspects of Wage Forms in Europe since 1500*, jointly edited with P. Scholliers (Berghahn, 2004) and 'Residential leisure towns in England towards the end of the eighteenth century', *Urban History*, 27 (2000), a theme that he is currently developing with Jon Stobart.

John Smith is Honorary Research Fellow at the Centre for Urban History, University of Leicester. His PhD was on the Governance of Wolverhampton 1848–88. He has published on various aspects of Urban History, particularly in relation to Victorian cities. Current research interests include crime and corruption in nineteenth- and twentieth-century public life.

Jon Stobart is Reader in Historical Geography at Coventry University. His research on urban and regional development in eighteenth and nineteenth-century Britain covers a variety of topics, from the role of towns in proto-industrialisation, to the spatial and social relationship between shopping and leisure. Recent publications include, *The First Industrial Region: NW England, 1700–1760* (Manchester University Press, 2004) and 'Leisure and shopping in the small towns of Georgian England', *Journal of Urban History*, 31:3 (2005).

Barrie Trinder is a freelance writer and lecturer whose teaching career has included fifteen years at the Ironbridge Institute (University of Birmingham) and, more recently, five years at University College Northampton. He has published extensively on the process of industrialisation, both regionally and nationally, and on market towns, and edited the *Blackwell Encyclopaedia of Industrial Archaeology* (1992). His current concerns include the growth of suburbs in provincial towns and the social history of river navigations.

Malcolm Wanklyn is Emeritus Professor of Regional History at the University of Wolverhampton. He was head of department for many years and managed the Port Book Programme. His principal publications on trade on the river Severn in Early Modern England are to be found in *Midland History* (1988, 1993) and the *Economic History Review* (1996). He is currently engaged with his first love, the military history of the English Civil War, with one book being published in 2004 (Pearsons) and another in 2005. He then intends to complete a major publication on the significance of the river trade to the English economy.

Christine Wiskin has taught modern history at the University of Warwick and University of Gloucestershire, specialising in women's and gender history. She is a contributor to the *New Dictionary of National Biography* and has written widely on English businesswomen in the eighteenth century.

Preface

This book owes its origin to the project on Urban and Industrial Change in the Midlands, 1700–1840, funded by The Leverhulme Trust, 1998–2001. The project team, led by Peter Clark along with Jon Stobart, Barrie Trinder, Leonard Schwarz and Neil Raven, brought together scholars from five universities across the Midlands and was based at the Centre for Urban History, University of Leicester. The project drew on long-standing research networks at the Centre, not least with scholars associated with *The Cambridge Urban History of Britain*, volume 2: *1540–1840* (Cambridge, 2000). Research for the *Cambridge Urban History* had helped to expose our continuing lack of knowledge about many aspects of the relationship between industrialisation and urbanisation, especially in the English Midlands – one of the cradles of European industrial transformation. It raised questions about the differential growth of towns, their varied experience of industrialisation, the role of endogenous and exogenous growth stimuli, the links between manufacturing and service economies and the relational nature of urban-industrial development. To answer these questions the project organised a programme of regional, local and thematic research. Research officers on the project were initially Penny Lane and then Andrew Hann, and we are grateful to them both for their work. New data sets were created and earlier ones held at the Centre were adapted. These included those relating to the project on Small Towns in England 1600–1850 funded by the Economic and Social Research Council (1985–93) and the European Urbanisation (EUROCIT) project funded by the European Union (1993–96). In addition to the research programme, the project organised two workshops at Leicester which attracted a wide audience and excellent contributions from academics outside the project. Revised versions of papers by Joyce Ellis and Malcolm Wanklyn have been included in this volume.

The editors are grateful to The Leverhulme Trust for funding of the project, and to Kate Crispin, Ralph Weedon, Richard Rodger and other staff at the Centre for Urban History for their help and support. We would also like to thank Stuart Gill for drawing the maps.

Abbreviations

BPP   British Parliamentary Papers
PRO   Public Record Office
RO   Record Office
UBD   *Universal British Directory*
VCH   *Victoria County History*

Introduction: industrialisation and urbanisation in a regional context

Jon Stobart and Neil Raven

Industrialisation: national and regional perspectives

When he coined the phrase in 1884, Arnold Toynbee saw the industrial revolution as the beginning of the modern age; a unique turning point in British economic and social history. It was a time when the old order was 'suddenly broken in pieces by the mighty blows of the steam engine and the power loom'.[1] The emphasis was on sudden and dramatic change engendered by technological innovation, but spreading to influence all aspects of society. Yet later historians, from Clapham onwards, have taken a seemingly more sober and considered view. In re-evaluating the industrial revolution, they have concluded that it was a time when 'less happened, less dramatically than was once thought'.[2] Early work uncovered considerable evidence that industrial expansion, organisational development and technological change were widespread before the middle of the eighteenth century.[3] This called into question the unique nature of the industrial revolution: the dramatic events of the period 1760–1840 appeared to be simply another peak on the long-term waves of economic innovation and development. More recently, this gradualist perspective has been reinforced by ideas of proto-industrial development and by the advent of econometric studies of industrial change. The former emphasise links and continuities between modern manufacturing industry and earlier systems of domestic production, both being seen as different stages in the long-term march of capitalist production.[4] The latter, in their painstaking reconstructions of occupational structure, capital formation, gross domestic product growth and so on, have questioned the extent of structural change or growth in the British economy before 1840.[5] Combining these with dual economy models that distinguish a dynamic 'revolutionised' and slow-growing 'traditional' sector of the economy, we almost inevitably reach the conclusion that 'much of England in 1850 was not very strikingly different from that of 1750'.[6]

This macro-economic gradualist approach has been important in emphasising the long-term causes and processes of industrialisation, many of which are examined in detail in the various contributions to this volume. However, it misses the importance of geography as a cause as well as an outcome of historical change. People were, of course, the ultimate agents of change; but their relationships with one another and with their economic, social and natural environments occurred in and through space as well as time. A growing recognition that industrialisation was a spatially uneven process has had three major impacts on the ways in which we study British economic growth.[7] First, drawing on the geographical tradition of regional analysis and the growing influence of proto-industrialisation, the object of analysis has changed from the nation to the region and locality. Predictably, growth regions have excited most interest, with studies of the Lancashire and Yorkshire textile districts being especially numerous; but others have explored the margins of industrialisation or areas of industrial decline.[8] Second, in narrowing the spatial focus, the ontological and methodological emphasis has switched from statistical analysis of nationally available indicators, and towards a fuller understanding of the complex make-up of regions and localities. This reflects a so-called 'cultural turn', which emphasises that the economic is firmly embedded in the cultural and that both have related and particular geographies.[9] Regions, then, are more than simply 'convenient box[es] into which masses of descriptive material is stuffed';[10] differences in their social, cultural and geographical constitution were important in moulding economic development. Third, in exploring more fully the causes and consequences of local and regional differentiation, there has been a growing attempt to theorise industrialisation. Drawing on new approaches to present-day economic processes and a redefinition of local history as more theoretically informed micro-history, this has highlighted the ways in which local and regional geographies shaped and were shaped by the timing and nature of economic development.[11] As Massey argues, a space economy comprises 'layers of investment' laid down during earlier production and consumption regimes. Thus, patterns and processes of industrial development are shaped by an already established socio-economic landscape.[12] These spatial arrangements are then cemented by cumulative causation that concentrates development into favoured core areas (*inter alia*, by forming pools of skilled labour, attracting subsidiary trades and focusing flows of information and capital) and creates a downward spiral of dis-investment and out-migration from the economic periphery.[13] This kind of spatial path-dependence underlined the nascent regional industrialisation of Britain. Yet these are, in reality, secondary causal factors, reinforcing already established patterns. How do we understand the underlying basis of local and regional development?

When it emerged in the early 1970s, proto-industrialisation was seen as offering both a coherent analytical framework for the analysis of regional development and a compelling logic for the kind of historical-geographical lock-in later theorised by Krugman and others.[14] The theory argued that regional growth and differentiation were the result of the 'rapid growth of traditionally organised but market oriented principally rural industry'.[15] This development was stimulated by the necessity to supplement household income because of under-employment on the land; it led to 'full' industrialisation via increasingly centralised control of production. However, whilst they were extensively applied in Europe – a point discussed by King in Chapter 14 – the highly variable nature of the pre-conditions, pathways and growth trajectories of proto-industrial regions have led most studies of British industrialisation to question its usefulness in explaining the processes and geographies of industrial development.[16] Instead, emphasis has been placed on the factors underpinning local economic growth. Some have argued the fundamental importance of natural resources in determining the growth and geography of British industrialisation. Coleman viewed these as the key to regional development, whilst Wrigley argued that it was coal that 'made possible the vast increase in individual productivity which was so striking a feature of the industrial revolution'.[17] In the present volume, Trinder and Stobart see the impact of coal and other mineral resources as central to urban-industrial growth in the Potteries and the Black Country (Chapter 7). In contrast, Trinder, Clark and Ellis follow Ogilvie, Hudson and others in highlighting the significance of the social and institutional environment in shaping access to resources and investment capital; developing diverse and complementary manufactures; and creating robust credit networks.[18] They were thus critical in shaping the timing and extent of major industrial development in places such as Nottingham and Loughborough (see Chapters 9 and 10) and in the smaller manufacturing enterprises seen across the region's lesser towns (Chapter 6).

Natural and human resources of this type can be viewed collectively as location factors. Traditional approaches to industrial location attempt to model the relative 'pull' of these different factors to determine the economically optimal location for a factory, firm or industry.[19] Arguing that many of these are fixed in space – at least in the medium term – regional growth theorists highlight three 'locational constants': resource sites, transport nodes and towns.[20] These drew together national and regional space economies and stimulated growth in particular localities. The explanatory power of these factors in understanding the geography and growth of industrialisation in the Midlands is explored in Chapters 2 and 5, but four points are worthy of note at this stage. The first is the extent to which these were, indeed, constants in the eighteenth and early nineteenth centuries. As the economy switched from an organic to a mineral base, the nature and location of key resources changed and with them the requirements and geography of the transport system. From being areal and diffuse, production became punctiform and concentrated: road transport was complemented and, to an extent, superseded by canals.[21] The second is that, notwithstanding these changes, both transport nodes and resources were increasingly focused onto towns, thus effectively collapsing all three constants onto the same urban locations. Third, as Lepetit argues, towns were much more than concentrations of a group of production factors: the passive arenas in which processes took place. Rather, they were active agents in economic, social and cultural change, creating favourable conditions for investment and growth.[22] Fourth, towns were not isolated points of activity, but were linked together by flows of goods, capital, information and people. The importance of these interactions is apparent from the analysis of Midlands transport networks presented by Raven and Stobart in Chapter 5 and from the external linkages that shaped the fortunes of the individual towns examined in Part II. These make it abundantly clear that we must not only recognise the town as an active agent in industrial change, but should also move away from static notions of location factors, and towards dynamic understandings of the urban network as a functioning system. Over twenty-five years ago, Wrigley suggested that important insights into modernisation could be gained from a fuller understanding of the relationship between towns and economic development.[23] To achieve this, we must re-examine our approach to urban history.

Urbanisation: economic and cultural approaches

English urban growth was one of the phenomena of the eighteenth century.[24] The near-fourfold increase in urban population between the Restoration and the start of the nineteenth century took the country from the margins to the very heart of European urbanisation.[25] Of course, not all towns were growing rapidly: selective growth made this 'one of the most mutable periods in English urban history', and transformed the urban hierarchy and geography of the country.[26] Growth was concentrated into the coalfield areas of the Midlands, the North-West, west Yorkshire and central Scotland, where Birmingham, Liverpool, Manchester, Leeds and Glasgow all grew strongly as regional centres, surrounded by networks of generally buoyant smaller towns. Yet, as Langton argues, the broad causal processes which underlay growth in, and geographical and hierarchical change of, the urban system are both well established and widely debated.[27]

At a national level, there is an orthodoxy of industrial-based urbanisation which meshes closely with the narrative of change presented in many economic histories. From Daunton through Corfield and Wrigley, to more recent studies by Clark and Langton, manufacturing industry has remained central to explanations of urban growth.[28] The focusing of manufacturing onto key resource, skill or transport sites caused urban settlements to grow up rapidly around them. Growth in the English Midlands and the North is explained in terms of their coal-based industrialisation, whilst the slow growth of many southern towns is seen as reflecting the lack of widespread and sustained industrial development in what remained principally agricultural counties.[29] Following this argument, the urban-industrial link is thus clear in spatial and causal terms. Industry was both necessary and sufficient for urban growth: 'new manufacturing' towns outstripped their more established neighbours, which were often spectators in the industrialisation process. As a result, urban history has long suffered from a traditional stereotyping between 'old' stagnant or slow-growth centres and 'new' dynamic places. Recent studies, however, have begun to question this convention, suggesting that many towns were growing strongly before the rapid industrial growth of the early nineteenth century and that they were closely involved in shaping and forming that economic change.[30] Towns have long been recognised as 'nurseries of skill' and often acted as finishing or co-ordinating centres for rural manufacturing.[31] These activities engendered economic prosperity and demographic growth in established towns such as Wolverhampton and Leeds, and burgeoning centres like Blackburn and Bradford. They also served to encourage local and regional development and to structure this around such urban centres.[32]

If the direction of the causal link between industrialisation and urbanisation has been challenged in this way, the two processes are largely uncoupled in a parallel analytical framework in which factors such as leisure, trade and consumption are seen as central to a process of urbanisation that was complex, multi-faceted and diverse. Here social and cultural change replaces economic growth as the driving force behind urban development. Borsay in particular has argued for a post-Restoration urban renaissance driven by societal shifts occurring in response to the rise of the middling sorts.[33] This comprised the (re)definition and expansion of polite society, and the emergence of a new urban material culture encompassing consumer goods and urban spaces. Politeness can be seen as a mechanism for aligning the growing commercial middle class with the social elite by conveying upper-class values and manners to a wider elite whose only qualification was money. It broke down barriers between the aristocracy and gentry and a new middling sort of professionals and tradesmen. Great emphasis was placed on appearance and behaviour, so that, as Defoe remarked, 'anything that looks like a gentleman, has an address agreeable, and behaves with decency and good manners, may single out whom he pleases'.[34] Appropriate genteel manners and behaviour were honed through social interaction, civility and sociability often being seen as the defining aspects of politeness. These were linked to new forms of social activities and institutions – including assemblies, promenades and theatres, but also libraries, coffee houses and shops – which allowed people to meet and converse with one another in appropriate social and physical settings. Politeness was thus closely linked with the new material culture, encompassing both the urban environment and tangible possessions.[35] Borsay details the 'improvements' made to towns across the country in terms of civic institutions, commercialised leisure, domestic and public architecture and the physical environment.[36] These combined with a growing consumerism in which the acquisition and ownership of particular goods helped to define politeness and respectability for individuals and groups. Sometimes consumption was driven by fashion and more arguably emulation, sometimes by the desire for novelty, and always by the social and cultural utility of the item.[37]

These transformations had a strong gender dimension, with women seen as central to processes of consumption and to many of the practices and pursuits that helped to define politeness.[38] This point, amongst others, is reiterated in the analysis offered by Christine Wiskin in Chapter 4, which argues that women were important in supplying as well as consuming novel goods. However, both consumption and politeness also had an important urban component. Towns provided access to the key consumer goods and formed the setting for new forms of behaviour, making them arenas of public consumption. Moreover, urban life informed the social and cultural norms of polite society. Indeed, for contemporaries and historians alike, 'politeness was a quintessentially urban concept': good company and good manners were to be found in towns and in urban institutions.[39] That said, not all towns were seen as being equally polite, and there were certainly differences in the provision of goods and services between different places. Stobart and Trinder demonstrate in Chapter 7 that industrial towns often had a growing range of leisure facilities and shops, whilst Smith argues persuasively for the coalescence of a new and polite elite in late-eighteenth-century Wolverhampton (see Chapter 8). But the consensus at the time was that commercial and manufacturing functions were essentially incompatible: new money was spent without taste, and industrial towns were too full of the lower orders to be truly polite.[40] In contrast, resorts and county towns – places often at the margins of industrialisation – prospered on their image as centres of polite leisure and taste. Their renaissance was based on their ability to service the needs of the middling sorts from the town itself, from the surrounding countryside and from neighbouring centres: a point explored by Schwarz in his analysis of Lichfield

(Chapter 11).[41] These rural-urban and inter-urban linkages were underpinned by the growing specialisation of towns, a point noted in Chapter 2, where Raven and Hooley highlight the increasing differentiation between urban economies. This brought with it greater interdependence and interaction of the kind that Ellis notes occurring between Nottingham and its region (see Chapter 9).

This inter-urban linkaging can be theorised in spatial-systematic or social-institutional terms. The former accommodates a 'whole range of towns and their territories in a system of interrelations',[42] and looks to understand urban growth, and its relationship with industrial, social or cultural change, in terms of the structure and dynamics of that system. This, in turn, focuses attention on the ways in which urban systems are organised and how growth stimuli are transmitted through the network of towns. Attempts to model the hierarchical and spatial structure of urban systems are often traced back to Christaller.[43] He argued that the size and importance of a town or central place was effectively governed by demand from its hinterland, including the countryside and smaller towns. Central places would be arranged in a regular isometric lattice, hinterlands for smaller places being nested within those for larger centres. This produces a rigid hierarchical and spatial arrangement with growth stimuli passing up the hierarchy from one 'order' of settlement to the next. Although some commentators reject this model as rigid and static,[44] it remains useful in conceptualising the spatial and hierarchical arrangement of service functions and is drawn on by Hann in his assessment of retailing in the Midlands (see Chapter 3). What Christaller's vision of central places cannot accommodate is the type of specialisation that prompted much inter-urban interaction: the emergence of ports, resorts, administrative centres and, of course, a huge variety of manufacturing towns. More useful here is Simmons's industrial specialisation model: one stage in his larger theorisation of the long-term development of the North American urban system.[45] In this, growth is based on the agglomeration advantages accruing as particular functions concentrate into certain places. However, local specialisation is dependent upon intra-regional trade and the effective integration of the space economy, a point highlighted by Wanklyn's emphasis on the importance of internal as well as overseas markets for industrial goods manufactured in the Midlands (see Chapter 12). In such a system, growth in one place will help to stimulate development elsewhere, making patterns of development highly sensitive to transport, business and personal networks. The first of these is explored by Raven and Stobart in Chapter 5, where they underline the significance of relative size, but also specialisation, in determining a town's position in the regional transport system. The second two types of network return us to the role of social-institutional linkages in drawing centres together.

As part of so-called 'new institutional' economics, personal networks are increasingly recognised as an important form of business as well as spatial integration. Indeed, they were central to Putnam's notion of social capital as a means of improving economic performance.[46] Networks offered a range of benefits to their members and, by association, the places in which they resided. First, they formed business opportunities: links to supplies, markets, capital and information. It is in this light that Raven and Stobart examine the importance of the business network of John and Thomas Wedgwood to their pottery manufacture (Chapter 5). Greefs, Blondé and Clark take a similar approach in exploring the role of key industrialists in the development of textile manufacturing in Flanders and Brabant (Chapter 13). Second, interaction and association within the network helped to create a common value system based on shared attitudes, goals and aspirations. This established trust and mutual regard amongst members of the network and facilitated joint action, of the type noted by Clark in the actions of the town trust in investing in the urban infrastructure of Loughborough (see Chapter 10). It also helped to bind together urban elites, such as the gentlemen merchants in Leeds and Liverpool or the traders and manufacturers in Wolverhampton (see Chapter 8).[47] Third, notions of reputation and trust led to the 'information benefits' of networks. Knowing where information could be acquired and the extent to which it can be relied upon as full and accurate is vital to all business: it reduces transaction costs resulting from uncertainty.[48] What cemented these networks were close personal relationships sustained by regular contact. These were often built on family ties, but, as various contributions to this volume clearly demonstrate, they also coalesced around urban institutions including improvement commissions, town trusts and cathedral deaneries.

A regional approach to urban-industrial development

The region offers a context in which industrial and urban histories can be brought together in a way that ties them closely with the English experience of socio-economic change in the eighteenth and early nineteenth centuries. Linking urban and industrial development at a regional level allows us to theorise these processes in new ways and creates a useful dialogue between the national and the local. As we have seen, regions were not simply inert containers for historical-geographical processes: they had their own economic, social and spatial structure. Thus, the regional space was not only the 'geographical site of action', but also the 'social possibility for engagement in action'.[49] In other words, the geography of the region shaped the nature, pace and timing of economic and social change. This moves the question of geography beyond simplistic conceptions of scale and pattern (the outcomes of economic and social change) and reconstitutes it as a functioning and meaningful context for urban and industrial growth: a key causal factor in change. We argued above that regional geography can be conceived in terms of location constants, but is more usefully theorised in terms of dynamic networks of towns and individuals. These systems helped to communicate growth stimuli through the regional space, their structure determining and reflecting local specialisation and the spatiality of development. Importantly, this systematic perspective facilitates comparative and relational analysis: it focuses attention beyond the particular and the individual, and onto the inter-relations and interactions between people, towns and regions. This approach is central to the analysis of industrial specialisation, service provision, business activities and transport networks offered in Part I of this volume, but it also informs the analyses of individual towns offered in Part II. However, it becomes most explicit in Part III, where the Midlands region is set into a broader relational and comparative framework. As Wanklyn demonstrates in Chapter 12, the trading links tying the Midlands economy to the wider world were essential in stimulating regional industrial and urban development: their communication through networks of roads, canals and towns helped to determine the local impact of such trade. The examination of industrial development in Belgium offered by Greefs, Blondé and Clark (Chapter 13) affords useful parallels with the Midlands experience. Like the Midlands, this region contained a number of distinct but related economies as well as towns that provided specialist service functions to neighbouring industrial districts. Whilst such comparisons might seem contrived and trivial, they are important for three main reasons. First, at a basic level, they allow us to judge the extent to which the experience in one region reflects that seen elsewhere. This focuses attention onto questions of the universality or uniqueness of place and process.[50] Second, and more specifically, they make it possible to identify those factors of universal importance in shaping development processes. Transport, urban and personal networks, for instance, appear as constants in the structuring of urban-industrial change; the availability of natural resources and links with agricultural change appear more variable.[51] Third, they highlight the way in which similar structures and institutions could have very different effects in different cultural or political contexts. The obvious example here is the way in which the civic magistracies of many continental towns were relatively closed with 'conservative' economic agendas. Those in the Midlands – even in towns at the margins of industrialisation (such as Lichfield) – were extremely energetic in promoting economic development.

It is surprising, then, that this kind of approach remains rare: there continues to be a strong tendency to divorce towns from their regional context, hinterlands and neighbours. The 1960s and 1970s saw considerable interest in urban hierarchies and systems, especially in North America, but these generally made little attempt to establish links between urban and economic processes and structures.[52] This makes it difficult to explore the linkages between urban growth and wider economic change, especially industrialisation. In the 1980s several innovative studies focused on the development of this interrelationship in various British regions. Most notable here is Noble's analysis of east Yorkshire in which she highlighted the importance of location, nodality, externality, competition and economic structure in determining local growth within the regional urban system.[53] However, the focus here, as in other studies from this time, was on small towns and/or regions at the periphery of industrial development. Apart from Stobart's recent analysis of north-west England, there are no regional analyses which attempt to explore the complexities of urban growth within an industrialising region.[54] This volume begins to fill this significant gap in the history and historiography of urban-industrial change by offering a detailed, systematic and thematic analysis of the English Midlands.

The term 'Midlands' can be traced back to at least the seventeenth century, one of the first references appearing in Ogilby's *Britannia* (1698) and alluding to the chief trade of Bristol deriving from the Midland Counties, along with Wales.[55] Yet, whilst the Midlands is widely recognised as a spatial and social entity, it is far from easy to delimit its boundaries. In devising their series of regional histories, Cuncliff and Hey acknowledged that 'regional identities are imprecise' and that 'any attempt to define a region must be somewhat arbitrary'.[56] This problem is particularly severe in the case of the Midlands. The standard definition, based upon geography, is supplied by the *Oxford English Dictionary*. This refers to the counties located 'south of the Humber and Mersey and north of the Thames, with the exception of Norfolk, Suffolk, Essex, Middlesex, Hertfordshire, Gloucestershire, and the counties bordering on Wales'.[57] However, the extent to which economic and social trends conform to this area is a subject of much debate. Even amongst those historians who adopt a regional perspective for the Midlands, there is a noticeable lack of consensus over its boundaries. Although the counties are not identified, Langton's Midlands comprise the western constituents of England's middle counties but exclude north Staffordshire, which is considered a separate entity. Meanwhile, in examining the transition to the factory system in the Midlands, along with its subsequent decline, Chapman centred discussion on the counties of Staffordshire, Leicestershire, Northamptonshire, Warwickshire, Worcestershire, Lincolnshire, Shropshire, Nottinghamshire and Derbyshire. Within these counties, the cotton and worsted spinning industry was found to be 'an integrated manufacture'. Thus, excluded from this definition was the extensive parish of Glossop, which fell 'within the orbit of Manchester'.[58]

Although acknowledging that 'the historical midlands is a concept which is difficult to pin down', Dyer discusses the urban networks operating in the nine counties identified by Chapman, along with Rutland and Herefordshire.[59] Meanwhile one of the most extensive definitions is offered by the journal *Midland History*, which considers Dyer's eleven counties, along with Cambridgeshire, Oxfordshire, Hertfordshire, Huntingdonshire, Gloucestershire and Bedfordshire.

Thus historical commentators' definitions of the Midlands appear to be heavily influenced by the subject under examination, be it cultural and political activities, textile production, urban networks or the maximising of potential readership. Whilst this flexibility affords the opportunity to introduce a new definition, this volume seeks a close approximation with the Midlands considered by Chapman and Dyer. The urban economies and societies contained in the eight counties of Derbyshire, Leicestershire, Nottinghamshire, Rutland, Shropshire, Staffordshire, Worcestershire and Warwickshire will be the focus of this volume. As Dyer notes, natural upland features help determine the western and northern boundaries of this region, whilst the extent of London's 'primary commercial region' establishes its southern limits. However, Herefordshire was excluded from this classification because of its proximity to and association with central and southern Wales, and Northamptonshire because of the strengthening influence of the metropolis, whilst the perception of the Midlands as a landlocked area excluded Lincolnshire – always a problematic county in regional studies. This, however, should be deemed a working definition of one of the subtler of England's regions; the extent to which these eight counties shared urban economic and social characteristics will be determined in the analyses contained in the following chapters.

Structure and themes of the book

This book offers a detailed but wide-ranging analysis of urban-industrialisation in the Midlands and beyond. The various contributions are rooted in different disciplines and draw on a wealth of new empirical research. Through their varied perspectives, they emphasise the complex, multi-dimensional and often conditional relationship between urban and industrial change, highlighting in particular the link between socio-economic and spatial transformation. The book's overall focus on the region unites these contributions in a thematic and comparative framework, and provides the basis for a theoretically informed discussion of development processes. The varied causes, experiences and outcomes of industrialisation in Midland towns are thus related not only to their local and individual circumstances, but also to processes operating on a broader scale. Equally, the development and geography of industrial specialisms, retailing, transport services and so on are linked to one another and interpreted both in the context of the historiography of the Midlands and through spatial and development models.

To emphasise these various approaches and linkages, the book is structured in three sections. In the first, the region is treated as a whole, and various aspects of urban-industrial change are surveyed to outline and assess the general patterns and local variations in development. Each chapter takes an overtly comparative and relational approach, and explores how change in one place related to and influenced processes occurring elsewhere in the region. This focuses attention onto the ways in which internal/local and external/region-wide influences combined in different places to encourage or discourage economic activity and urban prosperity. It also prompts questions about the way in which the regional space economy was structured: what was the role of personal, business, transport and urban networks? Part II takes up these themes and aspects, and explores how development processes were played out in individual communities. There is a conscious attempt to survey a range of different 'types' of town – from *ab initio* coalfield towns, through established industrial centres, to places at the margins of industrialisation. However, rather than merely offer brief local histories, these studies focus on the ways in which local and regional stimuli combined in particular localities. They engage with important questions such as what it meant to be a town, the two-way relationship between industrialisation and social institutions and the role of elite groups in encouraging urban and industrial development, especially through their networking activities. The final part broadens the geographical and conceptual horizons of the analysis by placing the industrial and urban development of the Midlands into wider spatial and theoretical contexts. Again, the emphasis is on a relational and comparative approach. Here, attention focuses on the links which existed between developing regions and between growing industrial centres: the universality or uniqueness of place and process and the emergence of functional and conceptual regions. Ultimately, this part seeks to explore some of the fundamental questions about the interrelationships between urbanisation, industrialisation and regional development.

In Chapter 2, Raven and Hooley offer a systematic analysis of the urban and industrial geography of the Midlands. This reveals manufacturing as an integral part of the region's urban economies: one that witnessed growing levels of sophistication during the late eighteenth and early nineteenth centuries. Although much of this production was for local consumption, a number of the region's towns operated as industrial centres, manufacturing metalware, ceramics and textiles for distant markets. Whilst these included new towns, a number of settlements with long-established urban credentials also featured, amongst them old market towns and ancient county capitals. Moreover, the distribution of particular manufacturing activities amongst these settlements and the composition of associated trades suggests that towns played a key role in determining the character and fortunes of industry. In the following chapter, Hann examines the relationship between industrial growth and the development of urban services, focusing particularly on the retail sector. The evidence shows that rapidly growing industrial towns improved their service provision over time, but that the type rather than the size of town affords a better guide to levels of retail diversity, with county and market towns with industrial specialisms amongst the best provided. An important, although poorly documented, component in the service provision of Midlands towns were women like Ann Cresswell – a Wolverhampton bookseller and bookbinder who also sold stockings probably manufactured in the Nottingham region. Although the period under review saw female business proprietors clustered into an increasingly narrow range of trades, Wiskin shows that, as part of the family enterprise and as hired hands, women were active in the region's lace and metalware industries. Moreover, they played a vital role as investors in local businesses and in the region's developing transport network. It is the dynamics of this network which are captured by Raven and Stobart in their examination of road and water-borne services on the eve of the railway age. Birmingham emerges as the premier regional transport node, and a focal point for many extra-regional connections, but significant sub-regional variations are also identified. Carrier services formed a much denser network in the eastern Midlands, whilst in the west the tendency was for many more services to operate along the same routes. Differences in manufacturing organisation afford an explanation, with textiles and hosiery in the east Midlands relying upon outworkers and industrial production in the west involving 'high-intensity movements of goods and materials between specialised manufacturing centres'. Good communications were also important to the fortunes of towns not engaged in the region's industrial staples, and it is these towns that form the subject of Trinder's chapter. Here, manufacturing activities were to be found operating alongside traditional crafts and trades. Although supplying predominantly local markets, such activities could still be of considerable economic significance and, in the case of malting and tanning, conducted on a sizeable scale. Moreover, as the case of mechanical engineering witnessed, these activities could undergo significant developments during the industrial period.

The second part commences with Stobart's and Trinder's consideration of two new urban communities: the pottery town of Burslem and the metalware centre of West Bromwich. Both were transformed from small industrial villages to 'clearly identifiable towns'. Although their urban services initially lagged behind industrial and population expansion, provision quickened in the early nineteenth century, with both towns also acquiring an array of cultural facilities. By the close of the period each could claim a 'recognisable urban landscape'. Whilst external forces, noticeably transport, played an important role in facilitating this transformation, the other key influences varied. In West Bromwich, enclosure of the parish was significant in providing space for retailing and desirable middle-class residences; in Burslem, the conscious efforts of the local elite did much to promote civic development. In contrast to both of these cases, Smith explores the impact of industrialisation on the social institutions and geography of Wolverhampton, a town with long-established urban credentials. During the eighteenth and early nineteenth centuries it was 'transformed and greatly expanded' by metalware manufacture. With much of its population growth concentrated into a constrained area, the town experienced high mortality rates and a process of socio-spatial polarisation. Yet out of this morass arose a 'self-confident form of civic consciousness and pride' that, with the emergence of effective governmental machinery, led to a concerted campaign for municipal improvement. The analysis of Nottingham and the surrounding industrial districts offered by Ellis reveals that Nottingham does not fit 'the conventional model of the relationship between a textile town and its hinterland'. Instead, it formed an integral part of a 'wider and notably polycentric industrial region', comprising villages and small towns and involving complex flows of labour and capital. Yet Nottingham may well have exerted a decisive influence upon perceptions of the urban within this region. As environmental conditions visibly deteriorated in the town, associated settlements were re-classified as manufacturing villages, rather than towns. In the following chapter, Clark examines the role of Loughborough's elite in encouraging urban industrial development. Whilst externalities, most noticeably the construction of the Soar Navigation, were important in this transformation, it was the town trust that did much to facilitate change through its investment in the urban infrastructure, and by providing an 'institutional focus for entrepreneurial networking'. Conversely, Clark argues that the continuing prosperity of Loughborough's traditional marketing and agricultural sectors operated to contain the extent of industrialisation by presenting alternative opportunities for commercial investment. Towards the other end of the small-town industrial experience stood Lichfield. During this period, the Staffordshire town saw a decline in its manufacturing sector, principally the result of the decay of the leather industry. Yet Schwarz shows that Lichfield was able to handle marginalisation rather well. The growth of shopping and service functions suggests the maintenance of prosperity; an interpretation underpinned by continuing population growth. The explanation for this successful transition was the growth of local demand generated by agricultural expansion, a phenomenon likely to have been associated with rapid urban-industrialisation occurring in other parts of the region. Thus Lichfield may have been marginalised from this process, but it was in no way isolated from it.

Wanklyn opens the final part of this volume by tracing the markets for the industrial staples of the Midlands. Whilst coal and agricultural surpluses were retained largely within the region, to feed and fuel economic and industrial expansion, metalware, ceramics and textiles found their way onto more distant markets. North America and continental Europe were important destinations for the region's industrial products. Yet it is argued that industrial products were consumed at home – a finding that has considerable implications for the standard-of-living debate and the pessimistic stance on levels of domestic demand. Greefs, Blondé and Clark take up the question of how industrial and urban developments in the Midlands compared with those in other regions in Europe. Belgium affords a suitable comparison as the 'first nation on the continent to follow the modernising footsteps of the British economy'. From the industrial regions explored, the authors are able to draw out a number of factors driving industrialisation that were also shared by the Midlands, including transport, technological innovation and entrepreneurial leadership. However, they also highlight the importance of institutional factors and conservative urban economic agendas in limiting the urban component of industrialisation. A very different comparative approach is adopted in the final chapter when King explores the wealth of continental literature devoted to regional industrial history. In contrast to the 'English tradition', towns do not feature prominently in continental models of regional economic development. A discussion of these models offers a salient reminder of the need to adopt a critical approach to the role of towns and to explore alternative explanations of regional development. Yet it is equally feasible that differences in historiography may reflect differences in the 'actuality' of the British and continental regional experience and, therefore, to claim that the first industrial revolution was a distinctly urban phenomenon.

Each chapter thus offers its own perspective on urban and industrial change. Overall, the chapters highlight a number of key ideas, central to a fuller understanding of the complex relationship between towns, regions and industries. First is the local and regional differentiation of urban and industrial growth. That different towns prospered for different reasons, and that different industries flourished in different locations, is an apparent commonplace. And yet traditional approaches to urbanisation and industrialisation have plotted a simple causal line between the two, often tracing both back to the availability of key natural resources. The region-wide analysis and the individual town studies underline the need to move away from traditional dichotomies of 'old' stagnant and 'new' dynamic centres and to a fresh understanding of the complex range of urban industrial activity that characterised the eighteenth and early nineteenth centuries The different local experiences also suggest that the issue of regionality has to be interpreted with care. Analysis offered here reveals significant differences between the economic structures of east and west Midlands, and between a core area centred on Birmingham and more peripheral districts. Whilst local economic specialisation may have undermined the identity of the Midlands as a functional and cognitive region[60] – different experiences of work leading to divergent local cultures – the evidence presented here points towards strong spatial integration of the regional space. This was affected through retail hierarchies, transport services and business networks. In short, and notwithstanding east–west and core–periphery distinctions, the Midlands possessed an integrated urban system.

This leads to the second major theme of the book: the way in which the regional urban system and its individual constituents both responded to and shaped processes of industrialisation. The analyses offered in Parts I and II reveal how the urban system at the regional and sub-regional level played an important and active, but differentiated part in the industrialisation process. This reflects Stobart's analysis of north-west England, which demonstrated that economic specialisation and growth were predicated on and structured by effective spatial integration through the regional urban system.[61] Indeed, we can go further and follow de Vries in arguing that a 'mature urban system is a ... necessary preparation for entry to the modern industrial world'.[62] In other words, spatial integration through a network of towns not only shaped the geography of industrialisation; it was fundamental to the very process.

In effect, interaction through the urban system can be viewed as communicating external influences on growth and helping to realise the potential of those internal to particular places. The balance and relationship between these externalities and internalities forms the third theme highlighted in these chapters. This echoes Noble's findings on urban growth in east Yorkshire and moves us still further away from simplistic arguments wherein industrial location is determined by static location factors.[63] Of course, the economic structure of a town was important in determining its growth and prosperity, but so too were its nodality in transport systems, competition from neighbouring towns, and the extent and nature of linkages with its hinterland. Specifically, we stress the significance of local and regional networking by civic, social and business elites. The importance of such groups in stimulating urban and industrial growth comprises the fourth main finding of this book. In many different types of town, elites banded together to promote industrial development, construct or improve urban infrastructure, or facilitate local and regional inter-linkages. This is not to suggest that these men – and they appear to have been almost exclusively men – were behaving in an altruistic manner. The town trust in Loughborough, the 'shopocracy' in Wolverhampton and the leading potters of Burslem were intent on enhancing their social status and promoting their individual and collective business interests. However, in their associations, investments and networking, they not only helped to create and sustain important social institutions, but also improved external linkages with other elites and other places.

This serves to underline the fourth aspect of urban and industrial development highlighted here: the interlinking of economic, social and cultural change. At the local level, this can be seen in the associational activities of elites and the increasingly commercialised provision of leisure that gave prosperity to a number of towns more marginal to industrialisation. Leisure thus became an alternative industrial specialism in places such as Leamington Spa, Worcester and Lichfield. At a broader level, the consumption of novel and fashionable items – so much a part of polite living in the eighteenth century – provided a growing domestic market for the products of Midlands industries.[64] Coffee pots from West Bromwich and porcelain from Burslem found their way into polite drawing rooms across the country, whilst Derby silk stockings, Nottingham lace and Worcester gloves adorned the bodies of their wealthy owners. Matching supply with demand through shops formed another important mainstay, indeed the defining aspect, of many urban economies.

Finally, and underpinning all these other themes, the importance of comparative and relational analysis is emphasised. A comparative approach to urban and industrial change throws into sharper relief the conditions that promoted development in one place and limited it elsewhere. It allows us to highlight – as we have just done – the key components of change, and the extent to which these were particular to certain places or generalised across them. This is true at an intra- and inter-regional scale, a point emphasised by the regional survey at the start of the book and the European and theoretical comparisons at its end. But comparison is not enough. Effective analysis must also be relational in both a functional and a spatial sense: linking cause and effect, urban with industrial change, economic with social transformation, and change in one place with that occurring elsewhere. It is in this light that we should seek to understand the towns, regions and industries of the eighteenth and early nineteenth centuries.

Notes

1 Toynbee, *Industrial Revolution*, p. 31.
2 Clapham, *Economic History*; Cannadine, 'British history', p. 183. For more

general reviews of the changing perspectives on industrialisation, see King and Timmins, *Making Sense*, pp. 10–32; Hudson, *Industrial Revolution*, pp. 9–36.

3 Unwin, *Industrial Organisation*; Carus-Wilson, 'Industrial revolution'; Nef, 'Industrial revolution reconsidered'.

4 Mendels, 'Proto-industrialization'; Kriedte, Medick and Schlumbohm, *Industrialization*.

5 For example, Crafts, *British Economic Growth*; Lindert and Williamson, 'English workers'.

6 Musson, *Growth of British Industry*, p. 149.

7 For a review of these arguments, see King and Timmins, *Making Sense*, pp. 33–66; Stobart, *First Industrial Region*, pp. 1–8. National econometric studies remain an important feature of British economic history. See, for example, Mills and Crafts, 'Trend growth in British industrial output'.

8 For example, Timmins, *Made in Lancashire*; Gregory, *Regional Transformation*; Hudson, *Genesis of Industrial Capital*; Short, 'The de-industrialisation process'; Richards, 'Margins of the industrial revolution'.

9 See Peet, 'Cultural production'.

10 Hudson, *Regions and Industries*, p. 30.

11 Stobart, 'Geography and industrialization', pp. 691–2. See also Massey, *Spatial Divisions*; Hudson, 'Regional and local history'.

12 Massey, *Spatial Divisions*, pp. 117–19, 196–215.

13 See Dicken and Lloyd, *Location in Space*, pp. 239–52, 384–91.

14 Krugman, *Geography and Trade*, pp. 36–54; Arthur, 'Competing technologies'.

15 Mendels, 'Proto-industrialization', p. 241.

16 See, for example, Coleman, 'Proto-industrialization'; Berg, *Age of Manufactures*, pp. 70–6; Hudson, 'Proto-industrialization in England', pp. 58–61; Timmins, *Made in Lancashire*, pp. 61–82.

17 Wrigley, 'Raw materials', p. 12.

18 Ogilivie, 'Social institutions', pp. 23–38; Hudson, *Genesis of Industrial Capital*, pp. 105–208; Berg, *Age of Manufactures*, pp. 255–79; Muldrew, *Economy of Obligation*, pp. 123–57.

19 The classic model is that of Alfred Weber. For a summary of this and other approaches, see Hayter, *Industrial Location*, pp. 112–17.

20 Richardson, *Regional Growth Theory*, pp. 172–3.

21 Wrigley, *Continuity*, pp. 68–97.

22 Lepetit, *Urban System*, pp. 81–93.

23 Wrigley, 'Parasite or stimulus', p. 308.

24 This section draws on discussion in Stobart, 'In search of causality', pp. 149–51.

25 De Vries, *European Urbanization*.

26 Corfield, *English Towns*, p. 11.

27 Langton, 'Urban growth', pp. 465–75.

28 Daunton, 'Towns and economic growth'; Corfield, *English Towns*; Wrigley, 'Urban growth'; Clark, 'Small towns'; Langton, 'Urban growth'.

29 Berg, *Age of Manufactures*, pp. 57–9; Langton, 'Urban growth', pp. 466–8.

30 For example, Clark, 'Small towns'; Langton, 'Urban growth'; Stobart, 'In search of causality'.

31 Everitt, 'Country, county and town', pp. 79–108.

32 These arguments are developed more fully in Stobart, *First Industrial Region*.

33 Borsay, *English Urban Renaissance*. See also Langford, *Polite and Commercial People*, pp. 1–7, 59–122.

34 Quoted in Borsay, *English Urban Renaissance*, p. 227.

35 Estabrook, *Urbane and Rustic England*, p. 7; Sweet, 'Topographies of politeness', pp. 355–7.

36 Borsay, *English Urban Renaissance*.

37 See Glennie and Thrift, 'Consumers'; Smith, *Consumption and Respectability*; Berg, 'New commodities'.

38 Finn, 'Men's things'; Vickery, *Gentleman's Daughter*.

39 Sweet, 'Topographies of politeness', p. 355.

40 Sweet, 'Topographies of politeness', pp. 364–6. See also Stobart, 'In search of a leisure hierarchy'; Stobart and Hann, 'Retailing revolution'.

41 This is an idea implicit, but not fully explored, in Borsay, *English Urban Renaissance*. It is dealt with more explicitly in Stobart, 'Leisure and shopping'.

42 Lepetit, *Urban System*, p. 97.

43 For a useful summary of Christaller's ideas, see Carter, *Urban Geography*, pp. 25–98.

44 Richardson, *Regional Growth Theory*, p. 76; Lepetit, *Urban System*, p. 180. But see Stobart, 'Spatial organisation'.

45 Simmons, 'Urban system'.

46 See Putnam, *Making Democracy Work*. For excellent summaries of these ideas, see Casson and Rose, 'Institutions'; Pearson and Richardson, 'Business networking'.

47 Wilson, *Gentlemen Merchants*; Stobart, 'Culture versus commerce'.

48 Burt, 'The network entrepreneur', pp. 286–8; Casson and Rose, 'Institutions', pp. 3–4.

49 Arnade, Howell and Simons, 'Fertile spaces', p. 518.

50 This question was implicit in the analyses offered in Hudson, *Regions and Industries*.

51 This might further question the general usefulness of proto-industrialisation theory, whilst underlining the value of an urban systems approach to change in the regional space economy.

52 For a review of these studies, see Stobart, *First Industrial Region*, pp. 9–31.

53 Noble, 'Growth and development', pp. 18–19.

54 Stobart, *First Industrial Region*.

55 *Oxford English Dictionary* (second edition, Oxford, 1989), vol. 9, pp. 747–8.

56 'General Preface', in Beckett, *East Midlands*.

57 *Oxford English Dictionary*, pp. 747–8.

58 Chapman, *Factory Masters*, pp. 11–13.

59 Langton also adopts this broader definition. See Dyer, 'Midlands', pp. 93–110, Langton, 'Town growth', pp. 7–47.

60 Stobart, 'Regions and industrialisation'.

61 Stobart, *First Industrial Region*, esp. pp. 175–218.

62 De Vries, *European Urbanization*, p. 10.

63 Noble, 'Growth and development', pp. 18–19.

64 Berg, 'New commodities'.

PART I

*The Midlands:
an industrial region*

2

Industrial and urban change in the Midlands: a regional survey

Neil Raven and Tristram Hooley

Introduction

Recent contributions to the historiography of Britain's industrial revolution have pushed towns to the margins of the industrialisation process. Indeed, for Charles More urbanisation was merely the consequence of an industrial revolution that owed its genesis to invention and market expansion.[1] Meanwhile, Snooks emphasises the need to look at 'the production and export of rural products in tracing the origins of the British Industrial Revolution'.[2] And whilst in Timmins's study of Lancashire, the presence of industry in towns is acknowledged, greater importance is attached to rural production and the role of powered machinery, credit networks and improved transport links.[3] However, there is a tradition in economic and social history that portrays towns as centres of industrial activity and as one of the key initiators of the industrialisation process. In this respect, Snooks acknowledges the work of 'early observers', amongst them Mantoux and Nef, as well as a 'later generation of scholars' including Landes.[4] To these can be added Corfield, whose study of eighteenth-century towns portrays these places as key facilitators of industrial change. More recently, in a survey of the period from the seventeenth century to 1841, Langton argued that the processes of urban and economic growth were inextricably linked.[5] Yet largely absent from the defence mounted by those who champion the role of towns is evidence from systematic regional investigations. As observed in Chapter 1, the few studies that have been conducted have tended to focus on regions peripheral to the industrialisation process.[6] The present chapter begins to address this omission by employing late-eighteenth- and early-nineteenth-century trade directories to examine the urban economies of more than ninety Midlands towns. Later chapters build upon this foundation by exploring key themes in urban economic development and by drawing upon the findings of detailed case studies. Here, we set the context for these local analyses.

Sources and methods

Investigations into urban economies during the industrial revolution have long been hampered by a paucity of empirical data. Many of the sources used by early modern urban historians, such as apprenticeship indentures, wills and freeman's lists, are less readily available from the late eighteenth century onwards. However, one source that does emerge at this time is the trade directory.[7] Initially, coverage was restricted to London and a number of larger provincial centres,[8] but with the publication of the *Universal British Directory* (*UBD*) in the 1790s, many smaller urban centres received attention. It is with the *UBD* that this survey begins, and from it that the selection of towns to be examined was determined. In total, the *UBD* afforded details of traders operating in ninety-seven Midlands towns, representing over half the region's urban settlements.[9] To establish the extent of urban economic change by the start of the Victorian period, data for the same set of settlements was gathered from Pigot's directories of the early 1840s.

As Figure 2.1 illustrates, these ninety-seven settlements included a wide spectrum of town sizes and were distributed throughout the region. There were, however, some absences which need to be kept in mind throughout this survey, and when considering the findings in Chapters 3 and 4 of this volume. For example, coverage in Derbyshire excluded Belper and Matlock. By the start of the Victorian period the former was amongst the largest towns in the county, housing a number of Strutt's cotton mills. One explanation for its omission may lie in what made towns worthy of attention. To the gentlemen and merchants who represented the *UBD*'s principal subscribers, these were likely to have been places full of traders and manufacturers. Perhaps Belper, dominated by its large mills, did not meet these criteria. Alternatively, the *UBD*'s coverage may have filtered out some of the newer, possibly fastest-growing towns of the region. However, the exclusion of Matlock, a town of long-standing urban status, suggests that selection may have been more random than this, depending upon the reliability of the agents that were claimed to have been appointed to every town.[10] Another problematic issue is the depth of coverage, as the *UBD* often underestimated the true range and number of a town's traders. This said, it probably represents the best survey of urban economies available in the eighteenth century. Although it excludes a number of businesses advertising in the Oxfordshire newspaper *Jackson's Journal*, Walton found that the *UBD* recorded a significantly higher number

Figure 2.1 *The surveyed towns of the Midlands*

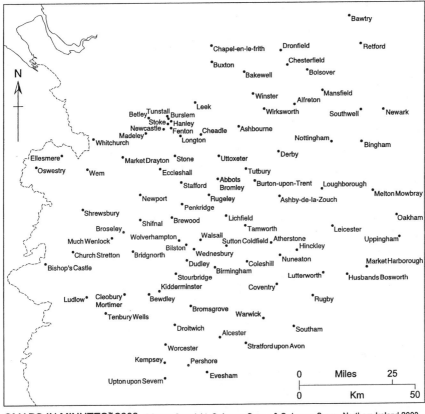

©MAPS IN MINUTES™ 2003. ©Crown Copyright, Ordnance Survey & Ordnance Survey Northern Ireland 2003 Permit No. NI 1675 & ©Government of Ireland, Ordnance Survey Ireland.

of town-based traders and professionals than were found in the newspaper or in Bailey's directory of the 1780s.[11]

Despite these reassuring findings, inherent problems remain when comparing data from two sets of distinct directories. Shaw emphasises the need, where possible, to use work from the same directory company.[12] However, with few exceptions, any survey of the industrial period that wishes to capture the late eighteenth as well as the early nineteenth century will need to consider data from various directory companies, including the *UBD* or one of Bailey's regional directories. Moreover, there is a firmly established precedent for employing the *UBD* in conjunction with early-nineteenth-century directories. Wilde, for instance, used it along with directories for 1828 and 1834 in his comparative analysis of the industrial structure of three south-west Pennine

silk towns.[13] For the current survey, directory material for the early 1840s
has been collected from those surveys conducted by Pigot and Co. Norton
considers Pigot and Co. to be amongst the most reliable of early-nineteenth-
century directory compilers, not least because they employed their own agents
to collect information. Certainly, the data which their directories contained
was accurate enough to ensure commercial viability and the production of a
number of editions.[14]

   To identify manufacturing concerns recorded in the directories, the
Booth–Armstrong classification scheme was used. This divides occupations
into fourteen broad classes, which are then subdivided into seventy-four
groups according to the type of service offered or product manufactured.[15]
This decision was, in part, influenced by the existence of a large database produced by the National Small Towns Project, which had used the
Booth–Armstrong scheme, and from which the present survey was able to
acquire data for sixty-eight of the region's towns. Moreover, it has been widely
adopted, ensuring potential for comparison.[16] One problem of applying this
scheme to directory material is that it was devised for occupational data; the
directories, in contrast, record businesses.[17] In consequence, the four 'occupational' classes dealing with employees remained unused: labour, [domestic]
service, independents and dependents. That said, Booth–Armstrong not only
identifies manufacturers as a distinct class, but also subdivides them into
thirty-one separate groups, allowing detailed analysis of manufacturing specialisms across the region.[18] Importantly, the scheme includes craft activities
such as tailoring and shoemaking within this class, effectively labelling them
as manufacturing. We follow this convention here: crafts are included in our
analysis and we use 'manufacturing' to refer to all trades covered in that class
of the Booth–Armstrong scheme. However, we do subsequently make a distinction between locally oriented industry and that aimed at distant markets.

The urban business community in aggregate

For Clark, the late eighteenth and early nineteenth centuries formed a time
when many of England's smaller towns – numerically the largest urban class
– faced mounting 'problems and challenges'. In particular, he argued that their
economies 'suffered' from the 'fierce industrial competition' of larger towns.
As a consequence, many lost their industrial functions and were reduced to
the status of market towns.[19] Does this story fit the evidence from the Midlands? In aggregate, the region's urban economies appear to have experienced
substantial expansion between the 1790s and 1840s, rather than stagnation or
contraction. Indeed, during this half-century the number of urban businesses
more than trebled, with manufacturing industry playing a vital role in this

growth. In the 1790s, 37 per cent of urban businesses were involved in some form of manufacturing, ensuring that manufacturing was returned as the largest class with services second. This pre-eminence was maintained into the 1840s, when manufacturing claimed 34 per cent of businesses. This class also grew in complexity over the period, with the average range of manufacturing activities increasing from 22 per town in the 1790s to 60 by the early 1840s: a rate of diversification greater than that experienced by the urban business community as a whole. In the 1790s the average range of trade-types for a town was 67; by the 1840s it was 116.

Such aggregates may well hide the experiences of smaller urban communities, yet taking as examples three small towns from across the region, the evidence would appear to support the aggregated findings: all three sustaining a sizeable manufacturing presence. In the 1790s, the Rutland town of Uppingham − for which the 1801 census reported a population of 1,393 − returned 36 per cent of its businesses in manufacturing, a figure that had changed very little fifty years later. Similarly, the proportion of manufacturers in Stratford upon Avon (1801 population: 2,418) showed only a modest fall, from 36 to 31 per cent, whilst the Shropshire town of Much Wenlock (1801 population: 1,981) saw a growth in its manufacturing sector, from 41 to 44 per cent. Manufacturing in all three towns was growing in sophistication. In the 1790s, Much Wenlock returned 21 different manufacturing trades, Stratford 32 and Uppingham 15. By the 1840s, the corresponding figures were 24, 47 and 27 respectively, with manufacturing concerns in the three towns ranging from bakers and blacksmiths to tailors and tanners. Moreover, in the composition of its manufacturers each town showed signs of embracing trends evident at a regional level. By the 1840s, printing trades were returned in Much Wenlock and Uppingham, and coal-related trades were recorded in Uppingham and Stratford. Thus manufacturing appears to have remained an important activity to the economies of many of the small towns of the Midlands throughout the period of the classic industrial revolution, and one capable of experiencing change. The case of Penkridge affords a measure of the vital role such industrial activity could play in the fortunes of smaller urban communities. It was one of the few small towns in the region to have experienced a decline in the proportion of its manufacturers, from 45 per cent of businesses in the 1790s to 29 per cent by the 1840s. During this period, it lost the trades of glover, hatter, peruke maker, rope maker, currier, tanner and turner. This experience may explain why, in 1851, White observed that, although an 'ancient town' with a 'spacious market place', Penkridge's market had become 'obsolete'.[20]

Despite the local importance that can be attached to manufacturing activity, none of our three case-study small towns was recognised by contemporaries as an industrial centre. According to Pigot, Much Wenlock possessed 'little man-ufacturing', Stratford could boast 'few notable manufactures' and Uppingham's business was 'principally of a local nature'.[21] Here, the directory compilers were drawing on a particular meaning of 'manufacturing', shared by Snooks, More and others: it was large-scale production for extra-local consumption. The three towns were well represented in a number of widespread but locally ori-ented manufacturing activities, most notably dress – the most common manu-facturing group throughout the period of analysis – and drink – the fourth largest. Indeed, by the 1840s, each boasted a percentage of businesses in these sectors that was either equal to or higher than that for the region as a whole. In dress the regional average by the start of the Victorian period was 34 per cent. Both Stratford and Uppingham claimed an almost identical percentage to this, whilst Much Wenlock returned 42 per cent. Much Wenlock and Upping-ham possessed a larger proportion of drink-related businesses than the regional average, with 11 and 9.5 per cent respectively, compared with the Midlands average of 6 per cent by the 1840s. Of course, the obvious corollary of this is that these towns were under-represented in a number of other important man-ufacturing classes, most noticeably in iron and steel – the second largest class by the 1840s – and copper and tin – the sixth largest class. At a regional level, iron and steel accounted for 8 per cent of urban manufacturers in the 1790s and 10 per cent by the 1840s, whilst for copper and tin the corresponding figure was 5 per cent for both dates. In contrast, Much Wenlock witnessed a decline in its iron and steel manufacturers, so that by the 1840s they represented just 5.6 per cent of the town's entries. Similarly, copper and tin accounted for 2.4 per cent of the Shropshire town's businesses in the 1790s and 1.6 per cent by the 1840s. Likewise, in Stratford iron and steel comprised 7 per cent of entries in 1840, with copper posting 3.6 per cent. Moreover, none of these towns were witness to the rapid expansion of the region's other major industries including earth-enware, lace and hosiery. During the period under investigation, earthenware rose from the fourteenth to the tenth largest class – accounting for 2 per cent of all urban manufacturing businesses by the 1840s – whilst lace leapt from twenty-fifth to twelfth position. In fact, these two industrial classes, along with cotton and silk – which accounted for 1.3 per cent of businesses in the 1840s – were entirely absent from the businesses recorded in these three towns. Yet it was in metalworking and earthenware, hosiery and lace making, cotton and silk manufacture that the Midlands gained recognition as an industrial region. These are the industries highlighted again and again in local and regional analyses of the Midlands economy.[22] Their absence from Stratford, Uppingham and Much Wenlock suggests that these small towns, and others like them, were being by-passed by the processes of industrialisation that increasingly characterised the region.

Large-scale manufacture for distant markets is often associated with specialisation in production, as tasks are subdivided and as high levels of demand
facilitate the manufacture of an expanding range of product-types. In the directories this phenomenon should manifest itself in a wide and growing array of
business types associated with those industrial classes engaged in large-scale
production.[23] Throughout the period under review, iron and steel returned the
largest range of trade types (52 in the 1790s and 76 by the 1840s), with copper and tin in close contention (32 and 50). Tools (32 and 51), machinery (18
and 39) and watches (26 to 50) – classes that, as will be shown, were often
associated with iron and steel and copper and tin – also ranked highly. Meanwhile, earthenware (from 15 to 31) and lace (2 to 13) featured amongst those
witnessing the most rapid growth in trade types, and were accompanied by
printing (3 to 12) and the rather smaller class of chemicals (9 to 22). In contrast, some of the slowest growth in trade diversification was to be found in
dress manufacture (29 to 43), drink (8 to 10) and food. Indeed, the number of
trade-types recorded by the latter remained unchanged throughout the period
(at 13).

A more refined method of highlighting levels of specialisation, and one that
affords a greater degree of comparison between classes, is to calculate the ratio
of trade-types to the number of businesses. By the 1840s, those classes with
the highest ratios included copper (1 trade-type to every 16 entries), iron (1:20),
earthenware (1:12), lace (1:13) and cotton and silk (1:10), along with watches
(1:11), machinery (1:8) and tools (1:4). Those with the lowest ratios comprised,
predictably enough, food (1:80), drink (1:96) and dress (1:122). Many of the
businesses featured in these three categories were pretty much ubiquitous and
catered for local markets. Prominent amongst these were bakers and confectioners, maltsters and brewers, shoemakers and dressmakers, and milliners and
tailors. Moreover, in iron and steel and in copper and tin, representation in
the three selected settlements tended to be in those activities common to most
towns. For instance, the only iron and steel entry found in Uppingham's 1840
directory listing was that of blacksmith: a trade found in most small towns
and many villages by the start of the Victorian period.[24]

The directory evidence considered so far suggests that industrial activity was
concentrated in a number of the region's towns, but how can these settlements
be identified? One method is to calculate the coefficient of variation (CV) for
each manufacturing class. By expressing the standard deviation as a percentage of the mean for each class, this calculation reveals the distribution of
manufacturing across the region's towns.[25] The more concentrated or uneven
the distribution, then the higher the CV score will be. As would be expected
from the foregoing discussion, those manufacturing classes with the highest
CV scores in the 1790s were iron and steel, copper and tin, and cotton and

silk. Indeed, all returned scores of over 200 when the regional average was only 100, whilst watches, machinery and tools, and wool also featured prominently. By the 1840s, lace and earthenware had joined iron and steel and copper and tin (all with scores of more than 200), and machinery, printing, wool, watches, dying and tools were only slightly below this level. By highlighting the occupational groups displaying the greatest unevenness of distribution, this calculation enables us to identify the towns characterised by industrial concentrations: in other words the places that might be labelled as the manufacturing towns of the Midlands. Before turning to the results, though, it should be remembered that industrial activity is recognised in this exercise by the number rather than the size of manufacturing concerns.[26] That said, the approach adopted here does possess certain advantages over previous methods that have relied upon settlement descriptions. There is evidence to suggest that some of these descriptions were 'borrowed' from existing accounts, whilst the brief nature of many others affords little insight into the true character of urban industrial activity.[27]

The industrial towns of the Midlands

Using the CV analysis for the 1790s reveals that the main industrial towns of the Midlands were spread across the region (see Figure 2.2). In the west Midlands, Birmingham, Wolverhampton, Bilston, Walsall, Stourbridge and Dudley accounted for more than 64 per cent of the region's iron and steel entries, with trade-types ranging from buckle and chape makers to key makers, bolt and nut makers, saddlers, ironmongers and candle-snuffer makers. Wolverhampton also featured strongly in a number of related areas of manufacture and had the largest number of tool as well as watch and toy manufacturers. This specialisation was well recognised by *Pigot's Directory* which noted that the town was 'justly celebrated' for its manufacture of 'iron articles, and almost every description of goods used in building and cabinet furniture; edge and various other tools; brass and iron founding, in its greatest variety'.[28]

These metalworking towns were accompanied by others specialising in textiles. Coventry, Nottingham, Derby, Nuneaton, Mansfield and Leek together accounted for 85 per cent of silk and cotton entries, although the types of product manufactured varied from one town to the next. Coventry's entries in this class were dominated by ribbon makers, as were those for Nuneaton and Leek, whilst Derby returned mainly silk throwsters, and Mansfield and Nottingham cotton manufacturers and hosiers. These industrial concentrations were certainly apparent to contemporaries such as the historian of Nottingham John Blackner, himself a framework knitter, who wrote in 1815 that Nottingham was so dependent on the 'stocking frame and its

Figure 2.2 *The industrial towns of the Midlands, c. 1790*

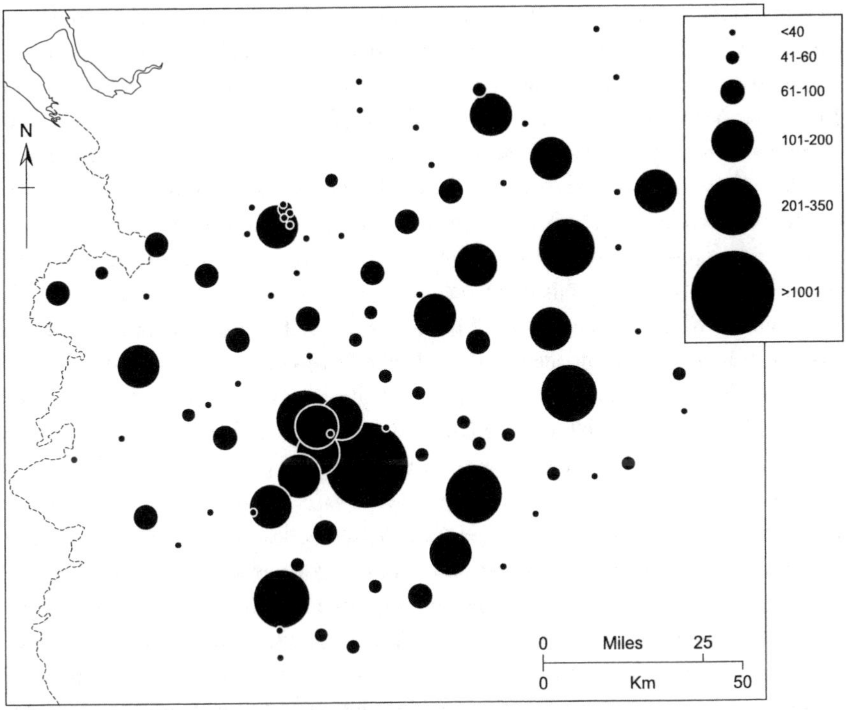
N
<40
41-60
61-100
101-200
201-350
>1001
0 Miles 25
0 Km 50
©MAPS IN MINUTES™ 2003. ©Crown Copyright, Ordnance Survey & Ordnance Survey Northern Ireland 2003
Permit No. NI 1675 & ©Government of Ireland, Ordnance Survey Ireland.

Shows number of businesses.
Source: *Universal British Directory*.

appendant machines that if it stood still, all other business must stand still also'.[29] The towns of Kidderminster and Leicester returned large concentrations of woollen manufacturing concerns. Indeed, between them these two claimed 26 per cent of the region's entries in this class. Most of the wool entries appearing in Kidderminster were involved in carpet and rug making, whilst many in Leicester were worsted manufacturers. The latter undoubtedly represented some of the seventy hosiers that were said to be operating from Leicester in 1792, and who employed '3000 frames in the town and surrounding villages'.[30]

Other, more localised, concentrations can be identified from detailed study of trade-types. These included Ludlow, with a concentration of glove makers, and Rugeley and Newcastle-under-Lyme, both of which had large numbers of hatters. In addition, significant numbers of hosiers were recorded in Loughborough, Ashby and Hinckley, with the *UBD* describing hosiery production as the 'chief manufacture' of the last of these.[31] In addition, Worcester was famed at home and abroad both for its porcelain and for the 'beauty and quality' of its gloves, and the seventy glovers listed in 1835 may have been the tip of the iceberg, as Pigot estimated that the industry gave employment to 'between seven and eight thousand persons in Worcester'.[32] Finally, in Burton-upon-Trent and Mansfield the directories listed large numbers of common brewers and maltsters respectively.

The 1840 map of industrial towns in the Midlands displayed many of its predecessor's characteristics. Birmingham, Wolverhampton, Bilston, Walsall, Stourbridge and Dudley continued to stand out as iron and steel centres, but were now joined by Walsall, Wednesbury and, to the east, Nottingham. Between them, these nine towns claimed in excess of 66 per cent of the region's iron and steel entries. Moreover, there had been considerable expansion in the actual number of businesses listed in this sector since the 1790s. According to White, many of the furnaces that had 'stimulated the rapid growth' of Bilston (from a population of 6,914 in 1801 to 20,181 by 1841) had 'commenced during the present century'.[33] Similarly, Walsall saw a fourteen-fold increase in the number of iron and steel manufactures recorded in the directories, and also witnessed substantial growth in copper and tin businesses. Much of this expansion resulted from an increase in the number of buckle makers, bridle cutters and stirrup makers, many of whom were associated with the town's carriage and harness production. According to White in 1851, Walsall was 'celebrated for the manufacture of saddlers' ironmongery, and other hardware'.[34] Wolverhampton specialised in the manufacture of small luxury goods such as watches, toys and spectacles (see Chapter 8), and by the 1840s the town boasted sixty-five businesses of this kind. Yet, despite Wolverhampton's fame in this area, other places in the Midlands also had similar specialisations. Coventry, for example, experienced considerable growth in this type of manufacturing, and by the 1840s there were sixty-eight manufacturers of small metal items in the town, most specialising in watchmaking or associated trades. Other prominent trades in Wolverhampton included machinery manufactures, principally involved in the making of agricultural machines and vices, and tool makers, of which there were sixteen different types, the most prominent being file and rasp makers. Other towns returning significant numbers in these two classes were Dudley, with a noticeable concentration of vice makers, and Walsall, where tool makers, notably blade makers, were prominent.

Elements of change and continuity also characterised silk and cotton production. Where six towns had accounted for the bulk of entries in the 1790s, now four – Coventry, Leek, Nottingham and Derby – returned 80 per cent of all silk and cotton manufacturers. The census of 1831 estimated that some

2,000 males of twenty years and upwards were 'employed in making ribbons' in Coventry.[35] More dramatic still, the directory evidence suggests that five lace-manufacturing centres had appeared since the late eighteenth century. Between them, Nottingham, Derby, Loughborough, Mansfield and Leicester accounted for 95 per cent of entries in this class. According to the 1831 census, the 'great increase of population' that had been experienced by Loughborough parish during the previous decade was, in part at least, 'attributed to the extension of the lace manufacture'.[36] Likewise, by 1853 White was describing Nottingham as 'the principal seat and emporium of the lace and hosiery manufactures', adding that the 'busy sounds of industry from the noise of the stocking frame and lace machine, are heard through the town and adjacent villages.'[37] The previous half-century had also seen the continued growth of Leicester as a hosiery centre. In 1815 Leicester was reported to have 'a very considerable trade in cotton and worsted hosiery', and by 1831 it was estimated that the town contained 'around 3,000 stocking makers'.[38] Hinckley also shared this industry. In 1835 Pigot noted that a 'large quantity of cotton and worsted hose, especially the former, is manufactured here', adding that 'the number of frames in the town and adjacent villages [is] upwards of 2000'.[39] Similarly, carpet manufacturing continued to feature in Kidderminster, where, according to the 1831 census, '2300 men [were] employed in making carpets and preparing materials for that manufacture'.[40]

Finally, new to the directory analysis of the 1840s were the six pottery towns of Burslem, Fenton, Hanley, Longton, Stoke and Tunstall, which together claimed 97 per cent of the region's earthenware producers. The importance of this manufactory to Burslem was noted by Pigot, who in 1835 commented on the town's 'many admirably arranged manufactories, numerous dwellings for the workmen [and] many good houses for the superintendents' (see also Chapter 7).[41] The corresponding population growth was noted in White's directory, which observed that whilst in 1801 the parish had contained a total of 6,578 inhabitants, by 1841 this had risen to 16,091.[42] Elsewhere, the number of businesses involved in the drink industry had doubled in Burton-upon-Trent, leading Pigot to describe it as 'justly celebrated' for the 'great quantity' of ale that it produced annually.[43] Both in the 1790s and 1840s, then, the Midlands had a number of specialist urban industrial centres, many of which witnessed considerable expansion in their manufactories during this period. How can they be classified, and to what purpose?

A typology of industrial towns

Amongst those who have argued for an active role for towns in the industrialisation process there has been a tendency to portray industrial towns as new, dynamic centres, and to contrast them with 'old, slow growing towns' that failed to develop manufactories. Both Corfield and Trinder make reference to these claims, with Corfield noting that this argument derives from the belief that 'controls and regulations' exercised by guilds and corporations were responsible for impeding the economic performance of old towns. However, both these authors reject this stereotyping and carefully select examples of 'old' incorporated towns that experienced rapid growth: places such as Liverpool, Preston and Wigan, as well as 'quiet' towns like York whose industrial activities have been overlooked.[44] A consideration of the range and variety of industrial towns within the Midlands affords the potential to examine Corfield's and Trinder's criticisms and to suggest a new typology of industrial towns.

Amongst the industrial towns of the Midlands there were a small number of settlements best described as new or *ab initio* urban centres, some coming to prominence during the period under examination (see Chapter 7). In iron and steel manufacture they included Bilston and Wednesbury. The latter had not featured as an industrial centre in the 1790s, and according to White it was not until 1824 that Bilston acquired the rights to hold a market; until then it had 'enjoyed the reputation of being one of the largest villages in England'.[45] Also claiming recent urban status were the pottery towns of Longton, Burslem, Tunstall, Stoke, Fenton and Hanley (see Chapter 7). Pigot in 1835 described the last of these as a 'modern market town', and noted that in 1812 'an application was made to Parliament for power to enlarge the market and market place'. The same directory also drew attention to the 'opulence' recently generated by the potteries of Longton and Stoke.[46] Tunstall, meanwhile, according to White had 'risen during the present century from the rank of a small village to that of a town of about 10,000 inhabitants'.[47]

Amongst the ranks of Midlands industrial centres, however, there were a number of older market towns with growing industrial specialisms (see Chapters 8 and 10). Indeed, as a class, these easily outnumbered the new industrial centres, and included Leek, Kidderminster, Stourbridge, Loughborough, Burton-upon-Trent, Nuneaton, Birmingham, Wolverhampton, Coventry, Dudley and Walsall. In 1851, White described Walsall as 'an ancient borough', Wolverhampton as a 'borough and market town of considerable antiquity', and Newcastle-under-Lyme as 'an ancient market town'.[48] For some of these towns the acquisition of their industrial specialisms had occurred within living memory. The *UBD* outlined the recent history of the silk industry in Coventry, observing that '[a]bout ninety years ago, the silk manufacture of ribbons was introduced here; and for the first thirty years it remained in the hands of a few people, who acquired vast fortunes; since which it has extended to a great degree'. Indeed, the directory suggested that 'at least ten thousand people' were now employed in silk manufacture.[49] However, for others in this class, industrial activity had a longer heritage. The *UBD* referred to 'an incorporated company of felt-makers' in relation to Newcastle's hat manufactory,[50] whilst White claimed that the distinction Wolverhampton gained for 'the skill and ingenuity of its artisans', especially in the making of locks, had derived from 'early times'. As evidence of 'the early celebrity' of this town's locksmiths, White referred to the observations of Dr Plot in his 1686 *History of Staffordshire*, who noted the 'excellency' of Wolverhampton's artisans, whose locks 'seemed to be preferred to all others'.[51]

In addition, a number of the region's county towns possessed industries (see Chapter 9). At the start of the period, Worcester returned a large concentration of glovers and Nottingham a sizeable contingent of cotton spinners and manufacturers, whilst Leicester claimed many worsted manufacturers and Derby a number of silk throwsters. However, far from stagnating, many of these places prospered as industrial centres over the next fifty years. Nottingham blossomed as a hosiery and lace-manufacturing centre: in the 1790s, the *UBD* listed only two lace makers in the town; by the 1840s the number had increased to over 200. Similarly, the period under review saw a rapid expansion in the number of Leicester's hosiers so that by the 1840s this trade was amongst the most numerous in the town. Likewise, the decades following the 1790s saw the expansion of Derby's silk industry. By 1835 Pigot considered 'the number of men, women and children employed in it' to be 'very considerable'.[52] Even though Worcester appears to have witnessed less rapid industrial growth, the 1831 census estimated that 'nearly 1000 men and a much greater number of females are employed in making gloves in the town and its suburbs'. Moreover, the town also made the 'finest china-ware' in which 'about fifty men and many females' were employed.[53]

Finally, when compiling a revised typology of industrial towns, some consideration should also be given to those places that witnessed industrial decline: a subject of much neglect (though see Chapter 11). Included in this category would be Newcastle-under-Lyme. By the time White produced his 1851 directory the town's long-standing hat trade had been 'depressed for some years'.[54] Similarly, Rugeley had lost half its hat makers over the same period, whilst by the 1840s only three glovers were recorded in Ludlow. Even new towns experienced industrial decline in this period. Bilston saw a fall in the number of iron and steel manufacturers and by the 1840s had lost all its chape and steel buckle makers. Significantly, it was not alone in this fate. A similar process, although on a more modest scale, had been witnessed by Bolsover in Derbyshire.[55] The industry in both towns was highly dependent on the near-universal wearing of shoe buckles that had dominated the fashion of all classes from the later seventeenth century.[56] By the late 1790s the shoe buckle had gone out of favour, precipitating a collapse in the number of buckle manufacturers. Unlike Bolsover, however, Bilston was able to benefit from the expansion of other metalware manufacturing, including iron and tin plate working and japanning.

The role of towns in the industrialisation process

So far, our analysis of the trade directories has identified a number of towns in the Midlands, including old market centres and county towns as well as so-called new industrial towns, which acted as sites of industrial activity. Such findings may require Snooks and More to revise their claims, but not neces-sarily to abandon them. These towns may have acted merely as the recipients of industry whose rise is best explained by external forces. One long-recog-nised influence in determining the location of industry is coal and its cheap availability. In this respect, Trinder profiles the fortunes of Liverpool's man-ufactories. From the 1770s, Liverpool 'flourished as a manufacturing city', thanks to cheap coal delivered by an expanding canal system. However, as the competitive advantage of coalfield towns increased, so Liverpool's manu-factories declined.[57] In outlining 'a simple model of regional [industrial] development', More also emphasises the influence of coal, a point recently reiterated by Langton.[58] Analysis of the location of the industrial towns of the Midlands by the 1840s suggests a strong correlation with the geography of the region's coalfields. The metalware towns of the west Midlands were within easy reach of south Staffordshire's coalfields, and the Potteries were proximate with those of north Staffordshire, whilst the main industrial cen-tres of the east Midlands, Derby, Leicester and Nottingham, were close to the Nottinghamshire and Derbyshire seams.[59] However, such a reading of industrial location is overly simplistic. Proximity to coal deposits cannot explain the variety of urban manufacturing activity recorded across the region's towns by the directories. As will be explored in subsequent chapters, and as we have glimpsed with Wolverhampton, local skills and artisan tradi-tions could play a vital role. Similarly, as Chapters 7 and 10 will show, local elites were often highly influential in establishing manufactories, as well as in creating commercial conditions favourable to industrial expansion. White, for instance, notes the role played by 'the eminent potter' Josiah Wedgwood in championing the construction of the Trent and Mersey canal.[60]

What this regional survey also reveals is the part played by clusters of towns in nurturing industrialisation. They created the critical mass of skills, capital and entrepreneurship that Pollard argues was instrumental in promoting sus-tained industrial growth.[61] In this respect, a number of distinct urban industrial districts can be identified. Concentrated along the Worcester and Staffordshire border were the Black Country metalworking towns of Dudley, Stourbridge,

Walsall, Bilston, Wednesbury and Wolverhampton, all linked with Birmingham to the east; in north Staffordshire were the pottery towns of Burslem, Fenton, Hanley, Longton, Tunstall and Stoke, whilst in north Warwickshire Coventry and Nuneaton comprised a separate silk manufacturing district. In addition, in the eastern part of the region were various, sometimes overlapping, groups of textile towns. These included the lace centres of Nottingham, Loughborough, Derby and Leicester, as well as Chesterfield and Mansfield, the cotton and silk production centres of Nottingham, Derby, Mansfield and Leicester and a hosiery district consisting of Nottingham, Leicester, Derby, Hinckley and Loughborough.[62] There is also evidence for the existence of other urban industrial districts whose membership was only partly located in the region. From a Midlands perspective, Leek would appear to represent a lone industrial town, yet just across the Cheshire border were Congleton and Macclesfield, which, together with Leek, comprised 'the silk towns of the south-west Pennines'.[63] Such clustering points to the role of the dissemination of ideas and capital in the spread of industrialisation. Illustrating this is the story of John Heathcoat, who had 'for many years' worked as a 'setter-up of machinery at Nottingham'; but on acquiring a patent for an 'improved twist lace frame' he built a factory at Loughborough.[64] Similarly, the directories reveal manufacturers who had established centres of production in more than one town in each cluster. By 1851, a number of Wolverhampton's hardware merchants and factors also had Birmingham addresses, including Joshua Schofield and Sons of Horsley-fields, and Walker and Fleeming of Berry Street.[65]

A consideration of trade-types suggests that, in promoting their own industry, towns in these clusters sought to complement the output of their neighbours rather than competing against it. This can be most clearly seen amongst the metalware towns of the Black Country. Here each town came to specialise in its own range of products. In iron and steel, Bilston recorded the largest number of iron founders and iron masters, Walsall the largest concentration of bit, curb and chain makers, as well as saddlers' iron-mongers, and Dudley the greatest number of nail factors and chain makers. Meanwhile, steel toy manufacturers and steel pen manufacturers, as well as fender manufactures and wire manufacturers, were numerous in Birmingham, whilst nailers predominated in Stourbridge, turnscrew makers in Wednesbury, and key and thumb latch and wood screw makers in Wolverhampton.[66] Similar distinctions can also be made for copper and tin. In Bilston tin plate workers and japanners were prominent, whilst in Walsall it was buckle makers and plated ware makers, and in Wolverhampton brass founders. The means of facilitating such co-operation may well have included the Ironmasters' Quarterly Meetings, which were held alternately at Walsall, Wolverhampton, Birmingham, Stourbridge and Dudley.[67]

Further evidence of intra-urban industrial co-operation can be found in the structure of urban hierarchies. For each cluster the directory evidence suggests the existence of one or two towns that functioned as organising hubs. It was these towns that returned the largest array of trades in the principal manu-facturing activity, including allied trades and those associated with later stages in the production process. In the potteries, Hanley and Burslem possessed the broadest range of earthenware trade-types, and the same towns were pre-emi-nent in related trades, being the only ones to possess, for example, colour manufacturers. Similarly, in the east Midlands lace-manufacturing district, Nottingham claimed the largest range of lace trades. A number of these, such as those of lace dresser and bobbin manufacturer, were servicing the lace mak-ers; others were involved in the later stages of production, including lace stamper, singer, patten maker and pearl lace manufacturer. None of these trades were recorded in any of the other lace towns. The same pattern is repeated in the metalware towns, where Birmingham and Wolverhampton predominated, as well as in the hosiery district of the east Midlands. Indeed, in some cases this hierarchical relationship included towns acting as little more than industrial outposts. This appears to have been the case with Market Har-borough, where Pigot recorded that the 'chief trade now carried on ... is an extensive one for the manufacture of carpets and worsteds, by Messrs. Clark and Sons'. This firm, Pigot added, had its principal establishment at Burton Latimer Mills, near Kettering.[68] The forging of a similar relationship may have helped Newcastle-under-Lyme recover from the decline in felt hat production, with White observing in 1851 that 'many of the [town's] inhabitants [now] find employment in the Potteries'.[69]

Finally, such hierarchies could also embrace the surrounding countryside. Whilst some of the ironwork for Wolverhampton's lock, buckle, steel toy and japan-ware manufacturers was made in the town, the *UBD* noted that 'the chief part of it [is produced] by the farmers for several miles round', adding that 'in this country every farm has at least one forge; so that, when the farm-ers are not employed in the fields, they work as smiths at their forges'.[70] Such urban-rural links were perhaps strongest in the hosiery industry of the east Midlands (see Chapters 9 and 10), where they endured into the Victorian period. Yet even in the Black Country, White noted large villages situated in a 'small basin between Dudley and Wolverhampton' whose populations in the mid-nineteenth century were employed in 'the smelting and rolling of iron'.[71]

Conclusion

The evidence presented in this chapter suggests the need to restore the urban dimension to recent accounts of the industrial revolution. Towns were important sites of industrial activity, with many witnessing considerable industrial expansion during the course of the late eighteenth and early nineteenth centuries. Moreover, this study has highlighted the range of urban types that experienced industrialisation. The prominence in this survey of old urban centres, including a number of shire towns, has underpinned calls to dispense with the traditional stereotyping between old slow-growing towns and new dynamic industrial centres. Beyond this, the directory and census evidence discussed in this chapter reveals that towns also acted to influence the character and fortunes of industry. Subsequent chapters will add colour and detail to these region-wide outlines. However, the broader perspective offered by this survey has highlighted the role played by clusters or networks of towns in shaping and promoting industrial development. The linking of towns (and town and country) through interactive spatial-economic systems was central to the articulation of the local specialisms noted in this survey. It also helped to construct the critical mass of activity necessary for sustained industrial growth. This subject has been little explored by economic and social histories,[72] but will be returned to in Chapter 5 and is a theme that runs through many of the contributions to this collection. Finally, whilst much of the focus of this chapter, and indeed of this book, is on large-scale industry and its production for extra-regional markets, this regional survey has also shown that industry could manifest itself in more modest forms, for local consumption. Although industry in this guise has attracted far less attention from contemporary observers and historians, its importance to the fortunes of individual urban communities, like Much Wenlock, Stratford and Uppingham, should not be ignored; accordingly, it is a subject that will be returned to when we consider the fortunes of Lichfield (Chapter 11).

Notes

1 More, *Industrial Revolution*, pp. 3–5, 164–5.
2 Snooks, *Industrial Revolution*, pp. 10–11.
3 Timmins, *Made in Lancashire*, pp. 35–60, 85–143.
4 Snooks, *Industrial Revolution*, pp. 10–11.
5 Langton, 'Urban growth', pp. 805–29; Corfield, *English Towns*, pp. 17–33.
6 Noble, 'Growth and development', pp. 1–21; Marshall, 'Rise and transformation'; Raven, 'De-industrialisation', pp. 46–69. The one notable exception is Stobart, *First Industrial Region*.
7 Raven, 'Manufacturing and trades', pp. 2–6.
8 Corfield and Kelly, 'Giving directions'.
9 Clark and Hoskins, *Population Estimates*.
10 A point acknowledged by Norton, *Guide to Directories*.
11 Walton, 'Trades and professions'.
12 Shaw, 'Trade directories'. See also Norton, *Guide to Directories*, pp. 1–24.

13 Wilde, 'Business directories'. In a study of Birmingham, Duggan ('Industrialisa-
    tion') notes that 'directories offer much insight into the process of change within
    such vital urban institutions as the business community'. See also Raven, 'Man-
    ufacturing and trades', pp. 251–69.
14 Raven, 'Manufacturing and trades', p. 117.
15 For details, see Armstrong, 'Information about occupation'.
16 See, for example, Clark, 'Small towns', pp. 733–73; Reeder and Rodger, 'Indus-
    trialisation and the city economy', pp. 553–92.
17 Raven, 'Trade directory'; Mills, *Rural Community History*.
18 It was decided to exclude the extractive industries category from detailed inves-
    tigation, principally because the focus for this study is urban manufacturing
    industry.
19 Clark, 'Small towns', pp. 756–63.
20 White, *Staffordshire* (1851).
21 *Pigot's Directory* (1841).
22 See, for example, Beckett, *East Midlands*, pp. 274–93; Millward and Robinson,
    Landscapes of Britain, pp. 52–6; More, *Industrial Revolution*, pp. 116–18.
23 Duggan, 'Industrialisation', pp. 457–65, discusses such a process occurring in
    Birmingham, on the basis of directory evidence.
24 Mills, *Rural Community History*, pp. 53–64.
25 Blalock, *Social Statistics*, p. 84.
26 Whilst it is possible to gauge the size of individual concerns through analysis of
    rate-books, this is not a practical option at a regional level. For discussion of the
    scale of manufacturing operations, see Chapters 7, 9 and 10.
27 Clark, 'Small towns'; Chilton, 'Universal British Directory'.
28 *Pigot's Directory* (1835), p. 480. See also Chapter 7 of this volume.
29 Blackner, *Nottingham*, p. 54. Nottingham's importance to the hosiery trade is dis-
    cussed more fully in Chapter 9 of this volume.
30 White, *Leicester and Rutland* (1846), p. 66.
31 *UBD*, vol. 3 (1794), p. 268.
32 *Pigot's Directory* (1835), p. 667.
33 White, *Staffordshire* (1851), p. 138. A summary of the range of metalware trades
    and numbers of males, aged over twenty, engaged in each of these is supplied in
    the census enumerations for 1831. The total, estimated to number more than 5000,
    can be doubled if those engaged in Birmingham's 'handicrafts' are included:
    'brass-workers, gunmakers, jewellers, whitesmiths, glass-cutters, japanners, sil-
    versmiths, and toymen'. Population Abstract, 1831, Enumeration, vol. 2 (1834),
    pp. 604–5.
34 The same directory added that '[a]mong the staple manufactures of Walsall, are
    buckles, chains, curbs, bits, spurs, stirrups, plated and other mounting bridles,
    saddles, harness, collars, etc, and every description of saddlers' and coach-mak-
    ers' ironmongery, for which Walsall stands unrivalled'. White, *Staffordshire*
    (1851), p. 635.
35 Population Abstract, 1831, Enumeration, vol. 2 (1834), pp. 680–1.
36 Population Abstract, 1831, Enumeration, vol. 1 (1834), p. 317.
37 White, *Nottinghamshire*.
38 *Leicester Directory*, p. 9; Population Abstract, 1831, Enumeration, vol. 1 (1834),
    pp. 326–7.

39 *Pigot's Directory* (1835), p. 118.

40 Population Abstract, 1831, Enumeration, vol. 2, pp. 726–7.

41 *Pigot's Directory* (1835), p. 426.

42 White, *Staffordshire* (1851), p. 269.

43 *Pigot's Directory* (1835), p. 400. Mansfield, the other prominent town in this class, witnessed a modest decline in its maltsters.

44 Corfield, *English Towns*, pp. 90–1; Trinder, 'Industrialising towns', pp. 805–29.

45 White, *Staffordshire* (1851).

46 *Pigot's Directory* (1835), p. 426.

47 White, *Staffordshire* (1851), p. 287.

48 White, *Staffordshire* (1851), pp. 71–3.

49 *UBD*, vol. 2 (1797), p. 615.

50 *UBD*, vol. 4 (1798), p. 101.

51 White, *Staffordshire* (1851).

52 *Pigot's Directory* (1835), p. 39.

53 Population Abstract, 1831, Enumerations, vol. 2 (1834), pp. 726–7.

54 White, *Staffordshire* (1851).

55 See Raven, 'Small towns of Derbyshire'.

56 Whitehead, *Buckles*, p. 7.

57 Trinder, 'Industrialising towns', p. 818.

58 More, *Industrial Revolution*, p. 115; Langton, 'Urban growth'.

59 Stobart, 'Regions and industrialisation'; Langton, 'Town growth'.

60 White, *Staffordshire* (1851), p. 270. Although Wedgwood is often overplayed as a heroic figure of the industrial revolution, there ample evidence that his actions were typical of a manufacturing elite vital to the growth of the Potteries as an industrial conurbation: see Chapter 7 of this volume.

61 Pollard, *Peaceful Conquest*, p. 39.

62 The fluid nature of industrial regions in the east Midlands is discussed in Chapters 9 and 10. See also Stobart, 'Regions and industrialisation'.

63 Wilde, 'Business directories'.

64 White, *Leicester and Rutland*, p. 272. For a fuller discussion, see Chapter 10 of this volume.

65 White, *Staffordshire* (1851), p. 130.

66 Amongst businesses appearing in the latter, White notes the presence of Messrs Chubb and Son, who 'have long been celebrated for their patent detector and other locks': White, *Staffordshire* (1851), p. 72.

67 White, *Staffordshire* (1851), p. 59.

68 *Pigot's Directory* (1835), pp. 153–4.

69 White, *Staffordshire* (1851), p. 301.

70 *UBD*, vol. 4 (1798), p. 810.

71 White, *Staffordshire* (1851), p. 59.

72 See Stobart, *First Industrial Region* for a rare exception.

3

Industrialisation
and the service economy

Andrew Hann

The main function of towns since their inception has been as service centres for a surrounding hinterland. In England many owed their existence to the establishment of a market during the medieval period, and occupational surveys show that, despite growing industrial specialisation, craftsmen and tradesmen continued to predominate in many towns well into the nineteenth century.[1] As argued in Chapter 1, traditional narratives of urban growth, with their focus on industrial development, have tended to marginalise the role of the service sector, although recent emphasis on leisure, trade and consumption has gone some way to redressing this imbalance. Certainly, the expansion of shopping and leisure facilities was a key element of the eighteenth-century urban renaissance identified by Borsay.[2] Shops, theatres and pleasure gardens were points of access not only to new goods and services, but also to the consumer lifestyle that went with them. Their proliferation was thus central to the redefinition of many town centres as polite spaces.[3] Yet much of this work lacks an overt spatial dimension, despite clear evidence that not all towns had similarly developed service sectors or were regarded by contemporaries as equally polite.[4] This chapter uses directory data to explore the relationship between industrial growth and decline, and the development of urban services within towns across the Midlands, focusing in particular on the retail sector.[5] Rapid population growth during the early stages of industrialisation has often been linked with a general deterioration of service provision. Indeed, some have suggested that industrial development was incompatible with a polite lifestyle.[6] Here it will be argued that the experiences of individual towns varied considerably as a result of both internal and external influences. The nature of service provision depended not just on the rate of urbanisation and character of industrialisation, but also on a town's position within the urban hierarchy and how transport, social and business networks linked it into the wider region.

In order to explore this variation in provision a spatial-systematic approach has been adopted. Following Christaller, towns can be conceptualised as central places, arranged in a hierarchy on the basis of their service functions.[7] A broad definition of the service sector is used, incorporating all those involved in the provision of goods and services to the local population. This covers all listed 'public service and professional' occupations, plus most of those classified as 'dealing', and a significant part of 'manufacturing', specifically craftsmen-retailers.[8] Demarcation of the boundary between craft production for the local market and manufacturing for wider distribution is clearly problematic as the directories rarely make this distinction explicit. Here the assumption has been made that production activities such as tailoring and shoemaking, found throughout the Midlands, were being conducted on a craft basis, whilst those concentrated in particular towns were on an industrial scale and could be excluded. Similarly, retailers have been included, but not wholesalers or those who dealt in raw materials. Of the groups selected, the professions and high-status retailers are comprehensively covered by both directories, but the coverage of other branches of the service sector is more patchy. The *UBD* omits many low-status service providers, particularly petty retailers and craftsmen. Pigot's 1840s directories were more comprehensive, but probably still understate the numbers involved in lower-status occupations.[9]

Level of service sector provision

The level of provision in a town can be measured by comparing the number of people listed in service occupations in the directories with population figures drawn from the 1801 and 1841 censuses. Table 3.1 provides a summary of these figures, grouping towns according to population size, the rate of population growth and the type of town.[10] Overall service provision seems to have improved for most Midlands towns during the study period, matching findings from other parts of the country.[11] In the 1790s the mean ratio between total population and the number of service providers stood at 39:1, but this had fallen to 27:1 by the early 1840s. Improvement appears to have been particularly marked amongst the largest towns. As they were initially the most poorly served, this suggests that the expansion of the service sector may initially have lagged somewhat behind population growth. Indeed, there was an inverse relationship between service provision per capita and town size in the 1790s, a pattern that had become much less apparent by the 1840s. Moreover, if towns are ranked according to their rate of population growth between 1801 and 1841, the fastest-growing quartile has a higher population:service provider ratio than the slowest-growing one, a distinction that is more marked in the 1790s than in the 1840s.

Table 3.1 *Population per service provider in Midlands towns,
1790s and 1840s*

Category of town	Number of towns	Mean ratio – population (1801): service providers (1790s)	Mean ratio – population (1841): service providers (1840s)
Town population (1841)			
<2,000	23	34.9	24.5
2,000–5,000	39	32.2	23.1
5,000–10,000	17	43.2	34.7
10,000+	17	56.1	31.9
All towns	96	39.0	27.1
Town growth (1801–41)			
Fastest growing	20	64.3	36.6
Slowest growing	20	36.8	23.9
Town grouping			
Ab initio industrial towns	11	102.4	52.9
County towns (industrial)	5	36.8	28.0
Market towns (industrial)	29	38.3	27.5
Other county/market towns	51	28.6	21.0

Sources: The size of the service sector was calculated from the *UBD* (1790s) and *Pigot's
Directory* (1841–42); population: census, 1801 and 1841.

Most of the fast-growing, service-poor towns can be characterised as emerging industrial centres or market towns with industrial specialisms according
to the criteria set out in Chapter 2. The majority of their slow-growing,
service-rich counterparts were established towns with limited industrial development. Those worst served in the 1790s and the 1840s were the new industrial
towns, found within two rapidly urbanising industrial districts, the Black
Country and the Potteries.[12] Hanley, for instance, had only two surgeons, one
chemist and an attorney in the 1790s, despite its population having reached
about 7,000. Market towns with substantial industrial sectors were far better
served, but still had population:service provider ratios that were considerably
higher than those for towns without any major industries. This lends further
support to the argument that the rapid population growth associated with
industrialisation led to a general deterioration in the level of service provision

in industrial towns during the late eighteenth and early nineteenth centuries that had only been partially addressed by the early 1840s. Places that were already established market centres were better able to meet the challenge of urban and industrial growth than those that had only recently attained urban status or were subordinate to a larger neighbouring town. Thus, Wednesbury had only one service sector worker for every 134 citizens in the 1790s, whereas nearby Wolverhampton had one for every 35. County towns undergoing rapid industrial development, such as Nottingham and Leicester, appear to have been able to maintain relatively low population:service provider ratios.

The level of service provision was clearly determined not only by the population of a town, but also by its status prior to industrialisation; the nature and extent of its hinterland, and its position within the urban hierarchy. For instance, Wolverhampton was, after Birmingham, the highest-order town in the central west Midlands with a well-developed service infrastructure. By 1798, it had carrier connections with London and major towns in the surrounding counties, and had been a favoured meeting place for the south Staffordshire gentry since the late seventeenth century.[13] Wednesbury, on the other hand, had a more lowly position within the urban hierarchy, with no recorded carrier services in the 1790s, and only three in 1835: to Wolverhampton and Birmingham.[14] Demand for services increased in most towns in response to urbanisation and in particular to the expansion of the urban middle class.[15] Established market centres were best placed to tap into this increased demand since they could exploit their existing reputation as service providers: they already had the necessary infrastructure and stocks of social capital, and could draw on extensive external networks and connections. These were advantages that emerging industrial towns did not possess. Not all established towns, however, shared in this urban renaissance: some, in fact, suffered from deteriorating levels of service provision between the 1790s and the 1840s. Although often exacerbated by high levels of population growth, in the majority of cases this trend reflected a real diminution of service function. In the case of Newcastle-under-Lyme this may have stemmed from the growing encroachment into its hinterland by the expanding service sectors of neighbouring Potteries towns, such as Burslem and Hanley. Certainly, Ingamells describes Newcastle as 'the market town for a large district on all sides except that of the Potteries'.[16] Improved transport and communications also played a part, allowing people to travel further in search of the better facilities and wider range of services available in the great provincial cities or even London.[17] Outside the main industrial districts, market towns could find themselves increasingly isolated as economic and social backwaters. Indeed, for many of the smaller centres, declining service provision marked a loss of urban status itself. Winster, for instance, is described in

Pigot's 1835 directory as 'an inconsiderable village' which had once been 'a market town of some note'.[18]

Diversity of service provision

Subdivision of the service sector into seven broad categories reveals the clear dominance of retailing (see Table 3.2). Around 50 per cent of recorded service personnel came under this heading in both the 1790s and the 1840s. The next largest grouping, craftsmen-retailers, stood at around 26 per cent, followed by professionals, at just under 15 per cent. The overall impression is that the balance between the various categories changed relatively little between the two periods, banking and retailing increasing slightly at the expense of craft-retailing and the professions. However, the composition of the service sector does appear to have differed substantially between different types of town. In general, industrial towns had a larger proportion of their service providers engaged in retailing and provisioning than their non-industrial counterparts, with correspondingly fewer professionals and retail craftsmen. These distinctions were most pronounced for new industrial towns, where retailers constituted around 60 per cent of all service personnel, producing a rather unbalanced service profile. Professionals were particularly under-represented here since many chose to reside in the more genteel surroundings of neighbouring market towns, particularly those where the holding of assizes or quarter sessions ensured a regular influx of gentry customers. For instance, attorneys and surgeons working in the Potteries appear often to have lived in Newcastle-under-Lyme, although the figures suggest that this was changing by the 1840s.[19] To some extent these contrasting service sector profiles were a reflection of the differing service requirements of Midlands towns. All towns provided a wide range of services to their hinterland populations, but only those with substantial manufacturing sectors had large numbers of wage labourers dependent on shops for basic provisioning. In the case of newly established industrial towns this was coupled with recent acquisition of basic urban infrastructure and often relatively limited hinterlands, all of which contributed to the prevalence of low-order services such as petty retailing and provisioning.

A few towns stand out as exceptions to these general patterns: Buxton, for instance, with its large concentration in lodging, making up 35 per cent of all service workers in 1842, and Southwell with its unusually large number of professionals. In both cases such anomalies can be put down to specialist functions. The *UBD* noted that Buxton was already 'supposed, during the season, when full, to accommodate about five hundred persons besides the inhabitants of the place', and the town continued to develop as a resort during the

Table 3.2 *The composition of the service sector in Midlands towns, 1790s and 1840s (percentages)*

Service category	All towns		'New' industrial towns		Established industrial towns		Other county/ market towns	
	1790s	1840s	1790s	1840s	1790s	1840s	1790s	1840s
Banking and finance	1.0	3.8	1.6	2.8	0.8	3.7	0.7	3.5
Craftsmen-retailing	27.2	25.6	22.0	21.3	27.5	27.5	30.9	29.8
Lodging	0.0	0.6	0.0	0.1	0.0	0.3	0.0	1.0
Other services*	2.1	1.8	0.9	2.3	1.7	1.8	1.8	1.6
Professions	15.3	12.0	14.6	8.2	15.9	12.5	18.4	14.3
Public service**	4.5	3.5	2.7	3.4	4.3	3.5	3.5	4.2
Retailing	49.9	52.7	58.2	61.9	49.8	50.7	44.7	45.6

Sources: *UBD* (1790s); *Pigot's Directory* (1841–42).
Notes: * Other services included those providing a personal service e.g. hair dressers.
** Public service included government and municipal workers.

nineteenth century.[20] Similarly, the minster church dominated Southwell, explaining why the *UBD* listed twenty-two clergymen in the town.[21] Other places with unusual service sector profiles included Melton Mowbray, which drew much of its wealth from hunting, and Stratford upon Avon, which benefited from its association with Shakespeare. Many county towns, particularly those that failed to develop significant industrial sectors, also developed their role as social centres for the county elite.[22] Directory entries for these towns often include references to a wide range of leisure facilities, such as theatres, billiards rooms and picture galleries, which were rarely found in smaller market towns or industrial centres. Worcester, for instance, had a large ballroom in the guildhall, a 'neat and commodious' theatre and a library containing 'upwards of 4000 volumes'.[23] Such specialisation in service functions was rarely as apparent as that in manufacturing, but did become increasingly common during the late eighteenth century as towns sought to project a strong cultural identity through the provision of leisure facilities.[24]

The relationships between towns, their hinterlands and the development of their service sectors were clearly complex. A town's position within the urban hierarchy was clearly important, as was its level of specialisation, the nature of its hinterland linkages and the state of the transport infrastructure. Many of these issues are addressed here through an analysis of one important element of the service sector, retailing and provisioning.

Retail and provisioning

Historians are generally agreed that industrialisation had a significant impact upon the nature of retailing in England. There is, however, less of a consensus about the exact timing of this change and indeed whether it marked a transformation of the retail system or merely one stage of a much longer evolutionary process. Until the 1960s the established view was of a retail sector slow to respond to the consequences of industrial development. Fixed shops, it was argued, did not come to replace a system based on markets, fairs and chapmen until the middle of the nineteenth century.[25] Re-appraisal by researchers such as Davis and Alexander pushed the origins of modern retailing back to the decades around 1800, but still maintained that it was essentially a product of industrialization.[26] Shops prior to this were seen as being 'few in number, highly specialised, and run by "producer-retailers", rather than by middlemen'.[27] There is now enough evidence that shops were widespread during the pre-industrial period to refute this argument.[28] Yet the late eighteenth and early nineteenth centuries are still regarded as a time of significant change in the nature and organisation of retailing, during which many innovatory practices such as fixed prices, advertising and branded goods emerged.[29]

The response of the retail sector to urban and industrial change is explored here through an analysis of the number of shops, their increasing variety and the growing complexity of their operations. A fairly narrow definition of retailing has been adopted covering only those occupations which primarily involved the sale to end-consumers of goods produced by others. This excludes producer-retailers such as tailors or shoemakers and those operating largely in a wholesale capacity, both groups which have been included in other directory-based studies.[30] Tradesmen dealing exclusively in foodstuffs, such as bakers and butchers, have been included, however, in order to explore the role shops played in the supply of basic provisions. Despite the emphasis on industrialisation as a watershed, few studies of retail change have examined differences between towns that developed significant manufacturing sectors during this period and those that did not. Most focus on a particular town or seek to identify national patterns from aggregative analysis of data drawn from towns scattered across the country.[31] The large database used here offers more scope for comparative study, whilst the focus onto a spatially coherent region makes it possible to ascertain the extent to which retail development was influenced by each town's position vis-à-vis neighbouring centres.[32]

Studies of retail change have conventionally focused on the number of shops and the ratio of shops to population. There are thought to have been comparatively few shops in the early seventeenth century, but numbers increased substantially after the Restoration, so that by 1759 there was approximately one shopkeeper for every 46 inhabitants.[33] These figures, of course, relate to the population as a whole, so it can be assumed that the actual level of provision in towns was better still. The introduction of a tax on shops in 1785 provides an opportunity to examine urban retailing in more detail, since shops were enumerated at the township level.[34] The tax was levied on 'every building or place used as a shop only, and every house or building any part of which was used as a shop publicly kept open for carrying on any trade, or for selling any goods, wares or merchandise by retail', and was charged according to the yearly rent or value of the premises on a sliding scale.[35] Only fixed-shop retailers fell within the remit of the tax, not wholesalers, itinerant dealers or those who kept market stalls and booths. Properties with a rental value of under £5 per annum were also excluded, as were bakers, provision dealers and alehouse keepers.[36] The shop tax therefore provides a useful indication of the relative size of the retail sector in each town, but cannot be used to measure the total number of shops. Moreover, for most Midlands counties the surviving documents record only the level of tax paid in each township, not the number of shops taxed. There are, though, several comprehensive tax listings that can be used to calculate ratios of population per shop. One such set of accounts, drawn up in 1785 prior to the passage of the act, notes the number of shops liable to taxation in London and thirty-one selected provincial towns.[37] The seven Midlands towns listed had a mean ratio of 57.5 persons per shop, but ranged from 19 in Worcester to 91 in Birmingham, suggesting wide variations in the level of urban retail provision. In general, the highest ratios were found for towns with sizeable industrial sectors such as Coventry (89 persons per shop) and Nottingham (73), whilst the lowest were for those with little industry, like Ludlow (33) and Warwick (45).

A second set of assessments, also from 1785, records the actual number of shops on which tax was paid in Worcestershire and parts of Warwickshire (Table 3.3). Most of the ratios calculated from these figures are somewhat lower, indicating perhaps that these smaller towns were better provided with retailers. Again the highest ratios are for industrial centres and the lowest for Worcester itself. These results must, however, be treated with caution as rates of population growth varied considerably between towns during the late eighteenth century. Some places, particularly the larger industrial centres, were significantly smaller in 1785 than they were in 1801, introducing a considerable upward bias into the ratio calculations. Indeed, the two Worcestershire towns with the supposedly worst levels of provision, Dudley and Kidderminster, are also the ones that were undergoing the most rapid population growth. Moreover, if the two assessments for Worcester are compared, it appears that only around two-thirds of liable shops were actually taxed in 1785.[38] Were the figures to be adjusted to take both these factors into account most towns

Table 3.3 *Number of assessed shops and population per shop in selected Worcestershire and Warwickshire towns, 1785*

Town	Number of assessed shops	Ratio of persons per assessed shop	% growth in town population (1801–11)
Alcester	52	31.3	14.6
Bewdley	61	60.2	−5.9
Bromsgrove	75	33.8	17.5
Droitwich	43	42.9	12.7
Dudley	44	229.7	37.8
Evesham	72	39.4	8.1
Kidderminster	56	122.9	28.4
Pershore	41	46.6	14.1
Stourbridge	60	57.2	18.7
Stratford upon Avon	35	69.1	17.5
Tenbury	24	37.7	1.3
Upton upon Severn	47	39.5	8.9
Worcester	394	29.1	20.4
Mean	77	64.6	14.9

Sources: Shops: PRO, E182/1062, 1123; Population: census, 1801.

would have ratios of around twenty to thirty persons per shop. Given that many petty shopkeepers were excluded from the tax, levels of retail provision in late-eighteenth-century Midlands towns were clearly very high indeed, although there is some indication that rapidly industrialising and growing centres such as Dudley may have been falling behind.

Table 3.4 shows figures for the same Worcestershire and Warwickshire towns derived from trade directory data. These seem to suggest a slight decline in the level of retail provision in many of the towns during the 1790s and probably for the following two decades, followed by significant improvements by the 1840s.[39] A cautious approach to these findings is necessary, however, given the uncertain reliability of early directories. Fowler, for instance, in her study of Southampton in the 1790s, estimated that as many as 30 per cent of retailers might be missing.[40] This is hardly surprising as small shopkeepers were unlikely to have been considered worthy of inclusion in what were publications designed primarily for the use of tradesmen. Indeed, the number of

Table 3.4 *Number of shops and population per shop in selected Worcestershire and Warwickshire towns, 1797–99 and 1842*

Town	Number of shops		Ratio of persons per shop	
	1797–99	*1842*	*1797–99*	*1842*
Alcester	48	57	33.9	42.1
Bewdley	27	99	136.0	34.3
Bromsgrove	61	129	41.5	32.2
Droitwich	22	60	83.9	46.1
Dudley	68	496	148.6	63.0
Evesham	72	79	39.4	53.7
Kidderminster	62	229	111.0	68.7
Pershore	37	65	51.6	43.3
Stourbridge	74	274	46.4	27.3
Stratford upon Avon	62	110	39.0	30.2
Tenbury	25	58	36.2	20.3
Upton upon Severn	37	53	50.2	50.9
Worcester	216	655	56.9	41.2
Mean	62	182	67.3	42.6

Sources: Shops: UBD (1797–99); *Pigot's Directory* (1842); Population: census, 1801 and 1841.

licensed tea dealers documented in late-eighteenth-century excise records confirms that petty shopkeepers were inadequately covered by both the shop tax and the *UBD*, and their numbers were probably somewhat understated by Pigot's directories too.[41] Allowing for the shortcomings of these sources, it would be unwise to claim a significant improvement in the general level of retail provision over the first half of the nineteenth century, and in many cases the situation may even have deteriorated.

Whether retail provision was adversely affected by the rapid population growth during the early stages of industrialisation cannot be firmly established from ratios of population per shop as the comparability of the sources is in doubt. There is, however, sufficient internal consistency within each source to allow measurement of the relative level of provision between towns.[42] This has been achieved by ranking towns according to the amount of shop tax paid in 1785 and the number of retailers listed in the two sets of trade directories. The retail rankings can then be compared with population rankings based on the 1801 and 1841 censuses. The figures confirm the impression that levels of retail provision varied considerably amongst Midlands towns. Some, including Market Harborough, Oswestry and Bishop's Castle, have a far higher retail ranking than their populations would suggest. Others such as Burslem, Hanley and Wednesbury have a much lower ranking than expected, indicating low levels of shop provision. As with the service sector in general, those towns identified as deficient in retail services, particularly in the late eighteenth century, were the emerging industrial centres. County and market towns that had developed industrial specialisms were rather better provided, except where growth had been precipitate, as in the case of Dudley. Most places with unusually high levels of provision were slow-growing established towns with little industrial development. There is also a geographical element to these distinctions, with most poorly served towns concentrated in the central and north-west Midlands, whilst their well-provided counterparts were primarily situated in the east, far west and south-west. Many of the towns showing under- or over-provision of retail services continued to do so throughout the study period, suggesting that these are genuine patterns. Nevertheless, over time there appears to have been a gradual improvement in the general level of provision shown in the closer match between retail and population rankings. In 1785 the mean deviation of rankings was 17.3, whereas in the 1790s it was 15.1 and in 1841–42 only 8.9. The difference between the first two figures may partly be accounted for by varying rates of population growth over the period from 1785 to 1801. The difference between the 1790s and 1840s was, however, much larger and surely reflected a genuine improvement in retail provision particularly within the rapidly growing industrial towns. That said, these findings support the view that, even in the late eighteenth century, established market towns remained 'the focal points of retail trade', regardless of whether they were becoming industrialised or not.[43] By the 1840s, however, the imbalance between population and retail services caused by rapid urbanisation was clearly being addressed. What this means is that the period between the 1790s and 1840s saw not so much a general improvement in the level of provision as a reduction in the diversity of provision.

Recent research suggests that changes to the structure and organisation of urban retailing during the late eighteenth and early nineteenth centuries were at least as important as the growth in the number of shopkeepers. Studies have focused on the greater diversity of shops, the balance between different branches of retailing and new developments in retail practice.[44] Simply counting the number of retailers conceals many aspects of this change, since what was really significant was the type of goods that each outlet sold.

The overall figures have therefore been disaggregated, allowing separate analysis of the various retail categories. Businesses have been grouped according to both the nature of their trade and their degree of specialisation.[45] These data are used to explore two specific questions. First, to what extent was there an expansion in the range of shops found in Midlands towns? And second, how did the balance between retail occupations vary over time and between the different types of town?

As Table 3.5 indicates, no place with pretensions to urban status was without an alehouse or grocer by the 1790s, and only the very smallest centres lacked a baker, butcher or draper. However, specialised retail outlets such as booksellers, chemists and china and glass sellers were restricted to higher-order centres.[46] By the 1840s specialist retailers were more widespread, although a number of categories were still found in fewer than 50 per cent of towns. Particularly notable was the increasing proliferation of shops selling finished goods such as furniture, clothing and jewellery, clearly a consequence of the gradual transition from producer-retailer to specialist shopkeeper, one of the most significant developments in retailing during the nineteenth century.[47] For instance, Alcester in Warwickshire had no such outlets in the 1790s, yet by 1842 there were three earthenware dealers, three watchmakers and clockmakers, one furniture dealer and a cabinet maker.

Table 3.5 *Proportions of towns containing each retail category,*
1790s and 1840s (percentages)

Retail category	All towns		'New' industrial towns		Established industrial towns		Other county/ market towns	
	1797– 99	1841– 42	1797– 99	1841– 42	1797– 99	1841– 42	1797– 99	1841– 42
Bakers and flour dealers	88	95	45	91	95	97	91	94
Butchers	88	98	45	100	89	100	96	98
Grocers and tea dealers	94	96	82	100	95	100	96	92
Confectioners and specialist bakers	38	63	9	55	55	85	30	51
Butter, cheese and milk dealers	24	33	9	55	39	47	15	20
Specialist food dealers	24	53	9	45	34	71	19	43
Tallow chandlers	64	74	27	82	74	88	64	63
Chemists and druggists	67	95	55	100	76	100	62	90

Retail category	All towns		'New' industrial towns		Established industrial towns		Other county/ market towns	
	1797–99	1841–42	1797–99	1841–42	1797–99	1841–42	1797–99	1841–42
Inns, ale and eating houses	96	100	82	100	95	100	100	100
Beer retailers	n/a	84	n/a	100	n/a	91	n/a	78
Wine and spirit merchants	49	73	27	73	68	82	38	67
Tobacconists	10	15	0	0	16	29	9	8
General shopkeepers	60	80	45	100	61	85	64	73
Mercers and drapers	91	96	82	100	92	97	91	94
Clothes dealers	17	30	9	55	26	50	11	12
Clothing accessories dealers	82	71	27	73	92	85	87	61
Milliners and dressmakers	80	83	27	91	92	91	83	78
Ironmongers and hardwaremen	68	86	27	82	71	94	74	82
Silversmiths and jewellers	24	46	0	45	34	56	21	39
Watchmakers and clockmakers	76	80	36	82	87	85	77	78
China, glass and earthenware dealers	36	71	9	64	42	85	38	63
Furniture dealers	1	29	9	27	0	47	0	18
Cabinet makers and upholsterers	54	69	36	91	66	74	49	63
Booksellers and stationers	59	81	27	73	71	88	57	78
Nurserymen and seedsmen	33	73	9	55	42	85	32	71
Itinerant dealers	9	9	9	0	21	29	0	0
Pawnbrokers	20	34	27	55	39	62	2	14
Total number of towns	96	96	11	11	38	34	47	51

Sources: *UBD* (1797–99); *Pigot's Directory* (1841–42).

Although population size explains some of these variations in retail profiles, the type of town and its position within the urban hierarchy also played an important role. In the 1790s, the range of shops was greatest in county towns and higher-order market centres that had developed industrial specialisms: places like Wolverhampton, Coventry and Stourbridge. Indeed, nineteen of the twenty-seven retail categories were found more frequently in established industrial towns than in those without a substantial interest in manufacturing. The distinction between the two types of town was particularly notable for itinerant traders, clothes dealers, pawnbrokers and dealers in fresh produce, all of whom drew their clientele predominantly from the labouring population.[48] Anomalously general shopkeepers seem to have been marginally more common in market towns, although this may reflect the low status of many such places. Moreover, trades usually regarded as catering mainly for the middling sort such as booksellers, confectioners and tobacconists were also more likely to be found in industrial towns. Most emerging industrial towns, however, had a far narrower retail base. Only 27 per cent had a resident wine and spirit merchant compared with 68 per cent of more established manufacturing towns. Industrial development and population growth seem to have occurred in such places before the acquisition of the basic trappings of urbanity. Stoke, for example, is described in the UBD as being 'intended for a market town, as there is a new market-house building, but the market-day is not yet fixed', yet its population already stood at over 2,500.[49] A limited range of shops was also found in small declining market towns such as Bidford and Betley, many of which had populations of 1,500 or fewer. Almost all places had increased the diversity of their retail provision by the 1840s: forty-five now had twenty or more different categories of shopkeeper compared with only thirteen in the 1790s. Industrial towns continued to consolidate their position at the top of the urban hierarchy at the expense of those county and larger market centres that had failed to industrialise: of the twenty highest-ranking towns, only one now lacked an industrial specialism. Moreover, the distinction between established and emerging industrial centres was now less obvious since the greatest improvement in provision came where it had previously been poorest. For instance, in Longton the range of shop categories rose from nine to twenty-three, and in Wednesbury from seven to twenty-one. Places with limited retail diversity were now overwhelmingly small market towns.

Overall the range of retail functions found in a town and the manner in which they developed appear to have depended to a large extent upon its pre-existing position within the Midlands urban hierarchy. Significantly, the type of town was a much better predictor of the level of retail diversity than population size, particularly in the late eighteenth century. The improvement in provision seen in manufacturing centres by the 1840s does suggest that the

Table 3.6 *Changing balance between different retail categories,*
1748–1840s (percentages)

Retail category	1748–70	1790s	1828–29	1840s
Bakers and flour dealers	4.7	11.5	9.5	8.1
Butchers	–	10.7	12.1	11.5
Grocers and tea dealers	15.2	15.6	12.0	9.2
Other dealers in consumables	12.9	12.2	13.2	12.8
Subtotal	32.8	50.0	46.8	41.6
General shopkeepers	8.8	5.5	9.4	17.8
Dealers in cloth and clothing	45.6	25.2	23.4	19.9
Dealers in metal goods	6.4	10.2	8.5	6.3
Dealers in household furnishings	3.6	4.0	5.3	6.7
Other retailers	2.8	5.1	6.6	7.7
Total number of retailers	283	5,195	2,147	15,263

Sources: Mui and Mui, *Shop and Shopkeeping*, pp. 62–3 (1748–70); *UBD* (1790s);
Pigot's Directory (1828–29; 1840s).

urban system was capable of adaptation to changing circumstances. However, those industrial towns that made the transition earliest and most successfully were ones such as Wolverhampton and Dudley that were already substantial market centres with relatively well-developed trading linkages within the region. This clearly demonstrates that external factors such as the configuration of hinterlands and level of network connections played a significant role in determining the course of retail development.[50] Emerging industrial towns faced competition from existing centres and could acquire specialist retail functions only once these connections had been recast and hinterlands realigned. There were also significant changes over time in the proportion of shopkeepers involved in the each branch of retailing (Table 3.6). Shops selling cloth and clothing formed the largest single group in the mid-eighteenth century, constituting 46 per cent of all shops outside London according to figures drawn from bankruptcy records.[51] By the 1790s, however, around half of all town-based retailers in the Midlands were selling consumables and only 25 per cent clothing. Figures taken from *Pigot's Directory* (1828–29) indicate a similar pattern, although both branches had declined in relative terms owing to growth in the number of both specialist outlets and general shopkeepers, a trend which continued into the early 1840s.

Table 3.7 *Variation in the retail profiles of different types of town,
1790s and 1840s (percentages)*

Retail category	'New' industrial towns		Established industrial towns		Other market towns	
	1797–99	1841–42	1797–99	1841–42	1797–99	1841–42
Butchers and bakers	13.1	16.1	23.1	20.0	22.0	19.8
Grocers and tea dealers	26.5	9.8	15.2	7.9	14.9	12.3
Other dealers in consumables	11.8	11.3	12.4	12.3	11.7	14.2
General shopkeepers	13.6	29.3	5.8	18.6	3.9	11.6
Dealers in cloth and clothing	22.2	18.6	23.5	19.8	28.8	20.9
Dealers is metal goods	4.5	4.6	10.7	6.2	9.7	7.4
Dealers in household furnishings	3.7	6.4	3.5	7.0	5.0	6.2
Other retailers	4.6	3.9	5.8	8.2	3.9	7.6
Total number of retailers	221	1,381	3,238	9,978	1,736	3,904

Sources: *UBD* (1790s); *Pigot's Directory* (1841–42).

So far attention has focused on specialist retailers, yet Alexander suggests that the most significant change between 1750 and 1850 was the rise of the small general shopkeeper.[52] At 18 per cent of the total, general stores formed the single largest grouping by 1841–42, having accounted for under 6 per cent of retailers in the 1790s. This represented a nine-fold increase, compared with growth of only 73 per cent for grocers and tea dealers, and 96 per cent for mercers and drapers. The only other branches of retailing to approach this rate of growth were ready-made clothes dealers, furniture dealers and tobacconists, but they started from a much smaller base. To some extent this reflects more thorough coverage of petty retailers in the later directories, but inadequate recording cannot entirely explain a change of this magnitude. Moreover, Table 3.7 indicates that general shops were heavily concentrated in established and especially new industrial towns. By the 1840s they constituted 19 per cent of retail outlets here, compared with only 12 per cent in towns without a substantial industrial sector. In new industrial towns the contrast was even greater, with 29 per cent of retailers operating such stores – together with beer sellers they accounted for almost half of all shopkeepers. In comparison, other categories of shop were more evenly distributed across the different types of town, although there were some discernible patterns. For instance, dealers in cloth and clothing were more numerous in market towns, particularly during the 1790s, whilst dealers in metal goods were under-represented in emerging industrial centres. Figures drawn from the *UBD* also reveal an unusually high concentration of grocers in the latter, but given the limited retail provision in these towns at the time many of them may have effectively acted as general shopkeepers. Clearly urbanisation here was associated with an increasing demand for low-cost neighbourhood stores rather than specialist retail facilities.

Conclusions

The early nineteenth century witnessed significant improvements in service provision across the Midlands. The number of retailers more than trebled during this period whereas the urban population merely doubled. There were, however, considerable variations in the level of provision between different types of town. In many cases the development of retail and service functions lagged behind industrialisation and population growth, especially in new industrial towns, which had often attained a considerable size before they acquired many of the basic trappings of urbanity. The figures suggest that their retail structure was still at an embryonic stage in the 1790s, reaching maturity only in the mid-nineteenth century. Service provision more generally also failed to keep pace with rapid population growth in market centres that developed manufacturing specialisms during early industrialisation. These inadequacies of provision are clearly visible in the 1790s in terms of both the limited range of services available in many centres and the high ratios of population per service provider. By the 1840s, some of these shortcomings had been addressed and the distinctions between industrial and market towns were certainly less pronounced. Nevertheless, the various categories of town still had recognisably different service sector profiles reflecting the differing characteristics of the populations they served. External relationships played a central role in shaping the evolution of retail and service provision, reflecting the dynamism of the Midlands urban system. In the 1790s the most complete provision was found in county towns and higher-order market centres, much as Christaller's conception of a central place hierarchy might predict. However, by the 1840s, the urban system had been recast as towns that had not industrialised saw their position in the hierarchy and their traditional relationship with rural hinterlands undermined by competition from their more dynamic neighbours. The most highly developed service sectors were now found in those towns that were able to combine successfully the roles of manufacturing town and high order-service centre. These towns had both an expanding internal market for goods and services, and good external linkages with other parts of the region and beyond.

Appendix 3.1: Categories used to group retail occupations

Dealers in consumables

Bakers and flour dealers

Butchers

Grocers and tea dealers – including coffee dealers

Confectioners and specialist bakers – including gingerbread bakers, pastry cooks

Butter, cheese and milk dealers – including cheesemongers, milk sellers, butter factors

Specialist food dealers – including fishmongers, fruiterers, greengrocers, poulterers

Innkeepers, alehouse and eating-house keepers – including victuallers, coffee house keepers

Wine and spirit dealers

Tobacconists

Chemists and druggists – including apothecaries, patent medicine sellers

Tallow chandlers – including soap boilers, oilmen and colourmen

General dealers

Shopkeepers – including dealers in sundries, badgers, hucksters

Dealers in cloth and clothing

Mercers and drapers

Clothes dealers – including slop shops, clothes salesmen, old-clothes men

Clothing accessories dealers – including haberdashers, hatters, hosiers, glovers, small-ware dealers

Milliners and dressmakers – including staymakers

Dealers in metal goods

Ironmongers and hardwaremen – including cutlers

Silversmiths and jewellers – including toymen

Watchmakers and clockmakers

Dealers in furniture and furnishings

China, glass and earthenware dealers

Furniture dealers – including carpet warehousemen

Cabinetmakers and upholsterers

Miscellaneous

Booksellers and stationers – including law stationers, music sellers

Itinerant dealers

Nurserymen and seedsmen

Pawnbrokers

Notes

1 Ellis, 'Regional and county centres', pp. 684–90; Hopkins, *Manufacturing Town*, pp. 76–97; Simmons, *Leicester*, vol. 1.
2 Borsay, *English Urban Renaissance*.
3 Glennie and Thrift, 'Consumers'; Stobart, 'Shopping streets'.
4 Sweet, 'Topographies of politeness'.
5 The main directories used here were the *UBD* and *Pigot's Directory* (1841 and 1842).
6 Collins, 'Primitive or not'; Mitchell, 'Retailing', pp. 40–1; Klein, 'Politeness for plebes'.
7 Christaller, *Central Places*.
8 Occupations were grouped using a modified version of the Booth–Armstrong classification system. See Chapter 2 for further elaboration.
9 Walton, 'Trades and professions'; Shaw and Alexander, 'Directories'.
10 These town typologies are discussed in Chapter 2.
11 Alexander, *Retailing in England*.
12 These towns are explored further in Chapter 7.
13 *UBD*, vol. 4 (1798), p. 811; Blome, *Britannia*, p. 206.
14 *UBD*, vol. 4 (1798), p. 706; *Pigot's Directory* (1835), p. 471.
15 Borsay, *English Urban Renaissance*; Sweet, *English Town*.
16 Ingamells, *Newcastle-under-Lyme*, p. 20.
17 Ellis, 'Regional and county centres', pp. 680–1; Pawson, *Transport and Economy*, pp. 277–9.
18 *Pigot's Directory* (1835) p. 79.
19 In Burslem, Hanley, Stoke and Longton, professionals rose from making up an average of 8.5 per cent of directory entries in the 1790s to 9.2 per cent in 1842; in Newcastle, they fell from 13.2 per cent to 10.7 per cent.
20 *UBD*, vol. 2 (1797), p. 447.
21 *UBD*, vol. 4 (1798), pp. 433–6.
22 McInnes, 'Shrewsbury', pp. 54–65; Beckett and Smith, 'Nottingham', pp. 33–6.
23 Chambers, *Worcester*, pp. 301–3, 366, 371–5.
24 Clark and Houston, 'Culture and leisure', p. 613; Sweet, 'Topographies of politeness', pp. 367–71.
25 Jefferys, *Retail Trading*, pp. 1–13.
26 Davis, *Shopping*; Alexander, *Retailing in England*.
27 Benson *et al.*, 'Sources', p. 167.
28 See Cox, *Complete Tradesman*; Mui and Mui, *Shops and Shopkeeping*; Shammas, *Pre-Industrial Consumer*; Willan, *Inland Trade*.
29 Fowler, 'Provincial retailing', pp. 48–52.
30 Mitchell, 'Retailing'; Collins, 'Primitive or not'.
31 Fowler, 'Provincial retailing'; Scola, *Victorian City*; Alexander, *Retailing in England*, pp. 89–109.
32 See Stobart, 'Spatial organization'.
33 Cox, *Complete Tradesman*, p. 53 suggests a ratio of roughly one retailing tradesman to every 500 inhabitants in early-seventeenth-century Gloucestershire; Mui and Mui, *Shops and Shopkeeping*, 44.
34 The 1759 survey was based on excise collection districts only.

35 Dowell, *History of Taxation*, p. 10.

36 Artisans who worked for hire also avoided the tax, although those who kept a shop were included. Mui and Mui, *Shops and Shopkeeping*, pp. 34–6, 74.

37 PRO, HO 42/7, fols 247–253b. These accounts are examined by Mui and Mui, *Shops and Shopkeeping*, pp. 85–90.

38 In the pre-tax listing 602 retail premises in Worcester were deemed liable to the tax, of which 277 had a rateable value of less than £15. Many of these shop-keepers may in fact have avoided paying the tax.

39 Collins, 'Primitive or not', pp. 30–1, and Mitchell, 'Urban markets', pp. 247–61, both noted a rise in the ratio of persons per shop between the 1790s and 1820s – a worsening of provision which they associated with industrialisation and rapid population growth – but improvement in the following decades.

40 Fowler, 'Provincial retailing', p. 39.

41 Mui and Mui, *Shops and Shopkeeping*, pp. 163–72, argue that petty retailers were only adequately covered from the 1840s, when Pigot & Co. introduced a new cat-egory of 'shopkeeper' into their directories.

42 There are some doubts regarding the *UBD* in this respect, although retailers seem in general to have been consistently recorded. The few towns where this was not the case have been excluded from the analysis.

43 Cox, 'Retailing tradesmen', p. 15.

44 Fowler, 'Provincial retailing'; Stobart and Hann, 'Retailing revolution'; Walsh, 'Department store'.

45 The scheme used to classify retail trades is set out in Appendix 3.1.

46 For a comparable survey of specialist retail provision in north-west England see Stobart and Hann, 'Retailing revolution'.

47 Collins, 'Primitive or not', pp. 31–2.

48 Alexander, *Retailing in England*, pp. 61–86; Scola, *Victorian City*, pp. 234–53.

49 *UBD*, vol. 4 (1798), p. 109.

50 See Stobart, 'Spatial organization'.

51 Mui and Mui, *Shops and Shopkeeping*, pp. 49–61.

52 Alexander, *Retailing in England*, pp. 97–9.

4

Industry, investment and consumption: urban women in the Midlands

Christine Wiskin

Introduction

Women were part of the urban landscape of the eighteenth- and early-nineteenth-century Midlands, but it is uncertain how far or with what conviction their actions may be translated into meaningful conclusions about their role in the development of this region. Surviving primary sources tend to be incomplete; data collection during the period was often arbitrary and frequently gender-blind, so that much of the recording of women's economic activities is anecdotal rather than systematic.[1] There is also the problem of the universalism of women. How might a cohort of the population found throughout Britain influence change in a particular part of it? Their contribution to economic development could be attributed to a trajectory which affected all British women. Most of them participated in a life cycle of maiden–wife–widow irrespective of where they lived. The activities, status and experiences of Midlands women were similar to those of their female contemporaries nationwide. Examples of the businesswoman widow, the entrepreneurial spinster, the female investor, the craftswoman and the labouring woman found in this region were also present in towns throughout Britain. Wherever they lived, even apparently leisured women 'worked', managing large households as well as holding together social networks which supported, maintained and extended family interests in business.[2] Women of all ranks and conditions, whether from the wage-earning or capital-owning classes, were also consumers, part of new and large markets for non-essential goods and services. Whilst differences between those who made, those who sold and those who purchased might seem significant, this was not necessarily the case. All were united in a 'world of goods' where distinctions between the demand and supply sides of the economy could be merged. As a result, arguments have been made for connections between women's production of manufactured goods and their consumption of them in the eighteenth and early nineteenth centuries. Furthermore, it has been claimed that women's appetites for these new products, when coupled with their buying power, were a major spur to efficiencies and innovations in manufacturing which characterised industrialisation.[3] Acquisition of new manufactures and services was open to all, involvement in it being limited only by the size of an individual's disposable income or moral standards.[4] Even the poor were consumers of new or recycled goods produced in the region and beyond it. Their desires for finery, as well as the need to make a living, fuelled poor women's elaborate networks of informal marketing, based on pawning, pledging and petty crime, and were a feature of life in the Midlands, as they were elsewhere in Britain.[5] Female industry and consumption were also instrumental in urbanisation. The female urban population was far from uniform, but how should we interpret this diversity and what was its effect on the history of the Midlands? One way is to balance the universalism of their sex against local circumstances; but were these sufficiently exceptional that women's activities would make a difference?

Despite shortcomings in primary sources, it may be said with confidence that, in the Midlands, the presence of urban women was real, recorded in contemporary newspapers, directories and topographical and local studies, as well as in their personal writings. The *UBD* and *Pigot's Directory* included listings of women involved in an eclectic range of occupations and businesses, and women without occupational designation, who were presumably annuitants living on savings or investment income. Entries in these directories permitted urban women who could afford the fee to lay claim to a distinct identity within the towns they inhabited. Midlands urban women produced, sold and consumed goods made in their region: hosiery and lace, metalwares, and china and earthenware. They also made goods for export, and sold and consumed items produced throughout the country.[6] In this chapter, it will be argued that the things that Midlands women made, sold or purchased played an important part in the region and especially in its towns, where they contributed to the processes by which urban values came to dominate society. Whether they were labourers, business proprietors or investors, women were likely to be involved in these changes.

Regional overview

Studies of women's businesses in the Midlands have shown that they were the owners of real enterprises which were not merely personal services for discrete groups of friends, kin or connections. Analyses have involved the linking together of a wide range of documentary sources including wills, probate inventories, newspaper advertisements and parish and business records, as well as urban directories. Record linkage indicates that women owned the assets necessary to carry on business (stock, tools and premises) and used them to do so.[7] For the purposes of this chapter, analysis was carried out on women's entries in trade directories for eight specific towns in the region: Burslem, Lichfield, Loughborough, Nottingham, Wolverhampton, Coventry, Warwick and Worcester. The first five are discussed in Part II of this book; the last three are included for comparative purposes. The aim is to establish the extent of women's participation in the urban business communities in the Midlands, whether this changed over time and whether their presence in the first five towns was exceptional within the region.

Table 4.1 shows that in the eight towns selected, female businesses made up a mean of 6 per cent of all those listed in the late 1790s and 9 per cent in 1842. In the late 1790s, women accounted for at least 5 per cent of all businesses listed, except in Lichfield and Nottingham. The low values in these towns may be an under-representation, the result of shortcomings in the soliciting of orders by the compilers' agents, which, to judge from the greater uniformity of entries, had been addressed by the 1840s. Certainly, the data suggest that the percentage of businesswomen in the first five towns was not exceptional within the region, similar values being found for businesswomen in Birmingham, the region's largest town.[8] The data also indicate that businesswomen were a small percentage of the Midlands urban commercial community and that the women who paid to be listed were an even smaller proportion of the total female urban population, the majority of whom belonged to the labouring classes. Thus the ownership of sufficient assets to be one's own mistress in business was the exception in the experience of Midlands women.

Perhaps more surprisingly, with the exception of Loughborough, in 1842 businesswomen constituted a higher percentage of the urban business community in every town surveyed than they did in the 1790s. Moreover, female advertisers in 1842 were to be found in more occupational categories than they were in the 1790s (see Table 4.2), though it is debatable whether in the early decades of the nineteenth century women had more chance of self-advancement or might make a greater contribution to town life. Table 4.2 shows that in the late 1790s the majority of women's businesses were in the food and drink trades and in those relating to clothing and textiles; together, these accounted for more than half of all women's enterprises in both periods. However, the data for 1842 reveal three major changes: an alteration in the composition of that majority, an increased percentage of women running enterprises concerned with education and a decline in female ownership of manufacturing businesses.

Table 4.1 *Female advertisers in Midlands towns,
1797–1842: businesswomen advertisers as percentage
of all business advertisers*

Town	1797–99	1842
Burslem	7.8	10.1
Coventry	7.2	8.5
Lichfield	1.6	9.8
Loughborough	9.6	9.0
Nottingham	3.9	8.5
Warwick	5.0	10.1
Wolverhampton	6.2	7.1
Worcester	6.3	11.5

Sources: *UBD* (1791–99); *Pigot's Directory* (1842).

Urban businesswomen in the Midlands did not experience some sort of commercial new dawn in the early nineteenth century. They do not seem to have benefited from a widening economic sphere; rather, the opposite appears to have been the case. Whilst a greater percentage made or sold clothing and textiles, proportionally fewer were engaged in the food and drink trades or in retailing. By the early nineteenth century, women were less likely to be engaged in highly capitalised businesses that dealt with both male and female customers. In the eighteenth century, women proprietors in the service sector (particularly retailers or victuallers) had not been isolated commercially or socially from men. This meant that their customer bases and business networks carried with them the potential for expansion.

Thus, Ann Dunn, a Birmingham innkeeper, developed a coaching network that included male innkeepers on the route between Wolverhampton and London.[9] By the 1840s, fewer women ran large-scale innkeeping businesses. They were also less likely to be urban retailers of the eighteenth-century sort, their incidence having declined in the majority of the towns surveyed. Moreover, in the eighteenth century, women were also active in manufacturing at all levels of engagement: as craft and artisan producers or, exceptionally, as owners of large industrial concerns. Typically, eighteenth-century businesswomen who engaged in manufacturing operated on a small scale in their own workshops.[10] Changes in the ways manufacturing was organised, however, made it increasingly difficult for small producers to make a reasonable living, and by the 1840s women were less likely to be found running businesses engaged in craft and artisan production.[11] Even in towns such as Wolverhampton, where small-scale producers continued to make specialist metalwares, there was a decline in the percentage of women advertisers engaged in trade and craft production (see Table 4.2).

Data on the sample towns indicate that by the nineteenth century urban businesswomen were generally clustered in 'feminine' occupations. These were service sector activities regarded by contemporaries as 'women's work' – implicitly inferior to men's. This change reflected longer-established trends in London, where the general structure of women's occupations scarcely changed between the late seventeenth and the mid-nineteenth centuries, dominated as it was by domestic service, needlework, laundry and catering.[12] It might be expected that provincial businesswomen from the middle ranks would have had different experiences. Yet increasing female engagement in education, the making and selling of clothing and textiles for women, and public adminis-tration (mostly, for example, as matrons of workhouses or mistresses of houses of industry) conformed to stereotypes of womanhood: to care for those unable to look after themselves, to undertake work which required the femi-nine touch of fine motor skills or to take on work which closely resembled household tasks. This suggests that changes in women's occupations reflected the increasing importance of domestic ideology in governing what occurred in both home and workplace. As far as middle-class women were concerned, the acceptability of following a respectable trade had been over-ridden by aspira-tions to gentility. They were the occupational group most likely to have been influenced by new notions of female behaviour, where to work for one's liv-ing was to 'cease to be a lady'.[13] In the eighteenth century, there had been many trades and crafts in which women of the 'middling sort' could engage and still retain good reputations in the eyes of their contemporaries. By the early decades of the next century, however, gentility had replaced respectabil-ity as the epitome of true womanhood, and the desire of a middle-class woman to support herself was deemed inimical to such aspirations. Ann Bassett's busi-ness life and the subsequent fate of the enterprise after her death exemplified this change. Bassett, a Birmingham woman, inherited her brother's saddlery business, which she ran for thirty years with the help a foreman and her two nieces. After her death in 1811, Bassett's nieces gave up the trade, apparently motivated by their belief that it was an unladylike type of business. In their case, their aunt's enterprise provided them with sufficient funds to retire to the new and exclusive Birmingham suburb of Edgbaston.[14]

New ideas of womanhood were not the only reason for the concentration of women's businesses into 'feminised' parts of the service sector. Ann Bas-sett's nieces appear to have been the fortunate recipients of their aunt's hard work. However, there were many women who aspired to middle-class status

Table 4.2 Occupations of females in Midlands towns, 1790s and 1842 (percentages)

	Burslem		Coventry		Lichfield		Loughborough		Nottingham		Warwick		Wolverhampton		Worcester	
	1798	1842	1797	1842	1799	1842	1799	1842	1798	1842	1798	1842	1799	1842	1798	1842
Food and drink	47.1	41.1	37.8	25.9	0.0	38.5	62.5	38.8	20.0	22.3	41.2	33.9	45.7	30.9	38.9	22.8
Clothing and textiles manufacturers	41.2	25.5	29.7	35.9	66.7	32.1	8.3	39.7	36.0	54.5	41.2	32.4	19.6	29.5	23.7	45.5
Crafts	11.8	8.9	10.8	14.6	0.0	11.0	20.8	8.6	10.0	4.9	0.0	7.4	21.7	18.1	16.9	4.9
Retail	0.0	2.2	16.2	2.7	0.0	3.7	0.0	0.0	22.0	0.3	0.0	3.2	8.7	2.01	5.1	2.7
Education	0.0	17.8	5.4	15.1	33.3	11.0	4.2	8.6	4.0	14.3	11.8	13.9	4.3	15.4	8.5	17.1
Miscellaneous	0.0	4.4	0.0	0.0	0.0	0.0	0.0	0.0	4.0	0.7	5.9	1.5	0.0	2.01	5.1	3.8
Transport	0.0	0.0	0.0	1.4	0.0	0.0	0.0	1.7	0.0	0.3	0.0	6.2	0.0	0.7	1.7	2.2
Public administration	0.0	0.0	0.0	4.3	0.0	0.0	0.0	2.6	4.0	0.0	0.0	1.5	0.0	0.0	0.0	0.9
Pawnbroking	0.0	0.0	0.0	0.0	0.0	3.7	4.2	0.0	0.0	0.7	0.0	0.0	0.0	2.01	0.0	0.8
Total	100.0	100.0	100.0	100.0	100.0	100.0	100.0	100.0	100.0	100.0	100.0	100.0	100.0	100.0	100.0	100.0

Sources: UBD (1791–99); Pigot's Directory (1842).

and respectability but who nonetheless could not rely on kin to provide for them. Instead, they had to find ways to provide for themselves or risk increasing impoverishment. Thus economic imperatives as well as changing cultural values help to explain the increased percentages of women running 'feminine' businesses.[15] In the late eighteenth and early nineteenth centuries, declining opportunities had forced poor women to find new types of work in towns rather than in the countryside.[16] Gender imbalances in early-nineteenth-century Lichfield (see Chapter 11) suggest that such pressures were present in the Midlands. Such reactions to market forces were not restricted to the poor. They also affected middle-class women and go some way to explain the changing nature of their businesses. Concentrated into certain parts of the service sector, urban middle-class women's businesses in the 1840s corresponded closely to their domestic roles. They frequently translated traditional female familiarity with, and assumed expertise in, needlework, homemaking and caring for others into money-making enterprises. The increasing female population of towns needed to be clothed and shod, and satisfying the expanding demand presented commercial opportunities that could be united in an entrepreneurial manner with women's traditional needle skills. The enthusiasm of young women to be dressmakers was driven by the combined forces of economic need and new ideas of gentility. The making or selling of clothing and textiles was a form of economic enterprise sufficiently congruent with these criteria that it could be undertaken by middle-class women, for whom the ownership of a high-class dressmaking or millinery business could be simultaneously genteel, profitable and successful.[17] The structure of the lace industry in the east Midlands also provided economic opportunities for businesswomen. By the early nineteenth century, lace-net was machine-made, but women decorated it by hand in their homes. Nottingham businesswomen organised this, collecting net from manufacturers, distributing it amongst home workers and marketing the finished goods.[18] There were also, as Table 4.2 shows, substantial increases in the percentage of women advertising educational services as demand grew for formal education for girls and young women. Schools may have outwardly resembled domestic premises and required attributes associated with private life: discipline and instruction of children, cooking, cleaning and laundry. Yet these were real businesses in as much as they demanded the outlay of time, money and management skills in order to be successful. Proprietors owned or leased premises and employed staff, male and female.[19] Women, such as Mary Ann Phipson and her sisters, and the half-sisters Sarah Bache and Phoebe Penn, ran successful girls' schools in and around Birmingham in the early nineteenth century.[20]

It is evident that differences in the nature of urban women's businesses in the Midlands in the early nineteenth century were the result of the complex

meshing of factors. New notions of femininity and gentility, women's economic needs, structural changes within particular trades – these all affected
the types of business in which women were found and help to explain how
and why change took place.

The urban businesswoman

Women's occupations tended to be grounded in their family life, for it was by
working within its business or trade that they acquired the know-how to carry
it on and, in time, the assets with which to do so. Division of labour meant
that husbands and fathers undertook the majority of production, helped by
journeymen and apprentices. Wives and daughters were engaged in subsidiary
tasks, often connected with finishing processes. If the enterprise was large, the
female members might work at these subsidiary tasks, but might also keep
accounts and deal with customers.[21] Division of labour also occurred in the
service sector. In innkeeping, for example, wives and daughters had specific
tasks concerned with the care of customers and the payment of bills.[22]
Although inherently gendered, dividing up and allocating work in this way
could ultimately be to the advantage of women. It enabled them to build up
social capital in the form of knowledge of how the trade was organised and
the dynamics of the market in which its products were sold and distributed.
This was important as a business as well as a monetary asset.

This picture of family enterprise carries with it implications for the oppres-
sion of women and the suppression of their desires and aspirations in the
interests of kin unity. Payments were made to the male head of the household,
to whom common law and religious precept had given authority and power.
Recent research, however, has shown how the boundaries of men's authority
over their female relatives might be more fluid than strict readings of the law
would suggest.[23] Even if a woman was subordinated during marriage or the
lifetime of her father, bereavement might offer her different opportunities. The
death of the male head threatened the loss of financial and emotional support,
but it was a complex and problematic event, which might paradoxically prom-
ise women release from other constraints. For widows, there was the
expectation of reclaiming property which had been subsumed by coverture, as
well as inheriting at least part of the deceased's estate.[24] On the other hand,
the deceased might, by his will, attempt to continue to impose his authority
on those who survived him. He might require that his female relatives carry
on the enterprise in order to provide an inheritance for children or other kin;
alternatively, he might order the sale of his business and the investment of its
proceeds; he might even impose sanctions should his widow attempt to
remarry.[25] The responses of Midlands women varied widely. Some obeyed

instructions to wind up the enterprise and live on the sale proceeds. They realised the family enterprise and invested the sale monies in the new types of low-risk security to provide themselves with an unearned income. Particular opportunities were available to widows in Birmingham, the region's largest town, where the building and renting of houses was a popular form of invest-ment.[26] Others, driven by a combination of economic need, personal circumstances and inclination, continued the business that had passed to them, irrespective of the instructions of the deceased.[27]

Whatever the circumstances that propelled them into business activity on their own account, the relatively small scale on which most enterprises were conducted aided women's participation in urban commercial communities. The fact that the home usually also housed the workplace, combined with the modest capital requirements of many eighteenth-century enterprises, meant that these could be continued by widows and daughters, and stock, tools and premises were bequeathed to them on the assumption that they would do so. Possessed of these assets, they were in a position to carry on 'business as usual' with the same male staff or with new ones.[28] They might reasonably expect to make a living, given that credit was generally easily available.[29] Ann Rol-lason, a Coventry woman widowed with young children after the death of her husband in 1813, kept the books and managed his printing and bookselling enterprise, with the assistance of his former business partner, journeymen and apprentices. By doing so, she ensured that her son inherited it on her death over thirty years later.[30] A further group of urban women, wealthy widows or spinsters, who might have been expected to realise large-scale enterprises and live on the invested proceeds, also continued inherited businesses. Entrepre-neurial widows, such as Abigail Gawthern of Nottingham and Phoebe Webster of Penns, near Birmingham, ran industrial concerns inherited from their hus-bands. Gawthern was a white-lead manufacturer, running for fifteen years the works left by her husband, and Webster managed her late husband's iron-works for thirteen years until her son came of age. During the minority of the heir, management of the Coalbrookdale Company in Shropshire was carried on by Sarah Darby, the unmarried sister of two deceased brothers, Abraham III and Samuel, and their widows, Rebecca and Deborah, assisted by a male agent.[31] Doubts that women's businesses were commercial ones must be dis-pelled by the prosperity and the size of the firms that they ran. Like their male contemporaries in manufacturing, Gawthern, Webster and the Darby women suffered good and bad fortune. In the cases of Gawthern and Webster the dishonesty of clerks and managers, natural hazards such as flooding and the hostility of less successful local businesspeople were counterbalanced and eventually over-ridden by the loyalty of their workforces. All these enter-prising women succeeded in handing on valuable and substantial firms.[32]

Whether they were widows or daughters of entrepreneurs or tradesmen, women who continued inherited businesses had fulfilled an intricate set of public and personal obligations. They had ensured that public funds had not been required for their upkeep and often provided local employment. Widowed mothers, whilst experiencing the ambivalent nature of single parenthood, had raised young adults who might, in the future, be expected to take on the enterprise. These inheritance patterns were not unique to the Midlands, but were widespread amongst the urban middling ranks.[33]

Industry, consumption and investment

The foregoing are important issues in women's history, but there still remains the question of female contributions to the urban and regional economy more generally. Did the presence of women's businesses affect urban life or industrial development and, if so, how? What was the effect of women's participation in particular trades or sectors on urban life and the regional economy?

The majority of urban women were poor, living and working hand to mouth in order to survive. Because they existed on the margins of society, were impoverished and were oppressed by a double burden of legal constraints and the sexual division of labour, their lack of power and agency would appear to have deprived them of significance; but are these assumptions reasonable? At the bottom of the economic ladder, labouring women undertook all sorts of industrial production in factories and workshops, as well as in their own homes. Quantifying the importance of their work to industrialisation is hampered by the paucity of reliable or extensive data.[34] Yet the ways in which contemporaries saw women made their labour attractive. Women were deemed to be dextrous, skilful, quick to learn, unambitious and more docile than men. As workers, they were believed to be steady, reliable and cheap. These attributes endowed them with machine-like qualities: they could perform repetitive tasks, were obedient and were seemingly tireless.[35] Theirs were the hands which could implement the improvements, efficiencies and innovations which typified the first stages of industrialisation. They were, therefore, an ideal workforce as manufacturers increased the intensity and pace of work and, by technological changes and extensive division of labour, decreased even further women's control over how they worked.[36] These qualities were specific to women as a sex and could be applied wherever they worked. They were as appropriate to rural outwork, carried on in the home, as to urban workshops or factories.

There were multiple routes to industrialisation in the Midlands. Manufacturing was carried on in many ways, and the structure of the region's space economy was complex. Metalware production in the west Midlands, where the large factories of Boulton and Watt or James Taylor were exceptional, was generally small-scale and artisan-based. In the north of the region, pottery production in Staffordshire underwent structural change and became factory-based. On the other hand, mechanisation came late to the east Midlands, in most cases not until the 1840s.[37] Metalwares and pottery were amongst the 'dynamic' new consumer goods of the age, produced by industries with high levels of output.[38] This was achieved by efficiencies based on division of labour which could take place either within single sites, as in the case of Staffordshire potteries, or in many, as in the Birmingham toy trades.[39] Women were vital in these industries because production called for extreme division of labour and repetition of tasks. They decorated Wedgwood's chinaware, initially painting routine patterns but increasingly doing more elaborate work, in which they were 'steady, remorseless and efficient'.[40] In the Birmingham trades, the dexterity and adaptability which women workers were believed to possess made them a desirable workforce, sought by manufacturers and workshop owners. Women were in demand in trades associated with the manufacture of decorative metal objects – stamping and shaping metal, polishing and japanning, and making buttons and buckles. Conversely, the quantity, flexibility and cost advantages of female labour may have encouraged the continued use of hand techniques at the expense of mechanisation.[41] An east–west divide appears to have occurred in the Midlands. In the metal trades of the west, the use of female labour was accompanied by technical innovation as tools were modified for their use.[42] In the east, it is argued that an abundance of female labour discouraged employers in Nottingham and Leicester from investing in new technologies until this source of human capital had largely dried up. Here, hosiery and lace production still had an input of hand labour, supplied by women workers, even after other parts of each industry had been mechanised.[43] This, however, is only part of the story. Delays in mechanisation appear to have been multi-causal, as much to do with the strength of established local customs and violent artisan resistance to the introduction of machinery as with the availability of women's labour.[44]

Many of the goods produced by 'dynamic' Midlands industries were exported (see Chapter 12), but there was an important home market, where production, marketing and consumption were tied together by intricate bonds. There was an overlap between producers and consumers because those who made or sold goods were themselves consumers.[45] To sell at home, manufacturers needed urban retailers, in both London and the provinces. We know a great deal about the importance of male shopkeepers – and their male and female customers – to the growth of home demand for manufactures in eighteenth-century provincial England.[46] Yet the significance of women retailers to the economy, either local or national, has generated only limited comment. As advertisements in provincial newspapers indicate, women sold all sorts of semi-luxury goods in the English regions. Mary Rollason of Birmingham, Mary Stubbs of Wolverhampton and Elizabeth and Jane Parker of Coventry were but a few of many female shopkeepers whose presence was recorded in this way. The goods and services which they sold were the new consumer products of the time, including chinaware, books, perfumes, patent medicines, high-quality candles, insurance policies and lending libraries.[47] Advertisements also show us how urban retailers were integrated into complex, multi-layered networks of trade which linked together towns within and beyond the region. Inclusion in well-publicised and extensive business connections would be expected of the male shopkeeper. Bearing in mind orthodoxies about women's exclusion from the public sphere, their place in regional and national trade networks seems remarkable, but they were to be found there. Their presence reminds us that commercial networks both were gender-neutral compared with new, exclusively male urban institutions; and were sufficiently flexible to include businesswomen, who were increasingly marginalised from other types of urban network. For example, like many provincial booksellers, Ann Cresswell of Wolverhampton sold many other lines. The stockings that she sold were probably made in or around Nottingham, and the patent medicines, such as Dr Radcliffe's Purging Elixir, were produced by the London firm of Dicey and Co. She was also an agent taking in local advertisements to be published in Birmingham newspapers.[48]

Notices in the provincial press, particularly those inserted by manufacturers seeking national markets, told potential consumers what goods were on sale, and where. They reinforce historians' understanding of the importance of local stockists, male and female, in marketing what was new and fashionable. In the world of the urban shopkeeper, however, the new was combined with the traditional. Women were believed to be expert in buying, in seeking out the most appropriate goods at the most favourable prices. This tradition served the urban female shopkeeper well. Customers could enter their premises in the expectation of being offered not only a wide range of goods but also advice on selecting, buying and using them. What women retailers were selling was more than new goods and services, important though this function was to producers. As far as their customers were concerned, women shopkeepers were marketing a design for living, transmitting particular social values of taste and style to their customers, conveying to urban communities new ideas of what was polite behaviour. This was based on the new eighteenth-century fashion for commercialised leisure and display, in which shopping was treated as a pastime as much as a necessity. The matched sets of china sold by Mary Rollason and the hosiery available from Ann Cresswell's

shop served particular purposes in the hands of their eighteenth-century pur-
chasers. Possession and display of such items played a part in forging their
owners' identity as individuals of taste and prosperity. But there was more to
it than that. The existence of shops that sold these and other non-essential
goods helped the growth of cultural identities of comfort and order, in which
those who consumed could participate. As well as marketing the new norms
of urban material culture, women retailers transmitted new ideas about nurturing the mind and the imagination. Customers of Ann Cresswell or the
Misses Parker, who ran libraries on their premises,[49] entered a world that was
literally novel because access to libraries was now far more widely available
to urban populations than in the past.[50] These were urban experiences but
could be spread into polite rural society by non-resident, visiting consumers.
In marketing them, female shopkeepers were part of the processes of behav-
ioural urbanisation, of the diffusion of social and cultural characteristics of
town life rather than of rural.[51] Tales of the contrast between rustic simplicity and urban polish have always been part of European culture; what was
different in the eighteenth century was that urban sophistication might be
purchased by those willing to subscribe to its values.[52]

The existence of these shopkeepers suggests that participation in the new
world of semi-luxury goods and services was achievable by urban and rural
customers. Yet expecting that this was so is different from demonstrating it.
How were the new products received? Did urban values influence those living in the countryside? Evidence from testamentary documents suggests that
townspeople of middling wealth, and sometimes even those with very little to
leave, had acquired many of the new consumer goods. As well as fine clothing, both men and women owned china and glassware, ornaments and books.[53]
It has been argued that the complexity of how ideas spread beyond towns
makes it hard to establish to what extent and how quickly urban values influenced country people.[54] On the other hand, it seems that rural customers
recognised that town life had much to offer. They looked forward to visits
and planned them carefully, for they were opportunities to experience and
purchase things not available at home.[55] In the Midlands, women shopkeepers provided opportunities for browsing, comparing, selecting and purchasing
all sorts of goods and services. In Birmingham, for example, Mary Rollason
stocked many kinds of china, crockery and glassware and dealt with rural as
well as urban customers. The Revd J. Fenwick, the rector of Northfield, then
a village in the rural hinterland of Birmingham, was a frequent customer for
these goods.[56] Those living in the countryside around Coventry could share in
the new experience of belonging to a subscription library. Membership of the
Coventry Library Society, whose stock of books was held and administered
by the Parker sisters on their premises, was open to members living within

fifteen miles of the city.[57] In sum, acts of viewing, selling, buying and using united urban female shopkeepers with their customers, who were initiated into a new way of life in which urban values predominated.

Despite individual case studies put forward in this chapter, women in the Midlands, generally speaking, were poorer than men,[58] so it would be surprising if they made much difference to the amount of capital invested in the region. Nevertheless, the *total* value of women's investments in industrialising Britain was substantial.[59] In addition, recent research has confirmed that women's investments in the capital stock of the Midlands were far from being insignificant. As well as producing, selling and consuming goods made in the region, women invested in its infrastructure and provided money for industrial development. New houses (essential to the growth of the region's towns) for new urban populations were, as we have already seen, an important investment medium for Midlands women. Their capital also aided the building of regional transport links, especially local canals and railways. Estimates indicate that women comprised 18 per cent of investors in Midlands canal companies, 11 per cent of local railway investors and 17 per cent of investors who held both canal and railway stock.[60] Moreover, spinsters with disposable wealth made loans to local businessmen; for example, Mary Galton lent money to the Birmingham industrialist Matthew Boulton.[61] The development of local banking was equally important in the eighteenth-century regional economy because it provided a specifically provincial financial infrastructure.[62] Women were again active, being amongst the first customers of the Birmingham bank Taylor & Lloyd, and borrowing money for short periods at interest, apparently charged at the legal maximum of 5 per cent. In the early 1780s, women made up nearly one-fifth of all those borrowing from Taylor & Lloyd. Unfortunately, these records do not reveal why the loans were taken out, and record linkage indicates that fewer than 10 per cent of female borrowers are likely to have been businesswomen.[63] Whatever the purposes of the loans, women's regime of borrowing, repayment and paying of interest contributed to the growth of this bank as a local and national institution. Small-scale lending to large numbers of customers was a risk-averse strategy for Taylor & Lloyd, and the short duration of the loans aided its liquidity.

Individual case studies indicate that there were Midlands leisured women, including the amateur poet Anna Seward of Lichfield, who lived in comfort and some style on rentier income.[64] Others, such as Elizabeth Farquharson, possessed substantial and valuable portfolios of shares in Midlands canal companies.[65] It was also possible, as in the case of Mary Alt, for a 'middling sort' woman to be simultaneously a businesswoman and a local investor. She combined a public role as postmistress and a milliner in Ashby-de-la-Zouch with a more private one as an investor in the Ashby Canal.[66] Capital that belonged to local women appears, therefore, to have contributed to the Midlands economy, but there are other points which should be considered. We should enquire if they were responsible for choosing investments made in their names, because this would suggest a specifically feminine input to local economic development. Unfortunately, it is impossible to establish the extent to which women investors made their own decisions. Some Midlands women actively managed their portfolios, but others probably did not, even though many inherited property that was bequeathed specifically for their own use and benefit.[67] Furthermore, the fact that many female investors held only life interests in such property suggests that they relied on the advice of male trustees or family for investment decisions.[68] In this way, as in many others, Midlands women behaved in much the same way as those elsewhere. All over the country widows and spinsters looked for a secure home which would produce a regular income for their modest savings. Unsurprisingly, they placed them in local projects, usually managed by local people, whom they or their kin were likely to know.[69] Local loyalties also influenced women's financing of business: Birmingham women dealt with Birmingham businessmen, and those in Yorkshire put out money at interest with Yorkshire businessmen.[70]

Conclusions

Midlands urban women, whether they were labouring women, businesswomen or female investors, were part of the life of the towns and region in which they lived. Their contribution occurred irrespective of their economic position or social status. The effect of women's labour on industrialisation in the region was complex and ambiguous. The physical and mental characteristics attributed to them by contemporaries explain how they could simultaneously be an ideal industrial workforce and a proto-industrial one. We should not disregard, because we cannot conclusively measure it, the importance of their labour to the expansion of manufacturing output nor the impetus to industrialisation that their buying power encouraged. As far as urban businesswomen are concerned, it is impossible to quantify their contribution. Surviving records of women's businesses are generally extremely meagre and do not permit even the calculation of annual profit or loss. As a result, we cannot measure how their business activities added to capital invested or circulating in the region. However, estimates of women's investments in the transport infrastructure suggest that their funds were not insignificant, and this improved transport system was fundamental both to regional integration and to reaching wider markets.

It seems that, if we are to seek evidence of urban women's roles in the development of Midlands towns and the region in general, we must look for it beyond the graphs and calculations of quantitative history. To this end, a combination of production, distribution and consumption suggests a way forward based on qualitative criteria. Sales of matched sets of china or pairs of silk stockings were ostensibly trivial matters, but buying and using such semi-luxury goods helped to spread urban values at the expense of rural ones. Their manufacture provided work for thousands of people, and those who organised production made fortunes. It also fostered the expansion of towns, and their associated industrial hinterlands, which specialised in making them, thereby effecting long-term changes to the regional landscape.[71] Similar long-term change occurred with the building of those canals and railways, financed by female as well as male investors, which still criss-cross the region linking Midlands towns to each other, the region and beyond. Much of the urban housing paid for by Midlands women and many of the sites where they made the material decencies of eighteenth-century life have vanished, demolished to make space for modern schemes of urban regeneration. Yet tangible memorials to women's industry, investment and consumption remain, valorised in museum displays of metal buttons, fine china, silk stockings and delicate lace, and in networks of railways and waterways which are being restored and upgraded to meet twenty-first-century requirements.

Notes

1   Berg, 'What difference', p. 26.
2   Davidoff and Hall, *Family Fortunes*, pp. 215–17, 279–80.
3   Berg, *Age of Manufactures*, pp. 134–5.
4   McKendrick, 'Home demand', pp. 152–210; McKendrick, Brewer and Plumb, *Consumer Society*, passim.
5   Lemire, 'Theft of clothes'; Lane, 'Work on the margins'.
6   Berg, *Age of Manufactures*, pp. 156, 276–7; Berg, 'Women's consumption'; Osterud, 'Leicester hosiery industry', p. 45; Chapman and Sharpe, 'Women's employment', pp. 326–38.
7   See Berg, 'Women's property', pp. 248–9; Lane, 'Women and inheritance', pp. 177–83; Wiskin, 'Women and credit', pp. 15–17.
8   Wiskin, 'Women and credit', pp. 103–5.
9   *Aris's Birmingham Gazette*, 12 January 1784, 3 January 1785.
10 Berg, 'Women's work', p. 87.
11 Berg, *Age of Manufactures*, pp. 274–5; Berg, 'Women's work', pp. 87–8.
12 Earle, 'Female labour market'.
13 Sarah Stickney Ellis, quoted in Davidoff and Hall, *Family Fortunes*, p. 315; Pinchbeck, *Women Workers*, p. 315.
14 Hall, 'Middle-class women', p. 119.
15 Gleadle, *British Women*, pp. 61–2.
16 Sharpe, 'De-industrialization', p. 87.
17 Pinchbeck, *Women Workers*, pp. 287–9.

18 Chapman and Sharpe, 'Women's employment', pp. 326–38.
19 Skedd, 'Women teachers', pp. 101–25.
20 Davidoff and Hall, *Family Fortunes*, pp. 296–8.
21 Pinchbeck, *Women Workers*, pp. 282–3; Hall, 'Middle-class women', pp. 112–16; Gleadle, *British Women*, pp. 57–8.
22 Clark, *English Alehouse*, pp. 287–9.
23 Finn, 'Women and marriage', pp. 703–22.
24 Churches, 'Women and property'.
25 Lane, 'Women and inheritance', pp. 178–80.
26 Berg, 'Commerce and creativity', pp. 191–4.
27 Berg, 'Women's work', p. 97, lists thirty-seven women carrying on metalware businesses inherited from male relatives, including one passing from father to daughter. See also Lane, 'Women, property and inheritance', pp. 181–3.
28 Lane, 'Women and inheritance', p. 180; Berg, 'Women's property', pp. 243–4, 248–9; Wiskin, 'Women and credit', pp. 207–11; Pinchbeck, *Women Workers*, pp. 283–5; Berg, *Age of Manufactures*, p. 278.
29 Behagg, *Politics and Production*, p. 54; Wiskin, 'Women and credit', p. 44.
30 City Archives, Coventry, PA 506/235/66, papers of William George Fretton.
31 Raistrick, *Iron Founders*, pp. 218, 222, 244.
32 Henstock, *Abigail Gawthern*, pp. 59–63, 70, 112; Horsfall, *Iron Masters*, pp. 48–57.
33 Churches, 'Women and property'; Barker, 'Women and the industrial revolution', pp. 91–7.
34 Berg, 'What difference', p. 26.
35 Honeyman, *Women and Industrialisation*, pp. 42–5.
36 Berg, 'What difference', p. 35.
37 Berg, *Age of Manufactures*, p. 267; Beckett and Heath, 'Industrial revolution', p. 78.
38 Berg, 'What difference', p. 26.
39 Berg, *Age of Manufactures*, pp. 267–8; McKendrick, 'Josiah Wedgwood', p. 32.
40 McKendrick, 'Josiah Wedgwood', pp. 34, 37–8.
41 Berg, *Age of Manufactures*, p. 148; Honeyman, *Women and Industrialisation*, p. 13.
42 Berg, *Age of Manufactures*, pp. 276–7; Berg, 'Women's work', pp. 85–6.
43 Chapman and Sharpe, 'Women's employment', p. 326.
44 Berg, *Age of Manufactures*, pp. 253–4.
45 Berg, *Age of Manufactures*, pp. 134–5; Berg, 'Women's consumption'.
46 See McKendrick, 'Home demand'; Nenadic, 'Middle rank consumers'; Finn, 'Men's things'.
47 *Aris's Birmingham Gazette*, 20 December 1813, 19 September 1814; *Coventry Mercury*, 13 December 1790, 31 December 1792; Wiskin, 'Women and credit', pp. 21, 272; Wiskin, 'Urban businesswomen', pp. 108–9.
48 *Wolverhampton Chronicle*, 16 December 1789, 17 March 1790.
49 *Wolverhampton Chronicle*, 16 December 1789; *Coventry Mercury*, 29 August 1791.
50 Clark and Houston, 'Culture and leisure', pp. 595–7.
51 Langton, 'Town growth', p. 7.
52 Clark and Houston, 'Culture and leisure', pp. 584–95.

53 Berg, 'Women's consumption', table 2.
54 Weatherill, *Consumer Behaviour*, p. 89.
55 Finn, 'Men's things', pp. 139–42.
56 Birmingham City Archives, MS 1340/2, papers of Revd Fenwick of Northfield.
57 *Coventry Mercury*, 25 April 1791.
58 Lane, 'Women and inheritance', pp. 184–5; Hudson, 'Attitudes to risk', pp. 200–1.
59 Davidoff and Hall, *Family Fortunes*, p. 278.
60 Hudson, 'Attitudes to risk', p. 113.
61 Hudson, 'Attitudes to risk', p. 78.
62 Pressnell, *Country Banking*; Hopkins, *Manufacturing Town*, p. 35.
63 Wiskin, 'Women and credit', pp. 223–31.
64 Brewer, *Pleasures of the Imagination*, pp. 574–5.
65 Lichfield RO, B/C/5/1808/16, inventory of Elizabeth Farquharson (died 31 May
    1796).
66 Lane, 'Women and inheritance', p. 184.
67 Davidoff and Hall, *Family Fortunes*, p. 278; Berg, 'Women's property', p. 248;
    Hudson, 'Attitudes to risk', pp. 198–9.
68 Hudson, 'Attitudes to risk', p. 205.
69 Pressnell, *Country Banking*, pp. 381, 394.
70 Hudson, *Genesis Industrial Capital*, p. 394.
71 See Chapter 10 of this volume.

5

Networks and hinterlands: transport in the Midlands

Neil Raven and Jon Stobart

Introduction

The transport networks that criss-crossed the Midlands were vital in integrating the regional space economy – they linked sites of specialist production and consumption, and thus articulated spatial divisions of labour.[1] Roads, rivers and canals transported raw materials to factories and workshops, and took finished goods to markets and entrepôts; they carried passengers, newspapers and the mail, thus communicating information across the country. It is unsurprising then that the creation of integrated and efficient transport services is seen as being central to the construction of modern economies and modern attitudes to time and space.[2] Moreover, although it is difficult to disentangle cause and effect, transport innovation is viewed as an important factor in urban, industrial and regional development: *inter alia*, it created nexuses of information, privileged certain production locations, shaped business and social networks, and helped to mould coherent local and regional identities.[3] The eighteenth and early nineteenth centuries saw many developments in transport provision in Britain. Turnpike trusts and improvements in wagon- and coach-building technology brought greater speed, comfort and safety to road transport – changes that were matched by a huge growth in the amount of traffic on the roads. Navigation schemes were undertaken across the country, greatly extending the length of navigable waterway and reducing the seasonality of their use. Canal building became ever more ambitious and widespread following the financial and economic success of early cuts such as the Bridgewater and the Trent and Mersey. These brought water transport to previously land-locked sites, extending river systems and crossing watersheds to link together separate systems.[4] By the 1830s, carrier, coach and water transport were at their peak, forming an efficient and integrated system.

These developments are familiar enough, and it is not the purpose of this chapter to discuss such matters in any detail. Instead, we want to explore the geography and structure of the Midlands transport network around this date, and assess its link to urban industrialisation. Specifically, we want to examine two sets of relationships at the regional scale: those between transport provision and economic development, and those between transport and urban networks. This moves discussion beyond notions of location constants – a conceptualisation of the transport-economy-urban trialectic which, as was argued in Chapter 1, is too static for a period of immense change in transport infrastructure and technology. Instead, we look to assess the part played by transport in processes of regional and sub-regional integration. At a basic level, this would involve an exploration of links between town and country – between a central place and its hinterland. However, the growing efficiency, speed and affordability of transport in the eighteenth century effectively brought towns closer together so that hinterlands increasingly overlapped with one another.[5] Given this, bi-polar analysis of a single town and its hinterland will tell us much less about the regional space economy than multi-polar analysis of a network of towns and hinterlands.[6] Simmons offers a way of theorising these webs of interaction between places and links them to a broader development model in a manner that can be useful to our analysis. He hypothesises a sequence of spatial structures for urban-economic systems.[7] Of particular importance to analysis of the Midlands in the eighteenth and early nineteenth centuries are the middle two stages of his model, characterised by 'staple exports' and industrial specialisation. In the first of these, growth in the regional economy is dependent upon exporting a limited range of goods (in Simmons's formulation these were agricultural produce, but the products of rural industry fit the model just as well), and the urban system is characterised by hierarchical linkages focusing on a dominant centre which provides extra-regional links. In the second, growth comes from the productive interchange of goods and services between specialist (industrial) centres within the region, the spatial structure being determined by these specialisations rather than relative position in an urban hierarchy.[8] What can these theorisations tell us about the Midlands space economy in the early nineteenth century and the ways in which the geography of transport systems linked into such spatial structures?

Transport networks and spatial interaction

Pawson argues that the establishment of turnpike trusts generally reflected the intensity of road usage and therefore the level and type of local economic development.[9] It is possible to identify two different patterns of turnpike formation in the Midlands. In the first, a web of roads radiating from a town would be turnpiked as a group. These town-centred trusts were most commonly found in county or substantial market towns. The earliest example in the Midlands was in Worcester, where the 1726 act covered a group of about a dozen roads leading into the city, but this was quickly followed by Evesham (1728), Leominster (1729) and Hereford (1730), and later by Bewdley and Stourbridge (1753), Droitwich (1754), Ludlow and Much Wenlock (1756), Tenbury (1757) and Kidderminster (1760).[10] Pawson associates this with the agricultural prosperity of these areas, the aim of the trusts being to ease access to and thus enhance marketing activity in these towns. The resultant spatial pattern was a series of disjointed radial systems centred on individual towns. More widespread and more significant in the integration of the regional space was the turnpiking of high-intensity routes associated either with heavy loads of industrial raw materials or finished goods, or with long-distance traffic. The latter included wagons and coaches passing from the Midlands to other regions (especially London), but also a growing volume of through traffic on routes such as the Great North Road, the London–Manchester route and, rather later, Telford's new Holyhead Road. This last project was intended to improve links with Ireland, but brought great benefits to places along the route: Coventry, Birmingham, the Black Country, Wolverhampton, the Shrop-shire coalfield and Shrewsbury. Early activity was again in the west Midlands, much of it sponsored by local merchants and manufacturers, who stood to gain most from the improvements affected. For example, we see John Wedg-wood of Burslem investing in both the Leek and Nantwich turnpikes.[11] Such was the precocity of this activity that two routes from London to Birming-ham had been turnpiked by 1740. In contrast, it was not until the mania of the 1760s that turnpikes became widespread in the east Midlands. In the first half of the century, only routes to London had been subject to improvement, but a trickle of acts in the 1750s turned into a steady flow: roads linking Leices-tershire and Nottinghamshire to the west Midlands and others in the nascent industrial areas of eastern Derbyshire were turnpiked.[12]

The early and intense turnpiking of roads in the west Midlands reflects the extent and the nature of industrialisation in these areas. The punctiform pro-duction associated with mineral-based economies created intense traffic between sites of concentrated production. It follows, then, that the density of the river and canal network should also be greatest in those areas characterised by such manufacturing activity.[13] As with the turnpike trusts, support and cap-ital were generally local. Josiah Wedgwood, for example, is famous for his championing of the project to cut the Trent and Mersey Canal through the Potteries, whilst, at a more modest scale, Mary Alt, the postmistress of Ashby-de-la-Zouch, invested in the Ashby Canal.[14] In the last quarter of the eighteenth century, water transport systems were essential to link the indus-tries of areas such as the Black Country to wider markets; they were also central to processes of regional integration.[15] The former can be seen in the construction of a series of canals feeding into the river Trent: the Erewash, Derby and Cromford canals brought coal, iron and textiles from east Derbyshire and west Nottinghamshire; they were carried via the Trent to the coast and thence to London. Similarly – and of enormous significance for these landlocked areas – the Staffordshire and Worcestershire, and Worcester and Birmingham, and Droitwich canals linked the Black Country to the river Severn; the Birmingham and Fazeley Canal gave access from Birmingham to the Trent and Mersey Canal, which itself provided external linkages for the Staffordshire Potteries.[16] Internal integration was affected by the dense network of canals that tied together Birmingham and the Black Country towns. At a broader scale, the Trent and Mersey Canal and later the Grand Trunk Canal served to link together the east and west Midlands.

Vital as these developing networks were for the industrial and urban development of the Midlands, they can only indicate the potential for interaction. To explore the realities of spatial integration in more detail, we need to consider the services operating along these routes. This could be achieved by looking at the toll books of turnpike trusts or canal companies, but the survival of such material is patchy at best. For region-wide analysis we must turn to the listings of carrier, water transport and coach services that appear in *Pigot's Directory* of 1835. Although the comprehensiveness of their coverage has been questioned, particularly where local services are concerned, the use of directories for this purpose is now firmly established.[17] Moreover, Pigot and Co. were amongst the most reliable of early-nineteenth-century directory compilers.[18]

Carrier services: roads and canals

Given the spatial variation in turnpiking, it would follow that both the density and intensity of carrier services would vary across the region. Whilst this is true, the patterns of service provision stand in apparent contrast to those of network improvement: a broad distinction can be drawn between the east and west Midlands, but with a much denser network of linkages seen in the former. The nineteen towns with the greatest number of linkages were fairly evenly spread across the region, but included nearly half the east Midlands and only 14 per cent of the west Midlands towns listed in *Pigot's Directory*. For individual towns, differences in the density of carrier networks could be considerable (Table 5.1). Leicester, for example, had carrier services to 160 places, including over 100 villages and hamlets within a ten-mile radius of the town; Newark had services to sixty-eight places and Melton Mowbray to thirty-seven. In contrast, Shrewsbury was linked to only thirty-nine places and Newcastle-under-Lyme to just eight. Even Birmingham had a relatively

Table 5.1 *Carrier services from principal transport centres in the Midlands, 1835*

Town of origin	Destinations linked by direct service	Wagons departing per week	Wagons per destination
Leicester	160	541	3.4
Nottingham	125	338	2.7
Birmingham	105	579	5.5
Newark	68	166	2.4
Worcester	66	223	3.4
Derby	54	225	4.2
Warwick	54	124	2.3
Shrewsbury	39	95	2.4
Melton Mowbray	37	53	1.4
Loughborough	33	75	2.3
Wolverhampton	26	151	5.8
Mansfield	26	76	2.9
Market Harborough	18	40	2.2
Hinckley	16	45	2.8
Uppingham	15	34	2.3
Atherstone	14	34	2.4
Ashby-de-la-Zouch	13	31	2.4
Chesterfield	13	60	4.6
Stourbridge	13	42	3.2

Source: *Pigot's Directory* (1835).

low-density network, being linked to 105 centres, the majority of which were towns more than five miles distant. To an extent, this may reflect the fuller listing of services, especially those to neighbouring villages, in the volume of *Pigot's Directory* covering Leicester, Nottingham and Derby. For these three towns, the ratio of village:town services is 0.19, 0.18 and 0.33 respectively. This contrasts with ratios of 0.63 for Birmingham, 0.41 for Worcester and 0.56 for Shrewsbury. However, the dense networks centred on the county towns of the east Midlands also suggest a genuinely closer link between town and country in these areas. Indeed, the smaller market towns surrounding these centres were also the focus of dense networks of rural carriers.

Whilst the density of carrier services was greatest in Nottinghamshire and especially Leicestershire, the intensity of traffic in the two counties was

Table 5.2 *Carrier services from Leicestershire, Nottinghamshire and Black Country towns, 1835*

Town of origin	Destinations linked by direct service	Wagons departing per week	Wagons per destination
Leicestershire and Nottinghamshire towns			
Leicester	160	541	3.4
Nottingham	125	338	2.7
Newark	68	166	2.4
Melton Mowbray	37	53	1.4
Loughborough	33	75	2.3
Mansfield	26	76	2.9
Market Harborough	18	40	2.2
Hinckley	16	45	2.8
Uppingham	15	34	2.3
Ashby-de-la-Zouch	13	31	2.4
Oakham	8	24	3.0
Lutterworth	6	12	2.0
Retford	11	44	4.0
Bingham	4	22	5.5
Southwell	3	13	4.3
Black Country towns			
Birmingham	105	579	5.5
Wolverhampton	26	151	5.8
Dudley	5	19	3.8
Walsall	4	56	14.0
Bilston	4	17	4.3
West Bromwich	1	35	35.0
Wednesbury	1	9	9.0

Source: *Pigot's Directory* (1835).

relatively low (Table 5.2). In common with the principal transport centres across the region, east Midlands towns generally had fewer than three services running to each destination per week. This stands in stark contrast with the situation in the Black Country. With the exception of Birmingham and, to a lesser extent, Wolverhampton, these towns had services to only a handful of destinations, but traffic was intense on the routes where services were available. Walsall carriers, for example, ran a total of fifty-six services per week to Birmingham, Wolverhampton, Cannock and London; their counterparts in West Bromwich operated thirty-five wagons to Birmingham alone.

Two points are important here. One is the link between the density and intensity of traffic and the relative stimulus these gave to the creation of turnpike trusts.[19] The dense networks that characterised Leicestershire and Nottinghamshire carrier systems were reflected in the comparatively light use of most of these routes. Most services were linking villages to their market town or to the county metropolis – a system closely resembling the hierarchical arrangement of Simmons's staple export model. The principal manufactured products were mainly textiles or hosiery wares being transported between a large number of rural production locations and key organising centres.[20] This helps to explain the relatively late turnpiking of east Midlands roads, especially when compared with the situation in the Black Country. Here, the close interaction between towns stimulated demand for frequent services and encouraged the early, if piecemeal, turnpiking of local roads. These corridors of intense traffic generated income that was amongst the highest for turnpike trusts in the region. The second point, and one that is underlined by the intensity of traffic flowing into and out of Birmingham, is that the inhabitants of West Bromwich, Bilston, Wednesbury and the like largely relied upon Birmingham carriers to provide extra-local links.[21] Even for larger or more distant towns – amongst them Wolverhampton, Walsall and Lichfield – *Pigot's Directory* noted that 'the carriers to Birmingham forward goods to London'.[22] Thus, Birmingham stands out as an important regional transport node, a position underlined by the nature of its carrier services: many links were to towns beyond the local area and even the region. *Pigot's Directory* for 1835 lists services from Birmingham to London, Liverpool and Manchester, Leeds and Wakefield, Bristol, Cumberland and Westmorland, Edinburgh, Hull, Norwich and York, plus numerous intermediate towns. This reflects the complex nature of the economy in this part of the west Midlands, wherein different urban-economic systems were overlain upon one another. The intense traffic reflects the mineral-based economy of the area and the existence of local industrial specialisms, seen in the lock makers of Wolverhampton and Bilston, chain makers of Cradley and lorimers of Walsall. As Simmons argues, these would prompt high levels of interchange between the different centres within this system. At the same time, the predominance of Birmingham in the long-distance linkages echoes its role as a key 'gateway town' for a hierarchically structured export economy.[23]

The network and provision of water transport services varied across the region. Unfortunately, it is impossible to undertake the same detailed network analysis that was attempted for the road carriers. Entries in Pigot's frequently refer to a carrier serving 'all parts' or list a huge number of potential destinations, amounting to any reasonably large centres on the canal or river network, many of which would be reached only by connections to other carriers. Moreover, the directories include less information on the bulk trade in coal and iron than on the trade in sundry manufactured goods.[24] Nonetheless, sub-regional differences in provision are very clear. There was a much higher density of canals and services in the west than in the east Midlands. Although the precise nature of the figures is somewhat misleading, the provision in Warwickshire (185 specified services), Staffordshire (170) and Worcestershire (143) was at an altogether different level from that seen in Leicestershire (thirty-seven), Derbyshire (thirty-three) and Nottinghamshire (twenty-six). In reality, the concentration was still more pronounced than this suggests. Birmingham had 159 services listed in *Pigot's Directory*, Stourbridge had ninety and the Potteries sixty-eight; Leicester and Derby each had twenty-three services and Nottingham only 16. It would clearly be wrong to see canals as insignificant in the east Midlands. The waterways constructed to link towns and manufacturing districts to the Trent formed vital conduits for trade, carrying coal, iron and textiles to extra-regional markets.[25] However, as would be expected in a mineral-based economy, they were far more important in the west Midlands.[26] As Wanklyn discusses later in this volume, links to the Severn, Trent and Thames opened up new markets, and the increasingly dense network of waterways between specialist production locations in the Black Country prompted rapid industrial growth. By 1798 around 1,500 Black Country collieries and ironworks were linked by canals, and the Birmingham Canal alone was carrying 300 tons per day to London.[27]

Such local examples are underlined by the detail that was provided in *Pigot's Directory* of canal services in these districts. The intensity and geographical range of services had two effects on the west Midlands economy: the important links that these gave to the major coastal ports encouraged longer distance trade and thus stimulated production, whilst the local movements of coal, iron and so on nurtured spatial divisions of labour and reinforced regional integration. These twin processes can be seen in the services offered by canal carriers from Birmingham. Pigot lists 941 direct services per week to a total of forty-one destinations. These include a number of other west Midlands towns: a total of sixty-three boats a week travelled to Wolverhampton, forty-nine to Dudley and thirty-five to Leamington. But even greater numbers of boats were travelling to river ports on the rivers Severn, Trent, Mersey and Thames. There were seventy-seven trips per week to Worcester and Gloucester, forty-nine to Shardlow, fifty-six to Liverpool and forty-two to London. The importance of these places as key nodes on England's water transport system is clear from their general prevalence as destinations for canal and river carriers: Liverpool is mentioned seventy-six times, London fifty-two, Shardlow

Figure 5.1 *Pickford's canal and carrier network, 1834*

Source: *Pigot's Directory*, 1834.

twenty-six and Worcester twenty-five times. But we should not see these ports and entrepôts as isolated from road transport: roads, rivers and canals formed an increasingly integrated transport system. The trade directories list numerous local carriers operating to and from canal wharfs. For example, Peter Hilton carried goods three or four times per week between his warehouse in Shrewsbury and Edstaston wharf on the Ellesmere Canal. Some larger haulage firms offered their own connecting services: the Shifnal–Wolverhampton wagons of Crowley, Hicklin, Batty and Co. met their own fly boats destined for London.[28] Both the integrated nature of transport networks and their power to mesh together regional and national economies are clear from the route map of Pickford and Co. (Figure 5.1). This shows a carrier system incorporating both water and road transport and linking London to north-west England via a range of Midlands towns.[29] In operating at this spatial scale, Pickford's was typical of a growing number of canal carriers. Crowley Co. operated fifty-four services from thirteen towns in the west Midlands, Kenworthy and Co. had seventeen services from nine towns and Shiptons and Co. twenty-eight services from seven towns. Such firms were instrumental in linking the Midlands with the wider national and – via services to London and Liverpool, Gloucester and Hull – international economies, an aspect discussed in more detail in Chapter 12.

Coach services

As with carriers, the towns with the greatest number of coaching services were fairly evenly distributed throughout the region (Table 5.3): twelve were located in the west Midlands and eight in the east. Trinder has suggested that most large towns were centres of coach networks, and the evidence from the Midlands supports this.[30] Birmingham was by far the busiest, this fact underpinning its status as the principal regional node and gateway town: with 594 weekly services Birmingham boasted almost three times the number recorded by the second-ranked town of Wolverhampton. Moreover, 31 per cent of all the coach services listed by Pigot for the towns of the Midlands operated from Birmingham, and coaches from the town travelled to thirty-seven different destinations, compared with the fourteen claimed by Nottingham and Leicester. After Birmingham it is the region's county towns that stand out as coaching centres: Nottingham and Leicester had more than 100 services a week, whilst Worcester, Derby, Shrewsbury and Warwick all returned enough services to rank them in the ten busiest coaching centres. Only Oakham and Stafford were absent from this group. The proximity of Leicester may account for the former, but, in the case of Stafford, a number of other towns appear to have fulfilled the role of coaching centre, including

Table 5.3 *Services from the principal coaching centres of the Midlands,*
1835

Town of origin	Destinations linked by direct service	Coaches departing per week	Coaches per destination
Birmingham	37	594	16.1
Wolverhampton	6	202	33.7
Nottingham	14	131	9.4
Leicester	14	124	8.9
Newark	9	78	8.7
Worcester	10	68	6.8
Derby	7	60	8.6
Coventry	5	54	10.8
Shrewsbury	6	49	8.2
Warwick	5	49	9.8
Dudley	4	43	10.8
Retford	4	34	8.5
Buxton	3	28	9.3
Stourbridge	3	26	8.7
Mansfield	3	23	7.7
Atherstone	3	20	6.7
Stamford	2	20	10.0
Walsall	2	19	9.5
Newcastle-under-Lyme	3	18	6.0
Leamington	2	15	7.5

Source: *Pigot's Directory* (1835).

Wolverhampton, Dudley, Walsall and Newcastle-under-Lyme. More generally, the region's coaching towns were long-established urban settlements.
New industrial centres, such as Burslem and Wednesbury, returned far fewer
coach services; indeed, no services from the latter are listed in *Pigot's Directory*, although there was certainly some through traffic in the town. The
industrialisation experienced by these new towns does not appear to have to
generated demand for large numbers of coach services in the early nineteenth
century. This contrasts with the experience of another of the region's new
urban settlements. As a spa Buxton was well served with coaches, one coach
company running daily services to Manchester 'during the season'. Similarly,
following the establishment of the spa around 1802, coach services to and from

Leamington grew in number so rapidly that it ranked amongst the top twenty coaching towns by 1835.

If consideration is given to places visited by coaches operating from the region's towns, two contrasting trends emerge. The first underpins Birmingham's prominence. Most of the coaches issuing from neighbouring Wolverhampton and Dudley were bound for Birmingham, and the same was true for more distant west Midlands towns, including Shrewsbury and Worcester. Moreover, Birmingham featured amongst the main destinations for coaches leaving Leicester (11 per cent), Newark (17 per cent) and Derby (22 per cent). Whilst Birmingham's coaching trade may have helped to bind together the region, a consideration of other services suggests the operation of sub-regional networks concentrated in either the west or the eastern parts of the region. Besides Birmingham, Wolverhampton's coaches were mainly destined for Dudley, whilst Warwick's busiest coach routes were to Coventry and neighbouring Leamington Spa. Meanwhile, the main destinations for Nottingham's coaches were Derby, Leicester and Newark, whilst most of those from Leicester travelled to Nottingham and Ashby. There is also some evidence to suggest that, as with carrier activity, the greatest density of services was in the east Midlands, whilst the most intense activity occurred in the west. Coaches from Leicester were destined for fourteen separate towns, with the largest concentration of twenty-one (17 per cent) journeying to Nottingham. In contrast, Wolverhampton's coaches served only six towns, and 167 (83 per cent) of these went to Birmingham. Likewise, Warwick's coaches went to only five towns, and twenty-eight (57 per cent) of these were bound for Coventry. Beyond these regional patterns, the coaching towns of the Midlands were linked into a wider national network (Table 5.4). Prominent here was London, which accounted for 31 per cent of all extra-regional destinations, followed by Liverpool and Manchester, with more than 22 per cent between them, and Sheffield with 5 per cent. Other places enjoying twenty or more weekly services with Midland towns included Holyhead, Cheltenham, Bristol and Bath, Leeds, Cambridge, Hull, Oxford, Lincoln and Gainsborough and Southampton.

By plotting the routes taken by coaches operating across the region, and cross-checking these against lists of entries under individual towns, it is possible to identify the main thoroughfare towns of the Midlands – defined as places that gained a living from the passing coach trade. Table 5.5 records the twenty towns with the largest number of passing coach services. Once again, Birmingham's importance is evident, with 384 services calling on the town each week. The county towns of Leicester, Shrewsbury, Worcester, Derby and, to a slightly lesser extent, Warwick and Nottingham also feature: a pre-eminence consistent with Everitt's claim that they were foci for much coaching activity.[31] However, it is likely that thoroughfare activity had a greater impact

Table 5.4 *Extra-regional towns served by the coaches operating from Midlands towns, 1835*

Towns	Services per week	Coaches per week	% of services
London	59	370	33.4
Liverpool	22	141	12.7
Manchester	20	128	11.5
Sheffield	9	61	5.5
Holyhead	7	47	4.2
Cheltenham	7	45	4.1
Bristol	6	39	3.5
Leeds	6	37	3.3
Cambridge	9	36	3.2
Hull	4	27	2.4
Oxford	4	26	2.3
Lincoln/Gainsborough	1	22	2.0
Southampton	1	21	1.9
Bath/Bristol	2	19	1.7
Aberystwyth	6	19	1.7
Doncaster/York	4	18	1.6
Edinburgh/Glasgow	2	14	1.3
Halifax	2	14	1.3
Hereford	2	13	1.2
Welshpool	2	12	1.1

Source: *Pigot's Directory* (1835).

on the economies of smaller centres, where the numbers of passing coaches were comparable to those seen in the larger centres. 190 coaches stopped off in Loughborough each week, 156 in Newcastle-under-Lyme and 148 in Newark. Even where totals were somewhat smaller, as in the case of Retford with 82 weekly visits, a considerable amount of business would have been generated, with each coach capable of carrying six passengers inside and up to twelve outside.[32] In this regard, Pigot in 1835 considered Loughborough to be 'a place of great thoroughfare'. Similarly, White in 1832 judged Newark to be a town that 'derives much wealth from its being a great public thoroughfare'.[33] Indeed, the large stream of temporary visitors brought in on these coaches appears to have had an impact on the character of these towns. White thought that Newark's thoroughfare cultivated a sense of 'cheerfulness' in the town,

Table 5.5 *The main thoroughfare towns of the Midlands,*
1835

Town	Coach services per week
Birmingham	384
Leicester	214
Shrewsbury	202
Loughborough	190
Worcester	182
Rugby	164
Newcastle-under-Lyme	156
Newark	148
Derby	140
Market Harborough	134
Warwick	122
Nottingham	120
Chesterfield	110
Dronfield	108
Southwell	94
Wolverhampton	94
Bakewell	84
Coventry	84
Wirksworth	84
Retford	82

Source: *Pigot's Directory* (1835).

whilst the 'great numbers of coaches and travellers' to Retford were said to 'impart a considerable degree of gaiety and bustle'.[34]

Barker and Gerhold emphasise the role of turnpike roads in the growth of the coaching trade.[35] In this respect, White considered Newark's success as a 'public thoroughfare' to have derived from its location 'at the junction of the great north road with turnpikes from London to Nottingham, Sheffield &c'.[36] Within the Midlands the later part of the eighteenth century was a time of much turnpike activity, and it seems likely that the prosperity these towns enjoyed as thoroughfares dated from this period. Certainly the *UBD* considered that Retford received 'great benefit by the passengers on the great north road'.[37] However, for many of these places the golden age of thoroughfare activity was to be a relatively short one, brought to a close by the arrival of the railway. By 1851, White was recalling how Newcastle-under-Lyme had been 'a great thoroughfare for coaches, wagons, vans, and travelers, till the opening of the railways, which have robbed it of this once important traffic'.[38]

Transport networks and urban-industrial development

Although transport is often seen as the dependent variable in its relationship with economic development,[39] specific locations might be advantaged by their position within transport networks. This was seen in a variety of towns across the Midlands. As we have already observed, county towns were the focus of many road transport services, especially coaches. They formed the principal nodes on webs of information and knowledge exchange, and were key points of access to new ideas, consumer goods and fashions. This served to underpin their economies as traditional industries came under threat from specialist manufacturing centres in the region and elsewhere. For example, in the early eighteenth century Shrewsbury was transformed from a centre of cloth making and leather working to a leisure town, drawing people from across Shropshire and mid-Wales.[40] Whilst they rarely developed the complex economic-cultural infrastructure seen in county towns, thoroughfare towns also benefited from coaching traffic. Here we see transport as a producer service: through their business strategies and entrepreneurial activities, the owners and operators of coaches, wagons and canal boats influenced the geography and operation of trade. They also encouraged the growth of a range of activities and industries, from inns and maltsters to wheelwrights and saddlers. The 'great numbers of coaches and travellers' that daily descended upon Retford help to account for the town's twenty-seven hotels, inns and taverns, seven maltsters and six wheelwrights, as well the host of luxury traders that included eight linen and woollen drapers and seven booksellers – many undoubtedly residing in the 'good shops' that lined the marketplace.[41] Inland ports prospered as key points of access to water transport networks or as points of transhipment between rivers and canals. They included places such as Newark and Burton-upon-Trent, but the importance of such centres is seen more clearly in the towns along the river Severn.[42] In this respect, Pigot considered a significant part of Bridgnorth's trade to have arisen 'from the navigation of the river, which affords every facility for the transit of goods'.[43] Canals also provided a huge fillip for towns served by this new transport infrastructure. This is perhaps most famously seen in the rise of Birmingham (although much of its trade and prosperity relied on transporting goods by road), but it is also apparent in the rapid industrial development seen in the Potteries, the Black Country and the Derby-Nottingham coalfield.[44]

At a more general level, it is clear that different types of town and modes of production were associated with different transport, interaction and urban systems. Moreover, these varied systems had their own sub-regional geographies. County towns were the focus of widespread networks, being linked to many places along low-intensity lines of interaction – a pattern seen most clearly in Shrewsbury and Worcester. Manufacturing towns were centres of geographically constrained, high-intensity networks of the type seen around Birmingham and the Black Country. This reflects the traditional role of county towns as centres of extensive, often county-wide hinterlands, whereas many newly emergent manufacturing towns had no natural hinterland – their interaction was dominated by high-intensity links with neighbouring and more distant industrial centres or with larger towns nearby. Thus, Burslem enjoyed close links with other north Staffordshire pottery towns and West Bromwich had intensive contact with Birmingham and Wolverhampton – relationships discussed more fully in Chapter 7. Such distinctions in transport and linkage patterns relate directly to the type of activities found in the different types of town. The administrative, cultural and social functions of county towns encouraged the development of and were underpinned by widespread and hierarchically structured interaction with other centres. These parallel Simmons's staple-export system, but, *contra* his model, flows were not uni-directional. Information, consumer goods, legislation and social mores generally passed down the hierarchy (often having been initiated in London), whereas such things as tax revenues, consumer spending and manufactures (especially semi-luxury goods) moved in the opposite direction. In manufacturing and commercial towns, such as Wolverhampton, Burslem and Loughborough, social functions were less prominent and their industrial activities principally generated flows of raw materials and finished goods. As spatial divisions of labour became ever more detailed, especially in the Black Country (see Chapter 2), these flows were concentrated along specific routeways between increasingly specialised production locations in a network resembling Simmons's industrial specialisation system.[45]

Considered in the abstract, this distinction seems sensible and logical. Moreover, it appears to be supported by the evidence from the Midlands, but only when it is viewed in a decontextualised and aspatial manner. When translated into patterns of connectivity and interaction within local and sub-regional economies, seemingly simple relationships become far more complex. First, there was an inevitable overlaying of these extensive-hierarchical and intensive-specialist systems. County and manufacturing towns were often neighbouring and naturally interacted with one another. Thus, for example, Newcastle-under-Lyme and Burslem, although functionally dissimilar and ostensibly part of different economic and interaction systems, enjoyed good transport links and close socio-economic ties with one another.[46] Second, as the analysis in Chapter 2 confirms, almost all towns contained some manufacturing activity and many places were specialised manufacturing as well as social, administrative and cultural centres. Birmingham certainly fell into this category as did some county towns in the west Midlands: Stafford was famous for shoemaking and boot making, whilst Worcester's porcelain and glove making industries had 'great repute at the foreign markets'.[47] As noted above, the overlaying of functions was strongest in the east Midlands, where the county towns were also the principal centres of manufacturing. As a result, extensive-hierarchical and intensive-specialist networks were mapped onto the same locations.

The third complication was that different forms of manufacturing were organised in different ways and often comprised specialised and discrete sub-regional economies. The nature of production could place profoundly different requirements onto transport networks and generate differently structured urban systems. In his theorisation of the industrial transformation of Britain, Wrigley contrasts the dense, but low-intensity interaction of an organic economy with the intense and spatially concentrated interaction associated with punctiform production within a mineral-based energy economy.[48] This dichotomy can be seen very clearly in the Midlands. Metalworking in the west Midlands formed the classic case of a mineral-based energy economy in the early nineteenth century. It depended upon heavy and bulky raw materials, used coal for heat and power from an early date, and was subject to detailed spatial divisions of labour. Combined, these necessitated high-intensity movements of goods and materials between specialised manufacturing centres, and thus encouraged the construction of a dense network of canals.[49] Textile and hosiery manufacture in the east Midlands relied on rural outworking well into the nineteenth century. The centralised organisation of production generated extensive, but lower-intensity linkages focused on key centres of control and often hierarchically structured (see Chapter 9) – much as Simmons's staple export model would suggest. Canals played a less significant role in such production systems, which relied instead on local and provincial carriers to link dispersed production to the organisational centres, principally Nottingham and Leicester.[50]

A final factor generating complexity in spatial interaction systems was that individual firms within particular local economies often drew on a variety of different transport modes and networks to gather market information, assemble raw materials and bring their goods to market. They thus placed themselves within different systems of interaction. This can be illustrated through the practices of John and Thomas Wedgwood, perhaps the most important earthenware manufacturers in mid-eighteenth-century Burslem. Like many other potters in north Staffordshire, they made a wide range of products for the 'universal' market and sold their wares to a variety of customers. What distinguished John and Thomas Wedgwood were the range and

Figure 5.2 *Customers of John and Thomas Wedgwood of Burslem, Stoke-on-Trent, 1755–77*

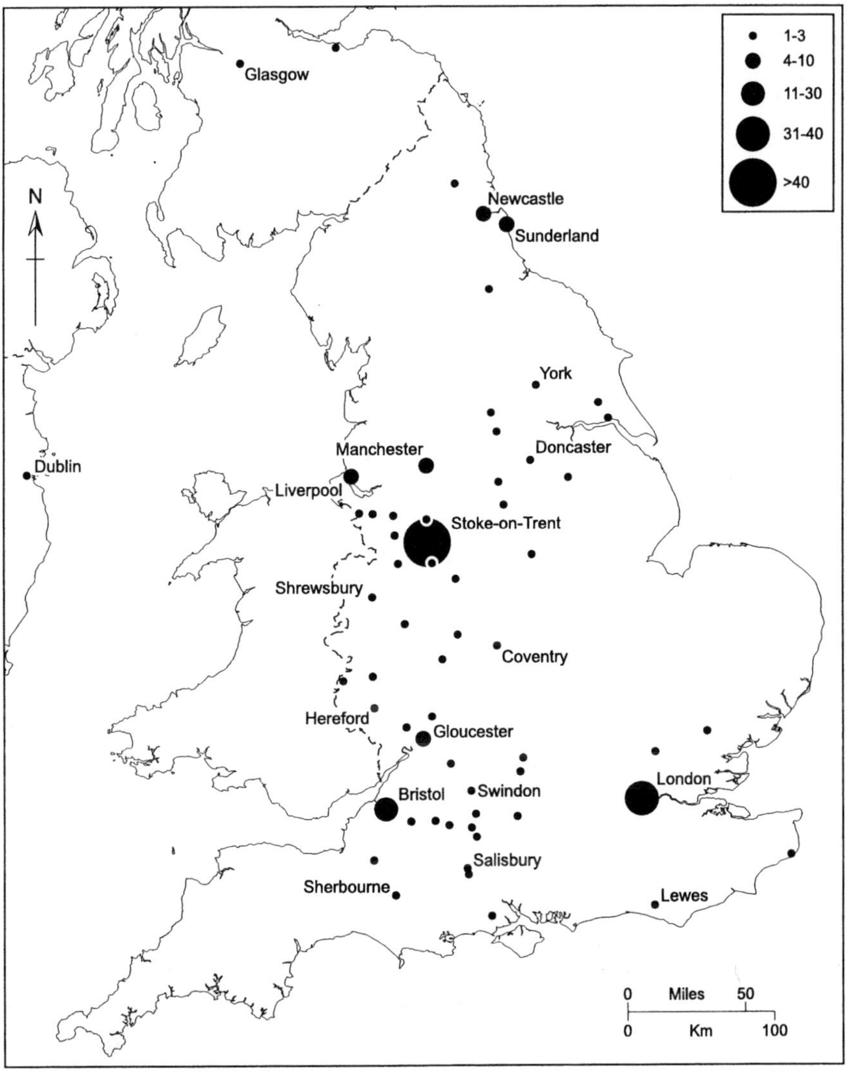

©MAPS IN MINUTES™ 2003. ©Crown Copyright, Ordnance Survey & Ordnance Survey Northern Ireland 2003 Permit No. NI 1675 & ©Government of Ireland, Ordnance Survey Ireland.

Source: John Wedgwood's Crate Book, Potteries Museum, Hanley.

scale of their local connections and merchanting activities. They had established a national network of customers by the 1750s, and between 1755 and 1777 dispatched consignments of earthenware to over 173 individuals in sixty-four places, from Glasgow to Dublin to Dover (Figure 5.2).[51] London (with

thirty-seven customers) and Bristol (with twenty-one) were particularly important markets, from which pottery was redistributed both nationally and
overseas.[52] Many of the London buyers (like William Hewson in the Strand)
placed regular orders with the Wedgwoods. Such men were generally wholesalers, but John and Thomas also sold to retailers like James Greenhalgh in
Manchester and Ann Else in Nottingham, and direct to the gentry, including
Sir Walter Bagot of Blithfield. As new institutional economics would argue,
this extensive network was essential to the operation of the Wedgwood's business[53] – bringing reliable information on demand for their wares – but also
articulated flows of capital and finished goods. To deliver their orders, they
used a range of carriers, mostly on road but also via the navigations of the
Severn, Trent and Weaver. Raw materials came via Liverpool and the river
Weaver to Winsford Bridge, from whence they were hauled overland to
Burslem. To collect payment they relied on kinsmen or made visits in person,
a practice underlining the importance of trust in unregulated markets – but at
the same time expanded that network of trust to encompass increasing numbers of people and places.[54] Personal visits were made by Thomas, who
regularly travelled to London and occasionally made longer journeys taking
in several centres. For example, between 22 September and 7 October 1761 he
went to Chesterfield, Sheffield, Hull, Beverley, Sunderland, Newcastle and
Leeds, collecting a total of £112 5s 2d from twelve customers. The Wedgwood's manufacturing activity and business world lay within an emerging
mineral-based energy economy, but drew on both intensive and extensive
transport networks. It relied on road and water transport, on local and
national carriers and on personal mobility on horseback and via public stage-
coaches. It formed a network of trust built on regular contact and often
personal relationships.

Conclusions

The 1830s formed the highpoint of road and canal transport before the coming of the railways. The analysis here shows a highly developed transport
network which afforded dense coverage and a geographically inclusive system
of linkages. The combination of coaches and wagons, river boats and canal
barges served to integrate the regional space economy and impacted on the
Midlands in five broadly defined areas. First, it allowed the efficient assembly of agricultural products and manufactured goods in key centres of
redistribution, thus helping to expand market areas and increasing the viability and competitiveness of Midlands producers. Second, extra-regional
connections provided a crucial link to national markets and supplies: both
were vital to a region which was heavily dependent upon export markets (a

point emphasised by Wanklyn in Chapter 12). Third, these transport services eased the distribution of incoming consumer goods through the region, encouraging the dissemination of new cultures of consumption by bringing novel and desirable goods to Midlands towns. Fourth, it facilitated the flow of capital, ideas and information across the region, allowing the expansion of credit networks and helping to spread market information, new ideas of fashion and so on. Fifth and most fundamentally, effective spatial integration made possible ever more detailed divisions of labour both within industrial sectors (as seen in the Black Country) and between centres of production and centres of consumption (witness the rise of Leamington Spa and Buxton).

Within the regional transport network, key centres are evident. Their functions structured the geography of the network, whilst their economies were boosted by the extra traffic which this brought. Birmingham was pre-eminent here: the centre of manufacturing systems and cross-regional and national movements of goods and people. Other manufacturing towns were generally less prominent, although important centres such as Wolverhampton do stand out as intersections on sub-regional systems. More significant were the county towns, around which many of the coach services were structured. However, there were important differences between those in the west and the east Midlands, Leicester, Nottingham and Derby having much denser networks linking them to their hinterlands. This points to a broader distinction between the space economies of the east and west Midlands. It also highlights the link between the socio-spatial organisation of systems of production and the geographical linkages which articulated those systems. Dispersed and often domestic production of the east Midlands with its hierarchical divisions of labour encouraged and relied upon a dense, hierarchically structured transport system centred on the organisational centres of Leicester and Nottingham (Simmons's staple export model). In contrast, the concentrated production and detailed spatial divisions of labour seen in Birmingham and the Black Country engendered corridors of intense traffic and encouraged the early construction of navigations and canals (industrial specialisation). In both systems, we can see transport networks as both the consequence and the cause of industrial organisation and industrial growth.

Notes

1 Spatial divisions of labour are discussed in historical and contemporary contexts by Stobart, *First Industrial Region*, chapter 1; and Massey, *Spatial Divisions*, pp. 117–19, 196–215.

2 See Thrift, 'Transport and communication', pp. 473–9.

3 Robson, *Urban Growth*, p. 140; Lepetit, *Urban System*. pp. 299–348; Turnbull, 'Canals'; Langton, 'Industrial revolution'.

4 See Dyos and Aldcroft, *British Transport*, pp. 81–109; Chartres and Turnbull, 'Road transport'; Turnbull, 'Canals'.
5 Stobart, *First Industrial Region*, pp. 1–8, 175–218.
6 Lepetit, *Urban System*, p. 97.
7 Simmons, 'Urban system', pp. 65–8.
8 For a fuller discussion of these models and their application to north-west England, see Stobart, *First Industrial Region*.
9 Pawson, *Transport and Economy*, pp. 135–45.
10 The Herefordshire turnpikes formed an important group, but were isolated from other Midlands turnpikes for several decades. See Albert, *Turnpike Road System*, appendix 1; Pawson, *Transport and Economy*, appendix 1.
11 Mountford, 'Thomas Wedgwood', p. 32.
12 Pawson, *Transport and Economy*, pp. 140, 151.
13 Wrigley, *Continuity*, pp. 7–33.
14 Hadfield, *West Midlands*, pp. 19–33; Lane, 'Women and inheritance', p. 184. See also Chapter 4 of this volume.
15 See Langton, 'Industrial revolution'; Turnbull, 'Canals'.
16 A number of these canals were not completed until the early nineteenth century: Stobart, 'Regions and industrialisation', p. 1, 315; Hadfield, *West Midlands*, pp. 70–2, 129–46.
17 Freeman, 'Carrier system'; Noble, 'Growth and Development', pp. 1–21; Raven, 'Manufacturing and trades', pp. 143–52.
18 Norton, *Guide to Directories*.
19 Pawson, *Transport and Economy*, pp. 15–21, 135–45.
20 Beckett, *East Midlands*, pp. 157–8, 284–5. See also Chapman, 'British hosiery industry'.
21 Hopkins, *Manufacturing Town*, p. 12.
22 *Pigot's Directory* (1835), pp. 492, 419, 468.
23 Simmons, 'Urban system', pp. 65–8.
24 For more discussion of this distinction and the traffic in sundries, see Trinder, *Shropshire*, p. 129.
25 Beckett, *East Midlands*, pp. 145–54 and 260–7; Hadfield, *East Midlands*, pp. 49–79. See also Chapter 12 of this volume.
26 Simmons, 'Urban system', p. 68; Wrigley, *Continuity*, pp. 7–33.
27 Rowlands, *West Midlands*, pp. 232–4.
28 *Pigot's Directory* (1835), pp. 371, 380.
29 See Turnbull, *Traffic and Transport*.
30 Trinder, 'Industrialising towns', pp. 822–3.
31 Everitt, 'Country, county and town', pp. 11–40. See also Barker and Gerhold, *Rise and Rise*, pp. 52–61.
32 Barker and Gerhold, *Rise and Rise*, p. 55.
33 *Pigot's Directory* (1835), p. 141; White, *Nottinghamshire*, p. 604.
34 White, *Nottinghamshire*, p. 302.
35 Barker and Gerhold, *Rise and Rise*, pp. 52–61.
36 White, *Nottinghamshire*, p. 603.
37 *UBD*, vol. 4 (1797).
38 White, *Staffordshire* (1851).
39 See, for example, Chartres and Turnbull, 'Road transport', pp. 72, 94–7.

40 McInnes, 'Shrewsbury'. See also Ellis, 'Regional and county centres', pp. 673–84.
41 White, *Nottinghamshire*, pp. 302–29.
42 Wanklyn, 'Water transport'.
43 *Pigot's Directory* (1842).
44 Hopkins, *Manufacturing Town*, pp. 28–30 and 78–9; Stobart, 'Regions and industrialisation', p. 1,315. See also Chapter 7 and Chapter 9 of this volume.
45 Large, 'Urban growth', pp. 169–89; Simmons, 'Urban system', pp. 65–8.
46 Weatherill, *Pottery Trade*, pp. 112–28.
47 *Pigot's Directory* (1835), p. 443.
48 Wrigley, *Continuity*, esp. pp. 7–33.
49 Turnbull, 'Canals'.
50 This east–west distinction was beginning to break down by 1840s, especially in the Nottingham-Derby-Loughborough triangle, where coal and iron industries were developing rapidly. See Beckett, *East Midlands*, pp. 276–84.
51 Potteries Museum, Hanley, John Wedgwood's Crate Book.
52 Mountford, 'Thomas Wedgwood', pp. 64–6.
53 See Casson and Rose, 'Institutions'; Pearson and Richardson, 'Business networking'.
54 Mountford, 'Thomas Wedgwood', pp. 13, 37, 93–6; Pearson and Richardson, 'Business networking', pp. 657–60.

6

Towns and industries: the changing character of manufacturing towns

Barrie Trinder

Examining urban and industrial change in the context of the Midlands has prompted a re-thinking of some of the ideas that I expressed in volume 2 of the *Cambridge Urban History*.[1] New data have been assembled and some significant questions have come to light about the patterns of thought followed in analysing the fortunes both of towns and industries. There is growing awareness of the potential of trade directories not just as a source of statistics, but also as a means of gaining acquaintance with patterns of economic custom (see Chapter 2), and as a source of evidence on the obscure origins of some far-reaching changes in trading or manufacturing patterns. New light has also been shed on census data, raising questions about the aggregated figures in the printed volumes, and demonstrating the value of detailed study of enumerators' returns in illuminating national and county-based statistics, and in revealing the nature of the economies of particular towns. This chapter also makes use of literary evidence – in particular of the workings of towns revealed in popular novels – and of archaeological evidence, from maps, pictorial evidence and surviving buildings. The study concentrates on questions about towns rather than those that concern the growth of particular industries.

Points of departure

One of the starting points for any analysis of industrial growth in the Midlands in the eighteenth and nineteenth centuries must be Langton's examination of the towns that grew most rapidly between the time of the hearth tax returns and the census of 1841,[2] and in particular his conclusion that 'by far the biggest effluxion of new towns was ... on and near coalfields'. Langton has pointed out that there was no simple distinction between regions that were industrialising and those that were not, but that different kinds of industrial growth were taking place in different regions.³ In some respects the differences between towns that lay within or near to the major coalfields and those that did not were more marked than those between the east and west Midlands. There was much in common between the principal coalfields: those in east Shropshire, the Black Country, the Potteries and the Derbyshire–Nottinghamshire border all benefited from the growth of coke-based ironmaking, the expanding markets for domestic fuel created by the waterways network and a range of ceramics manufactures from porcelain through brown stoneware bottles to blue engineering bricks. There were also differences: hosiery and lace making, almost universal accompaniments to the mining of coal in the east Midlands in the period under review, were unknown in the Black Country or Shropshire, while the manufacture of metal components and consumer goods that blossomed in Birmingham and its adjacent coalfield had few parallels in the east Midlands. The coalfield that lay on the border between the two sub-regions, in north Warwickshire, was a significant source of fuel for towns in the immediate locality and those that could be reached by the Oxford and Coventry canals, but had no substantial iron or ceramics industries. Other coalfields, like that which lay around Shrewsbury, were of minimal economic significance and were incapable of fulfilling the energy requirements of their immediate localities.⁴

A second starting point for this study is an assumption about the narrow range of the economic changes that took place during the classic period of the industrial revolution between 1750 and 1850. By participating in the prospering Atlantic economy, the coalfields of England experienced extraordinary growth in textile manufacture, coke-based iron production, mechanical engineering, which provided machinery for those industries, and civil engineering, which established a transport infrastructure. By contrast most consumer goods, garments, furniture, footwear and foodstuffs continued to be produced on a small scale, in many cases being supplied directly from producers to customers. Even in the most rapidly expanding new towns of the industrial revolution period, like West Bromwich (see Chapter 7), there developed a pattern of small-scale shoemakers, cabinet makers and tailors, alongside such retailers as grocers, drapers and druggists, not significantly different from that which can be observed in the most venerable of the primary towns of England. Crafts has observed that 'much of British "industry" in the first half of the nineteenth century was traditional and small-scale, and catered to local domestic markets. This sector, responsible for perhaps 60 per cent of industrial employment, experienced low levels of labour productivity and slow productivity growth – it is possible that there was virtually no advance during 1780–1860'.⁵ One purpose of this study is to examine the origins of the large-scale manufacture of consumer goods and to look forward into the second half of the nineteenth century, and more widely into some of the counties peripheral to the Midlands.

A third starting point is the hypothesis that the production of goods for distant markets has been a constant factor in the history of English towns, even of the smallest of them. The authors of early-nineteenth-century trade directories found it essential to define the 'manufactures' of a town. Even the occasional apology that a town lacked manufactures can be taken as an admission that it ought to have had them. The use of the word 'manufacture' usually implied the production of goods for distant markets. Malt and shoes, for example, were made in every town, but when eighteenth-century writers regarded malt in Newark or Mansfield, or footwear in Northampton or Stafford, as 'manufactures', they implied that production was for more than local requirements.[6] Alan Everitt in 1974 noted that 'the evolution of manufactures in the old market towns of England that did not develop into factory cities is unfortunately one of the most neglected aspects of industrial history', and noted that manufactures 'in the aggregate ... constituted something considerable, something essential in the economy of the town'.[7] This study attempts to place industrial activity in a broad urban context and to show that particular manufactures, while unimportant on a national scale, may have been of considerable significance in the context of an individual town. Steel manufacture in Woodstock did not rival that in Sheffield, but such trades were part of the essence of urban England.

Inheritances

Manufacturing, like any other urban activity, is shaped in part by a town's inheritance, by tangible and intangible factors that form what Massey called 'layers of investment' (see Chapter 1). A town's topography may have been shaped by a cruciform pattern of Roman streets, as in Chester or Towcester, or it may, as a consequence of medieval planning, form a neat pattern of burgage plots, as at Leeds or Ludlow. In towns of Saxon foundation, such as Shrewsbury or Northampton, the topography seems to follow no particular plan. Other topographical or architectural legacies may be the remnants of fortifications, the effects of great fires, as at Nantwich or Loughborough, or the legacy of a destructive siege during the Civil War, as at Banbury or Bridgnorth. Fine architecture from past periods of prosperity, like the houses of the late fourteenth century in Ludlow or the late sixteenth century in Shrewsbury, or the consequences of eighteenth- or early-nineteenth-century improvement acts might also influence a town's development.[8] There were also less tangible legacies. The influence of a great house on the edge of the town, like Burghley House at Stamford, might provide capital for new developments or might stifle enterprise. Trading in coal, timber and grain on navigable water-ways might lead families into banking and in due course to investment in manufacturing.

It was recognised in the early nineteenth century that a town was an agglomeration of particular functions. Everitt, in discussing Charlbury, remarked that it was 'as small a place as can properly be called a town, but during most of its history it has born the essential characteristics that distinguish every town, however small – namely the possession of trading rights and functions independent of farming activities'.[9] The trading status of a town might be measured by the degree of specialisation of its shops – in a very small place like Mark Rutherford's 'Cowfold', shops diverged towards 'general' trade, with drapers selling footwear, and grocers drugs and stationery,[10] whereas in assize towns and cathedral cities there might be such specialists as law stationers. There were cricket bat dealers in Oxford and Cambridge, and importers of diamonds and precious stones in resort towns such as Cheltenham or Leamington Spa. Towns were also places of religious diversity, most having a range of dissenting congregations by the 1830s, and retailing was often polarised around religious and political divisions. The more substantial market towns were centres for cultural and social organisations. These might be centrifugal, town-based bodies like mechanics' institutes or temperance societies, which perceived themselves to be duty-bound to spread messages in the surrounding countryside, or centripetal assemblies of countrymen, like farmers organising agricultural shows or rural clergy raising money for the mission to Jerusalem. In towns where society was polarised there might be parallel bodies pursuing similar aims whose membership was divided along political and religious lines. Towns provided meeting places for such bodies: these included assembly rooms in inns (some quite magnificent, as at the Lion in Shrewsbury, and others rather dowdy, like that described by Elizabeth Gaskell in *Cranford*), as well as theatres, corn exchanges, temperance halls and mechanics' institutes.[11]

A further feature of towns was the presence of the professions and in particular of doctors and lawyers. In *Catherine Furze*, Mark Rutherford discusses the differing shades of respect granted to the doctor, the lawyer and the clergyman in a town in the eastern Midlands in 1840.[12] A writer in 1865 observed that the outskirts of a county town might be dominated by four large buildings: the union workhouse, hospital, gaol and lunatic asylum.[13] The first two might be found at the edge of many market towns, and all were likely to be new developments of the first half of the nineteenth century. All four provided openings for the clerical, legal and medical professions that were fiercely contested. The proliferation of country banks was more significant to industrial growth.[14] By the 1830s, there were banks in almost every settlement that in qualitative terms might be classified as a town. They might be banks of local origin or branches of those in nearby larger towns, but all offered prospects of capital for manufacturers. Yet many bankers were members of families long established as lawyers, and to some extent banks continued an older tradition, previously pursued by solicitors, of guiding capital into the hands of those anxious to use it.

Transport facilities, like a situation on a main road, might be part of a town's inheritance, but increasingly they were the result of investment which might be locally based, as with some canals, and of political agitation, as was the case with most turnpike roads. One of the consequences of road improvements after 1750 was the development of networks of carriers' carts.[15] An extensive carrying network was a sign of a town's trading vitality, and some, like Banbury and Cirencester, attracted numbers of carriers out of all proportion to their populations. Some questions relating to the chronology of the development of carrying networks remain to be answered. The apparent sparse networks of some towns in the early nineteenth century may be the result of incomplete recording in trade directories, but the more dense networks revealed in directories of the 1850s and 1860s may reflect a real expansion of this form of trading. The waterway network provided most towns with access to coal and to carrying companies that provided an effective means by which manufacturers and importers could distribute small consignments of goods to shopkeepers. Some towns that lacked direct access to waterways were nevertheless linked by road transport to wharves a few miles away. Much of Ludlow's coal came from a wharf at Woofferton, while the traders of Bicester reputedly gained great advantages from the wharf at Lower Heyford on the Oxford Canal.

Most market towns were to some extent places of resort, and in the early nineteenth century there was a tendency to build speculative dwellings of a prestigious nature, like 'The Terrace' in Rutherford's 'Eastthorpe',[16] or Rutland Terrace on the western edge of Stamford. These might accommodate professional families or prosperous traders, but they could also attract people with income from private investments who might otherwise settle in Bath or Cheltenham. Banbury was a town which singularly failed to attract such people, perceptively defined by its local newspaper in 1852 when it remarked, 'we have workers and those who are seeking to get money in abundance; and it must be a wise step to encourage the residence amongst us of those who come to spend and not to get money'.[17] Stamford was a more attractive resort, and in 1851 thirteen of the twenty houses in Rutland Terrace were occupied by female fundholders, annuitants or property owners, the seven male householders comprising a solicitor, a banker, a retired grocer, a former naval officer, a proprietor of houses and two clergymen. The inhabitants of most fictional towns included aged gentlewomen living off income from property. Similarly, most towns portrayed in novels included a particular form of resort development, boarding schools, which provided trade for those who fed and clothed pupils and staff, and congregations for parish churches or dissenting chapels. Such schools were features of the early stages of growth of West Bromwich, emphasising the fact that they were an essential element in the perceived pattern of urban activities. In some Midlands towns, like Rugby, Shrewsbury and Uppingham, the expansion of ancient boarding schools created service industries of considerable local significance during the nineteenth century, stimulating the development of particular trades, just as cathedrals did in other cities.

Crafts and manufactures

Most consumer goods in the decades before 1840 were manufactured by craftsmen, the chief of whom occupied premises in the central areas of towns. The structures of trades like shoemaking and tailoring were complex: much work was put out by master tradesmen to others, who might themselves be masters or work consistently for more prestigious tradesmen. The role of women was often assumed but undocumented. Long before the advent of the sewing machine, the Banbury shoemaker George Herbert, when establishing his business after his marriage in 1838, set his wife to learn to bind shoes.[18] It is evident from the study of census returns that some enumerators recorded 'shoemakers' wives' as a distinct category, which appears in the aggregated returns, while others consistently failed to note occupations for women employed in the home. The dividing line between 'pure' retailers and craftsmen was often indistinct. In the eighteenth century mercers who sold tobacco often processed the dried bundles or 'hands', which involved the use of a sizeable 'tobacco engine'.[19] Many nineteenth-century ironmongers also made candles, knives or nails, while some drapers employed milliners and dressmakers, accounting for the considerable numbers of employees claimed by some shopkeepers in towns of fairly modest size. For example, John Cavell had twenty-four workers living in his household in Magdalen Street, Oxford, in 1861, while Charles Smith of Stamford employed forty-one, of whom nine lived in. A move by a retailer towards manufacturing for wider markets could therefore be a relatively small step.

Some local trades, by their very nature, required large-scale premises. A corn mill, most commonly operated by water power, was part of the very essence of a town in the Middle Ages, as evidenced by places like Bridgnorth and Wellington, which, lacking water power within their own boundaries, had legal access to mills at a distance.[20] Some urban mills were adapted in the eighteenth century to service the needs of other industries, particularly textiles and papermaking, but they remained constant factors in the urban economy nevertheless. Relatively few English towns were endowed with substantial numbers of mill sites, Derby and Ludlow being two of the most conspicuous in the Midlands, and their relative patterns of growth do not suggest that water power was the most vital factor in urban industrial expansion. Malting also required distinctive premises, since barley needed to be laid out on extensive floors to make it sprout. Malting was one of the quintessential urban occupations in the first half of the nineteenth century. There were malthouses in every market town, even those of the highland zone. A distinction should be made nevertheless between towns where maltsters simply supplied the needs of local brewers and those from which malt was despatched to the breweries of the largest cities and to such brewing towns as Burton and Tadcaster. In the second half of the nineteenth century malting disappeared from some towns, like Ellesmere, where it had previously been significant, but expanded in others, like Sleaford, Newark and Grantham. Some very large malting establishments were constructed, but, equally, small ones were being built in Shrewsbury as late as 1888.[21] Tanning was another trade that flourished in most towns in 1800, but which in the course of the nineteenth century disappeared from many, as tanneries using imported hides expanded in London, particularly in Bermondsey, on Merseyside and in Leeds.[22] Neither tanning nor malting was labour-intensive, but both required considerable investment in buildings and materials. Much the same could be said of rope making: most urban roperies supplied local needs, which were obviously greater in coastal communities or river ports.

Around 1800, there were also numerous 'manufactures' – goods produced for national or international markets – for which particular towns were famous. Daventry, for example, was celebrated for its whips: an appropriate trade for a town of great thoroughfare and doubtless of economic significance in a town that in 1801 had fewer than 3,000 inhabitants, but it is doubtful whether the number of whip makers extended far into double figures. Similarly, spring makers in Pershore supplied main springs for watches to the clockmakers who proliferated in towns all over England from the first half of the eighteenth century, but the numbers engaged in the trade were probably never very large in a town that also had fewer than 3,000 inhabitants in the early nineteenth century. Certainly, by 1835 just one spring maker remained in Pershore.[23] Some manufactures, like that of cakes in Banbury, which were being sent abroad in the 1830s, were of ancient origin,[24] but others originated in the period under review. In Wellingborough the most celebrated manufacture of the first half of the nineteenth century was a patent embrocation made by one John Whitton, which was said to be 'distributed to all parts of the kingdom'.[25] Many manufactures were textiles. Notwithstanding the prodigious growth of the cotton, woollen, flax and silk industries in the North and east Midlands, an astonishing variety of textile manufactures remained in English towns in the second half of the nineteenth century. Even Lichfield had a mill for the spinning of worsted yarn in 1835. Some mid-nineteenth-century textile mills were the surviving portions of once substantial regional industries that had suffered decline, like the remnants of Sir Robert Peel's cotton enterprises in Tamworth. Some, like the manufacture of blankets in Witney, carpets in Kidderminster or waistcoating in Kendal, were enterprises that had success-fully captured substantial niche markets. Some were the chance outposts of the main centres of the industry, like the flax mill in Shrewsbury that was a branch of Marshall & Co. of Leeds, while others were small mills, like those in Church Stretton and Knighton, catering for local needs in the same man-ner as the custom weavers of earlier generations. Redundant textile mills offered inexpensive accommodation for manufactures of many kinds.

New urban industries

In most towns of consequence three new forms of industry were established between 1780 and 1850, commercial breweries, mechanical engineering works and coachmaking establishments. Most beer in the mid-eighteenth century was still brewed at home or in the public houses where it was consumed, which in part explains the ubiquity of malting businesses. Some provincial towns, like Derby, had a reputation for supplying beer to national markets, but very large brewing establishments were essentially a feature of the capital. From about 1780 breweries developed in many market towns. By 1840 about thirty breweries in the provinces were producing more than 20,000 barrels of beer per annum, which may be taken as a benchmark for a concern that was of more than local significance,[26] but in most towns there were smaller estab-lishments, catering for their own public houses. Both in *The Revolution in Tanner's Lane* and in *Catherine Furze*, Mark Rutherford regarded the pres-ence of a nouveau riche brewer as one of the characteristic features of a small town in the 1830s or 1840s. Similarly, he saw the operation of a foundry by the ironmonger father of the heroine of *Catherine Furze* as unremarkable. The proliferation of mechanical engineering works depended on several techno-logical factors. First the growth of overall production in the iron industry increased supplies of pig-iron for foundries and wrought iron for forges, while the development of the inland waterways network enabled the efficient dis-tribution of iron and the coke necessary for the operation of foundries. From the 1790s foundry masters were able to use the cupola furnace to re-melt pig-iron or scrap, while the supply of machine tools from Henry Maudslay in

Lambeth and subsequently from works in Manchester and elsewhere improved during the first half of the nineteenth century. By 1850 it was possible to make castings and forgings, machine them and assemble them into threshing boxes or railway locomotives in almost every town in England. A parliamentary report of 1849 shows that foundry owners in all parts of the country were able to exercise choice in their pig-iron (from that produced in South Wales, Shropshire, Staffordshire or Scotland) and in their coke, most of which came either from Elsecar in south Yorkshire or from County Durham. The catalogue of the Great Exhibition of 1851 lists mechanical engineering works in most English market towns.[27]

Rutherford's easy assumptions illustrate one of the essential features of brewing and mechanical engineering, and one that applies to some of the consumer goods industries that developed in subsequent decades. Most large commercial breweries developed from the brewhouses of public houses whose owners began to supply other pubs and subsequently built up their production and acquired more outlets. Similarly most urban mechanical engineering works grew from foundries established by ironmongers, like Mr Furze; by millwrights, who decided to make their own castings; or by blacksmiths, who chose to produce cast-iron as well as wrought-iron goods. The process of growth was evolutionary rather than revolutionary. The first products of most market town foundries were agricultural implements, but some began to specialise in producing plant for other local manufacturing industries, like biscuit-making apparatus in Reading or machines for producing wooden bobbins in Kendal. Others developed products that were supplied to national and even to international markets, like the cranes made by Stothert & Pitt at Bath, the kitchen ranges made by several firms in Leamington Spa, the fairground equipment made by Frederick Savage at King's Lynn or the showmen's engines that were produced by Charles Burrell at Thetford. The evolutionary nature of market town industry is illustrated by the early history of the Neneside works in Thrapston, which until the 1990s supplied world markets with pulleys. William Langford Fisher took over the ironmongery shop of his uncle in nearby Oundle in 1841. Ten years later he was trading on the river Nene at Thrapston in coal, iron, seeds, oilcake and timber, and within a few years he set up a foundry on a riverside wharf. He died soon afterwards and the works was taken over by Robert and Nathaniel Smith, natives of Kettering who had been working in a foundry in Stamford. They employed twenty men and six boys by 1861, making a range of products including steam engines, hay mowers and oilcake crushers.

The proliferation of mechanical engineering works depended on the migration of skilled individuals as well as the availability of raw materials. Detailed studies of particular towns show the migration patterns of moulders, turners, fitters and pattern makers as they gained experience in the celebrated works on the coalfields and in the great cities, and before settling in towns which had previously lacked engineering traditions. Richard Jefferies observed in the 1870s that

> country towns of any size usually possess at least one manufactory of agricultural implements and some of these factories have acquired a reputation which reaches over the sea. The visitor to such a foundry is shown medals that have been granted for excellence of work exhibited in Vienna, and may see machines in process of construction which will be used upon the continent ... Busy workmen pass to and fro, lithe men, quick of step and motion, who come from Leeds, or some similar manufacturing town, and whose very step distinguishes them in a moment from the agricultural labourer.[28]

Similarly coachmaking, which flourished as the numbers of road vehicles used to transport passengers to railway stations increased, can be seen as the development of the wheelwright's trade, as well as the spread through the provinces of techniques practised in London, where coachmaking had long prospered. There were coachmakers in almost every town by 1850, and their number tended to expand during the half-century that followed. Most employed no more than a dozen people, but some concerns, like that which occupied Brunel's one-time Great Western Hotel in Bristol, could be very large.

The expansion of engineering, brewing or coachmaking, as of older industries that came to require larger premises, depended on the availability of space. It was possible to establish a small foundry on the burgage plot behind an ironmonger's shop, but new premises, preferably with access to water or subsequently to rail transport, and with room for a spacious erection shop, were desirable for the iron founder who wished to establish a substantial business. The sudden growth of new metal-using industries in West Bromwich that followed enclosure and the building of the Birmingham Canal illustrates the way in which growth could quickly follow the creation of sites for manufacturing. Most towns, regardless of their previous population histories, began to burst their medieval bounds in the closing years of the eighteenth century. This might lead to the construction of elegant terraces for those with incomes from investments or the establishment of industrial premises. Most of the zones of dense industrial activity in Midlands towns before 1840 were centred on rivers and canals. Rivers had traditionally provided water power, but navigable waterways could also deliver power in the form of coal. In several large Midlands towns it is possible to observe concentrations of manufacturing along the waterways and new developments in the suburbs. In late-eighteenth-century Shrewsbury a line of industrial concerns, including a textile mill, a tannery and a foundry, was established along the banks of the Severn, while two large flax mills were built on land that had previously been ill-drained meadow on the northern side of the town. The map produced for the Board of Health in Derby in 1852 shows a concentration of manufacturing activity around the confluence of the Derby Canal with the river Derwent: textile mills, including the celebrated silk mill of 1721, three foundries, a lead works and a paint and colour factory. There were also large-scale manufactories in the suburbs of Derby, including a lead works and two large silk mills on the Normanton Road.

Consumer goods industries

The final section of this study will examine briefly the growth after 1850 of companies concerned with the manufacture of consumer goods, garments, footwear, furniture and foodstuffs. The history of the Co-operative Wholesale Society, established in 1863 to supply retail societies throughout England, provides evidence of the factories used in the production of consumer goods and of the technologies employed. It also illustrates the importance of marketing. Distributing consumer goods to retailers necessitated the development of trading patterns as well as the availability of transport systems, and while the links between the Co-operative Wholesale Society and retailing societies are well documented, those between other producers and the shopkeepers who sold their products are obscure.

The manufacture of hosiery, a substantial part of the clothing industry, was organised on a large scale long before 1850. The principal concentration was in Nottinghamshire, Derbyshire and Leicestershire, where production was organised on a domestic and workshop basis.[29] In the second half of the nineteenth century production became concentrated in factories. Lace manufacture in the east Midlands was similarly dependent on domestic and workshop units until the 1880s, when powered factories were built. Gloves were also produced on a large scale before 1840, but the industry was subject to foreign competition, and its fitful history was shaped by the imposition and removal of import duties. A directory of 1835 lists eighty-five glove manufacturers in Worcester. In Woodstock in 1851 one manufacturer employed 150 outworkers, and another seventy-six.[30]

The production of garments on a large scale had several false starts. Long's Building in Devizes has been called Wiltshire's first textile factory, but it lacked any kind of power system, and documentary evidence suggests that when built in the 1780s it served as a warehouse for the domestic production of garments.[31] The 1851 census in Abingdon recorded John Hyde as a 'Cloth Manufacturer, employing 1400 people making garments'. The enumerators' returns show that many women and girls in the town were employed as makers of waistcoats, jackets and shirts, but the industry appears to have disappeared from the town by 1861. A directory of 1830 lists Hyde as a clothes dealer, a category that appears in many towns in the 1830s, which may indicate a gradual growth of shops selling ready-made garments.[32] The writers of the reports on occupations in the censuses of 1881 and 1891 admitted that it was difficult to determine national trends in garment manufacture. Numbers of needle-workers were increasing at about the same rate as the population at large, but the increasing availability of machines meant that productivity was increasing rather faster. The principal concentrations of garment workers were in the great cities, but there were significant manufacturers in many other towns. There were stay-makers in most towns in the early nineteenth century. The industry was organised on a factory basis after 1850, particularly in the area between Kettering and Market Harborough, where it grew out of general manufacture of clothing. In 1851 some sixty-four women in Desborough were employed embroidering waistcoats. In 1856 Frederick Wallis set up a clothing business using sewing machines in a former silk works in Kettering, and by 1871 he employed over 150 workers. At about the same time John Turner Stockburn opened a factory in Kettering where stays were manufactured on sewing machines. He employed more than 100 people by 1871, by which time there were also factories in Rothwell and Desborough.[33]

The history of footwear manufacture after 1850 is one of concentration, although the numbers of individual craftsmen in market towns remained stubbornly high. Some towns were recognised in the eighteenth century as centres for the manufacture of footwear, often on the basis of large-scale contracts for the military. Stephen Whatley in 1751 observed that Northampton's principal manufacture was 'shoes of which great numbers are sent beyond the sea'.[34] However, Northampton's 1801 population was only just over 7,000, so that however high the proportion of shoemakers amongst its inhabitants, they could have produced only a tiny fraction of the national output of boots and shoes. Trade directories for Stafford in the early nineteenth century distinguish wholesale manufacturers from other shoemakers and reveal an infrastructure of curriers, leather-cutters and last makers.[35] During the first half of the nineteenth century agents began to market Northamptonshire shoes in London, and by 1851 some 13,254 people in the county, just over 6 per cent of the total population, were engaged in shoemaking. At that date the industry was organised on a domestic basis, but during the 1850s the first factories were constructed when sewing machines were introduced from the United States. Employment in the footwear industry almost doubled between 1851 and 1881, and exceeded 40,000 by the end of the century. There appears to have been a move away from domestic towards factory production in the 1890s, and by the turn of the century there were nearly 400 factories in the county.

Northampton, Kettering and Wellingborough all saw substantial growth – the population of Kettering increasing from just over 5,000 to almost 30,000 between 1851 and 1901 – but some villages were transformed into industrial communities. Most notable was Rushden, where population increased from 1,460 to 12,453 in the fifty years after 1851. The Northamptonshire footwear industry thus grew from ancient origins, expansion accelerating after the introduction of the sewing machine. Machinery, often produced by locally based engineering companies, made possible the large-scale employment of women and children in factories, and by 1901 some 30 per cent of workers in the industry were female. Shoemaking developed in communities where there was space for expansion. The estate in the north-eastern quarter of Kettering, made available for development at auction in 1876, remains a landscape in which the feverish pace of economic growth in the 1880s and 1890s can be appreciated. The streets are laid out on a grid pattern and lined with red-brick cottages, many of them with garden workshops; alleyways to these provided means of conveying baskets to and from the three-storey factories, which, with dissenting chapels and rifle-and-band clubs, stand on many of the corners.[36]

The furniture trade was also transformed after 1850. There were cabinet-makers and chair makers in every town in the first half of the century. A few producers on a relatively large scale, such as Waring & Gillow of Lancaster, supplied national markets with high-class furniture.[37] Chair making, utilising parts made by 'bodgers' in the Chiltern woodlands, was the principal manu-facture in High Wycombe by the 1830s, when a directory listed twenty-one chairmakers.[38] The trade grew with the introduction of machinery from the 1860s and benefited from well-publicised orders for chairs for great events in London.[39] One chairmaker in 1861 employed 160, but the median size of a factory labour force was around thirty, of which young women formed a sig-nificant proportion. Specialist manufacturers provided chair backs, cane and varnish, and local engineers were producing chair-making machinery.

Two substantial consumer goods industries developed in the nearby county town of Aylesbury. The book-printing works of Hazel, Watson & Viney moved to Aylesbury from London in 1867 and employed over 200 people a decade later. Compositors were recruited from places as distant as Lewes, Liverpool and Dublin, but the factory also employed many young females, chiefly in folding, binding and packing books. Hazel, Watson & Viney was one of several book-printing companies to move from London to the provinces in the late nineteenth century. At least one of the others, Clowes at Beccles, Suffolk, invested heavily in American technology.[40] The Anglo-Swiss Con-densed Milk Co. established a canal-side factory in 1870, continuing the town's traditional trade of supplying dairy products to London. The company utilised processes for condensing and canning milk that were invented by an

American, Gail Borden, in the 1850s and perfected during the Civil War.[41] In 1871 the factory had about twenty employees and was managed by another American. By 1881 the labour force had increased to about fifty, many of them young females involved in filling, sealing, labelling and packing tins of milk.

The food industry in other towns displayed similar patterns. The manufacture of pork pies in Melton Mowbray reached its peak in the last thirty years of the nineteenth century, when there were three factories supplying customers in many parts of Britain. Growth was stimulated by well-publicised orders for special events – 30,000 pies for the Preston Guild in 1881 and six tons for the Royal Show at York in 1883 – together with contracts for military exercises and for Leicestershire Cricket Club matches.[42] Bacon production in Calne was initially dependent on a technology observed in 1847 by George Harris in New York State. Within a few decades the town's manufacturers were using the railways to supply consumers all over Britain.[43] Biscuit making in Reading was a small-scale regional speciality in the early nineteenth century – there were three biscuit bakers in the town in 1830, and others in Newbury, Windsor and Wokingham.[44] Its expansion also owed much to the railway system, to imaginative marketing and to links with local engineers.

Conclusions

In terms of town populations and numbers employed, industry in the Midlands continued through the second half of the nineteenth century to be dominated by the great staples of the industrial revolution, as new areas like Cannock Chase and the Leen Valley were opened up for mining, iron and steel. While engineering was significant in most towns, most engineers worked in substantial establishments in the coalfields or the largest cities. The producers of consumer goods prospered in similar places: footwear and clothing manufactures flourished in Leicester, and in Tipton Palethorpes converted a redundant brewery into a model factory despatching 'Royal Cambridge' sausages by rail to all parts of the country. Nevertheless, many towns which were relatively unaffected by the industrial revolution continued to flourish and were increasingly concerned with the manufacture of consumer goods for national markets. Langton has pointed out the contrast between the county towns of the east Midlands, which grew rapidly in the period to 1841, and those of the west Midlands, which did not.[45] This trend broadly continued after 1841, but this does not mean that the economies of the west Midlands county towns were stagnant. Shrewsbury, after losing its flax industry in the 1880s, retained several engineering works, one a producer of agricultural implements of international esteem, and, as a result of the enterprise of William Jones & Son, its malthouses dominated the region.[46] Worcester had an even more dynamic and prosperous mixed economy. In the 1830s, there were traditional industries like malting and tanning, old-established specialisms like porcelain, new trades such as brewing and engineering and consumer goods industries producing clothing and food, particularly vinegar and British wine.[47]

The new consumer goods industries of the second half of the nineteenth century had several common features. Many were built on old foundations, drawing on the layers of investment represented by the availability of professional and financial services, manual skills, transport facilities and the generally pleasing environments of market towns. Some entrepreneurs established their companies by supplying local consumers, taking advantage of the position of a market town in Christaller's central place hierarchy, but subsequently progressed to supplying national and even international markets. They frequently opened employment opportunities to women, even in traditionally male-dominated trades like book printing. They depended on imaginative marketing, in many cases on exploitation of the publicity opportunities offered by large-scale contracts, and on the development of distribution chains, of which the railway network usually formed the principal part. Some were stimulated by technology from abroad, particularly from the United States, and especially in the form of the sewing machine, a key factor in both clothing and footwear manufacture. They were established not just in the major centres of industry in the Midlands but in many towns that were not regarded primarily as industrial centres, continuing to take their place in what Everitt, describing an earlier period, called the 'mixed economy of trades, crafts and manufactures' that characterised most English towns. This phenomenon can be interpreted as a continuation of the eighteenth-century concept of 'manufactures', but the scale had changed. Rather than the workshops of individuals making whips or watch springs, the characteristic units of the late nineteenth century were factories of modest size, employing between twenty and fifty people, units that were similar in many respects to the 'small-scale factories' that have been identified in the north-eastern United States in the first half of the nineteenth century. Berg has pointed out the significance of this kind of unit in the metalworking trades of Birmingham and Sheffield. It may also be helpful to see it as a characteristic feature of the growth of the food, footwear, furniture, clothing and printing industries in many English towns in the latter part of the nineteenth century.[48] C. G. Harper wrote in 1907: 'The days when Market Harborough was a little market town interested in nothing else but agriculture and hunting are done. It is now, indeed, a busy little place, and with its varied industrial enterprises, not so little as it was. Chief of these is Symington's corset factory, employing 580 hands, but elsewhere may be noted manufactories of rubber soles and heels, pea flour and numerous other articles of commerce'.[49] With its involvement in the manufacture of footwear, food and clothing, this modest Leicestershire town epitomised many of the industrial developments in Midlands towns of the previous half-century.

Notes

1 Trinder, 'Industrialising towns', pp. 805–29.
2 Langton, 'Urban growth', p. 467.
3 Langton, 'Town growth', pp. 7–47.
4 Trinder, *Shropshire*, pp. 77–82.
5 Crafts, 'British industrialisation', p. 425.
6 Trinder, 'Industrialising towns', pp. 807–8.
7 Everitt, 'Banburys of England', pp. 36–7.
8 Innes and Rogers, 'Politics and government', pp. 536–7.
9 Everitt, 'Banburys of England', pp. 28–9.
10 Rutherford, *Revolution in Tanner's Lane*, p. 233.
11 Trinder, *Victorian Banbury*, p. 65; Champion, 'John Ashby'; Gaskell, *Cranford*, pp. 161–2.
12 Corfield, *Power and the Professions*; Rutherford, *Catherine Furze*, p. 60.
13 Anon., 'The English Bastille', *Social Science Review*, 3 (1865), 193, quoted in Driver, *Power and Paupers*, p. 1.
14 Dawes and Ward-Perkins, *Country Banks*, vol. 2, pp. 15, 50.
15 Everitt, 'Country carriers'. See also Chapter 5 of this volume.
16 Rutherford, *Catherine Furze*, p. 12.
17 *Banbury Guardian*, 13 May 1852. See also Everitt, 'English urban inn', p. 114.
18 Herbert, *Shoemaker's Window*, p. 16.
19 Trinder and Cox, *Yeomen and Colliers*, pp. 38–9.
20 Trinder, *Shropshire*, p. 44.
21 Trinder, *Shropshire*, pp. 47–51; Clark, *Malting Industry*; Wright, *Lincolnshire Towns*, pp. 212–13; Alderton and Booker, *East Anglia*, pp. 31–2.
22 Gomersall, 'Departed glory'.
23 *Pigot's Directory* (1835), pp. 365–6.
24 Trinder, *Victorian Banbury*, p. 32.
25 Trinder, *Northamptonshire*, p. 26.
26 Gourvish and Wilson, *British Brewing Industry*, pp. 111–13.
27 Stratton and Trinder, *Industrial England*, pp. 74–89.
28 Jefferies, *Hodge and his Masters*, p. 36.
29 Campion, 'People, process', pp. 75–8. See also Chapters 9 and 10 of this volume.
30 *Pigot's Directory* (1835), p. 389.
31 Stratton and Trinder, *Long's Building*.
32 *Pigot's Directory* (1830), pp. 2–3.
33 Trinder, *Northamptonshire*, p. 33.
34 Whatley, *England's Gazetteer*.
35 *Pigot's Directory* (1835), pp. 158–65.
36 Campion, 'People, process', pp. 81–3.
37 White, *Lancaster*, pp. 99–100.
38 *Pigot's Directory* (1830), pp. 69–72.

39 Mayes, *History of Chairmaking*, pp. 35–6.
40 Clowes, *Family Business*, p. 61.
41 Trinder, 'British food industry'.
42 Hickman, *Melton Mowbray*, pp. 14–22, 49–87.
43 Corfield, *Wiltshire*, pp. 63–70.
44 *Pigot's Directory* (1830), pp. 17, 21, 15, 39.
45 Langton, 'Town growth', pp. 29–30.
46 Trinder, *Shropshire*, pp. 50–1, 60–1.
47 *Pigot's Directory* (1835), pp. 382–93.
48 Berg, *Age of Manufactures*, pp. 201–3.
49 Harper, *Manchester and Glasgow Road*, p. 156.

PART II

Industrialisation and Midlands towns

7

New towns
of the industrial coalfields:
Burslem and West Bromwich

Jon Stobart and Barrie Trinder

The growth and spread of manufacturing towns was one of the defining features of eighteenth- and early-nineteenth-century, urbanisation.[1] However, in
contrast with the later nineteenth century when railway towns, new ports and
iron and steel towns proliferated, few of these emergent seats of industry grew
ab initio. Even in the heartlands of the industrial revolution genuinely new
towns were comparatively rare. The question is not whether or even how
industrialisation stimulated urbanisation in a broad sense,[2] but to what extent
wholly new urban communities developed during industrialisation. Porteous
identified a handful of canal towns, and there were a growing number of spa
or sea-bathing resorts, but most new urban development was focused onto the
coalfields.[3] Even here, though, urbanisation was a patchy process: in Lancashire we can point to St Helens, Ashton-under-Lyne and Oldham; in
Staffordshire the Potteries were urbanising by the late eighteenth century. But
on the coalfields of Derby and Nottingham, Shropshire and South Wales urban
growth was constrained before 1840. Places such as Ilkeston, Dawley and
Ebbw Vale were too large, complex or economically influential to be regarded
merely as industrial villages. Yet whilst they possessed the basic city-forming
industries, the non-basic servicing industries, hinterlands and civic identity of
true towns were lacking.[4]

What led certain places to acquire such functions whilst so many others –
often neighbouring settlements – failed to graduate to urban status? Traditional explanations that draw on location factors such as natural resources,
or the availability of capital or labour, are useful in some instances, but rarely
give us the full picture.[5] In this chapter we explore this question in the context of two Staffordshire manufacturing centres that, during the course of the
first industrial revolution, passed from being small industrial villages to being
clearly identifiable towns. Burslem and West Bromwich illustrate well how

urban activities could coalesce around industrial development, building up, sometimes rapidly and sometimes more slowly, around a functional and spatial core. Both towns were associated with the classic features of industrial growth. They were situated in productive coalfields where iron-making prospered, and benefited from the construction of canals and the improvement of roads. They also show how the urbanisation of such coalfield industrial districts was not merely a natural process of accretion around a key manufacture, the product of natural location advantages. Rather, it was an active project, often led by local elites and heavily influenced by developments in neighbouring urban and rural settlements. As we shall see, it required nascent towns to be closely linked into dynamic networks of individuals and urban centres.[6]

Growing industrial settlements

Located at either end of the county, Burslem and West Bromwich reflected the full range of Staffordshire industrialisation. Burslem was essentially a pottery centre: although iron production was also important in the district there were no ironworks in the town itself. The earliest evidence of earthenware manufacture dates from the thirteenth century, but production remained small-scale and localised well into the early modern period: most potters combined manufacturing activity with agricultural pursuits.[7] Importantly for its new status as a town, Burslem emerged early on as a key centre in the pottery industry. By the second half of the seventeenth century, Burslem already had several 'master potters' producing a wide range of earthenware goods in centralised potworks and sending some of their wares to London.[8] During the eighteenth century, the pottery industry was increasingly locked into north Staffordshire through the local availability of coal and coal-measure clays (although not china clay and ball clay – which mostly came from Devon and Cornwall via the Weaver to Winsford or to the head of navigation on the Trent) and a skilled workforce. A retrospective survey undertaken by Josiah Wedgwood towards the end of the eighteenth century gives us a picture of the scale and importance of pottery manufacture in Burslem around 1715. It showed an industry already widespread and specialised, and wares including black, mottled, stone, cloudy, red and freckled as well as the traditional butter pots. Together these manufacturers had a turnover of around £6,500 per year. Burslem's development as an industrial centre of national importance gathered pace during the late eighteenth and early nineteenth centuries, particularly after the turnpiking of the main roads through the town in 1763 and 1765 and the completion of the Trent and Mersey Canal in 1777. Employment in the pottery industry of north Staffordshire grew from less than 100 in 1660 to around 7,000 by 1760, spread across around 150 potworks. By the turn of

the nineteenth century, the number of earthenware manufacturers in the Potteries had stabilised at around 140, but they were now employing between
15,000 and 20,000 workers. The small workshops of the seventeenth century
were being replaced by large-scale potworks employing scores or hundreds of
men and women in increasingly divisions of labour.[9] Moreover, these works
were making a wide range of products for national and international markets,
with the emphasis increasingly on tableware, underlining the link between economic growth and the broad patterns of cultural change.[10] The collieries
feeding these works were ranged to the north and east of Burslem, controlled
by a handful of wealthy coal proprietors, who numbered no more than ten in
the early nineteenth century.[11]

In the eighteenth century West Bromwich was a 6,000-acre parish of hamlets scattered over heathland. The manufacture of iron products, particularly
nails, formed the mainstay of industrial development, but it was centred on
established Black Country towns such as Dudley and Stourbridge: a fact which
limited early urban development in the parish. There were only three ironmongers (in this sense, merchants putting out tasks to domestic workers) in
West Bromwich in 1775 and yet, as Arthur Young reported, the road through
the district 'for five or six miles [formed] one continued village of nailers ...
quite to Wolverhampton from Birmingham, I saw not one farmhouse'.[12] In the
1841 census, nailing still accounted for up to one-half of recorded occupations
in some townships, but from the late eighteenth century local metalworkers
were turning to more sophisticated products. Crucial here were the turnpiking of the Birmingham–Wolverhampton road in 1725, the completion of the
Birmingham Canal in 1769 and the enclosure of the parish in 1804, which provided improved access and created attractive sites for industry, particularly in
the western part of the parish.[13] This encouraged the migration of several manufacturers from Birmingham, including John Izon, who established his
foundry in West Bromwich in 1782, and Archibald Kenrick, who followed him
nine years later, specialising in light castings.[14] Some of the works clustered
around the turnpike road that was to become the town centre made components, either in cast iron or wrought iron, for the manufacture of road and
railway carriages, some made bayonets or gun locks, while others produced
such domestic items as coffee mills, spring balances and enamelled holloware.[15]
These works operated at an increasingly large scale, employing many hands.
Industry in West Bromwich had thus been transformed from proto-industrial
nail production to the disciplined manufacture of components and consumer
goods demanding consistency of quality and delivery. As in Burslem, this burgeoning industrial economy was dependent upon the local supply of coal: by
1837 there were twenty-one collieries arranged in a broad arc to the west of
the nascent town. Growth was also stimulated by the development of two

exceptionally large enterprises within a mile of the new centre: the glassworks of Robert Lucas Chance in Oldbury (opened in 1822) and the Birmingham and Staffordshire Gasworks at Swan Village (1825), which supplied Birmingham, Bilston and Darlaston and was reckoned the largest in Britain in 1850.

This industrial expansion promoted strong population growth (Table 7.1). Burslem was already the largest of the pottery communities by the 1730s, and by the late eighteenth century it was probably also larger than neighbouring Newcastle-under-Lyme. Expansion was initially concentrated within the bounds of the seventeenth-century village, houses, workshops and kilns being built in the numerous gardens and crofts which still characterised Burslem in the mid-eighteenth century. Subsequently, there was growth at Cobridge to the south and along the road joining the two settlements, especially after it was turnpiked in 1765. But most expansion took place in the new satellite settlements of Longport, Middleport and Newport, ranged along the Trent and Mersey Canal (opened in 1777) to the west and south-west of Burslem. Despite this, Burslem was the slowest-growing of the pottery communities through the eighteenth and nineteenth centuries: its demographic and physical expansion was overshadowed by that seen in neighbouring settlements. Two miles to the south Hanley grew rapidly during the second half of the eighteenth century, from just 2,000 or so in 1762 to 7,940 by 1801, by which time it was clearly the largest of the pottery towns. A little over a mile to the north, Tunstall grew at a phenomenal rate especially in the early nineteenth century, doubling in size between 1801 and 1811 and again by 1831. That said, Burslem was one of the twenty fastest-growing Midlands towns during this period and certainly grew much faster than its more established neighbours such as Newcastle-under-Lyme, Cheadle and Stone, which grew by only around 30 per cent during this period.

Table 7.1 *Population totals for Burslem and West Bromwich, 1738–1901*

	1738	1762	1801	1811	1821	1831	1841	1851	1901
Burslem	1,800	2,800	6,486	8,478	9,815	12,572	16,091	19,725	40,234
West Bromwich	–	–	5,687	7,485	9,505	15,327	26,121	34,591	65,175

Sources: Weatherill, *Pottery Trade*, p. 113; Ward, *Stoke*, p. 43; population census of England and Wales.

Early figures for West Bromwich are less reliable, but its maximum expansion clearly coincided with industrial diversification in the 1820s and 1830s. West Bromwich was the fastest-growing parish in a region where population was expanding rapidly. The total population of nine Black Country parishes that were not subjected to early-nineteenth-century boundary changes (Darlaston, Dudley, Rowley Regis, Sedgeley, Tipton, Walsall, Wednesbury, West Bromwich and Wolverhampton) was 79,170 in 1801. This rose to 223,272 in 1841 and 284,365 in 1851 – increases of 182 per cent and 259 per cent respectively. West Bromwich increased by 360 per cent and 508 per cent over the same period. The emergence of the urban community, which comprised a relatively small proportion of the parish, contributed to the overall growth of population, and at the same time was a consequence of it. Both settlements, then, were increasingly populous and contained dynamic industrial sectors, but were these enough to make these places towns? When did recognisably urban functions and characteristics appear and why did they cluster in these places?

Urban services

The development of service functions lagged some way behind the growth of manufacturing activities. In mid-eighteenth-century Burslem, 'there was nothing like a respectable shop for grocery, or drapery goods, in the Town; but most articles of family use were fetched weekly from Newcastle'.[16] And as late as the 1790s, West Bromwich was still 'an open common where rabbits burrowed in large numbers'.[17] The lack of established external linkages and the internalisation of trading activities within individual manufacturing partnerships meant that Burslem's service sector grew largely on the basis of demand within the town. Despite rapid population growth, the expansion of services was slow before the late eighteenth century, with retailing and professionals overshadowed by neighbouring Newcastle. From this time, though, the pace of growth quickened: by 1809, Burslem had grocers, hairdressers, gardeners, an organist, wine merchants, a printer and bookseller, drapers and druggists, plus surgeons, a postmaster and at least one attorney.[18] It could not match the number, range and quality of services and goods available in Newcastle, but it is clear that even wealthy residents could supply many of their needs in Burslem. A bundle of John Wood's bills and receipts dating from 1797 and 1798 reveals an individual making a range of purchases, many of them in Burslem, for items including picture framing, clothing and wines and spirits.[19] In the early nineteenth century, Burslem increasingly emerged from the shadow of Newcastle. In 1818, there were over 115 retailers in the town, including tea dealers, a publisher, milliners, a fire-insurance agent and a glass dealer. Equally, the range if not the number of professionals increased to include accountants, architects, bankers and music teachers.[20] By 1842 the two towns were far more equal in terms of servicing functions; Newcastle remained the dominant centre for north Staffordshire, and the quality of its shopkeepers was still above that of Burslem. However, most goods and services could, by then, be acquired within the pottery town itself. Burslem had clearly become a substantial market and service centre, able to supply its own population and provide for the needs of its growing suburbs.

Commercial development began even later in West Bromwich. The enclosure of the parish and transport improvements stimulated growth and served to focus activity onto the area on either side of the turnpike road extending about a mile from the edge of the Earl of Dartmouth's Sandwell Park in the east to Carters Green, where the Dudley and Wolverhampton roads bifurcated. The enclosure commissioners laid out a network of new roads in the area, a grid that can still be recognised in the landscape, and it is evident from the award that the land passed to a variety of owners. Commercial and industrial development was quickly stimulated, and in 1836 a local historian recalled the time immediately after the enclosure when building land had sold for up to £1,000 an acre.[21] Growth was centred onto the newly named High Street. In 1834 this had 'many well-stocked shops occupied by drapers, grocers, druggists &c, giving the whole the air and bustle of a market town',[22] and by 1841 more than 120 properties had been built on what had previously been open heathland. They were occupied by a middle-class urban community that was evidently prospering. Retailers included nine grocers, four of whom employed at least three people, and two of them more than six, and ten drapers, six of whom had at least three employees. There were also chemists, bakers, butchers, shoemakers supplied by a leather seller and a currier, tailors, watchmakers and clockmakers, hairdressers, pawnbrokers, a wine merchant and a printer. The professions were represented by three doctors, two solicitors, a surveyor, an auctioneer, an accountant and a veterinary surgeon; and local businessmen enjoyed the services of the Dudley & West Bromwich Bank. Shops continued to proliferate and to grow in size during the following decade. In 1851 five grocers and two drapers each employed at least five people, while one chemist had seventeen staff. Shopkeepers were drawn to West Bromwich from all over England. Of the thirty-four principal grocers, drapers and chemists, only six were born in the parish, and nine in Birmingham and the Black Country, while others originated from places as far afield as Mildenhall, Wisbech, Manchester, Cheltenham, Llanymynech and Appleby. The eight doctors and four solicitors practising in the town in 1851 included men born in Manchester, Hull and Ramsbury, Wiltshire.

It was, of course, the burgeoning population that underpinned this growth in service provision, but the catalyst to development was very different in the two towns. In Burslem, the establishment of a market by the local manufacturing elite in 1761 not only provided a regular supply of food, but also a physical and symbolic focus for an expanding range of shops and professionals. In contrast to this internally initiated growth, service development in West Bromwich was prompted by enclosure and by the improvement of the main thoroughfare as part of Telford's Holyhead Road from 1815.[23] The strong focus provided by this busy thoroughfare concentrated the district's service provision into West Bromwich and limited its development in neighbouring settlements such as Tipton and Oldbury. Burslem fared less well. Growth in its service sector was more than matched by that in Hanley, just over a mile to the south-east. By the 1780s, Hanley was already emerging as the principal service provider in the Potteries, and the subsequent growth of marketing functions in Tunstall, just to the north, further restricted development in Burslem.

Institutions and elites

Population growth encouraged service provision of a different kind with the construction of many places of worship in both Burslem and West Bromwich in the 1820s and 1830s. St John's, the original parish church in Burslem dating from 1556, was enlarged in 1788 and joined in 1831 by St Paul's and ten years later by Christ Church. By then, there were also chapels in the town for Wesleyan, New Connexion and Primitive Methodists, Independents, Baptists and Roman Catholics. As with other aspects of its urban development, growth began later in West Bromwich, but then progressed more rapidly. Christ Church, built on the High Street to supplement the distant parish church, was completed only in 1828, but by the mid-1830s there were Wesleyan, Primitive Methodist, Baptist, Independent and Roman Catholic places of worship in the vicinity of the High Street. Other cultural institutions were slower to develop. In Burslem the difficulty again lay in the proximity of Newcastle and the rivalry between Burslem and the other pottery towns. When developments did take place from the 1820s and 1830s, the emphasis was increasingly on personal improvement and rational recreation. Hence, Burslem acquired a newsroom at the town hall in 1834, a Literary and Scientific Society in 1838, and a growing number of institutes, libraries, museums and galleries from the 1850s onwards. There was a short-lived choral society in about 1824, and a number of dining clubs existed from the early nineteenth century. By the 1850s there was a recognisably urban landscape of public buildings, and many of the potworks were rebuilt or refronted with classical facades. Critical here was the emergence of a strong civic culture, fuelled by rivalries with Newcastle and increasingly with other Potteries towns.[24] The development of cultural facilities in West Bromwich came rather later and was, to some extent, a conscious copying of the municipal gospel preached by the Chamberlains in Birmingham. This stimulated the building of a town hall, school of art, library, public baths and general hospital in the 1870s, all on the Lodge estate, sold in 1867 by the Izon family, the iron founders. Development was further stimulated by the granting of a borough charter in 1882; certainly it was the last two decades of the nineteenth century that saw the full flowering of civic culture in the town, when its most notable citizen was Alderman Reuben Farley, iron founder and investor in a variety of other businesses, five times mayor, and active in the poor law union, the building society, the mechanics' institute, the YMCA, the choral, temperance and horticultural societies and the football club.[25] Farley believed that 'It was a man's duty in his native town ... to do all he could to improve the condition of the people ... to make the lives of the people brighter and happier'. The principal social centre in earlier times was the Dartmouth Hotel, adapted from the older Bull's Head tavern in 1834. In Burslem, much development preceded the granting of official urban status in 1878. Before then a series of quasi-urban authorities (market trustees from 1761, an Improvement Commission from 1825 and a Board of Health after 1850) proved very effective in encouraging the creation of both urban infrastructure and an urban identity.[26]

Crucial in the development of retail, professional and cultural activities was the presence of a resident elite. This is what was missing in so many of the growing coalfield settlements of the industrial revolution. The master potters of eighteenth- and early-nineteenth-century Burslem were often very wealthy, but all lived within the town. In 1751 John and Thomas Wedgwood built a substantial house – the Big House – next to their principal potworks right in the centre of town. Some forty years later, Enoch Wood included a house and grounds for himself within his newly built Fountain Place Works; he lived there until his death in 1840. It was not until the middle decades of the nineteenth century that elite migration out of town was discernible on any scale. Indeed, at this time, many industrial towns were still seen as desirable places to live: Runcorn, for example, was described as the Montpellier of England owing to its 'agreeable situation and the good air of the place'.[27] Similarly, West Bromwich formed an attractive 'west end suburb for the retired and thriven iron and coal masters, carriers and factors of the mining district which surrounds it'.[28] Wood's map of 1837 shows fourteen mansions, mostly owned by industrialists.

The relationship between urban-industrial development and these elites appears to have been different in the two towns. Their presence in West Bromwich reflected the new locational advantages of the town and its links to dynamic urban-industrial systems: the industrial and residential plots made available by enclosure and improved accessibility afforded by the canals and turnpike roads. In Burslem the pottery manufacturers were central to the construction of urban and commercial infrastructure. The majority of the £506

16s 6d raised for building the first town hall was pledged by thirty-four individuals, twenty-three of whom were earthenware manufacturers.[29] In the third quarter of the eighteenth century, John Wedgwood invested £550 in the Leek and Nantwich turnpikes and over £2,000 in the Trent and Mersey and Cauldon canals. A generation later John Wood was similarly engaged in developing local infrastructure, his transactions including a loan of £275 to the trustees of the Lawton Trust Turnpike and the purchase of seven quarter-shares and two half-shares in the Trent and Mersey Canal, costing a total of £8129 4s 3d.[30]

By the mid-nineteenth century the rich were moving away from West Bromwich. The fourth Earl of Dartmouth ceased to live at Sandwell Park in 1853, and made his home at Patshull Hall, which allowed building on the fringes of the park, including the construction of the middle-class dwellings in Beeches Road from the 1860s. Archibald Kenrick (1760–1835), founder of the hardware company, lived at Springfields on Roebuck Lane, but his two sons both had houses in the fashionable Birmingham suburb of Edgbaston. The Izons family sold the Lodge estate in 1867. Reuben Farley was an outstanding leader in industry, local government and the voluntary sector, but most of the leading manufacturers of subsequent generations in West Bromwich tended to live outside the town. The mansions of the mid-nineteenth century, occupied by manufacturers and those living on invested funds, had either been along the western fringe of the parish, where their tranquillity was threatened by the development of collieries, by ironworks and perhaps most of all by large-scale workings for clay, or on plots along the High Street, where rising land values offered a continuing temptation to sell for commercial development. Nevertheless, the presence of wealthy families living in and around the new town had been a significant factor in its development in the first half of the nineteenth century.

Externalities: transport and hinterlands

Canals were, of course, central to the industrial development of many coalfields in England. In West Bromwich, as we have already seen, the Birmingham Canal served to open up the area to Birmingham manufacturers as well as providing improved access to wider markets for local coal and ironware. A similar process occurred in Burslem with the completion of the Trent and Mersey Canal. In broad terms, this cemented the association between north Staffordshire and earthenware manufacture and allowed for the rapid expansion of production. More specifically, it encouraged a growth in the scale of production with the opening of several large works in canal-side locations. Yet it is easy to become too focused on the impact of canals on the development of coalfield settlements as *towns*: roads often played a more important role.[31] They brought in goods, people and information which were vital to the manufacturers of consumer goods, defined hinterlands and provided the spatial focus for service activities. These processes were most evident in West Bromwich, where Telford's Holyhead Road generated a hugely increased volume of traffic through the district and defined the spine of the business district. In 1818 there were six stage-coach services a day to London, six to Shrewsbury, and one each to Holyhead, Liverpool, Chester and Manchester, as well as several departures a day to Birmingham. Services improved remarkably over the next sixteen years. By 1835 there were hourly departures to Birmingham, seven departures a day to Shrewsbury, three to Liverpool, three to Manchester, two to the Potteries, one to Chester and one to Holyhead, as well as shorter runs to Bridgnorth, Brierley Hill, Walsall and Stourport. Contemporary commentators recognised the impact of this on West Bromwich: 'the life that is infused into it by the several coaches passing through continually to all parts of the north and south of the kingdom imparts to it that air and bustle which is recognised in a flourishing, respectable and populous market town'.[32]

A similar, although less dramatic, process can be identified in Burslem. Given its new growth, geographical and competitive position in relation to other Potteries towns, and its historic subordination to Newcastle, Burslem had no 'natural' local hinterland in the eighteenth and early nineteenth centuries. Goods and services (both producer and consumer) were offered essentially to the town's own population together with those of a small number of surrounding villages. The lack of a developed hinterland is evident from the transport services available from Burslem in 1835. The Legs of Man inn was served by one daily coach service to London, one to Birmingham, one to Liverpool and one to Manchester, but long-distance carriers tended to run to and from Hanley, and the Potteries lacked the network of regional coach services that had developed in the Black Country in the pre-railway era.[33] Even this limited provision formed a considerable improvement on earlier years and represented a breaking of Newcastle's stranglehold on transport in the region. The key here was the turnpiking of the roads to Lawton to the north-west, Shelton – and thence the Newcastle–Derby turnpike – in the south, Leek to the east and Congleton to the north, all during the course of the 1760s. The expanding sphere of influence which these transport services both reflected and enhanced can be gauged by their position in the formation of poor law unions in the 1830s. In a petition sent to the Poor Law Commissioners in 1837, Burslem's churchwardens and overseers were keen to assert their independence of the authorities in Newcastle, with which, they argued, the populace of Burslem had little common cause. However, they were equally anxious to exploit the opportunity to expand the influence of their town and their offices by underlining the geographic and economic links held with the neighbouring parish of Wolstanton.[34] West Bromwich too became the centre of a poor law union in the mid-1830s, something that would have been unthinkable a generation earlier. These external links were just as important as the availability of natural resources to the emergence of Burslem and West Bromwich as towns. They defined a relationship with surrounding settlements and helped to generate an urban identity.

Conclusions

The emergence of Burslem and West Bromwich as genuinely new towns owed much to the industrial developments taking place in and around them during the eighteenth and early nineteenth centuries. The economies of both moved decisively from proto-industrial activity to new forms of manufacturing, often prompted by changing cultural contexts including fashion.[35] In Burslem this involved a growth in the scale of production and a shift to tablewares for national and international markets: in essence, an eighteenth-century transformation. Change was later in West Bromwich, but more dramatic, domestic production of nails giving way in the early nineteenth century to the manufacture of consumer goods and components. Yet it was not this manufacturing activity that made Burslem and West Bromwich urban: many coalfield settlements were transformed in industrial terms and yet did not become towns. Rather, it was the agglomeration of service functions and the construction of an urban identity and image that marked out such places. Of course, the development of primary and secondary industries in the locale served to stimulate demand for retailing and professional services. However, their crystallisation in time and space was determined by other factors. In West Bromwich enclosure provided space for retailing and for desirable residences for a middle class of professionals; Telford's road focused this development and created the bustle and activity associated in the contemporary mind with towns. In Burslem urbanisation appears to have been a more conscious process: a local elite of manufacturers promoted civic development through the creation of a market and various instruments of urban government. In this, their own social ambitions were reinforced by strong rivalry with neighbouring centres. This competition helped to create an urban identity in Burslem by 1800, but probably served to limit subsequent development – the Potteries towns were arguably too densely grouped for a dominant centre to emerge. In contrast, the dynamism that developed on the plots created by the enclosure commissioners enabled West Bromwich to outstrip the older urban centre of Wednesbury and to emerge as the principal town in the district by the middle decades of the nineteenth century. In a broader regional context it could not rival Birmingham, but it was by 1840 indisputably a town in the full sense of that term.

New industrial towns are more readily identified in the second half of the nineteenth century than in the classic period of the industrial revolution. Railway engineering works revived the moribund urban economies of Swindon and Ashford, and created wholly new towns at Crewe and Wolverton, while Birkenhead and Middlesbrough are outstanding examples of ports that grew up in the period. The examples of Burslem and West Bromwich show that *ab initio* urban growth was possible between 1700 and 1850, given favourable circumstances. They also show that this was a comparatively unusual phenomenon. Much of the urban growth of the industrial revolution period, even in coalfields that saw the most rapid rates of industrialisation and population increase, came in places that enjoyed legacies from earlier centuries of urban facilities, markets and spaces for markets, concentrations of shopkeepers, the presence of the professions and traditions of cultural vitality. This is true of towns like Wellington in Shropshire, Dudley, Stourbridge, Walsall and Wolverhampton in the Black Country, Chesterfield in Derbyshire and Burnley and Blackburn in Lancashire. Equally, there were settlements in every coalfield – parishes like Tipton, Dawley and Madeley – that experienced rapid growth in industrial activity and in population, but without the development of urban facilities. The development of towns during the industrial revolution, as in other historical periods, depended on fortuitous circumstances and on human creativity. The character of Burslem in the second half of the nineteenth century is perhaps best epitomised in three buildings, its market, its town hall and the extraordinary Wedgwood Institute.[36] That of West Bromwich is best encapsulated not in buildings, but in the fertile career of Alderman Reuben Farley. That career and those buildings provide clear evidence of the urban nature of the communities that had developed by 1850.

Notes

1 Corfield, *English Towns*; Langton, 'Urban growth'.
2 Fuller discussion of this relationship can be found in Stobart, 'In search of causality'; Langton, 'Urban growth'.
3 Porteous, *Canal Ports*; Borsay, 'Health and leisure resorts'.
4 Carter, *Urban Geography*, pp. 45–6.
5 See Hudson and King, 'Industrialising townships'.
6 See Stobart, *First Industrial Region*, pp. 175–218; de Vries, *European Urbanization*, p. 10.
7 *VCH Staffordshire*, vol. 8, pp. 131–2.
8 Weatherill, *Pottery trade*, pp. 76–101; Weatherill, 'Middlemen', pp. 51–76.
9 Angerstein, *Industry in England*, pp. 338–40; Whipt, *Patterns of Labour*, p. 18; Aikin, *Country round Manchester*, pp. 523–35.

10 For details of wares sold in the mid-eighteenth century, see the appendices in Mountford, 'Thomas Wedgwood'.

11 Parsons and Bradshaw, *Staffordshire*.

12 Young, *Tours in England*, pp. 140–2.

13 This new availability of land and transport links undermines their traditional status as (spatial) constants in determining industrial location; see the discussion in Chapter 1.

14 Church, *Kenricks in Hardware*; Jephcott, *House of Izons*.

15 *Pigot's Directory* (1835), pp. 187–92. This forms another link to cultural change.

16 Ward, *Stoke*, p. 235.

17 White, *Staffordshire* (1851), p. 460.

18 Stobart, 'Burslem as a town', pp. 132–3.

19 Hanley reference library, D4842/14/4/7.

20 Parsons and Bradshaw, *Staffordshire*.

21 Reeves, *West Bromwich*, p. 12.

22 White, *Staffordshire* (1834), p. 460.

23 Trinder, 'The Holyhead Road', pp. 52–4.

24 Stobart, 'Building an urban identity'.

25 Trainor, *Black Country Elites*.

26 Stobart, 'Building an urban identity'.

27 Porteous, *Canal Ports*, pp. 77–8.

28 *Staffordshire Advertiser*, 22 December 1849.

29 Ward, *Stoke*, pp. 235–6.

30 Hanley reference library, D4842/13/4/4.

31 See the discussion of the business activities of John and Thomas Wedgwood in Chapter 5.

32 *Pigot's Directory* (1835).

33 *Pigot's Directory* (1835).

34 PRO, MH12/11196, correspondence with poor law unions: Wolstanton and Burslem.

35 See Chapter 13 for more general discussion of this transition.

36 Stratton, *Terracotta Revival*, pp. 63–7.

8

Industrialisation and social change: Wolverhampton transformed, 1700–1840

John Smith

During the eighteenth and early nineteenth centuries Wolverhampton was transformed and greatly expanded by manufacturing based upon various types of metalwork. In the ranking of British towns by population Wolverhampton, which had been 111th in the 1660s, advanced to fourteenth in 1801 and tenth in 1841.[1] Despite this remarkable progress, Wolverhampton was not a new town, but a well-established and flourishing market centre. In medieval times, Wolverhampton had been an entrepôt for the wool trade. There was a continuous history of general trading especially with the rural hinterland to the west in Shropshire and Wales. By the 1830s, Wolverhampton market was said to have a trade which 'was not surpassed in extent by any other town of similar size and population'.[2] However, the principal industry of Wolverhampton was metalwork: well established before the end of the sixteenth century, it had become by the eighteenth century the mainstay of local commerce, generating considerable prosperity from the manufacture and distribution of products including such specialities as buckles, locks and keys.

From the mid-eighteenth century onwards the gathering pace of the industrial revolution changed the face of Wolverhampton. The natural advantage represented by the remarkable ten-yard-thick coal seam, which came close to the town, was exploited to the full. Collieries and ironworks of all sizes proliferated, and converted the area immediately east of Wolverhampton into part of the ravaged landscape which from about 1850 became known colloquially as the Black Country.[3] By the 1860s Wolverhampton was described confidently as 'the capital of the Black Country'.[4] The joint effects of commercial growth and widening markets required improved services of communication and transport: roads were turnpiked, canals were constructed and railways were built. There was growth in financial, legal and service facilities, and, although metalwork remained the dominant theme of local manufacturing, new industries were introduced which were often highly skilled, including japan-ning from the 1720s, enamelling from the 1740s and varnish making from the 1770s. By the middle of the nineteenth century, Wolverhampton was at the forefront of a new urban experience, truly a 'shock city' of the industrial rev-olution. The downside of this manufacturing success, and its associated demographic explosion,[5] was that the eastern districts and some central areas of the town became desperately overcrowded, polluted and very unhealthy. The responsibility for governing the town passed in 1777 from the high con-stable, who acted under the direction of the county magistrates, to commissioners appointed from among the leading citizens under the terms of a local act of Parliament. In Wolverhampton at that time there was a relative absence of local aristocracy or even of especially wealthy gentry, so that the commissioners and other urban elites were left to construct their own culture and tradition. Particularly prominent within the moral background of many of the elites was a powerful strain of nonconformist religiosity which was usually associated with Liberalism.

The aim of this chapter is to establish how the economy, society and envi-ronment of Wolverhampton changed between 1700 and 1840, and to examine the process of government by its commissioners. The intention is to define the priorities of administration in a town characterised by massive industrialisa-tion and increasing environmental polarisation between east and west, and having as a moral influence a remarkably high level of religious observance. The analysis not only brings together a consideration of internal and external influences on urban-industrial development, but also seeks to place economic change within the contemporary cultural and political milieu. It thus argues that the most significant development of the period 1700–1840 was the growth of a self-confident form of civic consciousness and pride which, from the mid-nineteenth century, became the main driving force for municipal improvement.[6] It was the growing strength and the social inter-linked net-works of this elite that helped to make Wolverhampton such a dynamic industrial centre through the eighteenth and early nineteenth centuries.

Industry and economics

From the mid-eighteenth century onwards the massive increase in manufac-turing activity associated with the period of the industrial revolution transformed Wolverhampton from a market town into a centre of production and commerce second only to Birmingham within the Midlands.[7] Indeed, it was written that 'if Birmingham had not existed, Wolverhampton would have been Birmingham'.[8] Moreover the nature of the industrial revolution as it affected Wolverhampton was similar to the corresponding situation in

Birmingham: the introduction of new machinery such as Nasmyth's steam hammer was of great benefit but few large factories were established.[9] In Wolverhampton, as in Birmingham, this was a handcraft- and workshop-based revolution distinguished principally by vastly increased production. The industry was supplied with iron which was smelted using coke at Bilston, three miles to the east of Wolverhampton. The rich Black Country coal seam was conveniently close to large deposits of iron ore.[10] Until the coal seam became exhausted, or at least prohibitively difficult to work, after 1860, it was the foundation of most of the wealth of Wolverhampton.[11]

Metalwork of various kinds had long been a Wolverhampton speciality. The wide range of products included 'every description of iron and brass goods ... and almost every article in which the anvil, the forge and the foundry can be employed to advantage'. Because much of this work could be carried out as a cottage industry, some of those involved were able to operate a dual economy. Thus in the early nineteenth century it was reported that 'most of the farmers in the neighbourhood have their forges where they work when not employed in the field and take their work to market as regularly as other farmers do their corn, where it is readily bought up; many of the women are assistants in these manufactures and work at the file'.[12] However, the general trend away from the dual economy to an industrial economy, 'already perceptible by 1720', was very dominant by 1820, when manufacture in Wolverhampton was 'chiefly that of hardware for which it has long been celebrated'.[13] In 1792, approximately half of those listed in the town rate-book under the category of trades and occupations were involved in activities concerned with metalwork.[14]

Trade associated with iron expanded at a phenomenal rate. As early as 1726, the road between Wolverhampton and Birmingham was described as 'dangerous and almost impassable by reason of the great number of carriages constantly employed in carrying of iron, and iron goods, and coal'.[15] By 1802 there were forty-two blast furnaces in or near Wolverhampton, the number increasing to 129 by 1829. Production of iron continued to increase to a peak in 1858, after which it declined. At maximum capacity in 1871 the Wolverhampton area was capable of producing 20,000 tons of iron weekly, nearly one-third of national production. However, it was in the boom period of the 1820s to 1860s that the town flourished as a manufacturer of all kinds of metalwork, ranging from crude iron bars and sheets to tools and decorative items in iron and brass.[16] The range of hardware products was extensive but became increasingly specialised. In 1800 the product range included small metal goods in iron and brass, japanned iron and tin plate and papier-mâché ware. All these manufactures required relatively high levels of skill, and this was a feature of work in Wolverhampton. Even in the old-established trade of lock making, the town was known for producing the most advanced locks in the Black Country.[17] In fact the work done in Wolverhampton tended increasingly towards higher skill to the exclusion of low-skill work such as nail making, 'the part-time resort of the very poor', which drifted out of Wolverhampton in the early eighteenth century.[18] As manufacturing expanded, becoming more skilled and complex, so an associated business structure developed in the town. In the directories of the 1790s, 53.2 per cent of listed businesses were involved in manufacturing, but an appreciable 28.8 per cent were concerned with 'dealing'. In this connection a major contribution to Wolverhampton's prosperity was derived from its role as entrepôt for the locksmiths and nail makers of the Black Country.[19] The associated increase in business transactions was illustrated by the rising number of attorneys practising in the town: there were two in 1770, ten in 1805 and twenty-three in 1839.

It has been claimed that at the end of the eighteenth century, three-quarters of the trade of Wolverhampton was for export, and this demanded continuous improvement in the systems of local transport.[20] The roads to Birmingham and Stafford were turnpiked, and in 1772 construction of the canal network began when the Staffordshire and Worcestershire Canal was opened, providing a connection with the Trent and Mersey Canal and the river Severn at Stourport. The Birmingham Canal, which was mainly intended to give access to the Black Country coalfields, was opened in 1762 and extended in the 1790s. The last canal to be built, which connected to Chester, was opened as late as 1835.[21] Arguments between competing contractors, which had delayed the construction of canals, also obstructed progress in the building of railways. The Grand Junction Railway, which connected Birmingham with Liverpool and Manchester, opened in 1837, but because of the rising cost of land in the town centre, the original station was a mile and a half out of Wolverhampton. Thereafter, the Shrewsbury and Birmingham Railway and the London and North Western Railway made connections to Wolverhampton which were completed in 1851, but only after organised violence between these opposed companies had necessitated a reading of the Riot Act. Finally in 1854 the Great Western Railway opened its line from Birmingham which linked up to the Shrewsbury line, and so, despite there being two central stations, the railway network for Wolverhampton was effectively complete.

In general the magnitude and diversity of trade, combined with improving transport linkages, provided growing prosperity. However, there were inevitably interludes of depression, which were often related to the reliance upon export. As early as 1736–39 disputes with France and Spain disrupted trade to the West Indies, and poor law payments in Wolverhampton rose by a factor of four.[22] Both the War of American Independence and the Napoleonic Wars had serious effects: after the end of the latter in 1819 poor law payments in Wolverhampton reached record levels. Recovery in the 1820s was followed by recession in the 1830s; brief prosperity and then recession again ensued in the early 1840s, when local banks collapsed and several manufacturers became bankrupt.[23] It has been argued that only in the periods 1834–37 and 1845–55 could there be claimed to have been full employment.[24] These vicissitudes undoubtedly caused much social tension, but nevertheless labour relations in Wolverhampton were not unduly antagonistic. There were sporadic conflicts but relations between employees and masters were less prone to confrontation than in the surrounding districts. It may well be that the custom of manufacture in small workshops, combined with the high level of skill required in much of the work, encouraged a more conciliatory attitude in Wolverhampton.[25] Although Chartism was quite active in the town, its supporters were less inclined to violent protest than those elsewhere in the neighbourhood (for example, Bilston), and they were criticised for their relative inaction by Chartists in Birmingham. Remarkably in 1842 the Wolverhampton Chartists came very close to reaching an historic agreement of common interest with local employers.[26]

Demography and space

From the early eighteenth century to the mid-nineteenth century the rapid and sustained increase in manufacturing caused the population of Wolverhampton to rise correspondingly. The rate of increase peaked during the early years of the nineteenth century; between 1821 and 1851 the population was doubling every twenty years. The rate of increase between 1831 and 1851 was exceptionally high, exceeding the corresponding figures for Birmingham, Glasgow, Leeds and Sheffield. Between 1831 and 1841 the decennial rate of increase (47.1 per cent) exceeded that of Manchester, which never reached 45 per cent at any time during the nineteenth century. Weber commented in 1899 that only London, Portsmouth and Wolverhampton of his 'seventeen great cities' attained a higher rate of growth in 1841–51 than in 1821–31. In the case of Wolverhampton, Weber attributed this accelerating expansion to 'the opening of railways, with the concomitant development of the iron industry'.[27]

This explosive expansion was accompanied by what David Reeder described as 'the self-evident products of the urban process, the massing of physical structures and the social massing of the people'.[28] However, not only were building costs high; Wolverhampton also had severe limitations placed upon the availability of land for building.[29] The population increase between 1750 and 1841 appears to have been accommodated because the number of persons per inhabited house remained constant at 5.2, but the quality of the new housing was very poor indeed. In 1834 it was claimed that half of the houses in the town 'were deliberately built to squalid specifications'.[30] Comparison of the street maps of 1750 and 1850 shows little change in the total area of building despite an increase in population by a factor of seven. Apart from some movement of the relatively prosperous towards the district surrounding St John's Church (opened 1760) to the south-west of the centre, most of the new housing was built by infilling, cramming courts at maximum density into any available gaps. Thus arose notorious slum areas, particularly in relatively low-lying central districts close to the canal.[31] Although high building costs were a relevant factor, the main reason for this housing congestion lay in the details of land ownership. Data accompanying the tithe map of 1842 shows that ten owners held more than 66 per cent of tithable land and were very reluctant either to sell freehold or to grant long leases. Much of the remaining central land was owned by the Church; deeds of ownership had lapsed into obscurity and there was much derelict property.[32]

The congested infilling of the central district and inadequate drainage of the streets and courtyards meant that living conditions deteriorated sharply. A description of the area written in 1843 for the Parliamentary Commission on Children's Employment referred to 'small workshops at the back of houses so that the places where children and great bodies of operatives are employed are completely out of sight in its narrow courts, unpaved yards and blind alleys ... the great majority of yards contain two to four houses, one or two of which were workshops or have room in them for a workshop.' The writer went on to comment that because of this undesirable infilling, 'the circumference of the town remained the same for a long time'.[33] Not surprisingly, disease was rife. In 1840 Dr E. H. Coleman drew attention to the open sewers which were close to overcrowded courts and commented that 'when this town was attacked by the cholera (1832) it was very prevalent in this vicinity ... the only place in which any of the more respectable families were attacked by that disease'.[34] In his report to the Chadwick Commission of 1840, Dr J. Dehane wrote that fever, primarily typhoid, had been 'constantly present' in Wolverhampton for the past twenty years.[35] Dehane considered that, although the position of the town centre on a high sandstone ridge 530 feet above sea level would assist drainage and ventilation, this natural advantage was vitiated by the density of housing and the common disregard of any basic hygiene. Most of the local doctors reporting to Chadwick gave realistic accounts of the problem but tended to regard much of the remedy as lying in the education of the poor into cleaner habits. An honourable exception was the surgeon John Talbot Cartwright, who, in a list of 'causes amongst the poor which operate against a good state of health', included the following perceptive comment: '1st the want of proper food, at all times scarce among the very poorest classes, but more particularly when there is little or no demand for labour'.[36] Thus in 1840 Wolverhampton had growing slum areas and insufficient drainage and sanitation. Moreover, the town water supply was inadequate in both quantity and quality. These problems were major contributors to the high death rate of east Wolverhampton, which from 1841–50 was standing at 32.0 per thousand compared with 21.3 per thousand in west Wolverhampton and a national average of 22.4. The environmental and social polarisation between east and west would affect the fortunes of Wolverhampton for the remainder of the nineteenth century and beyond.[37]

Commissioners and elites

By 1777, when the commissioners were first appointed, Wolverhampton had become a town with widely divergent levels of wealth. From the early eighteenth century the relatively well-off townspeople were supplied by an increasing number of shops selling a wide range of merchandise.[38] Some retailers held inventories exceeding £1,000 in value, and at that time very few manufacturers could emulate the wealth of these early members of the shopocracy. However, the advent of the industrial revolution ensured that through various forms of manufacturing centred upon metalwork, families could move 'in three generations from comparative obscurity to wealth, gentry status and positions of considerable local influence'.[39] These opportunities transformed the structure of society and resulted in what was considered by 1872 to be a town of self-made men.

It was largely from the ranks of the self-made men that the commissioners were appointed. Their authority rested upon the local acts of Parliament of 1777 and 1814 which conferred upon them powers over streets, markets and public buildings and also over the general sanitary provision of the town. They had to be men of some standing, qualified either by ownership of property having a yearly rateable value of £12 or by possessing £1,000 value of real or personal estate.[40] Their meetings were informal and even disorganised; attendances were poor, and the high membership figure of 125 at which the commission was maintained reflected the wish to guarantee a quorum of seven to thirteen, rather than any real numerical requirement.[41] It has been claimed justifiably that there was no suggestion 'that the commissioners represented anyone except themselves'. The most influential commissioners were merchants and manufacturers, and inevitably their commercial interests predominated. In 1838 John Lewis complained to his fellow commissioners that 'when a rate was to be laid or a job to be transacted they had plenty of commissioners but when the poor were to be heard, they had none'.[42]

The effective power of the commissioners was always held within clearly defined limits. Their facility for borrowing to finance civic improvement was never more than £20,000, raised either by annuities or by mortgages on the town rates. Acts of Parliament restricted the rates themselves, and the net effect was that the commissioners were in debt throughout their period of office. Moreover, they had no judicial power to enforce their edicts. One of their first major actions (in 1787) was to clear the congested and insanitary central area around the old market hall, which was itself demolished. It is symptomatic of the financial constraints which applied to the commissioners that a new market hall was not built until 1851 when the elected borough council had taken over. Financial constraints also limited the extent to which the commissioners were involved in the supply of gas: although they arranged for the laying of mains, they could not afford to purchase the gas works. The water supply also remained outside the commissioners' authority because its capital value (£26,000 in 1844) exceeded their buying power. On the question of sanitation, the commissioners had no effect beyond sweeping the streets and disposing of refuse: the provision of sewerage was regarded as the responsibility of private property owners. In 1838 the commissioners threatened that, unless private owners built the necessary sewers, they would take action against them; but there was no power of enforcement available and this was an empty threat. Probably the major achievement of the commissioners was the negotiation with the Earl of Darlington which resulted in the purchase of land enabling the construction of Darlington Street, opened in 1823: this new wide main street by-passed the deteriorating slum of Salop Street and gave a more direct trade route to Shrewsbury and Wales.

In the 1840s the commissioners were beginning to appear out-dated. Their decisions were mainly influenced by the priorities of manufacturing and trade, which were not necessarily those of the general population of Wolverhampton. For example, although the town was expanding rapidly, there were no building regulations. Furthermore the profit from public utilities such as gas and water went to private individuals (who were frequently also commissioners). The commissioners were vulnerable to charges of apathy, inertia and self-interest; they had 'lost the confidence of the inhabitants'.[43] There was a new political atmosphere in the town: 'the spirit of reform was in the air'.[44] The Municipal Reform Act of 1835 had given towns the opportunity to apply to become incorporated and to have elected councils. It was a natural development that agitation for incorporation would be prevalent in Wolverhampton. In 1838 the commissioners suffered a serious setback when their move to impose a church rate was defeated. They attempted to improve and stabilise their situation by trying to compose a new act of Parliament which would have materially increased their powers, but in the event this was never presented. Serious divisions became apparent among the commissioners themselves with increasing numbers backing the campaign for incorporation.

Commissioner Joseph Walker, a nail manufacturer and 'a man of broad and liberal sympathies', told his fellow members that they 'were a self-elected body and as such did not possess the confidence of the ratepayers'.[45]

By the 1840s there was a rising determination among the citizens of Wolverhampton that they should seek incorporation in order to run their own affairs. It was particularly irksome that the policing of the town was responsible to county authorities in Stafford; it was written in 1847, 'we may blush to own that we are subjugated to a rural police'.[46] Any reservations which ratepayers might have had about the expense of incorporation were countered by quoting the example of Manchester, which, having bought the gas company, made an annual profit of £30,000 which was spent on improvement in the city.[47] Many commissioners and other local elites supported the views of the attorney Mr T. Bolton, who 'contended that no one could say that in a population of over 36,000 they did not possess among them men with qualifications sufficient to manage their local affairs ... the town of Wolverhampton possessing the three necessary qualifications of wealth, intelligence and population'.[48] The petition for incorporation was presented to the Queen in 1847, and after an official enquiry had been held in Wolverhampton, all opposition was withdrawn and incorporation proceeded. The first borough council was elected in May 1848 with many former commissioners among its first members.[49] This new governing body would be obliged to balance the necessity of civic improvement against the associated costs, which would fall upon the ratepayers.

Social networks

In the mid-eighteenth century the educated and wealthy people of Wolverhampton had an active and enlightened associational culture. There was a flourishing debating society which allowed women 'of rank and distinction' to become members.[50] However, as the eighteenth century progressed and 'self-made' men gained increased influence, there appears to have been a decline in meetings for cultural association, a trend not reversed until the 1860s, when new cultural and recreational societies were founded enthusiastically. In so far as there was a continuous thread of association between the mid-eighteenth and nineteenth centuries, it was provided by religious affiliation, which was particularly evident in Wolverhampton. The town became a stronghold of dissent and there were sporadic outbreaks of sectarian conflict. John Wesley visited Wolverhampton frequently from 1760 onwards and encountered mob violence; he wrote of 'this furious town'.[51] By 1800 a wide range of nonconformist denominations – including Congregationalists, Irvingites, Methodists, Quakers, Trinitarians and Unitarians – had established chapels or meeting houses, often receiving support from local manufacturers. By 1830, however, the Church of England still had only two central churches even though the population of the town was approaching 30,000.[52]

In the 1851 religious census, Wolverhampton registered a notably high attendance for an industrial town. However, breaking down the constituent figures showed that this attendance was principally contributed by nonconformists at 57 per cent of the total, compared with 36 per cent for the Church of England and 7 per cent for Roman Catholicism.[53] The Church of England was closely associated with the Conservative cause, and nonconformity with the Liberals. In a town where the new borough council of 1848 decided to eschew any association with party politics, religious affiliation often provided the only indication of political sympathy among council members, who all stood nominally as independents. After incorporation in 1848 local government was increasingly influenced by religious morality. Nonconformists were particularly active in promoting campaigns for the welfare of the people, especially by establishing facilities for education and leisure. Congregationalists, who were the dominant nonconformist group, became very influential in borough politics: indeed they were later instructed by their ministers that they should actively seek such involvement as a religious duty. However, they attracted much criticism for their strict and puritanical attitudes, displayed in such actions as their campaign for temperance in the 'notoriously drunken town' and their ill-judged attempt in 1876 to abolish the traditional Town Fair.[54]

Conclusions

Despite the various conflicts and oppositions which were inevitable in the 'shock city' between 1700 and 1840, it is possible to identify a constructive and unifying attitude which became clearly apparent from the early nineteenth century onwards: this was a rising self-confidence which manifested itself as civic pride. The economic success of Wolverhampton and its explosive expansion to a high position in national ranking by population conferred a strong sense of achievement. Although intensive industrialisation had polarised the town into ravaged east and pleasant west, there had not been excessive social disorder.[55] In the county of Staffordshire, although Stafford was the administrative centre and Lichfield was probably regarded as the social and intellectual centre, Wolverhampton was undoubtedly the most important town, and regarded itself as such. Within this, the role of the town's elite – especially its set of commissioners – was central. In common with those of other Midlands towns (see Chapters 10 and 11), they did much to create a dynamic civic pride. As the nineteenth century progressed, the powerful Liberal nonconformist faction in particular initiated steady improvement. The self-made men who had undertaken the responsibility of governing Wolverhampton either as commissioners or later as councillors could derive much satisfaction from what they had achieved. They had constructed their own civic culture without any significant involvement from external influences – either of aristocracy or local gentry, both of whom were largely absent from the district. The new civic pride was readily justifiable. When the institutions and health of the town came under external criticism from the mid-nineteenth century onwards, what started as a defensive reaction evolved by the late 1860s into a genuine desire and indeed a feeling of obligation for civic improvement. This reforming zeal, confirmed and legitimated by the royal visit of Queen Victoria in 1866, led to a sustained programme of improvement for what was often referred to with pride and affection as 'the good old town'.[56]

Notes

1   See Langton, 'Town growth', pp. 14–18.
2   Hardcastle, *Old Wolverhampton*; Mander and Tildesley, *Wolverhampton*, p. 35.
3   Among the first writers to use the expression 'Black Country' were White, *Round the Wrekin*, and Burritt, *Black Country*. The Black Country is defined conveniently and concisely as 'a rectangular area bounded on the north by Wolverhampton and Walsall and on the south by Stourbridge and Smethwick': Barnsby, *Working Class Movement*, p. 1.
4   *The Standard* quoted in *Royal Visit* (Wolverhampton, 1867).
5   Sustained expansion of manufacturing activity ensured that the town attracted high levels of inward migration. Between 1801 and 1851 the population rose by a factor of four from 12,565 to 49,985.
6   For an extended version of this argument, see Smith, 'The governance of Wolverhampton'.
7   For general accounts of the development of Wolverhampton see Mander and Tildesley, *Wolverhampton*, Mason, *Wolverhampton* and Upton, *Wolverhampton*.
8   *Illustrated London News*, 8 December 1866.
9   See Berg, *Age of Manufactures* and Hopkins, *Manufacturing Town*.
10 Burritt, *Black Country*, wrote that 'the iron ore, coal and lime ... were all deposited close at hand ... in almost the very proportion for the furnace', p. 3.
11 This resource was acknowledged when an arch of coal was built to greet Queen Victoria on the royal visit of 1866. The event is described in *Illustrated London News*, 8 December 1866 and in *Royal Visit*.
12 West, *Picturesque Views*, p. 16.
13 Rowlands, *Masters and Men*, p. 43; West, *Picturesque Views*, p. 16.
14 Roper, *Trades and Occupations*.
15 Hopkins, *Manufacturing Town*, pp. 12–13.
16 For a classified list of these metalwares, see Jones, *Borough Politics*, p. 20.
17 As early as 1686, Wolverhampton was noted for 'the greatest excellency of the locksmith's profession ... preferred above all others': Rowlands, *Masters and Men*, p. 28. The more basic locks were made in surrounding villages, such as Bilston, Sedgley, Wednesfield and Willenhall.

18 Rowlands, *Masters and Men*, pp. 129–30.
19 Clark, 'Introduction', p. 28; Trinder, 'Industrialising towns', p. 819.
20 Upton, *Wolverhampton*, p. 53.
21 Upton, *Wolverhampton*, pp. 63–6.
22 Rowlands, *Masters and Men*, p. 121.
23 Mason, *Wolverhampton*, p. 48; Smith, 'Wolverhampton Old Bank'.
24 Barnsby, 'Standard of living', pp. 220–39.
25 These possibilities are discussed in Smith, *Conflict and Compromise*.
26 Barnsby, *Working Class Movement*, p. 95.
27 Weber, *Growth of Cities*, pp. 40–57.
28 Reeder, 'H. J. Dyos', p. xv.
29 Wolverhampton was not unusual in this respect. National difficulties with land availability, rising costs of building, the prevalence of small builders and the unsatisfactory quality of much of the resultant housing are described in Rodger, *Housing in Urban Britain*, pp. 13–27.
30 Barnsby, *Housing in Wolverhampton*, p. 8; Huffer, 'Growth of Wolverhampton', p. 10.
31 The high density of infilling is apparent on the tithe map of 1842 and is illustrated by the data in Roper, *Trades and Occupations*. The worst slum, Caribee Island, was not cleared until 1877.
32 Huffer, 'Growth of Wolverhampton', p. 13.
33 See Horne, Report to the Children's Employment Commission, 1843, for this and much more informative comment on working and social conditions in this 'extremely rich' town. BPP, Children's Employment, 2, 1843, pp. 1–38.
34 Dr E. H. Coleman, letter to the Poor Law Commissioners, 25 January 1840, BPP, Chadwick Report Health General 3, 1840, p. 222.
35 Dr J. Dehane, letter to the Poor Law Commissioners, 20 January 1840, BPP, Chadwick Report Health General 3, 1840, p. 218.
36 J. T. Cartwright, letter to the Poor Law Commissioners, 25 January 1840, BPP, Chadwick Report Health General 3, 1840, p. 222.
37 Barnsby, *Housing in Wolverhampton*, p. 18; Jones, *Borough Politics*, p. 33.
38 Collins, 'Primitive or not', p. 28, commented that in the eighteenth century 'the numbers of apothecaries, bakers, booksellers, butchers, chandlers, hatters and shoemakers point to an impressive shopping centre'.
39 Rowlands, *Masters and Men*, pp. 119, 49.
40 The total of 125 commissioners included 20 tradesmen, 16 manufacturers, 8 clergymen, 6 doctors, 4 attorneys and 3 publicans: Smith, 'Town commissioners'.
41 Mander, *Wolverhampton Antiquary*, vol. 1(1), September 1915, p. 19.
42 Mason, *Town Commissioners*, p. 1 and preface.
43 Jones, *Municipal Life*, p. 20.
44 Mander, *Wolverhampton Antiquary*, vol. 2(1), July 1934, p. 25.
45 *Wolverhampton Chronicle*, 10 February 1841, quoted in Mason, *Town Commissioners*, p. 66.
46 *How Shall the Town be Governed?*, pp. 3–12.
47 *How Shall the Town be Governed?*, p. 9.
48 Jones, *Municipal Life*, p. 22.
49 The deed of transfer, which conveyed all powers from the commission to the new elected council, was signed on 14 November 1848 by eleven commissioners,

of whom nine were members of the new council. See Mason, *Town Commissioners*, p. 71.

50　Clark, *British Clubs and Societies*, pp. 120–99.

51　Mander and Tildesley, *Wolverhampton*, p. 131. The Methodists were the largest single group of nonconformists.

52　In West, *Picturesque Views*, p. 17, it was noted that 'in a place of such extent, it was rather remarkable that there were only two Protestant churches'.

53　The Roman Catholic component was largely represented by the Irish immigrant community, which amounted to 12 per cent of the population in 1851.

54　This is how Mander described the town in the Wolverhampton Directory of 1770, reprinted as a supplement to Mander, *Wolverhampton Antiquary*, vol. 2 (1934); Jones, *Municipal Life*, pp. 203–7.

55　The combination of progress and stability continued after incorporation in 1848. See Trainor, *Black Country Elites*, p. 374.

56　'The good old town' was a frequent usage. See, for example, Jones, *Municipal Life*, p. 151.

9

Industrial and urban growth in Nottingham, 1680–1840

Joyce Ellis

The pattern of urban development in the east Midlands during the long eighteenth century ran counter to many significant national trends.[1] In particular, the increasing prosperity and continuing economic dominance of the county towns of Derby, Leicester and Nottingham appears to have had no parallel elsewhere in industrialising Britain. Although the urban system as a whole exhibited considerable continuity in the century and a half after 1680, there were major changes in the rankings of individual towns, changes which gathered pace in the late eighteenth century and undermined the relative prosperity of many county towns. The gradual provision of better transport and communications had initially given these established centres an advantage over smaller towns within their hinterlands by making them more accessible. As the pace and scale of improvement increased, however, they began to suffer from increasing competition as the roads, rivers and canals opened up the countryside, accelerating existing trends towards concentrating activity in bigger, well-positioned and increasingly specialised towns.[2] Their significance as social and cultural centres for the neighbouring gentry was eclipsed by the growing accessibility of London and the rise of fashionable leisure resorts. Meanwhile, their traditional role as the focus of their economic hinterlands was undermined by the rise of 'new' manufacturing towns and regional centres that successfully tapped into the rapid growth of industrial production. Traditional county towns therefore tended to dwindle into stuffy and increasingly faded gentility, overtaken by the 'mushroom' towns growing around them. Although very few actually declined in size, their rate of population growth began to fall markedly from 1750, so that they experienced the sort of relative 'failure' that had already afflicted York in the mid-seventeenth century. The county towns of the east Midlands, in marked contrast to those of the west Midlands, not only grew substantially in this period but also rose significantly up the urban hierarchy. Far from dwindling into insignificance, Derby, Leicester and Nottingham enjoyed a virtually unchallenged regional

pre-eminence, as both industrial and demographic growth continued to con-
verge in these traditional centres.[3] In this chapter, I explore some of the
economic, social and cultural issues raised by their exceptional experience by
examining the complex relationship between urban and industrial change in
the industrial region centred on Nottingham.

Nottingham: county capital and industrial town

In the late seventeenth century, Nottingham appeared to fit the conventional
pattern of county centres, deriving both its status and its livelihood from the
support of the county and combining a wide range of administrative, social
and cultural functions with interests in both manufacturing and trade. The
1674 hearth tax returns identify a substantial nucleus of resident gentry, in
addition to a prosperous 'middling sort' made up of wealthy merchants, craftsmen and tradesmen. A contemporary visitor confirmed that 'many people of
good quality from several parts, make choice of habitations here where they
find good accommodation, which must be no small advantage to the place ...
and great Traders besides these, concerned and owners in the town'.[4] A period
of sustained growth and prosperity ensured that Nottingham shared in the
cultural and material benefits of the urban renaissance of the late seventeenth
and early eighteenth centuries, developing a glittering social calendar patron-
ised by leading county families as well as by 'the genteel Part of the Town of
both Sexes', and investing heavily in the urban environment. Contemporaries
accepted that the town had achieved a rare combination of elegance and enterprise, building a reputation as 'the loveliest and the neatest ... of all the towns
I have seen outside London', while deriving substantial profits from industry
and its role as a major wholesaling and distributive centre for goods coming
upstream on the Trent.[5] As the period progressed, however, intensive industrial development began to destabilise this delicate balance between social and
economic functions. Surveying the 'numerous and noble Company' attending
the annual race meeting in August 1779, a report in the *Nottingham Journal*
proclaimed that 'it may truly be said Nottingham is now in the Zenith of her
Splendour'. Given that, a few weeks previously, the Forest race ground had
been chosen as the site of a mass protest meeting by discontented framework-
knitters, a meeting that failed to avert an outbreak of destructive popular
protest, the summer of 1779 may indeed have marked a symbolic turning point
in the town's evolution.[6] Rapid population growth combined with speculative
building within the congested city centre to produce an urban environment
that became notorious for its 'unparalleled overcrowding and squalor'.[7]

The key to Nottingham's transformation from county capital to industrial
town was increasing consumer demand for knitted fabrics. According to

Charles Deering, the town's first historian, there had been only two frame-work-knitters in Nottingham in 1641, whereas fifty years later Celia Fiennes was in no doubt that 'the manufacture of the town mostly consists in weaving of stockings, which is a very ingenious art'. A significant upturn in demand seems to have occurred in the 1730s with the introduction of cotton hose: between 1727 and the early 1740s, the number of frames at work in the town had risen from 400 to around 1,200, and the industry had clearly developed a mature organisation. A list of trades and manufactures drawn up in 1739 included fifty framework-knitters, fourteen framesmiths, twelve stocking-needle makers, eight setters-up of frames and a number of sinker makers, stocking trimmers and bleachers of cotton hose, to which must be added the hundreds of female seamers, sizers and winders who were employed in the finishing process. By the early 1740s there were, according to Deering, well over fifty 'Manufacturers, Employers of Frames, or as they are commonly cal-l'd Putters out' operating in the town, employing directly or indirectly a very high proportion of its working population; by 1754 a third of Nottingham's burgesses were hosiers.[8] Some of these were wealthy men, among them John Clee, who died in 1735 leaving an inventory valued at £147, which included forty-one pictures, five mirrors and a watch.[9] By the 1770s, the number of firms based in the town had nearly doubled, doubling again to around 200 by the end of the century.

Although eighteenth-century Nottingham seems to have had a relatively small professional sector, its merchants and bankers played a particularly important role in encouraging technical innovation in the industry, bringing both James Hargreaves and Richard Arkwright to town in 1768 in the hope that their experimental spinning machinery would raise the quality and reduce the price of cotton yarn.[10] Their arrival merely augmented the existing ferment of inventiveness among Nottingham knitters, as they strove first to improve the existing technology of stocking making and then to extend it to the pro-duction of machine-made lace. 'An enterprising spirit', it was observed in 1790, 'pervades every branch of the stocking manufactory, and industry is a mark-ing feature in the place'.[11] It seems clear, therefore, that the social and institutional environment of Nottingham played a crucial role in shaping the timing and extent of its industrial development. Surprisingly, Nottingham entrepreneurs failed to win many of the prizes offered by the Society of Arts for improvements on the basic stocking frame, while some of the key patents which revolutionised the hosiery industry were also taken out by entrepre-neurs outside the town. Jedediah Strutt, for instance, whose 1758 'Derby rib' attachment allowed ribbed stockings to made mechanically rather than by hand, moved to Derby from his farmhouse in Blackwell. John Heathcote, the first frame maker to succeed in mechanising the hand lace-making process, added insult to injury by moving his business *out* of Nottingham on the eve of his breakthrough, and then patenting his bobbin-net machine in 1809 under the name of 'Old Loughborough'. Only John Leavers's invention of the bobbin and carriage machine in 1813, a development of Heathcote's original concept, was unequivocally associated with Nottingham.

However, the complaints by Nottingham manufacturers that Heathcote owed his breakthrough to 'the Ingenuity, Talents, and Industry of others, (principally, if not wholly, People of the Town of *Nottingham*)' were undoubtedly very close to the truth.[12] The quality of the urban workforce was extremely high: employers based elsewhere in the region constantly bemoaned the drain of talent and energy towards the centre, where skilful workers could command high earnings.[13] These workers had a clear incentive to experiment and innovate, while the relative simplicity and low cost of the machinery employed in the hosiery industry meant that innovation was not dependent on access to large lumps of fixed capital. Discussion, comparison and experiment seem to have been rife in clubs, alehouses and workshops throughout the town; in fact one local inventor allegedly derived his inspiration from watching a child playing with a yo-yo in Sneinton Street.[14] Against this background of widely diffused mechanical ingenuity, minor technical advances could gradually accumulate until they inspired a significant leap forward, such as the invention of the eyelet-hole machine in 1764 and of the point-net frame in the later 1770s. The result was an ever-expanding range of patterns, styles and products, responding to but also stimulating changes in consumer demand. As this indicates, although elite groups within Nottingham's business community played a key role in stimulating industrial change, the diffusion of social capital among a pool of skilled labour was also instrumental in creating favourable conditions for innovation and growth.

The termination of Arkwright's patent in 1784 sparked off a boom in Nottingham's cotton-spinning industry, which reduced the price of cotton and worsted yarns and accelerated the expansion of framework-knitting within the region. By 1812, when there were 2,600 stocking frames operating in Nottingham, no fewer than forty distinct fabrics were being produced.[15] The slump in hosiery manufacture which was already starting to affect the local economy in 1812, as supply began to outrun demand, was mitigated by the growth of lace making. Most of the eighty-two small manufacturers known to be operating bobbin-net machines in 1819 were based in Nottingham, while the expiry of Heathcote's patent in 1823 stimulated a trade boom that became known as the 'twist-net fever'. By September 1829 there were 1,200 bobbin machines at work in Nottingham, stimulating a wave of in-migration that burst the town's medieval boundaries and prompted the development of new 'colony villages' just beyond the open fields.[16] The end of the twist-net boom in the 1830s, and particularly the chronic trade depression of 1837–42, temporarily reversed these trends, causing houses, shops and tenements to be abandoned in both the town centre and the new industrial suburbs that surrounded it.[17] It was not until the 1850s that prosperity returned to the lace industry and hence to the town as a whole, confirming the conditional nature of the relationship between urban and industrial change.

Nottingham's industrial region

Throughout the long eighteenth century, it is clear that a significant part of Nottingham's industrial and commercial strength derived from providing technical, financial and marketing services to the industrialising villages and small towns in its neighbourhood: settlements tied into the hosiery trade through a network of town-based warehouses and dealers. Deering, for example, noted that 60 per cent of the stocking frames directly employed by Nottingham manufacturers were located 'in the Villages about, who buy their Provisions and other Necessaries in this Town'.[18] It seems relatively straightforward, therefore, to see Nottingham as the focus of a recognisable industrial region, one in which innovation and success gravitated towards the core area before diffusing to the periphery through the multi-dimensional chains of contacts and relationships that bound the region together. By the same token, misery and depression tended to strike first at the fringes of this network, as falling demand reinforced the differentials between the low-cost, low-quality goods associated with village stockingers and the skilled work of their town-based competitors.

Going beyond these generalisations to hard, quantifiable evidence of the personal and business networks that identified and cemented this regional urban system is extremely difficult. Contemporary commentators found these relationships problematic, expending a great deal of time and thought in distinguishing between the interlocking hinterlands of the three county capitals. The trinity of Derby, Leicester and Nottingham – each of them deriving significant benefit from the same industry, yet each with its own industrial strengths and distinct socio-political character – prompted writers to emphasise the differences that contributed to an effective division of labour within an industrial region characterised by William Hutton as 'the stocking country'.[19] In the 1720s, Defoe had been content to report that Nottingham's branch of the hosiery industry was 'the same as at Leicester'.[20] Two decades later, however, local patriotism inspired Deering not only to highlight the growing specialisation in manufacturing silk hose in and around Derby, worsted around Leicester and cotton around Nottingham, but also to proclaim Nottingham's regional pre-eminence. Although he was ready to accept that 'of all these, none comes in Competition with Leicester for Quantity of Goods', he insisted 'but even this very Town ... must confess, that its best Goods are made at *Nottingham*, where by far the greatest part of the richest and most valuable Commodity, whether of Silk, Cotton, Thread or Worsted, is wrought'.[21] Although Deering was hardly a disinterested observer, Nottingham's relative economic success after about 1730 is reflected in the more objective and sophisticated scoring system devised by Sir Richard Phillips, the radical journalist. In the early years of the nineteenth century, he graded Nottingham's industrial performance at 8, compared with Leicester's mark of 6 and Derby's 5.[22]

It is possible to suggest the broad limits of Nottingham's industrial region by looking for evidence of an active hosiery industry working for the many manufacturers and wholesalers operating in the town, particularly before the widespread diffusion of cotton-spinning mills in the last two decades of the eighteenth century. This crude test reveals a pattern of activity that broadly corresponds with Nottingham's primary catchment area in terms of migration and with the carrier network (see Chapter 5), confirming that Hutton's 'stocking country' stretched no further north than Mansfield. Certainly Cathy Smith found no evidence of domestic hosiery production in Ollerton and only a token presence in Worksop, while one of the reasons for the failure of Cartwright's innovative 'Revolution' cotton mill in East Retford was that textiles had no strong roots in the town or its hinterland. Although the eastern part of the county was an important source of farm produce for Nottingham's markets from the early years of the eighteenth century, Newark's direct involvement in textiles came relatively late.[23] Basically, the stocking frame never dominated the local economy of northern and eastern Nottinghamshire. Instead, Nottingham's industrial region crossed the county boundaries and took in large stretches of south-east Derbyshire and north-west Leicestershire. The framework-knitters of Kegworth, for instance, seem to have been employed by firms based in Nottingham, rather than working to hosiers in Loughborough or Leicester.[24]

Refining this broad definition, however, requires an important caveat: that it is necessary to demonstrate that the hosiery industry in these supposedly 'satellite' communities was actually orbiting around Nottingham rather than one of the other urban centres involved in the industry. Indeed there are signs that, in the early years of the period, Nottingham itself was still partly within the gravitational field of Leicester; Deering certainly distinguished between manufacturers who had direct contact with merchant houses in London and 'those who only deal with *Leicester*'.[25] As cotton mills began to spring up in dispersed locations throughout the region, hosiers could easily step in and establish direct links with the pool of hosiery workers which grew up around the mills, as the firm of Ward, Brettle & Ward did at Belper in 1795. The mills' own labour forces were predominantly made up of women and children: Richard Arkwright's mills, for instance, employed only 150 adult men out of a total workforce of 1,150, while 48 per cent of the workers at Strutt's mills in Belper and Milford were children. Mill-owners desperate to recruit suitable workers stressed that they were looking for 'families' to settle locally and were often willing to offer them favourable terms of employment and attractive fringe benefits, since the alternative was the unwelcome prospect of housing, feeding and training hundreds of parish apprentices. Indeed, much of the housing erected by mill-owners for their workers was advertised as 'particularly adapted to stocking-makers', on the assumption that many male heads of household would occupy themselves as framework-knitters while their wives and children worked in the mill. Given this, it is not surprising that in the early years of the nineteenth century the largest concentrations of stocking frames in the east Midlands, outside Leicester and Nottingham, coincided with the large spinning mills.[26]

By the 1780s and 1790s, the hold of Nottingham over hosiery production within its region seems to have weakened; in effect, the urban system of the east Midlands was being reshaped by the dynamic processes of industrialisation. There were obvious practical difficulties in establishing and sustaining direct connections with workers scattered over an extended hinterland. We know, for example, that several Nottingham hosiers were interested in establishing connections with framework-knitters in the Alfreton area in 1757. The hosiers were desperate to take on extra hands to supply an 'exceeding brisk' market for cotton hose, while there was apparently a 'prodigious increase of stocking makers thereabouts'. However, these stocking makers clearly preferred dealing with their ultimate employers in Nottingham through a local agent, so that they could 'receive their money & so lay it out at the Market [in Alfreton] without more loss of time', while the hosiers were deterred by 'the great [expense] a week for Carrying goods and Letters', as well as by the difficulty of recruiting a reliable intermediary.[27] Knitters from market towns and industrial villages whose connection with Nottingham was mediated through locally based 'bag hosiers' do not fit the conventional model of the relationship between a textile town and its hinterland. This model is represented by William Felkin, who lived and worked in the village of Bramcote but travelled the five miles into Nottingham every second Saturday to collect his yarn and his earnings from Heard's and Hurst's warehouse in Hockley, have dinner with old friends from around the region who were in town on similar errands, and then pick up household supplies in the market on his way home.

The example of Felkin, however, supports rather than undermines the idea that Nottingham was only one part of a wider and polycentric industrial region. Felkin may have walked into Nottingham once a fortnight, but every single Sunday he turned in the other direction and walked across the county border to attend a Baptist chapel in Ilkeston.[28] This town, meanwhile, which lay ten miles from Derby and eight miles from Nottingham, was by 1831 sending its paupers to a house of industry in the Nottinghamshire 'village' of Basford.[29] It is abundantly clear that the clustering of urban centres in this particular part of the east Midlands encouraged a high degree of interchange and association between them, as their respective 'neighbourhoods' interlocked with one another. In terms of social and cultural interchanges among the wealthiest sections of regional society, this was reflected in the need to schedule the meetings of winter assemblies so as to avoid 'interfering with Others in the Neighbourhood'. In 1781, for instance, the promoter of Mansfield's assembly complained that the current programme made it 'impossible [for subscribers] without Fatigue to visit any but those of their own Town, and sometimes a Change would be very agreeable'. The rescheduling at Mansfield that he proposed, however, inevitably produced a knock-on effect on the timing of meetings at Southwell and several other neighbouring towns.[30] The complexities of the social calendar of polite society in Nottinghamshire thus provide further evidence of growing interdependence within the regional urban system, as the aristocracy and landed gentry met and mingled with the leaders of the professional and business communities in the genteel arena provided by urban social activities and institutions.

As Stanley Chapman demonstrated when studying the careers of the early factory masters, the entrepreneurs responsible for many of the successful developments in the east Midlands textile industry formed a closely integrated group, bound together by complex ties that combined business interests with family, social and religious affiliations and that seem to have taken relatively little account of narrowly defined civic loyalties. Following the movements of individual entrepreneurs around the region reinforces the impression that discussing Nottingham's industrial region in simplistic terms of a central core, surrounded by subordinate peripheral settlements, is profoundly misleading. John Heathcote, for instance, was born in Duffield in Derbyshire in 1783, was subsequently apprenticed as a stocking maker and framesmith in Hathern and Long Whatton in Leicestershire, and then moved to Nottingham to work as a skilled journeyman. This is the pattern of migration, gravitating towards the largest urban centre in the region, which might be expected from a young man with talent and ambition, and it is equally predictable that he succeeded in buying out his employer at the age of twenty-one. What spoils this paradigm of geographical and social mobility is that Heathcote then moved his business out of Nottingham, first to Hathern and then to Loughborough. The sources of finance upon which he drew were also interestingly varied, even if we discount the suggestion that one of his initial backers was a former Derby solicitor who was then living in Warwick. Nottingham sources certainly provided a substantial share of the development costs of his bobbin-lace machine, but he also raised money from a Kegworth attorney and from hosiery firms in Loughborough and Leicester. His partners in the firm that patented the 'Old Loughborough' lace-making machine included Charles Lacy of Nottingham and John Boden, a sales director in London, who was also a partner in the Leicester firm of Boden, Oliver & Cartwright, besides having a considerable stake in a lace factory in Derby.[31]

Urban development in the industrial region

This dispersal of capital and enterprise, together with the close integration of business and social ties among hosiers and knitters throughout the broad industrial region, seems to have contributed to a noticeably dispersed pattern of settlement. The east Midlands is often said to be exceptional in that its industrial dynamism in the eighteenth century was not accompanied by a marked degree of urbanisation. Although the population of established urban centres such as Nottingham, Leicester and Derby certainly grew appreciably in the eighteenth century, framework-knitting was an industry that fostered a 'thickening of the countryside', rather than the mushroom growth of urban populations. The regional space economy of the 'stocking country' was closely integrated with the processes of industrialisation. Moreover, the figures presented in Table 9.1 clearly demonstrate the enormous potential of new technology (in this case cotton mills and bobbin-net machines) in transforming the size and character of many existing settlements. Belper started with one mill in 1778 and added another in 1786; even before the West Mill was constructed in 1793–95, it was reported that 'every year, almost every month, new houses are rising up'. Messrs Strutts were probably the direct employers of at least a third of the population recorded in the 1801 census, while most of the remainder were indirectly dependent on the business generated by the mills and their workforce. In 1831, this one firm owned 1,482 houses in Belper – about 20 per cent of the total housing stock.[32] The annual growth rates recorded in Table 9.1 grossly under-estimate the sudden upward surge that took place at the turn of the nineteenth century. Villages on the outskirts of Nottingham grew just as fast and suddenly, but from an even lower base. Radford – described in 1790 as 'a little paradise' – grew so quickly after the opening of Radford mill in 1794 that an observer in 1815 reckoned that 'few villages in England have had so rapid an increase of population'. Basford's growth started a decade or so earlier but accelerated after the opening of Hall's and White's cotton mill in 1787; by 1790 Throsby considered that 'this village appears like a new town, in consequence of its manufactory and improvements'.[33]

The extent to which these settlements were 'urban' is one of the key questions in examining industrialisation and urbanisation in the east Midlands. The dominant position of the mill and mill-owners in such communities would seem to undermine their claims to urban status, given that variety and diversity, particularly in supply and service occupations, are conventionally regarded as critical in assessing such issues.[34] The close involvement of the Strutts in every aspect of life in Belper and Milford is well documented, including their provision of a 'dancing-room in their mill, where festoons of flowers are suspended, and a band of music is heard on holydays, as a substitute for the public-house to their female youth'.[35] Even in Arnold, however, which was only a few miles outside Nottingham and was served by three daily carrier services on every day of the week except Sunday, the mill-owners not only fed and housed 600 parish apprentices, but also ran their own farm to supply their workers, maintained their own grocer's and mercer's shops, employed their own miller and baker and issued their own token coinage.[36] On the other hand, a sharp dichotomy between town and village does not seem appropriate when looking at the 'colonies' of housing that grew so rapidly on the outskirts of Nottingham from the 1790s. New settlements in the parishes of Radford, Basford, Sneinton, Lenton and Bulwell may have been physically separated from main built-up area of the town, but their character and aspirations seem to have been overwhelmingly suburban. It is notable, for instance, that a contemporary directory referred to New Radford, a mile out of town, as 'Islington', while New Basford was apparently also known as 'Pentonville'.[37]

In these cases, the language used by contemporaries in characterising these settlements appears highly significant, an observation which also applies to small towns within Nottingham's orbit. Writers in the late eighteenth and early nineteenth centuries were concerned to demonstrate the essential 'urbanity' of these communities not simply in terms of crude population growth. Like modern historians, they were aware that a concentration of industrial labour was not enough to make a town, unless it was accompanied by the development of a wide spectrum of urban functions. It is significant, therefore, that Throsby referred to Basford's *improvements*, as well as to its manufactures, when discussing whether it qualified as a 'new town'. Contemporary praise of Belper, and even of Ilkeston, also hooked into this rhetoric of urban improvement, by which success was measured in terms of the active, commercial virtues extolled by William Hutton. So pre-industrial Belper, which had been a small market town before the Strutts began to pour investment into the area, was portrayed as 'a mere hamlet' or 'inconsiderable

Table 9.1. *Populations of the fastest-growing towns
in Nottinghamshire, 1660s–1841*

Town	1660s hearth tax	Rank	1801	Rank	1841	Rank	% growth rate per annum	
							1660s–1801	1801–41
Nottingham	4,264	1	28,801	1	52,360	1	1.4	1.5
Leicester	3,014	2	17,005	2	50,806	2	1.3	2.8
Derby	2,140	4	10,832	3	32,741	3	1.2	2.8
Radford (parish)	–	–	2,269	9	10,817	4	–	4.0
Newark	2,690	3	6,730	4	10,220	5	0.7	1.1
Belper	430	12	4,500	7	9,885	6	1.7	2.0
Loughborough	1,500	5	4,420	8	9,748	7	0.8	2.0
Mansfield	1,290	6	5,641	5	9,222	8	1.2	1.2
Basford (parish)	–	–	2,124	10	8,688	9	–	3.6
Sneinton (parish)	–	–	558	17	7,079	10	–	6.6
Hinckley	440	11	5,070	6	6,356	11	1.8	0.6
Lenton (parish)	–	–	893	15	4,467	12	–	4.1
Duffield	445	10	1,656	12	3,109	13	1.1	1.6
Heanor	810	7	1,061	13	3,058	14	0.2	2.7
Alfreton	710	9	815	16	2,683	15	0.1	3.0
East Retford	760	8	1,948	11	2,680	16	0.7	0.8
Ilkeston	420	13	963	14	2,188	17	0.7	2.1

Sources: Langton, 'Urban growth', pp. 453–90; *VCH Nottinghamshire*, vol. 2, pp. 307–17.

village', whose 'inhabitants were notorious for vice and immorality' as well as for poverty. In contrast, it was claimed, industrial expansion after 1778 had produced an urbane population, 'conspicuous ... [for] their industry, decorous behaviour, attendance on public worship, and general good conduct', while Belper itself was now ranked 'next to the capital of the county in extent of population, wealth, and intelligence'.[38]

The urban crisis of the 1830s and 1840s, however, produced a sea-change in these attitudes. In his passionate defence of the factory system, Andrew Ure praised Belper, not for becoming a successful small town, but for turning into a larger version of a traditional country estate, where a paternalist landlord presided over a population of happy industrial peasants: 'the pure unmixed effect of factory labour', he argued, 'is best and most easily found in the country – where it affords regular employment over the years to the same families'. Although Belper was described as a 'handsome town' in the early stages of this account, it was rapidly transformed into a 'manufacturing village', with 'quite the picturesque air of an Italian scene, with its river, overhanging woods, and distant range of hills'. Peter Gaskell, in his reply, accepted this premise, classifying Messrs Strutt as a 'country mill' and warning his readers against basing an entire argument on the experience of 'a few out-town manufactories'.[39] The second largest urban settlement in Derbyshire had thus been reclassified as 'the country'. To be urban was now to be dangerous, a shift which may well have been influenced by the notorious degeneration of Nottingham's own urban environment under the twin pressures of uncontrolled population growth and the hosiery industry's downhill lurch from crisis to crisis. 'Here is a *resurrection* of buildings', wrote one disgusted contemporary, 'seated like mushrooms in a field cast by chance'.[40] In the context, 'mushroom' had lost any positive sense of rapid expansion and had been reinterpreted purely as fungus, as a sign of decay. It is an image that is echoed in many other accounts of conditions in the town centre in this period, including a graphic description of life in a court in the Broad Marsh, 'let to many stockingers ... and there being many families, and even extra lodgers in all, it swarmed with population. Maggots in carrion flesh, or mites in cheese, could not be huddled more closely together'.[41]

The experience of Nottingham and its industrial region offers an interesting contrast to the situation in much of north-western England, where destitution, disorder and disease were increasingly associated with the rise of new industrial centres, rather than with established county towns. It is now generally accepted among historians that regional identity was growing in importance in the course of the eighteenth century, as long-established natural and socio-economic landscapes produced very different patterns of economic, social and cultural development. The industrial region, as Pat Hudson and others have argued, had 'a dynamic and operative function', with implications for the ways in which people thought about and organised both their work and their 'non-work' activities.[42] It is probable, therefore, that the dynamic industrial region, as conceived by economic historians, had equally significant implications for the ways in which people responded to urban growth, as well as a profound influence on the character and pattern of that growth. The processes of industrialisation and urbanisation in Nottingham were intimately associated with complex interlocking networks of economic, social and cultural innovation within an established regional context.

Notes

1 Langton, 'Urban growth', pp. 453–90.
2 See Ellis, 'Regional and county centres', pp. 673–84.
3 The general context for these developments is explored in Dyer, 'Midlands', pp. 93–110.
4 Thoroton, *Nottinghamshire*, p. 499.
5 Deering, *Nottinghamia*, pp. 6, 8–9, 75, 92; Moritz, *German in England*, p. 176.
6 *Nottingham Journal*, 7 August 1779, 12 June 1779.
7 Blackner, *Nottingham*, p. 66. For a fuller account of this transformation, see Beckett, *Nottingham*, pp. 189–208.
8 Deering, *Nottinghamia*, pp. 94–5, 72 and 101.
9 Nottingham Archive Office, inventory of John Clee, 1743. I owe this reference to Cathy Smith.
10 Henson, *Framework-Knitters*, vol. 1, pp. 364–8; Aspin, 'James Hargreaves', p. 121.
11 Throsby, *Thoroton's History*, vol. 2, p. 131.
12 *Nottingham Review*, 4 July 1817; Blackner, *Nottingham*, p. 231.
13 See Eden, *State of the Poor*, vol. 2, p. 574.
14 *Nottingham Journal*, 8 February 1835. Hosiers renting out large numbers of frames to stockingers, on the other hand, had a vested interest in opposing innovation, since they had little depreciation value: see Wells, *British Hosiery Industry*, pp. 64–5, 75.
15 Chapman, 'British hosiery industry'.
16 Felkin, *History of Hosiery*, p. 249; *Nottingham Review*, 11 September 1829.
17 Chapman, 'Working-class housing', p. 154.
18 Deering, *Nottinghamia*, p. 101.
19 Hutton, *William Hutton*, p. 110; Beckett, *East Midlands*, p. 5.
20 Defoe, *Tour*, vol. 2, p. 145.
21 Deering, *Nottinghamia*, pp. 100–1. Throsby, *Thoroton's History*, vol. 2, pp. 130–1, provides a later example of partisan comparisons being used to promote the reputation of Nottingham at the expense of Derby and Leicester.
22 Quoted in Clark, 'Introduction', p. 32.
23 Smith, 'English market town', pp. 135–42; Chaloner and Marshall, 'Revolution mill', pp. 281–303.
24 *VCH, Leicestershire*, vol. 3, pp. 3–5. Nottingham's catchment area for in-migration also corresponded with this region, although the twist-net boom of the 1820s drew in migrants from a much wider area.
25 Deering, *Nottinghamia*, p. 101.
26 *Nottingham Journal*, 13 and 20 December 1794, 2 February 1793.
27 Quoted in Fitton and Wadsworth, *Strutts and Arkwrights*, pp. 29, 32.
28 Chapman, 'Two framework knitters'.
29 Glover, *Ilkeston and Shipley*, p. 7.
30 *Nottingham Journal*, 16 November 1781, 8 December 1781.
31 See Varley, 'John Heathcoat'.
32 Pilkington, *Derbyshire*, vol. 2, p. 237; Glover, *Derby*, vol. 2, pp. 100–1.
33 Throsby, *Thoroton's History*, vol. 2, pp. 206, 230; Blackner, *Nottingham*, p. 391. The development of Radford is discussed in Smith, 'Population movements', pp. 56–64.

34 See, for example, Patten, 'Village and town'.

35 Quoted in Fitton and Wadsworth, *Strutts and Arkwrights*, p. 260.

36 *Nottingham Journal*, 6 October 1810, 6 February 1802.

37 *Nottingham Directory* (1818), pp. 75–6, 103.

38 Chapman, 'Two framework knitters', p. 96; Laird, *Beauties of England*, vol. 3, p. 520; Report of the Select Committee on Children employed in Manufactures, *Parliamentary Papers* (1815), vol. 2, p. 217; Glover, *Derby*, vol. 2, pp. 100–1.

39 Ure, *Philosophy of Manufactures*, pp. 342–4; Gaskell, *Artisans and Machinery*, pp. 90–1.

40 Laird, *Beauties of England*, vol. 2, p. 102.

41 *Nottingham Review*, 17 April 1829.

42 Hudson, *Regions and Industries*, p. 23; Langton, 'Industrial revolution'.

10

Elite networking and the formation of an industrial small town: Loughborough, 1700–1840[1]

Peter Clark

'A considerable market town ... a very great thoroughfare. Its manufactures are in a very flourishing state. A great part of the town has been rebuilt and much enlarged'.[2] Thus in 1822 *Pigot's Directory* lavished praise on the ancient town of Loughborough. How was this industrialisation achieved? Whilst bigger towns have attracted growing attention, small industrial towns have received little study, but their importance cannot be ignored. Up and down the country, and certainly in the east Midlands, the growth of new industries in old market towns was a vital feature of industrial transformation during the eighteenth and early nineteenth centuries. In this chapter, the concern is with seeing how Loughborough's position as a market town, embedded in the countryside of north-west Leicestershire, interacted with its industrial growth. What was the contribution of the regional economy and the immediate hinterland? How did the town's central place functions feed into new manufacturing activity? Most crucially, what was the role of the urban elite and elite networking? Underlying the analysis is the question of the extent to which the structural features of this small town both generated growth and put a ceiling on that success.

During the late Middle Ages Loughborough consolidated its position as one of the principal market towns in Leicestershire, winning the commendation of John Leland as a town 'in largeness and good building next to Leicester'. Nonetheless, its early growth was relatively modest, achieving only 1,290 inhabitants by 1563.[3] The most significant development was associated with the town trust. The original fifteenth-century endowment by Thomas Burton to improve bridges was enlarged in 1597 with a further bequest to extend repairs, establish a grammar school and relieve the poor. As in other Leicestershire towns, the feoffees of the trust (with its annually elected bridgemaster) steadily developed as the town's ruling group,[4] but for much of the sixteenth and seventeenth centuries, Loughborough was dominated by the Hastings family. Only during the eighteenth century, with the decay of the town's manorial courts, did the trust become the leading political and administrative body, working closely with the parish authorities.[5]

Fires badly affected the town in 1622, 1666 and 1761, and expansion may also have been retarded by high mortality.[6] By the accession of George III, Loughborough was probably starting to benefit from the new buoyancy of the regional economy, Nottingham and Leicester emerging as major centres of hosiery manufacture and traffic on the river Trent growing strongly.[7] Yet contemporary descriptions indicate that the town's performance was hardly impressive before the 1780s. One writer in 1770 claimed that the previously flourishing malt trade was in decline, 'nor is trade in general to be boasted of in this place'. As for the chief manufactures of wool combing and frameworkknitting, he added, 'I know not of any person that has made his fortune by either'. Many of the buildings appeared run-down and the streets were in bad shape. As late as 1795 these were 'rather narrow, dirty and irregular'.[8] Yet within a decade, the picture was changing. While remarking that 'the town in general has many bad thatched buildings', John Nichols noted that 'of late years [it] has been considerably improved'.[9]

The turning point for the town came with the construction of the Soar Navigation to the river Trent after 1776, making the town a terminal for river commerce and wholesale trade in the northern part of Leicestershire. Landowners led the way in this development: initial proprietors included the Earl of Huntingdon and six other major landowners with an aggregate investment of £2,000 (out of a total stock of £7,000). But Loughborough inhabitants, including local gentlemen as well as leading townsmen, were also prominent, twenty of them investing in all £3,900. Over time, Loughborough's role in the company increased, with a number of manufacturers and members of the town trust on the committee of proprietors which managed the canal. No less vital was the Erewash Canal, opened in 1779, which provided a link to the Derbyshire coalfield. Here again Loughborough inhabitants were active, as evinced by William Cradock, a Loughborough attorney and clerk to the Soar company, who was also treasurer of the Erewash Canal. By 1790 Throsby noted that 'the spirit and life of [Loughborough] is its navigation', which 'has enriched its inhabitants, aided the population of the place, and continues a source of multiplying benefits to almost every individual therein'.[10] Growth came quickly: by 1790 the town numbered about 3,900, in 1811 there were 4,500 inhabitants and in 1851 there were 11,172. During the 1820s and 1830s Loughborough became firmly established as the county's leading urban industrial centre after Leicester. In 1833 the town was said to be much improved 'by the erection of a new market-house and many handsome private edifices'.[11]

External linkages

How do we explain Loughborough's success? Clearly the expansive state of the regional economy was important for Loughborough, but none of the shire's other small towns did so well. Ashby flourished as a minor spa centre in the early nineteenth century, but its expansion was modest, rising from 2,674 in 1801 to 5,208 in 1851; Castle Donington, like Loughborough, profited from water navigation, but its population reached only 3,508 in 1841; Hinckley, which had prospered as a hosiery centre, suffered serious economic problems after 1811, and its population increased only marginally from 6,058 to 6,111 between 1811 and 1851.[12] What enabled Loughborough to outshine its neighbours? The boost given by the opening of the Soar Navigation was important, but so too were a range of factors, both external and internal, including its close links to its hinterland, its diversified economy, its urban networking and the elite's connection with the town trust.

Loughborough had an extensive hinterland. Mapping the wider territory is difficult, but if the Methodist circuit records are any guide, then the town's area included Shepshed, Diseworth, Thringston, Barrow-on-Soar, Mountsorrell, Castle Donington and Ratcliffe. The records of the General Baptist church, meanwhile, reveal close ties with Quorn but also with Woodhouse Eaves, Swithland, Barrow, Bedworth and Rothley. Voluntary society records suggest similar close ties to the hinterland. In 1821–22 a quarter of the membership of the Loughborough Association (a prosecution society) came from the surrounding area around, embracing Belton, Mountsorrell, Sutton Bonington and Burton-on-the-Wolds.[13] Within this hinterland, mainly to the south and west, was the wood and pastoral area of Charnwood, where livestock farming became increasingly mixed with coalmining. It contained industrialising villages such as Shepshed, Barrow and Woodhouse Eaves. On the eastern flank, the open arable fields were increasingly enclosed, often for dairy farming.[14] The agrarian sector was important for the town economy, because rising rents and land values, at least until after the Napoleonic Wars, boosted upper-class wealth, income and consumption. It is also likely that some townsmen engaged in commercial farming for the market, as happened in 1809 when part of the rectory lands were given over to cabbage and turnip cultivation to meet demand from a growing urban population. The town's canal link facilitated shipments downriver of agricultural goods, including wool sent to Gainsborough for the Yorkshire textile industry.[15] A number of the trust's principal officers were listed as farmers or graziers, including the Capps, the

Farrow family and Thomas Henshaw. Links to the food-processing industries were also significant, and several bridgemasters were maltsters with substantial landholdings.[16] After 1780 much of this malt was doubtless shipped along the Trent to Nottingham, Burton or London, but at least some was used by town brewers. The bridgemaster Harley family, for instance, combined malting with brewing, and in 1804 we hear of their 'magnificent brewery' with extensive buildings erected three years earlier.[17]

Internal dynamism

Loughborough's ancient role as a market centre remained strong. The market was held on Thursday and specialised in grain; there were also livestock and cheese fairs.[18] At the start of the nineteenth century the old market place and streets adjacent were crowded with inns and shops. The Bull's Head Inn in Highgate, owned by the Hastings family, was 'well situated in the town, long established as the principal inn and in full business', exploiting both the coaching trade as well as local commerce (see Chapter 5). Next door stood the Anchor, another substantial inn.[19] In 1770 the market place at the Cross was known only for a 'clump of miserable houses with petty shops belonging to them'. The 1785 shop tax also indicated that retailing was less advanced than in other Leicestershire towns (see Chapter 3). However, the growth of the Soar Navigation gave a boost to distribution so that, by the time of the 1811 census, we discover a clustering of retailing and service activities in the market area including three grocers and six linen drapers, alongside a butcher, an auctioneer, an apothecary, the postmaster and innkeeper, a surgeon and apothecary and a bookseller.[20] In 1789 the usually hard-to-please John Byng had praised Loughborough's bookseller, and the business clearly prospered in following years. Other specialist shops multiplied, such the Coffee, Spice and Foreign Fruit Warehouse with its appeal to the nobility, gentry and clergy, as well as the town public.[21]

Professional services in the town also expanded. Along with the grammar and elementary schools, Loughborough acquired a number of private academies. Lawyers were less prominent and their numbers remained modest, with about seven in the 1820s and eleven in the 1840s, but medical men were more numerous and a dispensary was established.[22] By the late eighteenth century these traditional central place functions of the town were interacting with and feeding into new transport and industrial developments. Lands of the Hastings estate were rented out in 1797 to the Soar Navigation and the Leicester Navigation Company, and in 1808, encumbered with debt, the Earl of Moira got parliamentary approval for the disposal of part of his Leicestershire property. In 1810 he sold off most of his holdings in the town, opening the way

for major industrial and commercial development.[23] Several of the agricultur-
alists, innkeepers and retailers in the town had considerable investments in the
canal companies and industrial activity. The innkeeper John Foster had shares
in the Soar and Erewash navigations, while James Douglas – bridgemaster in
1799, 1812 and 1823, and listed as a liquor merchant – was tenant in 1810 of
an extensive worsted mill, with engine house and workshop; he was also on
the committee of the Soar Navigation. William Knightley, landlord of the
Royal George Inn, was a lace manufacturer before his bankruptcy in 1837,
while Michael Ella, innkeeper at the Bull's Head, was an investor in the Soar,
Leicester and Erewash navigations, as well as a partner in a shipping company operating on the canals. Less certain is how far professional men
contributed to the industrial development of the town. Unusually, lawyers do
not seem to have been particularly important in the town elite, for instance
as bridgemasters, though one or two medical men served in that position. Nor
is there much evidence of their investment in business enterprises.[24] In general
there seems to have been a good deal of cross-investment and economic integration in the town, with profits from new sectors attracted back into
traditional activities. Several industrialists, like the hosier William Joseph Fry,
had considerable farm holdings, while Samuel Barnsdall, a boatbuilder, was
also engaged as a timber and coal merchant. The nature of the role of banks
in the town's economic growth is problematic. Loughborough had a private
bank by 1791, to which a second was added in 1822, but this was in line with
the trend in the other county market towns. More notably, Loughborough
acquired one of the first savings banks in the county (in 1816), and by 1841
the number of investors totalled a thousand, a tenth of the population (a much
higher proportion than in other places), indicating mounting affluence and,
arguably, economic dynamism.[25]

From the late eighteenth century hosiery was strongly established in Loughborough. In the 1790s the *UBD* declared that 'the chief manufactory ... is
woollen in the stocking-branch', and in 1804 Nichols confirmed that the
'hosiery business is carried on to a very great extent'. In common with hosiers
at Nottingham and Leicester, Loughborough manufacturers were busy putting
out work to framework-knitters in the adjoining countryside, villages such as
Shepshed, Diseworth, Mountsorrel, Woodhouse and Barrow becoming particularly important. Each manufacturer had his own network. John Watson,
who manufactured wrought cotton hose, reported that 'my hands are at
Thringstone, Whitwick, Belton, Long Whatton, Shepshed, Diseworth, Sutton
Bonington, and all on that side'; while a Barrow knitter remarked that the
firm of Cartwright and Warner had 'filled the town with work'. Though some
manufacturers in the region used middlemen, the Loughborough hosiers seem
to have put out work directly to knitters.[26] At the same time, Loughborough

was a considerable hosiery production centre in its own right. Most independent knitters worked narrow frames in their own homes, although some ran small workshops with up to six frames. Output, however, was increasingly controlled by the major manufacturers, who had 'got great capitals in the town'.[27]

From around the turn of the nineteenth century town producers started to innovate and diversify. Loughborough was an important source of new technical improvements in hosiery and bobbin-net manufacture. There was also a move from stockings into shirts and gloves, as well as a shift into new materials, including cotton, worsted and merino wool. Innovation and diversification helped the town to ward off the worst effects of the downturn in the hosiery trade during the early decades of the nineteenth century, which badly affected rural framework-knitting, especially in less diversified small towns such as Hinckley.[28] Even so, the depression took its toll: frame prices fell and the major hosiers bought up many, thus consolidating their control over the trade. Prices paid to knitters were reduced, more drastically than at Leicester and Nottingham. Robert Spencer, a Loughborough knitter, complained that the manufacturers 'have got the workmen a great deal under about here ... I believe they would be more spirited in Loughborough but it is the villages round about: they have been so oppressed that they are completely beaten down'. More pressure on the small knitters came from other directions. In the 1830s the Loughborough manufacturers introduced more efficient wide frames. By the following decade Loughborough had between 100 and 150 such frames, all of them owned by manufacturers and housed on their premises. Similar competition came from the expanding Leicester and Nottingham manufactories.[29] Finally, during the 1840s Cartwright and Warner opened the first power-driven wide frame factory in the county, and they were soon followed by the Pagets, who converted the Zouch Mills to steam. 'The steam and the scissors', it was prophetically said by one worker, 'are the ruin of the plain [traditional knitted] trade'.[30]

These developments at Loughborough conformed to the general European pattern in the urban textile industry from the late Middle Ages, particularly with regard to rural putting-out (see Chapters 13 and 14). Rural output was mobilised as a means of exploiting lower labour costs and providing flexible additional output for urban manufacturers: cheap-grade rural products complemented but did not compete with higher-quality, more diversified items made in town. However, as increased mechanisation enabled the making of cheaper mass-produced but varied goods in towns, rural producers were unable to compete. Industrialisation at Loughborough also benefited from the growth of related manufactures, particularly that of bobbin net-lace. Lace machinery was introduced by Heathcote and Lacey in 1809, and by the time of the Luddite riots the Heathcote factory was extensive, having about fifty to sixty machines with another five under construction, the whole costing between £5,000 and £10,000. Damage by the rioters was extensive, and Heathcote subsequently moved to Devon, but Loughborough remained a significant centre of the industry. During the 1830s there was a serious slump: in 1835 we hear that the bobbin-net industry had fallen into decay 'chiefly from over production'. The situation may have been compounded by dependence on Nottingham manufacturers, which left Loughborough producers exposed in periods of recession. Bankruptcies soared, and upwards of thirty twist-lace machines were being auctioned at one time.[31] On top of the problems in the hosiery industry there was an upsurge in distress at Loughborough. Nearly 200 unemployed operatives complained in 1837 of the 'present misery in the town and districts'. Distress among the traditional framework-knitters persisted into the next decade, with many rural workers flocking into town and living in wretched conditions.[32]

In terms of economic performance, lace making recovered and mechanisation boosted the hosiery industry, which remained the town's most important trade in the 1860s. At the same time, the economy continued to diversify. About 1840 the bellmakers John Taylor and Company moved their foundry from Oxford, taking over from an earlier firm which had been an offshoot of a Leicester bell foundry. As this indicates, part of the impetus for manufacturing growth continued to come from outside the town. In the case of textiles, there were connections to London, but most of the influence came from Leicester and Nottingham. Loughborough's Paget family had strong Leicester links, and the glove trade was shared with that city. The Cartwright and Warner hosiery firm had a strong Nottingham base, and Loughborough's shirt manufacture was a branch of the Nottingham trade. Nottingham's development as a lace-making centre also undoubtedly impacted on Loughborough, though the direct connections are less visible. Skilled workers moved fluidly between the three towns.[33]

Although industry was vital to Loughborough's economic success, it was only one dimension (see Table 10.1).[34] The importance of the textile industry is clear, with substantial numbers of framework-knitters and related trades, as well as lace makers. At the same time, tertiary-sector trades, including victualling, shopkeeping and transportation, appear in sizeable numbers. Once again the absence of substantial numbers of professional men is surprising, even if some may be hidden in the thicket of gentlemen.[35] Loughborough's broadly based economy thus drew on a number of sectors typical of a traditional market town. If these helped to buttress growth, they may have also served, through their competing demands and alternative options for profitable investment, to constrain concentration in one particular area and thus put a ceiling on the kind of high growth found in more specialist industrial centres, such as developed in the west Midlands. Also important was the fact that Loughborough seems to have been a relatively open community with a multiplicity of economic links to its hinterland, but also to the major urban centres of the region. Critical to this openness of the town and its commercial and industrial growth were good communications even before the Soar Navigation. Loughborough's main roads were progressively turnpiked in the early eighteenth century (to Leicester and the south in 1726, to Derby and the north in 1738, to Ashby and the west in 1757), and the town soon became a busy coaching station on the road between London and Manchester. In 1791 three different coach lines operated through the town from London to Manchester, offering fourteen services per week in each direction. In addition, a near-weekly service from Nottingham ran to the capital via Loughborough, while other regular services from Leeds, Derby and Sheffield stopped at town. By 1828 there were twenty-three daily services to London, Manchester and Leeds, as well as to neighbouring Leicester, Derby and Nottingham, alongside regular carrier services to much of the hinterland.[36]

After the late 1770s growing commerce on the river Trent and Soar Navigation complemented this overland traffic. There was a major expansion of the coal trade, with Derbyshire and Yorkshire supplies being transported on to Leicester and elsewhere, undermining the competitive position of Leicestershire coal. Leicester and the county's coal owners fought back with their own canal schemes, which culminated in the 1791 Leicester Navigation Act. The scheme included a canal link through Charnwood to the Leicestershire coalfields. Loughborough fought hard against the project and investment in the canal company by townspeople was minimal. The canal opened in 1794 but, unfortunately for the promoters, the Charnwood branch failed. Traffic on the new Leicester Canal was dominated by Derbyshire coal shipped via Loughborough.[37] In consequence, the canal navigation remained a golden goose for the town, and the area near the canals was bustling with wharves, warehouses and mills. In 1810 a sale catalogue for land near the New Bridge listed properties 'in a good situation for building'; another piece of land on the Derby road was 'used as a dockyard for building boats extending to the Loughborough Navigation'; and other land nearby was said to be in 'an excellent situation for forming a wharf'. Dividends by the Soar Navigation company rose from 30 per cent in the 1790s to 96 per cent in 1805; by 1824 a £100 share was worth £4,600. As already noted, the elite bridgemaster group were prominent investors in transport improvement.[38] Loughborough likewise did well from the Leicester and Swanington Railway, opened in 1832 by Leicestershire coalowners and linking the coalfields to Leicester. In reply, the Derbyshire and Nottinghamshire coalowners launched the Midland Counties

Table 10.1 *Principal occupations in Loughborough, 1811*

Occupation	%
Labourer	24.2
Framework-knitter	20.2
Woolcomber	7.9
Victualler/publican	6.3
Framesmith	4.2
Grocer	4.2
Cordwainer	3.6
Gentleman	3.6
Lace manufacturer	3.3
Tailor	3.3
Butcher	3.1
Joiner	2.7
Draper	2.7
Farmer	2.2
Bricklayer	2.2
Hosier	1.8
Carpenter	1.5
Carrier	1.5
Boatman	1.5

Source: Leicestershire RO, DE 667/188.
Note: n=331.

Railway in 1839, which the following year opened a connection to Leicester by way of Loughborough. Whilst coach and navigation traffic suffered, the town's carrying network survived, and Loughborough acquired a significant position in the railway network, on the lines to Nottingham, Derby, Leeds and eventually London.[39]

Although good fortune certainly favoured the town's development, along with regional economic forces and structural resources, it is important to recognise the contribution made by the town's leaders. Loughborough showed itself to be quick on its feet, flexible and responsive to new opportunities in both manufacturing and transport. Already in 1790 John Throsby noted how 'the people of Loughborough ... are remarkably studious for the interest and prosperity' of the town. No doubt he was thinking principally of the local elite. As noted in Chapter 1, 'personal networks are increasingly recognised as an important form of business as well as spatial integration'. Yet the precise role of local leaders in urban economic growth has been under-studied by historians, especially in small towns, where elites were more informal and documentation is sparser. The problem is complicated by the fact that there were often, as at Loughborough, several elite networks competing and overlapping with one another. Parish officials seem to have occupied their own circle, and dissenting congregations may also have had their own network of substantial inhabitants. The best evidence, however, comes from those leading townsmen associated with the town trust, which probably comprised the main elite group in the town.[40] What is striking about the trust is the wide range of occupations represented (Table 10.2). This reflected both the diversity and the strength of the town's economy by the start of the nineteenth century. As elsewhere, the elite circle was reinforced by shared office, family connections and economic and associational activity. The Capp, Farrow, Fowler, Paget, Wood and Burchill families all supplied three or more bridgemasters between 1780 and 1840. A number of the town trustees served on the Soar Navigation committee, and in the 1780s nearly a dozen bridgemasters were listed as subscribers to the Loughborough Association, concerned with prosecuting agricultural crimes and thefts from warehouses and shops in the town.[41]

During the eighteenth century the trust operated closely with the parish in the governance of the town. After 1749 the parish vestry was closed, matching the oligarchic nature of the town trust. About the same time, the trust paid the cost of a new workhouse which was built on its land at Sparrow Hill. A report from 1770 suggests the workhouse was run on business lines: the healthy poor were to work according to 'the usual working hours of handicraft trades', and it was stressed how 'order and good discipline is conducive to industry'. Trust expenditure on other forms of poor relief rose steadily from about £40 in 1735 to £120 in 1785, £225 in 1795 and £246 in 1805–6. In subsequent years it made an annual transfer to the parish overseers rather than relieve the poor directly, but during the eighteenth century the trust played a significant part in managing the social impact of economic growth.[42] By the late eighteenth century the trust was also funding a variety of economic activities, such as paying boys to be taught building crafts or writing and accounts, apprenticing boys (often to framework-knitters in Loughborough's hinterland) and purchasing spinning wheels for loan to poor women.[43] But most important was its rising expenditure on urban infrastructure, including bridges, roads and schools. Already in 1739 the feoffees complained of the 'great charge' of improving bridges, and the mid-century saw heavy expenses on the school. Infrastructure expenditure of this kind (plus administrative costs) rose from about £146 in 1734–35 to £244 in 1754–55, £333 in 1765 and £564 in

Table 10.2 *Occupations of Loughborough bridgemasters and feoffees, 1780–1840*

Occupation	%
Farmer	14.9
Hosier	11.1
Maltster	11.1
Linen draper	11.1
Grazier	11.1
Gentleman/esquire	11.1
Cutler/ironmonger	7.4
Liquor merchant	7.4
Yeoman	7.4
Brewer	3.7
Innkeeper	3.7

Sources: PRO, PROB 11/1650/606 (F. Harley, 1821); Nichols, *History*, p. 890.
Note: n=27; multiple occupations listed by each occupation.

1794–95. After the turn of the century the trust increasingly concentrated on this kind of work: about 1800 the main bridges to Nottingham were improved and widened, and in the 1820s especially there was a spate of investment in roads and schools.[44] Running the trust was not without its difficulties: late payment or arrears of rent caused short-term deficits. In the late eighteenth century incoming bridgemasters paid off the loans made to the trust by their predecessors. From the 1760s, expanded activity was also funded by borrowing at interest. All the indications are that the trust made an important contribution to improving the infrastructure and educational resources of the town. No less vitally, it provided an institutional focus for entrepreneurial networking and wider collaboration, and in that way created leadership and direction for a small community before the establishment of new municipal councils in the Victorian era.[45]

Conclusions

Loughborough by 1840 was evidently a substantial community where 'the inter-linkage of economic social and cultural change' had created a town with various trappings of modernity. A town library had been established in 1826 and a theatre followed a decade later. There were numerous voluntary associations, some of them linked to the Church or dissenting congregations.[46] By the 1830s gas had arrived: in the following decade the town was said to have 'a number of handsome streets paved and lighted with gas'. In 1837 a short-lived newspaper, the *Loughborough Telegraph and Advertiser*, was founded, although this carried only limited local news and eventually turned into a regional paper.[47] State action helped entrench the town's centrality. In the late 1830s Loughborough became the centre of a poor law union of twenty-three parishes straddling the Leicestershire and Nottinghamshire border – most of them 'connected with the manufactory'. About the same period, a court of requests was instituted in the town with an extensive jurisdiction covering nearly eighty places. In addition, Loughborough became a parliamentary polling station and a barracks town.[48] Not everything went smoothly. In the Luddite riots of 1816 Heathcote's lace factory was attacked, and the 1830s were a time of industrial depression which saw mounting tension between Anglicans and dissenters. Protests erupted over allegedly excessive rates and the abuse of the town trust and parish accounts. Other charges were made about selective admission to the free school. In the longer run, management by the town trust and parish authorities proved inadequate for controlling urban growth; by the mid-nineteenth century mortality was high owing to poor drainage and water supply, and a Local Board of Health was established in 1850. The town was chartered in 1888.[49]

Loughborough was never to become a Burslem or Wolverhampton with a soaring and specialist industrial economy (see Chapter 7 and 8), but the town's expansion and prosperity outshone that of other small towns in its area of the east Midlands. As we have seen, both external linkages and local dynamism were clearly important, in conjunction with a matrix of demand and supply factors. These included the links to regional production centres at Nottingham and Leicester and through them to wider markets, the availability of skilled rural labour linked to the putting-out industry, the ready movement of workers to and between urban centres and the investment in links to Nottingham, Leicester and local landowners, as well as capital supplied by traditional sectors in the town. All this supports the powerful argument made in Chapter 1, that 'spatial integration through a network of towns not only shaped the geography of industrialisation: it was fundamental to the very process'. Again, the interdependence of hosiery, lace making and the transport and service sectors also undoubtedly contributed. These factors seem to have been less positive for the other small towns of the area. Chance also played its part – not least the failure of the Leicester–Charnwood branch canal – but what was distinctive about Loughborough at this time was the entrepreneurial flair and innovation of leading townsmen. Here institutional factors were of special significance, the town trust providing both a focus for entrepreneurial networking and an engine for new investment in urban infrastructure. Whilst traditional structures and sectors helped to underpin Loughborough's growth, they may also have constrained its development, putting a ceiling on industrial specialisation by offering competing investment opportunities in the service sector. Nonetheless, there can be no question that by 1840 the town's industrial and economic position in the east Midlands was well established, with a diversity of trades, a broadly skilled labour force, a solid range of economic connections and a transport role which gave it the capacity to respond to new challenges, thus assuring its modest but continuing success in the urban system into the twentieth century.

Notes

1 I am grateful to Dr Andrew Hann for his help in preparing this chapter and to Professor Herman van der Wee for comments on a late draft.

2 *Pigot's Directory* (1822–23), p. 223.

3 Postles, 'English small town'; Smith, *John Leland*, vol. 1, p. 19; Clark and Hosking, *Population Estimates*, p. 93.

4 Leicestershire RO, Leicester, DE 664/30.

5 For the Hastings family see Moxon, 'Ashby-de-la-Zouch'; Leicestershire RO, DE 40/33/34.

6 Throsby, *Leicestershire Views*, pp. 266–7, Gräf, 'Leicestershire small towns', p. 106.

7 Dyer, 'Midlands', pp. 95–6 and 108–9; *VCH Leicestershire*, vol. 4, pp. 168–74.

8 Pochin, *Loughborough*, p. 6; MacRitchie, *Diary of a Tour*, p. 71.

9 Nichols, *History of Leicestershire*, p. 889.

10 Temple-Patterson, 'Leicestershire canals', pp. 67–9; PRO, RAIL 849/1, fols 7, 107, 342, RAIL 849/2, fols 1–2, 132, 157; Leicestershire RO, Misc. 110/1; Throsby, *Leicestershire Views*, p. 277.

11 Clark and Hosking, *Population Estimates*, p. 94; *Pigot's Directory* (1835), p. 141; Gorton, *Topographical Dictionary*, vol. 2, p. 706.

12 Clark and Hosking, *Population Estimates*, pp. 93–4; Granville, *Spas of England*, vol. 2, pp. 129–35; Lee, 'Market town'; Lane, 'Industrialising town', pp. 145–6.

13 Leicestershire RO, N/M 207/6, N/B 207A/80.

14 Leicestershire RO, 1097/11; Levine, *Family Formation*, esp. chapter 2; *VCH Leicestershire*, vol. 2, p. 229ff.; Nichols, *History of Leicestershire*, p. 888.

15 Palmer, *Aristocratic Estate*, pp. 56–68; Leicestershire RO, DE 667/186, DE 664/62; Nichols, *History of Leicestershire*, p. 895.

16 For a list of bridgemasters see: Leicestershire RO, DE 641/7 (front); for occupations see DE 664. Survey of wills from Leicestershire RO, PC series, and PRO, PROB 11.

17 PRO, PROB 11/1650/606 (F. Harley, 1821); Nichols, *History of Leicestershire*, p. 890.

18 *Pigot's Directory* (1822–23), p. 223.

19 Leicestershire RO, DE 4686; Pochin, *Loughborough*, p. 6; Nichols, *History of Leicestershire*, p. 890.

20 Pochin, *Loughborough*, p. 6; Gräf, 'Leicestershire small towns', p. 113; Leicestershire RO, DE 667/188.

21 Byng, *Torrington Diaries*, vol. 2, p. 82; Leicestershire RO, DE 113/14; *Loughborough Telegraph and Advertiser Loughborough T&A*, 6 January 1837.

22 BPP, A Digest of Parochial Returns made to the Select Committee [for] the Education of the Poor (1819), 9:1, 1819, p. 457; *Pigot's Directory* (1822–23), p. 223; *Pigot's Directory* (1840), pp. 304–7; Gorton, *Topographical Dictionary*, vol. 2, p. 706.

23 There are parallels here with the development seen later in West Bromwich.

24 Palmer, *Aristocratic Estate*, pp. 62–3, 68ff.; Leicestershire RO, DE 667/186, DE 4686; Leicestershire RO, PC 1782/81 (J. Foster); PRO, RAIL 849/2, fols 1–2, 10, 21, 23–4; *Loughborough T&A*, 6 January 1837. For lawyers in other urban centres see Clark, 'Small towns', pp. 753–4.

25 Leicestershire RO, PC 1842/71, PC 1810/13/1–2; *VCH Leicestershire*, vol. 3, p. 51; Keaveny, 'Urban expansion', pp. 6, 24–5.

26 *UBD*, vol. 3 (1798), p. 576; Nichols, *History of Leicestershire*, p. 890; *VCH Leicestershire*, vol. 3, pp. 5, 11; Levine, *Family Formation*, chapter 2; BPP, Report of the Commissioner appointed to inquire into the Condition of the Framework Knitters, Appendix to Report, 15:1, 1845, pp. 429, 418, 420–5, 429. This contrasted with the situation in Nottingham: see Chapter 9 of this volume.

27 BPP, Report ... Framework Knitters, Appendix to Report, 15:1, 1845, pp. 403–4, 407, 395.

28 BPP, Report ... Framework Knitters, 15, 1845, pp. 22–4; *Pigot's Directory* (1822–23), p. 223; Levine, *Family Formation*, esp. chapter 2; Lane, 'Industrialising town', pp. 145–6.

29 BPP, Report ... Framework Knitters, Appendix to Report, 15:1, 1845, pp. 394–5, 400–1, 424.

30 *VCH Leicestershire*, vol. 3, pp. 12 and 16; BPP, Report ... Framework Knitters, Appendix to Report, 15:1, 1845, p. 399.

31 Van der Wee, 'Woollen industries'; Leicestershire RO, 12 D36/2, 11, 17–19; *Pigot's Directory* (1835), p. 141; *Loughborough T&A*, 6. Jan 1837.

32 *Loughborough T&A*, 9 June, 23 June 1837; BPP, Report ... Framework Knitters, Appendix to Report, 15:1, 1845, pp. 411–12, 414ff., 427–8.

33 *Directory of Leicester and Rutland* (1861), p. 233; Jenning, *Master of my Art*, pp. 20ff., 27; BPP, Report ... Framework Knitters, Appendix to Report, 15:1, 1845, pp. 402, 394 and 404; Beckett, *Nottingham*, pp. 324ff.

34 Census enumeration data is drawn from Fishpoool Head, Wards End, the Market Place, Wood Gate, Baxter Gate and Sparrow Hill – a reasonably representative sample of the town as a whole.

35 Leicestershire RO, DE 667/188.

36 12 George I, Public Acts, no. 5; 11 George II, Public Acts, no. 33; 30 & 31 George II, Public Acts, no. 44; *UBD*, vol. 3 (1798), p. 576 ; *Pigot's Directory* (1828), pp. 496–7.

37 Temple-Patterson, 'Leicestershire canals', pp. 69–90; Leicestershire RO, 3 D 42/4/2, p. 7, 3 D 42/4/19/1, p. 19.

38 Leicestershire RO, DE 4686; Temple-Patterson, 'Leicestershire canals', p. 97.

39 Clinker, 'Leicester and Swannington railway'; *VCH Leicestershire*, vol. 3, pp. 110–18; Mason, 'Impact of the railway', pp. 8–9, 20, 35.

40 Throsby, *Leicestershire Views*, p. 277; Pearson and Richardson, 'Business networking', pp. 657–79. For Loughborough parish officials see Leicestershire RO, DE 667/63.

41 Leicestershire RO, Misc. 1097/9.

42 Leicestershire RO, DE 667/177, DE 664/14a, DE 664/34–6.

43 Leicestershire RO, DE 664/41b.

44 Leicestershire RO, DE 664/34–6, DE 664/31; Nichols, *History of Leicestershire*, p. 891; White, *Loughborough Schools*, p. 174.

45 Leicestershire RO, DE 664/31.

46 *Loughborough T&A*, 10 March, 5 May, 12 May, 9 June 1837.

47 *Pigot's Directory* (1835), p. 141; *Parliamentary Gazetteer* (1844), 2 (2), p. 305. The *Loughborough T&A* became the *Leicestershire, Nottinghamshire and Derby Telegraph and Advertiser for the Midland Counties* in late 1837.

48 *Parliamentary Gazetteer* (1844), 2 (2), pp. 305–6.

49 Deakin, *Loughborough*, pp. 21, 29–30, 32; PRO, MH 12/6523.

I I

On the margins of industrialisation: Lichfield

Leonard Schwarz

Lichfield was on the margins of industrialisation. It was one of the principal nodal points of pre-industrial England, where the main road from the east to the west Midlands met the road from London to Chester. In a region of small towns, sixteenth-century Lichfield was sufficiently important to undermine Stafford's pre-eminence in the county: too weak to dominate yet strong enough to deny primacy to any rival town, as Alan Dyer has put it.[1] It is described by Peter Clark as one of the 'larger, usually early established, centres, a number of them boroughs, benefiting from good communications and a variety of functions, sometimes overlapping with lesser county towns' and is compared to Chichester, Stamford, Huntingdon and Chelmsford.[2] In Blome's survey of 1673 it counted as a 'flourishing' town.[3] However, as the Midlands developed during the eighteenth century, more roads were built, and long before the railways it was becoming ever more marginalised. It was not sufficiently close to either the east or the west Midlands, while its nearest coalmines were seven miles distant at Rugeley. The town's relative decline during the eighteenth and nineteenth centuries is unsurprising. Its population of about 2,300 in 1664 placed it sixteenth in Langton's hierarchy of Midlands towns, yet this expanded only slowly, to about 3,800 in 1781, 4,712 in 1801 and 6,499 in 1831.[4] As a consequence, it ceased to be one of the top thirty Midlands towns.

However, Lichfield managed marginalisation remarkably well, with no depopulation and no very obvious signs of impoverishment. What this chapter shows is how a quite prosperous middle-sized eighteenth-century town with a large transit trade, some industry and serious pretensions towards being a leisure centre for its region could become quite a prosperous little nineteenth-century town with little industry and less transit. Such a transition was not uncommon, but has not been considered much by historians. It will be argued that Lichfield was an indirect beneficiary of the industrialisation of both the east and the west Midlands. It owed its function to its role in the urban network, and as this network changed, Lichfield changed with it. It may therefore be seen as typical of many small towns of nineteenth-century England that declined relatively but not absolutely and not particularly painfully. In this process, the role of its leisure sector needs to be set in context. Whatever might have been the case in Bath, or in a small *ab initio* leisure town such as Leamington Spa, in Lichfield social and cultural changes alone could never be the sole driving forces of economic development. Lichfield's leisure sector held only a regional attraction and could not compensate for a declining manufacturing sector and the loss of the town's position as a transport hub. However, it could help the town to develop its local links and to become the centre of a prosperous locality whose wealth was, in turn, dependent upon the rapidly growing urban markets of the east and west Midlands. The geography of the region was reformulated and Lichfield reflected this.

A service and communication centre

Lichfield's eighteenth-century development befitted a regional centre seeking to attract the gentry. Its musical society was founded in 1739, with public concerts from the 1740s, and long before then its cathedral had been used for concerts. It had a Society of Gardeners by 1769.[5] It had its races: by the early 1740s these were held in September and lasted for two days, this duration extending to three days in 1746.[6] Famously, it had Michael Johnson the bookseller – though it is worth noting that he took time off from his Lichfield business to sell books in neighbouring towns. It was also a useful regional shopping centre and, if its inhabitants sometimes felt the need to shop further afield by the end of the eighteenth century, usually they could get what they needed locally.[7] The *UBD* lists seventy-two different trades in the town in 1798, including the sort of shops and services needed for a genteel lifestyle – no longer that of Michael Johnson, but a couple of combined printers and booksellers, two silversmiths, a dentist, perfumer and toyman (all in one), a clutch of apothecaries, surgeons and doctors, an organist, five attorneys and a lunatic hospital. Certainly, Lichfield's occupations were as varied as those of any of the more prosperous eighteenth-century small towns examined by Corfield and Kelly.[8]

In addition to this, Lichfield had two distinctive characteristics. The first was its clergy, the locus of the fashionable part of the town being the Cathedral Close, physically separate from the rest of the town and with its own magistrates. Urban historians have not usually remarked much on the role of the Anglican clergy,[9] but in Lichfield they were inescapable. As far as wealth, let alone education, was concerned, the higher cathedral clergy were high on the county scales. White's directory of Staffordshire, 1834 estimated that the bishopric was worth about £6,000 per annum (the bishop was the brother of the Earl of Harrowby), and the deanery of the cathedral about £3,000 (the dean was the brother of the Earl of Carlisle); the average annual income of each of the six canons residentiary was about £800, and they all had free accommodation. The chancellor received £600 a year; the six vicars-choral had about £100 a year each with their accommodation. These figures may have been exaggerated – they were probably gross rather than net income and perhaps smacked a little of the not always reliable Black Books of the time – but they are indicative. The clergy's influence over the electorate could not be taken for granted, but their cultural influence was undisputed. Those who wished to pass as being really cultured lived in the Cathedral Close or, as the Close could take only some forty families, as near to it as they could. Cultural arrivistes such as Michael Johnson, who still had to make a living, lived by the market place. The wills of the clergy show them owning land in Warwickshire and Staffordshire and sometimes beyond, as well as buying inns in the town and shares in Staffordshire's canals.[10] It will be argued later that Lichfield had its limitations as a leisure town for a wider region, but it was a clerical leisure town. The clergy dominated Lichfield's public and professional sector. Throughout the eighteenth century they comfortably outnumbered all others in that sector. As late as 1818 they formed 40 per cent of the professions. In 1788 they launched an appeal for rebuilding their cathedral; a list of subscribers who raised about £3,000 included an enormous range of people, from the Duke of Devonshire (who gave £1,000) to Matthew Boulton. There was a separate 'Birmingham list' with fifty subscribers.[11] It was the combined efforts of the clergy, not the single-handed energy of Erasmus Darwin or the prolixity of Anna Seward, that ensured that the town was a cultural centre.[12]

The second distinctive aspect of Lichfield was its role as a transport hub. Until the mid-eighteenth century almost all coaches from London to the North-West passed through Lichfield, as did the coaches from Birmingham, Bristol and the South-West to Sheffield, Leeds and the North-East.[13] What happened after that has been described in detail by Phillips and Turton.[14] Essentially, alternative routes were developed through the east and west Midlands, and long-distance traffic increasingly by-passed Lichfield: carriers and post coaches from London to the North-West, for example, preferred to pass through Birmingham. In the long run there was nothing that Lichfield could do about it. It tried, of course: from the nadir of 1674, when the deputy postmaster-general saw fit to inform Lichfield's postmaster that 'your riders are oftener lost in the night, and have more unfortunate accidents happen to them on your roads than halfe Englande besides'; improvements were made, and at the turn of the eighteenth century Celia Fiennes found the road rather good.[15] During the course of the eighteenth century the town developed its own regional network, with the local shopkeepers, gentry and clergy investing in

Table 11.1 *Coach and carrier connections per week from Lichfield, 1834 (excluding mail)*

Destination	Coaches	Carriers
Birmingham	35	10
Liverpool	13	–
London	13	–
Sheffield (via Derby)	14	3
Rugeley	7	1
Manchester	7	0
Nottingham	7	0
Uttoxeter	0	2
Burton-upon-Trent	0	2
Needwood Forest	0	–
Walsall	0	3

Source: White, *Staffordshire* (1834), p. 162.

turnpike roads, but what Lichfield could do was very limited. Most of the turnpike roads that emanated from or proceeded through Lichfield had been completed by 1759; the last significant Turnpike Act provided the connection with Walsall, and that road was completed by 1769.[16] In 1797 Lichfield had twenty-one daily coach connections (including returns). This would have been respectable half a century earlier and compared favourably with the twenty-two services a week from Nottingham in 1751 or the thirty-one from Liverpool in 1753, but already in 1767 Birmingham had 160 services a week, provided by fifty-four firms.[17] By 1818 there were four coaches a day from Lichfield to London and another two to Liverpool as well as other Liverpool connections running four days in the week. To Manchester there was one daily connection and another for three days a week, while Sheffield had one daily connection. If the directories are to be trusted, this was not an overwhelmingly busy schedule. Table 11.1 gives Lichfield's coach connections in 1834, before the railway connections with the North-West were operational. It shows that Lichfield did not have many connections, although some were important and long-distance, going to London, Manchester, Sheffield and Liverpool.[18]

Unsurprisingly, Lichfield failed to obtain the most successful railway connections. In 1837 the London & Birmingham & Grand Junction Railway opened, followed shortly afterwards by the Birmingham and Derby Railway.

None passed through Lichfield. Local capitalists had chosen the wrong company: they sought instead to connect with the South Manchester Railway, which was to go from Manchester to the Potteries, Rugeley, Lichfield and Birmingham. The ostensible grounds were that these were the important places with which they had contact and, slightly desperately and revealingly,

> that Lichfield [was situated] on ... the main travelling lines between London, Lancashire and Ireland, and derives extensive profit from such a position that although manufactories are not carried on to a great extent, yet the very large expenditure of the annual revenue of the Inhabitants leads to a considerable ... trade and the central situation with respect to the general business of the County still further tends to make it a place of resort.[19]

The last London coach ran on 11 April 1838, whilst the railway did not arrive until 1847.[20] This was, however, merely the end of a long and gradual process.

A changing identity?

Between about 1780 and 1840 Lichfield's identity changed. It would be misleading to speak of decline: a town situated so near to so many flourishing urban centres and with a broadly based economy of its own was unlikely to decline during the eighteenth and nineteenth centuries. Yet Lichfield's aspirations towards being a regional centre did decline. Its manufacturing base changed orientation and its service sector was ever more localised. In short, it was being by-passed; but, as with transport, this was a slow process and Lichfield adapted itself quite successfully. Table 11.2 gives a number of different statistics of the town's occupations, but omits those workers who might be connected with agriculture – not only farmers but also labourers. Care must be taken to compare like with like: the census enumerators' books are reasonably complete; the baptism registers give the occupations of adult males, many of them young; the 1747 electorate was wide but obviously biased towards the wealthier inhabitants of the town, as were the directories, which also had a particular bias towards the more established shopkeepers. Before 1851, therefore, the figures should be regarded as indicative of broad long-run trends, but these trends are clear. The directories suggest that manufacturing involved some 40 per cent of those whom they listed between 1797 and 1834; the professions accounted for 10–15 per cent, whilst the figures for the dealing sector fluctuate more, but suggest an increase from 1747. The baptism registers – a much more widely based source than the directories and therefore more comparable to the census – suggest a distinct decline in manufacturing between 1813 and 1851, balanced by an increase in building, dealing and the professions. It can be misleading to focus excessively on these

Table 11.2 *Occupations of males in Lichfield, 1747–1851 (percentages)*

	1747 elec- torate	*1797 direc- tory*	*1818 direc- tory*	*1834 direc- tory*	*1813–14 baptism registers*	*1835–36 baptism registers*	*1851 census enumer- ators' books*
Building	8.5	5.9	13.4	9.1	12.4	16.1	13.9
Dealing	19.4	35.3	23.1	36.0	10.4	16.6	22.3
Domestic service	1.7	2.9	7.0	1.9	8.9	7.6	4.3
Manufacturing	54.4	40.4	42.7	41.8	51.9	47.1	37.1
Public service and professional	15.6	15.5	12.5	10.3	11.9	7.2	17.3
Transport	0.4	0.0	1.3	0.9	4.5	5.4	5.1
Total	100.0	100.0	100.0	100.0	100.0	100.0	100.0
Number	237	136	320	428	206	232	960

Sources: 1747 electorate: Stafford RO, D661/19/4/1; Baptism registers: Lichfield RO, 1851 census: Lichfield RO; 1851 census enumerators' returns: transcript in Lichfield RO. Directories: *UBD, General and Commercial Directory for 1818*, White, *Stafford-shire* (1834).
Note: The Armstrong–Booth classification has been applied: see Armstrong, 'Information about occupation'.

occupational data, which illustrate change without explaining it. This is clear when manufacturing is examined in greater detail. Between 1747 and 1835 the various sources consistently place manufacturing at around 50 per cent of the total. Thereafter there was a decline to 37 per cent in the census enumerators' returns for 1851.[21] It is dangerous to place excessive reliance on any one source, but it does appear that the decline in manufacturing's share came during the nineteenth century. Table 11.3 shows that most of this was caused by a decline in leather trades, which occupied 17 per cent of the electorate in 1747, 3 per cent of fathers in the baptism registers for 1813–14 and fewer in 1851. This was compensated by a rise in carriage and harness from 2 per cent to 10 per cent and by clothes finishing from 31 to 36 per cent of the enumerated male population.

Attempts to date the relative decline in Lichfield's manufacturing with greater precision are probably impossible and in any case miss the point. Regional economic development meant that the way for a town like Lichfield to position itself was to concentrate on up-market and/or finished goods.

Table 11.3 *Principal male manufacturing occupations in Lichfield,*
1747–1851 (percentages)

	1747 *electorate*	*1813–14* *baptism* *registers*	*1835–36* *baptism* *registers*	*1851 census* *enumerators* *books*
Food processing	12.4	5.7	4.4	8.0
Drink processing	4.7	1.0	1.1	4.0
Leather	17.1	2.9	6.6	1.4
Clothes finishing	31.0	36.2	26.4	32.2
Metals	8.5	7.6	9.9	5.1
Weaving	10.9	1.9	5.5	2.3
Dying	3.1	1.0	0.0	0.9
Carriage and harness	2.3	10.5	12.1	17.4
% of manufacturing included above	89.9	66.7	65.9	71.2
Manufacturing: number	129	105	91	351

Sources: see Table 11.2.
Note: Occupation categories are taken from the Armstrong–Booth classification: food processing MF 25 and 26; drink processing MF 27; leather MF10; clothes finishing MF23; metals MF4; weaving MF18; dyeing MF22; carriage and harness MF 15.

Already in 1747 it seems to have leant predominantly in this direction. Of the 129 voters who were involved in manufacturing, forty were involved in clothes finishing (mainly tailors and shoemakers), and another sixteen in food processing. The vulnerable sections were involved in leather, weaving and dying. As Table 11.3 shows, these were activities that declined. The directories give a similar picture. By 1797 employers in the leather trade had sunk to ten out of 140. only one of them a tanner, and there was only one employer in the weaving trade. A more complete directory of 1818 returned two tanners, four curriers and leather dealers and one dyer. However, it also returned two coachmakers, five clockmakers, a jeweller and three confectioners alongside ten shoemakers, ten milliners, nine tailors, seventeen bakers and eighteen maltsters.[22] In this respect Lichfield followed the Midlands pattern as revealed in Chapter 2 and discussed more fully in Chapter 6. Between the 1790s and the 1840s the number of producers of clothing in the Midlands grew while the number of producers of leather, fur and wool declined. A relatively small number of Midlands towns became more specialised; as a corollary most of the others tended to became less specialised and more similar to each other. For towns without coal this would usually involve a greater concentration upon the finishing trades, but these in turn were becoming more specialised. Rugeley lost half its hatters, Worcester half its glovers and Ludlow nearly all of its glovers. Leather moved more from Lichfield towards Walsall. Of course the trend was nuanced – Lichfield had a fulling mill from the 1790s and a woollen manufactory in 1809, both of which were still operational in the 1850s – but it was also clear: Sir Robert Peel established a cotton manufactory in 1802 but it did not survive.[23]

As Lichfield's role as a transport hub faded, other aspects of its economy revealed a similarly nuanced picture. The number of inns and public houses seems to have been declining from the late eighteenth century, eighty being recorded in 1732, but only fifty-four in 1818. However, this had risen to fifty-five in 1834 and to sixty-two in 1851.[24] Lichfield's role as a national transport hub faded gradually. Its significance in long-distance trade declined, but its role as a regional transport centre became more important not only to the town itself, but perhaps also to the town's wider agricultural region. Stage-coaching, mentioned in the directories, was only a part of the coaching trade: the provision of carts, coaches and horses for private hire was important and difficult to document.[25]

In contrast to its role in manufacturing and transport, Lichfield's role as a shopping and service centre does not appear to have declined. At the start of the nineteenth century the ratio of population per service provider, at 32.2, was exactly at the mean for Midlands towns of its size.[26] On the other hand, the ratio of persons per assessed shop (83.3) was significantly higher than the mean for Worcestershire and Warwickshire (67.3) and far above that of Worcester (56.9).[27] The 1785 shop tax gives a rather pessimistic picture. The statistics provide the total amount of taxation collected from Lichfield, but not the number of assessed shops, so it is not possible to make a direct comparison with Table 3.3 in this volume. However, it is possible to calculate the shop tax per capita, using the 1801 census. The results are in Figure 11.1. Lichfield was exactly on the mean for the combined towns of Worcestershire, Warwickshire and Staffordshire. However, the population of many of the towns to the right of Lichfield on the graph would grow very rapidly between 1785 and 1801, and they therefore had more shops per capita in 1785 than the graph implies. On the other hand, Lichfield had its specialist shops, and these grew in number. Between 1818 and 1851 the number of glass and china warehouses rose from two to four, and confectioners from three to six, to parallel the rise in plumbers from three to eleven and of surgeons from six to seven. The Lichfield Savings Bank was established in 1818 and had 722 individual accounts by 1827; there was also a small country bank and a branch of the National Provincial Bank that was established in 1834.[28]

Figure 11.1 *Shop tax per capita, 1785: percentage of mean for Worcestershire, Warwickshire, Staffordshire*

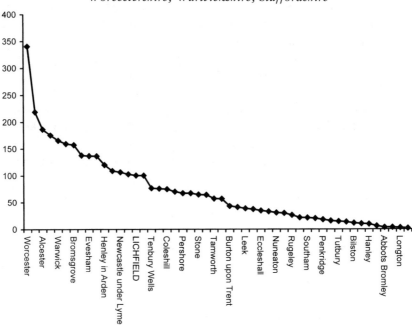

Source: PRO, E182 Shop Tax.

Significantly, during the first half of the nineteenth century Lichfield had a large female surplus in its population. The surplus was consistently larger than that of most Staffordshire towns or the county itself, and considerably larger than that of Rugeley, the expanding coal-based industrial town seven miles away. Young women would hardly migrate in large numbers to a declining town and, as Figure 11.2 shows, they were more inclined to migrate to Lichfield than they were to Rugeley, Stafford or West Bromwich. Despite the female surplus, Messrs Hitchcock and Sulzer, worsted spinners of Lichfield, felt confident enough to write to the Poor Law Commissioners in 1835 claiming that they were 'subjected to serious inconvenience in business from a scarcity of factory hands ... The description of persons most suitable for our purpose would be ... widows with large families or orphans of both sexes thereby furnishing a supply of young persons of the most use for employment agreeable to the provisions of the Factory Regulation Act ... We should use at the present time about fifty persons to set us through at liberty ... Our employment is regular and permanent.'[29] And in fact male wage rates in Lichfield kept up with the national trend, tending to rise gradually over the long run.[30]

Figure 11.2 *Sex ratios by age (females per 100 males) in Staffordshire and selected towns, 1841*

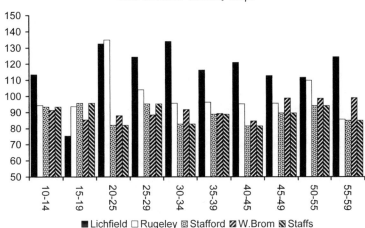

■ Lichfield □ Rugeley ▨ Stafford ▨ W.Brom ◩ Staffs

Source: 1841 census.

The female surplus in Figure 11.2 was not the result of male emigration: successive male cohorts in Lichfield were by no means depleted compared with those in the other towns represented there.

Lichfield's transition was not without pain. Transport, inns and leather did decline. Furthermore, there are signs that from about 1800 Lichfield was ceasing to maintain its attractions as a regional centre of fashion. The September races were a great event in the social calendar. In the mid-eighteenth century as many as 233 diners, including one duke, three earls, four other peers and sixteen baronets, had taken part in a race dinner.[31] In 1811 General William Dyott, a local notable and one of the trustees of the races, returned from the wars to start his lamentations in the privacy of his diary: 'with respect to carriages, compared with the races five-and-twenty years ago, when there were generally ten coaches and six, a dozen coaches and four; now the only set of horses was Lord Stafford's, and three or four coaches and four'. By 1825 Dyott was lamenting the failure of the aristocracy to attend the races, and he thought – wrongly as it turned out – that the 1842 meeting would be the last.[32]

Yet one of the main reasons why the pain inflicted by this decline was relatively limited was precisely that Lichfield had never been a very successful leisure town in the first place. Lichfield was categorically not what has been called a 'residential leisure town', defined as having thirty or more residential employers of taxable manservants in 1780. There were fifty-three such towns outside Middlesex and Surrey, nine of them with populations of less than 6,000

in 1801.[33] Lichfield, with a population of 4,712, had only twelve such employers, with another eight living very close to its boundaries. The combined total
of twenty put Lichfield eighty-seventh on the national list. Worcester had
sixty-six employers of manservants, Stafford thirty-seven and Derby seventy-
nine. This modest showing may have related to the lack of a large hinterland;
it was not helped by the bishop moving to Eccleshall early in the century,[34]
but even there he had only two manservants. Nor was Lichfield especially
well endowed with shops (see Figure 11.1), whilst improvements in urban
infrastructure were not enough to compensate for growing geographical
marginalisation – a process caused not only by transport links but also by
the growing attractions of other towns for the gentry. Erasmus Darwin of
Lichfield was one of the founders of the Lunar Society, but it was not acci-
dental that the society's meetings were so often held in Birmingham, or that
Darwin could raise only a small handful of members for his more local Botan-
ical Society.[35] A group of well-educated clergy in the Close was clearly not a
sufficient attraction. In any case, they had their limitations: Fanny Burney's
Evelina was published in 1778 but was unknown in the town in 1781 when
Samuel Johnson brought a copy.[36]

The town's governors did their best to improve amenities. However much
political animosity there may have been between town and Close, they co-
operated in making Lichfield more presentable. This was easy for both sides.
Lichfield was fortunate in having the Conduit Lands Trust, a body created in
the sixteenth century to supply the town with water. It came to be wealthier
than the corporation – the latter being 'too poor to be corrupt'[37] – and its role
increasingly overlapped with that of the corporation, indeed often seeming to
overshadow it. During the eighteenth century it had repeatedly paid for the
repair of the Guildhall. From the 1770s the trust provided the wealthier inhabitants with piped water, and during the same decade it agreed to a request
from Anna Seward and other inhabitants of the Close to 'serpentine' the river
outside the Close – Anna Seward being a great admirer of things metropoli-
tan and the trustees hoping that the gentry would think likewise. The trustees
were widening bridges and roads at least from the 1760s; they spent £488 on
paving in 1802 and were still paving streets during the 1840s, when they paid
a further £2,000 to repair the Guildhall. They contributed considerably
towards Lichfield's grammar school, to the great advantage of Garrick and
Johnson (both of whom studied there), paid some apprenticeship premiums
and also contributed towards poor relief. The Municipal Corporations Act led
to a radical corporation in 1835, which took over £22 in cash and a debt of
£260 from its predecessor. When it sought to take over the Conduit Lands
Trust's land, the latter withheld its grants for civic purposes, and the corporation rapidly retreated.[38] But whatever the corporation and the trust could

Figure 11.3 *Staffordshire turnpike trusts: income per mile, 1837–40*

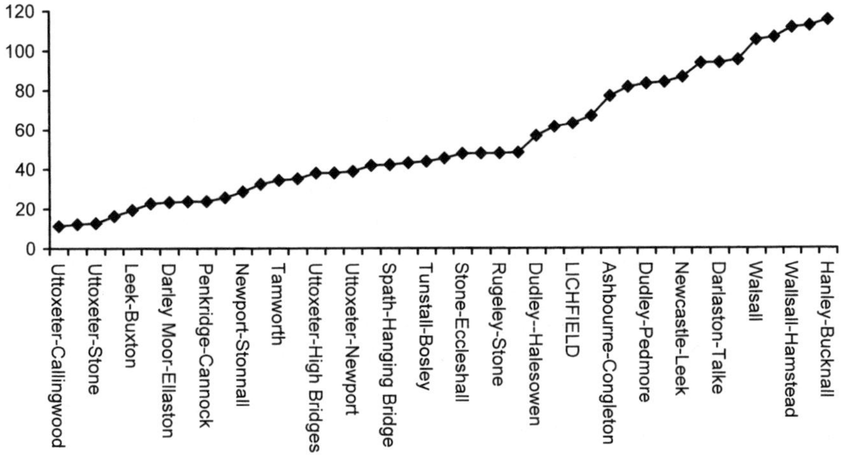

Source: Phillips and Turton, 'Staffordshire turnpike trusts'.

do between them was never enough. In the circumstances, Lichfield did as well as would be expected from a local centre that had lost its longer-distance trade and had never moved into the higher league of leisure towns. Like most other towns in the Midlands it depended largely upon local demand, and it is the growing local demand that provides the answer as to why so many smaller towns managed to prosper during the early nineteenth century. They were, of course, the indirect beneficiaries of regional industrialisation.

The expansion and the rural growth that industrialisation caused in its wider hinterland is difficult to quantify. Chartres has argued for a rapid growth in many rural services and crafts during the twenty or thirty years or so before 1851, especially in transport and in distribution: a natural function of urban expansion and transport improvements.[39] This argument is strengthened by the research of Phillips and Turton on the Staffordshire turnpike trusts. They have calculated the annual toll income per mile for the county's turnpike trusts for the years 1817–20, 1827–30 and 1837–40. The figures for 1837–40 are reproduced in Figure 11.3, which excludes the dense west Midlands urban network, where incomes were in excess of £120 per mile. Lichfield's position at this time was quite respectable. There were twenty-eight turnpike trusts with lower incomes per mile and only twenty-two with more. Its rank position had, of course, been falling during the 1820s and 1830s – in 1827–30 there were thirty-one turnpike trusts with lower incomes per mile, eleven with higher. Ten years earlier there had been twenty-six with lower incomes and ten with higher. Nevertheless, for 1817–20 annual toll income per mile was higher than in the Potteries, ten years later it was at the same level, and although by 1837–40 it was 50 per cent lower, this income was nevertheless 50 per cent higher than a Staffordshire average that excluded the Potteries and the Black Country.

Related to this, there are indications of the development of agriculture around Lichfield. The difficulties faced by wheat farmers after 1815 seem to have been countered by a growth of market gardening around Tamworth and Lichfield; there are reports of crops of peas, turnips and potatoes in 1818, and by the early 1830s 'immense quantities' of onions and carrots were being grown around Birmingham, Walsall and Wolverhampton. In general, land prices in Staffordshire were high in relation to rental value, and in 1833 they were higher still around Lichfield. An 1818 directory listed six market gardeners in Lichfield; an 1851 directory listed forty. In addition, in 1848 there were monthly or fortnightly cattle fairs at Lichfield, and at nearby Rugeley there was one of the largest horse fairs in the kingdom.[40]

The region's agriculture was at the core of Lichfield's adaptation. Lichfield had always held an important regional role and this continued. The town responded to changes in its environment: it was not and could not be an independent actor. In this respect Lichfield did not take an unusual path. It was gradually marginalised, but adapted itself without too much difficulty, and it did so by being an indirect beneficiary of economic development elsewhere. Its marginalisation was gradual, of long standing and obvious long before the railways. However, the period when this might have been expected to cause the most pain was the first half of the nineteenth century, particularly 1815–50. Yet the pain was not great: like many small towns Lichfield adjusted itself. Its manufacturing concentrated increasingly upon the finishing trades. Its shops and services still had their clientele. As a reflection of a reasonably successful transition, by the 1840s the ratio of persons per shop was just below the mean for Worcestershire and Warwickshire, while the ratio of population per service provider was nearly half that of towns of its size.[41] The larger part of Lichfield's adjustment was mediated through local small-town and agricultural development, itself largely dependent upon the rapidly growing conurbations of the east and west Midlands.[42] This led to a general increase of prosperity which, at least in the medium run, was able to override any depression in wheat farming. Industry and agriculture together created a wave upon which Lichfield floated, as did most of the smaller towns in the region.

Notes

1 Dyer, 'Midlands', p. 101.
2 Clark, 'Small towns', p. 736.

3 Clark, 'Small towns', p. 736.

4 Langton, 'Town growth', pp. 16–17; Thorpe, 'Lichfield'.

5 Reed, 'Small towns', pp. 135, 139.

6 VCH Staffordshire, vol. 2, p. 298.

7 Anna Seward complained of the Lichfield shops, but rather spoiled her case by comparing them with Bath: VCH Staffordshire, vol. 14, p. 21.

8 Corfield and Kelly, 'Giving directions'. See also Ellis, 'Regional and county centres', p. 685.

9 There are few references to the clergy in Sweet's chapter on 'urban culture and the urban renaissance' in her English Town. They are not in the index of Ellis's Georgian Town. In The Cambridge Urban History, vol. 2 references are sparse: there are hardly any in Clark's chapter on small towns and none in Borsay's on health and leisure resorts, although Clark and Houston discuss the vitality of eighteenth-century religion at some length: Clark and Houston, 'Culture and leisure', pp. 604–12. There are surprisingly few references in Borsay, Urban Renaissance to the role of the clergy in leisure towns. The nearest they come to being treated on their merits is in Ellis, 'Regional and county centres', Barry, 'Cultural patronage' and Gregory, 'Anglicanism'.

10 The Revd James Falconer, the cathedral chancellor, was a trustee of one of the local turnpike roads in 1764: Lichfield RO, D15/2/2. See also Lichfield RO, D15/12/20: account of expenses of Revd James Falconer, died 18 April 1809. His estate included seventy shares in the Grand Trunk Canal, which were sold in 1821 at £1,800 per share, three shares in the Wyrley and Essington Canal Navigation and a mortgage of £1,583 on the tolls on the Booth Lane Turnpike to Cheshire, as well as £347 with his bankers.

11 The Birmingham list included John Taylor (banker), Guest, Chance and Messrs Smith of Newhall Street: Lichfield RO, D30/6/1/11–12.

12 For Anna Seward, see Brewer, Pleasures of the Imagination, pp. 573–612. For a prolix account of the intellectual life of Lichfield see Seward, Dr Darwin.

13 Albert, Turnpike Road System, p. 35.

14 Phillips and Turton, 'Turnpike network'.

15 Quoted in Thorpe, 'Lichfield', pp. 182, 188, 189.

16 Phillips and Turton, 'Turnpike network'.

17 Barker and Gerhold, Rise and Rise, p. 27.

18 White, Staffordshire (1834), p. 153.

19 Lichfield RO, D 77/5/3, Lichfield Hall Book, 2 January 1837.

20 VCH Staffordshire, vol. 14, p. 25.

21 All the directories recorded some people working in agriculture, and the baptism registers and census enumerators' reports reported labourers, who have been omitted in Table 11.2.

22 General and Commercial Directory for 1818, part 2 (1818), pp. 183–93.

23 VCH Staffordshire, vol. 14, p. 28.

24 The directories used for this paper are: UBD; General and Commercial Directory for 1818, part 2; White, Staffordshire (1834 and 1851 editions). To study this in more detail would involve detailed work that distinguishes the larger inns from the smaller public houses and does not rely uncritically on the directories. Furthermore, these numbers were affected by changing licensing policies.

25 Trinder, Shrewsbury, pp. 15–16.

26 See Chapter 3, Table 3.1.

27 See Chapter 3, Table 3.4.

28 *VCH Staffordshire*, vol. 14, pp. 130–1.

29 PRO, MH12/1130, correspondence with poor law unions, Lichfield, 1834–38.

30 Based on a variety of sources: for Lichfield wage rates, Lichfield RO, D/16/5/9, D27/3/10, D/32/6/1/12, D661/8/1/2/6–7, D/126/3/2. These have been compared with Feinstein, 'Pessimism perpetuated' and Crafts and Mills, 'Trends in real wages in Britain'.

31 Hopkins, *Dr. Johnson's Lichfield*, p. 56.

32 Jeffery, *Dyott's Diary*, vol. 1, pp. 297, 315, 351, 370; vol. 2, pp. 37, 106, 228, 362, 374; *VCH Staffordshire*, vol. 14, p. 366.

33 Schwarz, 'Residential leisure towns'. The towns were Lewes, Peterborough, Stafford, Stamford, Chichester, Windsor, Winchester, Boston and Beverley.

34 *VCH Staffordshire*, vol. 14, p. 22.

35 Clark, *British Clubs and Societies*, p. 111.

36 *VCH Staffordshire*, vol. 14, p. 23.

37 *Lichfield Mercury*, 13 December 1833.

38 Laithwaite, *Conduit Lands Trust*, pp. 30–57, 81; *VCH Staffordshire*, vol. 14, p. 79.

39 Chartres, 'Country trades'. The chapter concentrates on the early nineteenth century, but p. 438 refers to the period 1750–1850.

40 *VCH Staffordshire*, vol. 6, pp. 106, 116.

41 For number of people per service provider, see Chapter 3, Table 3.1. The figure for towns with a population of 5,000–10,000 was 34.7 and Lichfield stood at 17.9. For number of people per shop, see Chapter 3, Table 3.4. The mean was 42.6; Lichfield's 163 retailers produced a figure of 41.6.

42 The state was of little help: it built a store for the militia in Lichfield, but barracks arrived only during the 1880s: *VCH Staffordshire*, vol. 14, p. 29.

PART III

The wider world: regional development in comparative context

12

National and international trade and the Midlands economy[1]

Malcolm Wanklyn

The Midlands, in the period 1760 to 1840 as today, was not a single economic region, but comprised a wide range of interlinked economies, some associated with *pays*, others with individual towns and their immediate environs, each of which produced a different surplus or mix of surpluses which were sold in a variety of markets, including the Midlands itself. Coal, for example, was very largely retained within the region: small quantities penetrated south-west England via the Severn, and a little from the east Midlands found its way into other parts of England and the Netherlands. This constriction in trade is, of course, evidence of competitors in the North-East and South Wales being better placed to cater for the coastal and overseas trade. Notwithstanding this, the output of the Midlands coalfields had increased very substantially by 1840 thanks to the demands of Midlands industry and the domestic fires of its expanding population. Moreover, extra-regional trade developed over time. The Grand Junction and Oxford canals opened up new markets for War-wickshire, Leicestershire and Staffordshire coal in the south Midlands and the Home Counties, whereas the Trent and Mersey Canal enabled Staffordshire coal to compete with Lancashire coal in Cheshire. The construction of rail-ways in the mid-nineteenth century further widened the market for Midlands coal in southern England.[2] In contrast, an increasing percentage of the agri-cultural surplus of the Midlands was retained to feed its growing population, though niche markets were retained or developed in fruit, vegetables, cheese and hops.

Selling in the home and the overseas market

For the Midlands manufacturing districts extra-regional and international trade were important, but the producers and distributors of the traded goods cannot be divided neatly into exporters and domestic traders, each with its own set of priorities, aspirations and experiences. The correspondence and account books of big producers for the home market, like Josiah Wedgwood, Matthew Boulton and the Darby family, show that they were heavily involved in exporting. Smaller producers may have been less so, but insufficient records survive to show how typical or untypical were men like John English, the Feckenham needle maker, and William Thursfield, the Broseley potter.[3] Moreover, the business practices employed in both types of commerce were not strikingly different.[4] Many involved in overseas trade appear not to have exported goods themselves. Instead their products went abroad through the auspices of merchants, like Richard Champion of Bristol and William Wilberforce of Hull, who assembled mixed cargoes of goods for export.[5] Producers also used intermediaries in the home market because of the difficulties in setting up an effective sales force of 'riders', whereas those who established display centres in London did not do so merely in the hope of attracting domestic customers.[6] Finally, improving communications with Bristol, Hull, Liverpool and London was not solely of value to those involved in the export trade. Moving goods coastwise was of vital importance in the operation of the home market for foodstuffs and coal. Also, the components used to make manufactured goods were often not native to the Midlands and therefore needed to be brought in from elsewhere in the United Kingdom or from overseas. Producers of better-quality ceramics in north Staffordshire, for example, were heavily dependent on clays from Devon and Cornwall from 1720 onwards, whereas the spinning mills of Derbyshire could not have operated without imported cotton wool.[7] The interest of manufacturers in promoting canal schemes reflects very clearly their ambition to have such bulky raw materials delivered to their doorsteps by water rather than hauled overland from the nearest ports on the Severn, the Trent or the Weaver. Similarly, traded goods despatched to other English regions were not necessarily for consumption in those regions. They might be carried overseas from there, as in the case of much Leicestershire hosiery, or employed in the manufacture of goods to be traded nationally and internationally. By 1760, for example, fire clay from Stourbridge was used in all parts of the country for making crucibles for glass manufacture.[8]

Towns within a region or *pays* can be conceived as being in a Darwinian struggle with one another for national and international trade in its various forms. Those successful increased in size and prosperity, whilst the unsuccessful ones degenerated into mere market towns. However, this notion of rivalry can be exaggerated. If they were not competing to market the same type of product, there was no reason why they should vie with one another for local commercial supremacy. Competition may have been more intense with towns in different parts of the country, sometimes in different parts of the world. For Kidderminster, for example, carpet-manufacturing rivals in the home market were in west Yorkshire and Scotland, not ten miles down the road; in the overseas market they were in the United States, France and Germany. Moreover, the most famous regional examples of battles of trade between towns – such as that between Bewdley and Stourport for the waterborne trade of Birmingham and the Black Country – turn out on closer examination not to be what historical legend has portrayed. Not only did Stourport remain a midget amongst towns, but Bewdley's economy did not go into decline until after 1825, fifty years after the construction of the Staffordshire and Worcestershire canals. The cause was not the loss of its function as a river port, but the collapse of its chemical and pewter industries.[9] Midlands towns often grouped together against the common foe, with the pottery manufacturers and some of the Birmingham metalware manufacturers making common cause through their proto-Chambers of Commerce against the emigration of skilled workers, the commercial treaty with France in 1786 and Orders in Council directed against the United States in 1810–12.[10] Long-distance transport undertakings were not intended merely to benefit the termini. The Birmingham–Liverpool railway scheme of 1824–26, for example, drew in Chester, the Potteries, the east Shropshire ironworks, Dudley and Stourbridge, which were to be linked to it by branch lines, even though the vast majority of the management committee and shareholders were from the Birmingham area.[11] Similarly, Birmingham metal goods manufacturers brought in their colleagues from Walsall and Wolverhampton to oppose the proposal to abolish the act forbidding the export of brass. They were also associated with the scheme to acquire a steady supply of copper via the Birmingham Mining and Copper Company.[12]

The importance of both internal and external trade to economic growth in England during the industrial revolution has been the subject of wide-ranging discussion for many years, but usually as a corollary to debates concerning the rate of economic growth and the standard of living of the working class. The significance of home demand in encouraging or nurturing industrial production has been touched on frequently, but academic comment has tended to be cautious rather than dogmatic and couched in terms of total demand, not that for manufactures.[13] Such caution is understandable given the absence of contemporary quantitative evidence as to the consumption patterns of workers.[14] Agricultural labourers, apart from those in high-waged districts adjacent to industrial areas, are thought to have been too poor to contribute anything substantial to the demand for manufactured items at any time between 1700 and 1840.[15] On the other hand, the ability of the industrial working class to do so may have increased so long as the price of foodstuffs remained low, that is until about 1790.[16] However, the extent to which they used their spare money to purchase more attractive foodstuffs like sugar rather than British manufactures is uncertain. For forty, fifty or possibly seventy years thereafter, the picture is one of gloom, rises in the prices of staple foodstuffs not being totally offset by reductions in the prices of fuel, sugar and tea.[17] Only workers with skills that were in short supply were able, though not necessarily willing, to increase their purchases of manufactures.[18] After 1830, there may have been an improvement in real wages, but there was not necessarily an increased propensity to purchase British manufactures. Indeed a recent contributor to the debate claims that the demands of other expenditure imperatives reduced the purchase of manufactures by the working classes.[19] As for the middle class, the consumption of farmers was probably of significance, particularly when food prices were high (as between 1790 and 1812), but even so higher poor rates over much of southern England caused by agricultural under-employment reduced their disposable income, as did rises in rents and the costs of inputs.[20] Of greater importance was probably the growth in urban 'white collar' employment, but in 1840 the numbers thus employed fell far short of those working in agriculture, mining or manufacturing.[21]

Given the level of pessimism amongst historians concerning home demand, it is difficult to explain the great increase in production of English manufactures between 1700 and 1840 without invoking export markets. There is no doubt that overseas trade experienced remarkable growth during the period, but it has been persuasively argued that this was a supply-driven rather than a demand-driven expansion. Significant changes in the technology and management helped entrepreneurs to operate larger units of production, and the resulting economies of scale enabled British goods to be sold at competitive prices on world markets.[22] But it was not merely a matter of price: British industry produced a succession of new lines that were attractive to fickle consumers. The corollary of this was that, without a secure market external to the United Kingdom, producers would have been faced with a crisis of overproduction, as cheapness had been achieved only by producing goods in such quantities as to swamp the home market. In other words overseas markets provided a lifeline to the English economy by taking an excess of goods that the domestic market could not absorb. Yet overseas markets were far from secure. Panicky petitions sent to Parliament from Midlands industrial districts when there was war, or the prospect of war, in important markets seem to provide evidence of over-dependence, but it is important to beware of overreaction on the part of the petitioners, whether deliberate or involuntary. One needs also to be wary of comments from individuals, however famous. As early as 1771 Josiah Wedgwood wrote that nothing but a foreign market would enable him to clear his stocks, but his concentration on the middle- and upper-class market, and his notoriously high prices, made him untypical.[23]

The language Sir Richard Whitworth employed in his pamphlet in support of canals written five years earlier emphasised that production would be encouraged because of cheaper inputs, not that excess output could be more readily moved to markets overseas: 'inland navigations will encourage old manufacturers to work with fresh vigour now that their materials come cheap to them'.[24] Only in the case of Worcester's trade in undyed cloth in the years before 1760 does there appear to have been an excessive, and ultimately disastrous, reliance on export markets.[25] Also, evidence that new technology resulted in crises of overproduction is less apparent in most Midlands industries than they are, for example, in Lancashire. In ceramics steam power was little employed, skill counted more than machinery and increases in output were achieved by building more, rather than significantly larger, plant.[26] In the east Midlands hosiery trades and in carpet manufacture a succession of small technological advances using existing plant and power sources appears to have been the pattern, though both benefited from cheaper inputs of factory-produced thread.[27] Cutting prices in the Midlands hardware trades appears to have been achieved largely by technical and organisational changes that were labour-saving, not by mass production using steam-powered machinery.[28] Of greater significance still for non-textile trades were developments in the transport infrastructure, in which entrepreneurs were enthusiastically involved. Their main object was to increase output because of the demand engendered by the lower prices at which they could now sell their produce beyond the bounds of their *pays* thanks to the lower cost of inputs.

Monitoring changes in the scale of domestic and foreign sales other than in very general terms is extremely difficult. Literary evidence is frequently skewed by the self-interest of the witnesses, and even when it is not, what exist are 'guestimates' based on the range of personal and second-hand data the writer could amass. The official record is superficially more impressive, but ultimately disappointing in its scope and accuracy. With regard to home trade, all that exists is information concerning the limited number of products that were subject to excise duties. In the case of exported goods, a wider range of sources survives, but all are to a greater or lesser extent problematic. In the first place, the statistics produced from customs records differentiate between London and the out-ports until 1782, but not between the out-ports themselves.[29] That said, in the case of certain commodities produced very largely in the Midlands – including carpets, hosiery and pottery – national figures for exports are a useful indication of overall trends. In addition, although overseas port books provide detailed information about items being exported and their destinations, they do not necessarily provide a complete record of trade even for commodities not likely to attract smugglers. Moreover, as most items were shipped overseas under the name of an exporting merchant, not that of the producer, it is impossible in many cases to identify their source. Nails exported from Hull, for example, could have come from the Black Country, from Derbyshire or from the villages around Sheffield; and glassware shipped to the West Indies from Bristol could have been produced in the Stour valley or in the city itself.[30] There are some exceptions. Droitwich salt bound for Virginia was shipped from Bristol under the names of John Chance, Edward Jackson and William Perkes, who operated fleets of boats on the river Severn. Other merchants including John Sandford, who specialised in gloves, William Turton, who only shipped nails, and Samuel Burgess, who specialised in hops, may also turn out to have an association with the west Midlands, but the prospects of major progress in this direction are limited.[31] Finally, for three of the four ports of the Midlands, Bristol, Liverpool and London, port books no longer survive, or are very uncommon, for the second half of the eighteenth century. Other sources can serve to some extent as substitutes. However, the Bristol Port Presentments, which survive for the periods 1773–80 and 1801–18, employ the same limiting conventions as the port books, whilst newspaper advertisements, which have been used to study Bristol's and Liverpool's trade after the port-book era, are more informative about the cargoes of ships carrying imports than about those of ships carrying exports.[32]

Demographic trends, if used with caution, can provide a crude, but more systematic, indicator of levels of economic activity. If correlated with reliable data concerning exports, they may also shed light on what was happening to the home market for certain goods. That there is a causal connection between population and economic activity is implicit in the frequent coincidence of demographic downturns with trading difficulties. Shrewsbury, for example, lost 5 per cent of its population between 1831 and 1851 owing to the eclipse of its coaching trade under the impact of the railways and the closure of one of its two linen factories.[33] Amongst smaller towns such as Broseley, Ludlow and Upton-upon-Severn, demographic stagnation in the second quarter of the century was associated with industrial or commercial crisis linked, respectively, with iron smelting, glove making and overland trade. Conversely the spectacular growth of small settlements like Kingswinford and Willenhall in Staffordshire, and Radford and Basford on the outskirts of Nottingham, was a direct consequence of rapid industrialisation.[34] Burton-upon-Trent's success in adapting to changed economic conditions is reflected in its population trends. In the second half of the eighteenth century its population had steadily risen as it responded to the demand for sweet, dark cask beer from the countries around the Baltic Sea. Between 1811 and 1831, when the town was losing this trade (owing to the erection of tariff walls by Baltic countries) and trying to expand its home market for lighter beers, its population increased by less than 10 per cent. In the next twenty years, however, it more than doubled thanks to the construction of large breweries to cater for the tremendous growth of exports of Indian pale ale, mainly to the Empire: a trade that had originated in London but which the Burton brewers were better able to cater for because of the qualities of the water they used. Expansion was assisted by the railways, which reached the town in 1839.[35]

Success in manufacturing and growth in population were not invariably linked. When powered machinery was introduced, it could be followed by a decline in the demand for labour leading to out-migration, as at Kidderminster after the introduction of the steam-powered carpet loom in the 1850s.[36] However, the principal examples of technology-related losses of employment were in branches of the textile industry which, if important locally, were not of great significance in the Midlands region as a whole. Indeed, in the case of machine-made lace, it was other parts of the country that suffered from the resulting concentration of the trade into the east Midlands. Population might also rise rapidly through natural increase even if there was long-standing under-employment, particularly if there were legal restraints on the mobility of labour and no opportunities for alternative employment at a reasonable distance. But this was not typical of the Midlands: the growth in population and lack of out-migration in areas where there was distress after 1815 suggests a different scenario, as will be discussed below.

The metal trades

The production of metalwares was probably the most important trade in the Midlands. It was centred on Birmingham and the Black Country, the combined population of which rose from about 30,000 in 1700 to approaching 500,000 in 1851.[37] Only a minority, however, would have been directly involved in making metal goods. Others were employed in ancillary trades, such as iron manufacture and coal-mining, which expanded considerably during the period. A third group were active in transport and retailing, which underpinned production and were dependent on industrial growth. Locally produced coal had long been important as fuel for domestic hearths and for heating and shaping iron and brass, and its production shadowed the growth in manufacturing. Moreover, it acquired new uses. For much of the eighteenth century metalworkers generally used malleable iron that had been smelted and refined using charcoal. Some was transported up the river Severn from the Forest of Dean; much of the rest came from Sweden and Russia via the river Trent or overland from London. This explains the enthusiasm for canals amongst members of the Birmingham and Black Country business community: they reduced the cost of transport of Swedish iron from the Trent by a quarter.[38] From about 1770, however, an increasing quantity of iron was smelted locally using coke, and from 1790 coke was also used more widely for converting pig-iron into malleable iron, thus cheapening costs, most notably that of transport.[39] In the nineteenth century the great increase in the production of iron goods of all sorts depended on local raw materials and producer goods, but it also created employment at a distance. By 1851 east Shropshire pig-iron, for example, largely helped supply the needs of the Black Country.[40]

The export trade was without doubt of great significance to the growth of population and trade in Birmingham and its environs. In the early 1720s, about 1,400 tons of iron and ironwares were shipped down the Severn to Bristol each year, just under half of the quantity the country exported.[41] The ratio between the Severn trade and the overseas trade does not seem unreasonable if one adds Sheffield's exports and Midlands ironwares sent to London overland for sale overseas, and then allows for the fact that some of the ironwares sent down the Severn were for home consumption in the west of England. By the late 1750s petitioners to the House of Commons were claiming that at least 20,000 people worked in the 'toy trade' in Birmingham and adjacent towns producing goods worth £600,000 a year, of which £500,000 was sold overseas. However, the total value of exports of wrought-iron goods and brasswares from England at this time was about £400,000 and included wares produced in the Sheffield region, in Shropshire, Bristol and London and elsewhere. Such discrepancies were often the result of customs valuations being lower than real valuations, but the difference was much less than that.[42] Fifty years later Thomas Attwood gave evidence to Parliament in connection with the Orders in Council directed against trade with the United States that Birmingham and district produced goods worth about £2,000,000 a year, of which about £1,300,000 was exported.[43] His reliability as a witness has been criticised, but the overall totals accord well with the national average figures for iron and ironware exports: about £2,700,000 for 1804–6.[44] However, Attwood's claims that £1,000,000 of the exports of the central Midlands went to the United States must be mistaken, as the average for 1804–6 for the whole of the country was well under half that amount. Both estimates therefore include an element of exaggeration. Inferences drawn from William Whitehouse's remarks concerning nailing made on the same occasion also raise considerable concern. He estimated that the home market absorbed about half of the output and the United States about a quarter. However, sales of nails to the United States had declined both numerically and as a percentage of the whole over time from between 40 and 50 per cent during the 1760s to 20 per cent in 1795 and 14 per cent in 1800. Moreover, the average quantity of nails exported annually to the USA between 1785 and 1800 was only half of what it had been in the period 1750–70, and not that much higher than in the first quarter of the eighteenth century.[45]

Unfortunately estimates for home consumption cannot be critically evaluated in a similar manner, but they seem unduly low given that on both occasions the country was involved in a major war. Despite Birmingham's reputation as a centre for the manufacture of guns and other weapons of war, its other trades were almost certainly damaged by disruptions to its European and American markets.[46] Rising food prices would also have served to restrict the domestic market. Trading problems therefore probably explain the relatively slow rate of population growth in Birmingham around the turn of the nineteenth century. In the 1790s the percentage increase may have been very small indeed, and in the following decade growth was only slightly higher than in the nation as a whole and well below the rate of increase for other large industrial cities like Manchester and Leeds. Moreover, the demographic experience of Black Country towns that produced metalwares (for example, Wolverhampton and Walsall) was very similar to that of Birmingham, and in marked contrast to that of other settlements (Bilston, Wednesbury and Dudley) that produced coal and iron. These experienced growth rates in excess of 20 per cent, whereas Rowley Regis, a nail-making settlement, had fewer inhabitants in 1811 than in 1801.[47]

The most recent assessments of Birmingham's economy in the early nineteenth century have nothing to say about the importance of its export trade after 1815.[48] National figures for the export of the types of metalware produced in Birmingham and the Black Country show a 30 per cent increase in value between 1814–16 and 1844–46, but a much more marked increase in the following decade. It has thus been postulated that the value of overseas sales of traditional hardware had doubled by 1854–56.[49] Yet this represents a much slower growth rate than had been the case in the late eighteenth century, and it has been claimed that trading problems, and the associated unemployment, explain political and social unrest in Birmingham in the thirty years after Waterloo. However, the population of the town continued to grow at above the national rate, and indeed more than doubled between 1811 and 1851, largely as a result of in-migration. Moreover, as a centre of the metal industries, it was not apparently losing ground to Sheffield, whose population increased at almost exactly the same rate.[50] This suggests a greater buoyancy in home than in export markets, but may reflect immigrant labour being attracted into Birmingham in periods of good trade like those that preceded the banking crises of 1827 and 1836. The paradox of immigration combined with complaints of poor trade may, however, be explained by the fact that some activities, like gun making, were doing badly because of lack of government orders, whilst others, like the manufacture of brass goods, were doing extremely well though the growth of steam power and of the gas industry.[51] The link between population and economic performance in Birmingham therefore merits closer investigation.

Ceramics

Evidence concerning the pottery industry shows similar discrepancies between some contemporary comments, the official figures for exports and a more recent attempt to assess growth in production based on plant. Two observations by Josiah Wedgwood, one made in the 1760s and one in the early 1780s, suggest that a very high percentage of the output was exported, though in the first case he may have been referring merely to the activities of himself and his partners. The employers' confederation known as the Potters' Committee repeated Wedgwood's assessment almost word for word a few years later at a time when the ceramics industries were apparently experiencing their first major surge in the overseas trade, and they are not likely merely to have been relying on his assessment.[52] Soon afterwards, however, the Revolutionary and Napoleonic wars apparently caused serious marketing problems, as much of the ceramics trade was with Europe. Such difficulties were compounded by conflict with the United States between 1810 and 1813 and by reduced demand in the home market. However, the latter is based upon estimates of production for the whole of the country that show a 25 per cent increase in the number of potteries in the Midlands between 1790 and 1810.[53] There are other signs of growth rather than stagnation in the home market. Ceramics were in the process of replacing pewter, partly because they were lighter and more attractive to the eye, partly because of the discomfort associated with trying to drink hot beverages like tea and coffee from metal vessels.[54] Moreover, as pottery was both cheap and easily breakable, home consumption per annum probably grew faster than the total population, though there are no figures whatsoever to support this hypothesis.

Absence of figures is not a problem with the export trade, but establishing the quantity of ceramics exported in the eighteenth century is impossible because customs records from before 1812 group together ceramics and glassware. However, such is the increase in the two combined that the trade in ceramics must have grown very fast, there being no reason for believing that the export of glasswares was increasing at an even higher rate.[55] What is somewhat surprising is the smooth upward curve in external trade. From between one and three million pieces per year for the period from 1710 to 1758, the annual average increased to between four and seven million between 1759 and 1779, to eight to fourteen million between 1780 and 1787 and to seventeen to thirty-three million between 1791 and 1808.[56] The relevance of export figures to the scale of manufacturing in the Potteries increased over time as the district increasingly dominated national production.[57] It is possible that the export figures from after 1765 underestimate the trade in pottery and glass. The exports of earthenware alone from the port of Hull amounted to over a third of the total number of pieces of glass and earthenware exported in 1770, a not unexpected figure given the importance of the European market, but 70 per cent in 1780 and about 85 per cent in 1787 seem far too high, even though there were few glassworks within the broad catchment area of Hull. This anomaly may have been the result of different practices in calculating how many pieces of pottery each crate contained, but this cannot explain an even more disquieting conclusion from the analysis of central government records, namely that the quantity of pottery exported in 1814, a moderately prosperous year, was higher than that for pottery and glassware combined in good years such as 1801–2 and 1806.[58] The export figures show a significant increase from then to the end of the period, with overseas sales of pottery more than doubling in quantity, a development that is more than matched by the growth of population in the three Potteries parishes, which rose from circa 42,000 in 1815 to almost 100,000 in 1851.[59] Given some economies in scale produced by such processes as the use of transfers for decorating cheaper wares, this suggests a buoyant home market, combined with growth in the service sector in response to variegated demands of a larger population of potters.[60] The emphasis which contemporary accounts placed on growth in the overseas sales may have been no more than a natural reaction to growth in the American market, which in 1850 took more than twice as much pottery in terms of value as it had done in 1814.[61]

Textiles

In the case of textiles and apparel, there were significant differences between the markets for the various branches of this industry, which included carpet making in Kidderminster and Bridgnorth, stocking weaving in Leicestershire and Nottinghamshire and in the valley of the Warwickshire Avon, silk manufacture at Leek, cotton spinning in Derbyshire, glove making in Worcester and linen manufacture for a time at Shrewsbury. For most, overseas sales were an important element, but some faced fierce competition in home markets from imports and from production elsewhere in the country. Improving communication by water was of less concern than was the case in many trades, although raw cotton was brought by canal and river to Strutt's mills in Derbyshire and yarn to the Kidderminster carpet and stuff manufacturers.[62] Entrepreneurs were interested in canal and railway schemes that would reduce the costs of coal, initially for their workforce's domestic hearths and later to power their steam engines.[63] Given the complexity and variety of the experience of the textile trades in the Midlands, discussion will focus on the most important sector in terms of employment and output, the hosiery and lace industries.

Woollen and silk hosiery produced on framework-knitting machines had been widely spread across the Midlands and south-east England in the first quarter of the eighteenth century, though with some concentration in Leicestershire, south Nottinghamshire and lowland Derbyshire. By 1800 this area dominated manufacture of such hosiery and a wide variety of other types of knitwear (see Chapter 9).[64] Little can be said about the home market for such goods, as contemporaries appear to have taken it for granted and there was not the avalanche of representations to the House of Commons as in the case of the metalworking trades. In 1812, however, an allegedly reliable witness estimated that just over half of the cotton hosiery was being sold at home.[65]

The export of men's woollen stockings through Hull was well established by 1702 – not surprising given the importance of central Europe as a market throughout the eighteenth century[66] – although some of these stockings may have been produced by the hand-knitters of Yorkshire and Cumbria. Subsequently most east Midlands hosiery intended for export appears to have gone overland to London. Stockings being sent abroad via Bristol probably originated in Tewkesbury, which was a significant centre of frame-knitting until the third decade of the nineteenth century.[67] The quantity of woollen stockings exported nationally remained remarkably stable throughout the eighteenth century, with a downturn in some European markets being offset by increased trade with North America. The importance of this Atlantic trade appears to have continued into the mid-nineteenth century, though the figures for before and after 1810 are not strictly comparable. What is clear, however, is that up to 1850 the volume of exports of woollen hosiery remained on a level. This would not have been possible, as contemporaries realised, without cuts in wages driving down prices; otherwise cheap European goods would have swept English woollens from overseas markets.[68] Surprisingly, the stagnation in overseas demand did nothing to stem a rapid flow of workers into the industry, underpinning Leicester's growth from 23,000 in 1811 to 61,000 in 1851, over twice the national average. Moreover, the number of stocking frames in the town may have increased by a factor of ten between 1800 and 1850. The missing element in the equation is probably a significant increase in home demand caused by the lower prices of knitwear, even though this was denied by a commission of enquiry, which reported in 1844 to the effect that demand was stationary.[69]

With regard to cotton knitwear, the picture is very different. In 1700 output had been small, but the much cheaper cost of thread brought about by the textile innovations of the eighteenth century brought down prices and made cotton goods more affordable.[70] Lower prices had some impact on home markets for knitwear, but between 1790 and 1840 working-class demand was held back, as manufacturers were well aware, by the high cost of foodstuffs, and the fact that, unlike cups and bowls, knitwear could be repaired.[71] Cheaper prices apparently had a more significant effect on exports, which rose very significantly between the early 1790s and 1808. On the supply side, sales in both home and overseas markets were also boosted by manufacturers producing new types of product which then became fashionable. However, a change in men's fashions in Europe and the Americas from breeches and long hose to trousers and short hose had a major effect on demand. Moreover, competition in Europe and the United States increased, and there were no major cost-cutting innovations available until the very end of the period.[72] As with the woollen branch of the industry, exports could be sustained only by taking advantage of the impact of excessive supply of labour on wage costs to reduce prices at which goods could be sold overseas. The results, however, were not at all impressive, as the average annual volume of exports increased by less than 10 per cent between 1814–16 and 1834–43. Once again, falling prices should have increased sales in the domestic market,[73] but the evidence is not convincing. One authority suggested an increase in production of three-quarters between 1812 and 1844; another that demand was stagnant. Moreover, as in the case of ceramics and metalwares, evidence as to the industry's fortunes in the overseas market gives cause for concern. It seems unlikely that only around 120,000 dozen pairs could have been exported in the best years just before 1810 and 376,000 per annum in 1814–16, a period of variable trade. Similarly a supposedly reliable witness, who estimated for a Nottingham newspaper in 1844 that the city and its environs sold half a million dozen pairs of socks per year in the United States, was guilty of extreme hyperbole. The total quantity of cotton hosiery exported per annum for the period 1834 to 1843 was 15 per cent below that figure.[74]

The fortunes of the knitting industry as portrayed in the literature are not those reflected in the population figures for the *pays* in which it was concentrated. The first decade of the nineteenth century was seen subsequently as a golden age, but this is not obvious from the census returns for 1801 and 1811. Only in Nottinghamshire was there a larger population increase than average, and this reflected the growth in exports of the cotton knitwear particularly associated with that county. Also, the percentage increase in population in the two counties most involved in the knitting industry, Leicestershire and Nottinghamshire, was below the national rate in the second quarter of the nineteenth century, seemingly reflecting stagnation in trade. On the other hand, the increase in the populations of the two county towns and of some of the industrial villages between 1811 and 1851 was equivalent to that of similar-sized settlements in Lancashire and Staffordshire.[75] Moreover, the number of frames in the Midlands counties increased by over 70 per cent between 1812 and 1844.[76] This development has yet to be convincingly explained in the context of a stagnant hosiery industry. Despite the evidence of under-employment, particularly in the period 1837–44, the implication is that production increased, which, given the flat export performance of the industry, can be explained only by greater sales in the home market, possibly of poorer-quality goods produced on the larger frames concentrated in the towns and big industrial villages.[77]

Conclusion

The population of the Midlands increased from about 850,000 in 1700 to about 2,250,000 in 1851.[78] Much of the increase was in towns with populations in excess of 15,000 and in the industrial districts.[79] In the absence of evidence of permanent industrial under-employment, other than possibly in declining trades in Birmingham and the east Midlands, it can be inferred that population increase was associated with a massive increase in productive employment, and thus in the quantity of goods being produced and sold. Beyond that the conclusions of this chapter can only be tentative because of the imperfections of the evidence currently available. All that one can say with confidence is that overseas trade was important for Midlands manufacturing industries, and that its significance changed over time, but that most of what was produced in most decades was probably sold in the United Kingdom. The home market tends to be overlooked by historians, not least because of the lack of quantitative data to compare with that generated by overseas trade. Moreover, qualitative sources tend to exaggerate the significance of exports, particularly when the audience being addressed was central government, whose policies affected the conditions under which overseas trade was conducted. However, if the home trade was as significant for Midland manufacturers in the period 1700–1840 as the incomplete and imperfect evidence currently available suggests, its scale and operations need to be re-investigated and re-evaluated, not least because of the contribution such findings may make to the ongoing debate over the standard of living.

Notes

1 I am most grateful to John Benson and Paul Henderson for their comments on a draft of this chapter.
2 Aldcroft and Freeman, *Transport*, pp. 128–9, 132–3.
3 Jones, 'The country trade', p. 26; Trinder, *Shropshire*, p. 86.
4 Weatherill, *Pottery Trade*, pp. 78–88; Reilly, *Josiah Wedgwood*, p. 217; Robinson, 'Boulton and Fothergill', pp. 65–79; Morgan, *Bristol*, p. 103.
5 PRO, E 190 359/6, Hull overseas port book, June–December 1726; Jackson, *Hull*, pp. 128–9.

6 Reilly, *Josiah Wedgwood*, pp. 40–3, 101–2, 223–5; Fitton and Wadsworth, *Strutts and Arkwrights*, pp. 47–50; Jones, 'The country trade', pp. 24–8, 32–9.

7 Hussey *et al.*, *Gloucester Port Books*, p. 83; Hussey, *Coastal and River Trade*, pp. 75–9; Beckwith, 'River trade', p. 7.

8 Chapman, 'British hoisery industry', pp. 14–15.

9 Pennell, 'Bewdley'.

10 Thomas, *Staffordshire Potteries*, pp. 141–67; Wright, *Chronicles*, pp. 11–15.

11 *Aris's Birmingham Gazette*, 13, 20 September 1824, 26 September 1825.

12 Wright, *Chronicles*, p. 15; Hamilton, *Copper and Brass*, pp. 219–20, 224, 233–4; Hutton, *Birmingham*, pp. 329–31.

13 O'Brien and Engerman, 'Income and its distribution', pp. 178–9.

14 Horrell and Humphries, 'Living standards', pp. 872–4, use extensive data from household budgets to shed light on expenditure, but the bleak findings do not inspire confidence. In the Midlands, most of the budgets analysed derive from the Leicestershire and Nottinghamshire hosiery district in the early 1840s, a particularly depressed period when real wages were at their lowest. Indeed it is unfortunate for historians trying to gain as representative a data set as possible that much of the quantifiable material was compiled in periods of great distress and related to those groups of workers that were most affected.

15 O'Brien, 'Agriculture', pp. 784–5. For the rest of the period their real income did not improve.

16 Eversley, 'Home market', p. 209; Cole, 'Factors in demand', p. 62.

17 Feinstein, 'Pessimism perpetuated', pp. 642–8; Clark, Huberman and Lindert, 'British food puzzle', p. 233.

18 Pottery workers in north Staffordshire, for example: see Botham and Hunt, 'Wages in Britain', pp. 392–3.

19 Horrell, 'Home demand', pp. 590–2. However, her conclusions are based on analysis of data sets very similar to those used in Horrell and Humphries, 'Living standards'.

20 O'Brien, 'Agriculture', p. 785; Chambers and Mingay, *Agricultural Revolution*, p. 118.

21 Lindert and Williamson, 'English workers'; Mitchell and Deane, *Historical Statistics*, p. 60.

22 Crafts, *British Economic Growth*, p. 48.

23 Reilly, *Josiah Wedgwood*, p. 217.

24 *VCH Staffordshire*, vol. 2, p. 287.

25 Mann, *Clothing Industry*, pp. 42–3.

26 Weatherill, 'Pottery industry', pp. 22–3.

27 Chapman, 'British hoisery innovation', pp. 25–8, 30–2; Bartlett, *Carpeting the Millions*, pp. 4, 9–15.

28 Weatherill, 'Pottery industry', p. 23; Berg, *Age of Manufactures*, pp. 203–4, 267–8. Thomas, *Staffordshire Potteries*, pp. 67–9, grossly overemphasises the employment of steam power by assuming that all the steam engines in Staffordshire were located in the Potteries.

29 Ashton, introduction to Schumpeter, *English Trade Statistics*, pp. 1–2.

30 Beckett, *East Midlands*, pp. 233, 288; Hey, *Rural Metalworkers*, pp. 43–4.

31 PRO, E176 1160/3, fols 13, 15, 19, 38, 43; 1189/1, fols 4, 7, Bristol overseas port books 1702, 1720.

32   Avon Central Reference Library, Bristol, B11126–11151; Hyde, *Liverpool*, pp. 34 and 221n.

33   Trinder, *Shrewsbury*, p. 19; *VCH Shropshire*, vol. 2, p. 227.

34   *VCH Staffordshire*, vol. 1, pp. 324, 326; see also Chapter 8 of this volume.

35   Matthias, *Brewing Industry*, pp. 175–91; *VCH Staffordshire*, vol. 1, p. 372; Owen, *Burton-on-Trent*, pp. 76–9.

36   Smith, *Carpet Weavers*, pp. 258–61, 272–3.

37   Rowlands, *West Midlands*, pp. 173–5; *VCH Staffordshire*, vol. 1, pp. 324, 326; *VCH Warwickshire*, vol. 2, p. 186.

38   Rowlands, *Masters and Men*, p. 62; Jackson, *Hull*, p. 20.

39   Court, *Midlands Industries*, p. 197.

40   Trinder, *Industrial Revolution in Shropshire*, pp. 144–5.

41   Hussey, *Coastal and River Trade*, p. 78.

42   Schumpeter, *English Trade Statistics*, pp. 20–1; Robinson, 'Boulton and Fothergill', p. 63.

43   *VCH Warwickshire*, vol. 8, p. 117.

44   Hopkins, *Manufacturing Town*, pp. 36–7, 72–3; Court, *Midlands Industries*, p. 197; Davis, *Industrial Revolution*, p. 96.

45   Court, *Midlands Industries*, p. 209; Schumpeter, *English Trade Statistics*, pp. 20–2, 25–8, 64; Smith, 'Market for manufactures', pp. 682, 687.

46   Hopkins, *Manufacturing Town*, p. 72–3.

47   Mitchell and Deane, *Historical Statistics*, pp. 19, 24–7; Hopkins, *Manufacturing Town*, pp. 73–5; *VCH Staffordshire*, vol. 1, p. 326; *VCH Worcestershire*, vol. 4, p. 472.

48   Hopkins, *Manufacturing Town*; Behagg, *Politics and Production*.

49   Davis, *Industrial Revolution*, pp. 26–8, 64.

50   Smith, *Conflict and Compromise*; Mitchell and Deane, *Historical Statistics*, pp. 24–6.

51   Hopkins, *Manufacturing Town*, pp. 43–8.

52   Reilly, *Josiah Wedgwood*, p. 217; *VCH Staffordshire*, vol. 2, p. 116.

53   Weatherill, 'Pottery industry', pp. 25–8, 40.

54   Thomas, *Staffordshire Potteries*, pp. 103–4.

55   Weatherill, 'Pottery industry', p. 16.

56   Calculations of the population of the 'Five Towns' give c. 4,000 inhabitants in 1732, c. 16,000 in 1785 and c. 31,000 in 1811: Stobart, 'Burslem as a town', p. 124.

57   Weatherill, 'Pottery industry', pp. 39–41.

58   Schumpeter, *English Trade Statistics*, pp. 20–2 and 25–8; Weatherill, 'Pottery industry', pp. 16, 24, 31–2. After 1814 the figures for exports are for ceramics alone.

59   *VCH Staffordshire*, vol. 2, p. 27. Lower population figures are cited in Stobart, 'Burslem as a town', p. 124, but the rate of growth was possibly even higher: c. 31,000 in 1811, c. 68,000 in 1841.

60   Thomas, *Staffordshire Potteries*, p. 103; Stobart, 'Burslem as a town', p. 133.

61   Weatherill, 'Pottery industry', p. 24, 31–2; *VCH Staffordshire*, vol. 2, p. 27.

62   Smith, *Carpet Weavers*, p. 25; Fitton and Wadsworth, *Strutts and Arkwrights*, pp. 289–91; Beckwith, 'River trade', p. 7; Jackson, *Hull*, p. 30.

63   Hanford, *Stroudwater Canal*, p. 316.

64   Beckett, *East Midlands*, p. 284; Chapman, 'British hoisery industry', p. 19.

65 Church, *Economic and Social Change*, p. 26; but one wonders how reliable the evidence is given the need of witnesses to provide simple and understandable explanations in order to be persuasive. The industry's problems on the demand side were complex, but one condition that was absolutely clear was that Britain was at war with its principal overseas customers for hosiery, the United States and a Europe dominated by Napoleon.

66 4,448 dozen pairs were exported in 1702: Jackson, *Hull*, p. 55; Schumpeter, *English Trade Statistics*, p. 69.

67 Kerridge, *Textile Manufacture*, pp. 133–4; Patterson, *Radical Leicester*, p. 65; Rath, 'Tewkesbury hosiery industry', pp. 149–51.

68 Schumpeter, *English Trade Statistics*, pp. 29–34; Church, *Economic and Social Change*, p. 20.

69 Beckett, *East Midlands*, pp. 286, 355; Chapman, 'British hoisery industry', p. 17; Brown, *Leicester*, p. 64.

70 Beckett, *East Midlands*, p. 285.

71 Wells, *British Hosiery Indusrty*, p. 110.

72 Chapman, 'British hoisery industry', pp. 29–30.

73 Church, *Economic and Social Change*, pp. 29, 31, 40–51.

74 Schumpeter, *English Trade Statistics*, pp. 39–43; Church, *Economic and Social Change*, pp. 28–9.

75 Beckett, *East Midlands*, p. 355; Chapter 8 above; Mitchell and Deane, *Historical Statistics*, pp. 24–6.

76 Chapman, 'British hoisery innovation', p. 19.

77 William Felkin, a local businessman, alleged that output increased by about 80 per cent between 1812 and 1844, but his figures have been dismissed as rough estimates and somewhat peripheral to the argument about the problems of the industry: Church, *Economic and Social Change*, p. 30. They may be incorrect, but they fit in well with the demographic record.

78 BPP, 1843, 22, pp. 36–7; Mitchell and Deane, *Historical Statistics*, pp. 24–6.

79 Beckett, *East Midlands*, p. 354; *VCH Staffordshire*, vol. 1, p. 320; *VCH Warwickshire*, vol. 2, p. 184; *VCH Worcestershire*, vol. 4, p. 446; *VCH Shropshire*, vol. 2, p. 219.

13

The growth of urban industrial regions: Belgian developments in comparative perspective, 1750–1850

Hilde Greefs, Bruno Blondé and Peter Clark

Introduction

Towards the close of the eighteenth century, isolated areas of advanced industrial production, manufacturing on a large scale for long-distance markets, multiplied across Europe. Some of the most extensive industrial areas emerged in Britain, enveloping, as we have seen in this book, much of an urban region such as the Midlands. Elsewhere the pattern was more uneven. Although some textile manufactures spread in northern Italy, especially in the small towns and villages in the triangle between Milan, Turin and Genoa, and also in Catalonia (in and around Barcelona), the most important industrial activity was to be found in western Europe. In the Northern Netherlands, the old textile towns of Leiden and Haarlem decayed, losing their manufactures to the countryside, but Germany saw rural charcoal iron production in the Sauerland and Siegerland, part of the future Ruhr area, and in the south traditional towns like Nuremberg maintained their metal crafts, whilst the textile putting-out system flourished in certain rural districts.[1] In revolutionary France we find cloth and cotton production in the countryside and small towns around Rouen and Lille, whilst to the south-east St-Etienne provided the focus for a number of industrialising small towns and villages, such as Rieve-de-Gier, St Chamond and Le Chambon-Feugerolles, increasingly engaged in metalworking and mining.[2] In addition, we must not forget the major manufacturing role of European capital cities, which were largely free-standing centres, with almost no industrial activity in their hinterlands.[3]

In much of Europe the pattern of advanced industrial output appears to have been largely decentralised and fragmented. Rural production, exploiting low wage rates, often had a tense and conflictual relationship with the guilds in bigger towns, although the role of small towns could be more important and productive. Industry in the towns was often traditionally structured and inward-looking, failing to generate interdependency with other sectors of the urban economy or with other urban centres. Competition rather than co-oper-ation predominated. With the decline of the Dutch network of so-called Randstad towns in the eighteenth century, few European countries had any real claim to regional systems of urban manufacturing before the late nine-teenth century. The major exception, however, was the Southern Netherlands (from 1830 the kingdom of Belgium). Though developments here were later, slower and less predictable than in the English Midlands, the study of nascent manufacturing regions in Belgium provides an opportunity to shed light both on the universalism (or otherwise) of factors generating sustainable industrial change and those retarding the development of urban regional systems, at least before the 1840s.

The second industrial nation of the world: a success story?

Belgium is well known as the first nation on the continent to follow the mod-ernising footsteps of the British economy. It was, indeed, an early industrialising nation. However, its path of development differed considerably from that of Britain. As a small country without any political power, Belgium had only limited access to the rapidly expanding Atlantic economy, for instance. Government policies and financial structures in the two countries were very different.[4] Moreover, however impressive the results achieved in some sectors and regions, Belgium's was a small economy. The first nation on the continent to really compete with Great Britain on a quantitative basis was Germany, where industrialisation broke through from the late 1830s onwards.[5]

Recent research has tended to qualify the growth experienced in Belgium. Average industrial production between 1811 and 1846 grew by only about 2.8 per cent a year. In 1846 the mechanised industries (cotton, iron, wool and coal) accounted for scarcely 10 per cent of gross domestic product, whilst its share in total industrial production was about 25 per cent. The proportion of the active population employed in industry is revealing too. In 1846, scarcely 4.8 per cent of the active population (or 13.5 per cent of total industrial employment) was engaged in modern factories.[6] Although by that time the numerical importance of the agricultural sector was definitely on the decline, it was not until the end of the century that there was an explosion of both the service industries and industrial employment.[7] In fact, an overwhelming majority of economic activities was not yet related to mechanisation: artisanal, small-scale and capital-extensive workshop production was still the rule, not the exception. Steam engines, for instance, were very slow to be installed in towns such as Antwerp, where they appeared only on a limited scale.[8] Although fairly modest from a quantitative viewpoint, the qualitative changes to Belgian industrial production which were initiated during this period had far-reaching importance.[9] The most important technological innovations took place before 1830 and can be divided in two broad phases. During the first period, from about 1800 until 1810, the textile industry was setting the pace of the modernisation process. During the years 1820–30, however, metal industry was the backbone of industrial development. The period from 1830 until 1850 can be viewed as a kind of consolidation period, though the economy of the country went through a deep crisis in the years following the independence of 1830. In these decades technological equipment, transport infrastructure and organisational and financial structures, however, were improved and economic growth was intensified. The steam engine was generally introduced and financial linkages between the heavy industry in the Walloon area and the capital of the country (Brussels) were firmly established.

The rapid industrialisation of the country was built upon the favourable heritage of earlier developments. The country was favoured by an abundant supply of natural resources such as coal and iron ore, and human resources of labour and capital were also readily available. The importance of favourable historical traditions should not be underplayed: a productive agriculture in Low and Middle Belgium, strong industrial and urban traditions, the existence of a well-developed commercial infrastructure focused on foreign and transit trade, excellent transport facilities (improved especially during the eighteenth century) and the country's central geographical position in western Europe together created a strong suit of economic trump cards. Pre-industrial relations between industrial activities, commerce and agriculture also help to explain a growing rural economy and urban demand for new commodities and services. Intensive husbandry, heightened by strong urban–rural ties, positively influenced the incomes of both farmers and urban landowners. In many Flemish and Walloon regions rural industry, often but erroneously depicted as proto-industrial, developed under the direction of predominantly urban trader-entrepreneurs and further intensified contacts and commercial bonds between towns and countryside.[10] An extensive integrated road and canal system, built under Austrian rule in the eighteenth century, facilitated the commercialisation of agriculture as well as a good circulation of goods and services, ideas and fashions.

Annexation to France (1795–1814) undeniably brought economic advantages. Under French occupation the country benefited from a large 'export' market – effectively a large toll-free commercial zone – and the early implementation of

French revolutionary laws. These laws abolished pre-industrial corporate or guild structures and implemented a new administrative, legal and civic regime. The military operations of Napoleon generated considerable backward linkages, such as contracts for metalwork products (including nails and weapons) and for textiles. At the same time, the continental blockade (1806–14) protected the fledgling Belgian industries from fierce British competition and facilitated import substitution.[11] Yet urban industrialisation in Belgium was slow to occur and showed significant regional and sectoral variations.[12] Structural changes occurred only in specific parts of the country, functioning in some measure as industrial enclaves or in Sidney Pollard's phrase as 'islands of modernity' amidst a largely traditional economy and agrarian society.[13] The three most important industrial areas to develop were clustered around the cities of Ghent and Lier in Flanders and Brabant (the Flemish speaking part of the country); the Verviers-Liège region; and the Hainault region with the Mons-Charleroi axis in the southern part of Belgium. Whilst none form direct counterparts to the English Midlands, all offer useful comparisons in terms of their industrial specialisms, resource base or developing infrastructure.

Textile industries in Flanders and Brabant: the failure of a leading sector?

As already noted, towns in Flanders and Brabant had a long-standing industrial and commercial tradition in textiles.[14] After 1650 these urban industries had to cope with growing problems, mainly resulting from difficulties of exporting to foreign markets, where mercantilistic policies developed by emerging nation states (such as England and France) rendered sales very difficult. In addition, the Southern Netherlands turned from being a leader to follower of a fashion. Changing consumer tastes, increasingly giving preference to exotic products or French fashions, also seem to have played an important role.[15] The political regime of the Austrian Netherlands prevented the country before 1748 from developing the necessary trade and tariff policies necessary to support industrial growth. After the Peace of Aachen (1748), however, textile industries in towns such as Brussels, Malines, Lier, Antwerp and Ghent showed a new dynamism. Some centralised textile enterprises emerged, specialising in the production of cheap and fashionable mixed cotton fabrics and in cotton printing.[16] The central government played an active role by implementing protective duties after 1748 and by granting patents. Local government contributed with social policies directed towards the compulsory employment of poor people at low wages.[17] Capital was supplied by merchant-entrepreneurs, who increasingly engaged in industrial activities; but they did so essentially in order to maximise profits in international trade.

Generally speaking, the cotton industry in Brabant and Flanders remained technologically backward, using simple hand-powered tools. It was only during the Napoleonic period that improved machinery was introduced. The town of Ghent was a centre of innovation. Often labelled the 'Manchester of the continent', it developed into a modern textile centre, thanks in large part to Lieven Bauwens. With the financial support of the French regime, Bauwens rigged up the different pieces of a smuggled English cotton mill in 1801 and installed the first spinning jenny on the continent.[18] Others followed his example, again benefiting from the continental blockade.[19] By 1810 some twenty-three mechanical cotton-spinning factories were in operation. These family business enterprises employed approximately 10,000 factory workers and even more home labourers.[20] Vertical integration occurred during the same period: into the traditional cotton printing factory of the Lousberg brothers, spinning-machines and hand-loom cotton weaving were introduced.[21] In the small town of Lier, near Antwerp, the factory system developed only a few years later. The firm De Heyder & Co., established by Antwerp merchants in 1757, started to manufacture 'siamoises'. In addition, a cotton-printing plant was set up in 1777. In 1807, De Heyder junior used a considerable part of his fortune to purchase sixty spinning mules, thus creating a fully integrated cotton mill, where spinning, weaving, dying, bleaching and printing were carried out under the same roof. As far as the equipment, turnover and size of the labour force was concerned, the Lier factory could compete with other firms in Belgium, France and Switzerland.[22]

After 1815, the market was flooded with cheap British products, stockedpiled during the blockade. Soon it became clear that the young textile industry was vulnerable to competition from the far more advanced British textile industries. Although a severe crisis hit the textile manufacturers, technological innovation continued in Ghent, thanks to the efforts of the cotton printer F. Voortman. He contracted English technicians in 1821 for the installation of steam engines, a washing-stool machine, ten dressing machines and, most importantly, 100 power looms, the first to be installed in Belgium. He thus became the owner of the first completely integrated and fully mechanised cotton-fabric factory on the continent. His competitors followed this example, and in 1829 about 600 power looms were in operation in the city of Ghent, though rural hand-loom weaving remained far more important.[23] Orders from the Nederlandse Handel-Maatschappij, a commercial company founded by the Dutch-Belgian King Willem I in 1824, boosted exports to the Dutch East-Indian colonies of textile products from both Ghent and Lier.[24]

The loss of these Asian markets after Belgium independence in 1830 caused a severe crisis in the Ghent industry. Textile manufacturers tried to survive by lowering wages, through the further modernisation of the cotton industry and the mechanisation of the linen industry.[25] The late modernisation of linen manufacture was largely due to the opposition of the rural population, who traditionally supplemented their agricultural income with flax-processing at home. This extra income became vital at this time, since rents were continuously rising and landholdings were increasingly fragmented. Flanders thus became the archetype of so-called proto-industrial production.[26] By the beginning of the nineteenth century, however, mechanised production was vital in order to withstand international competition. In 1837–38 the first two mechanised linen factories, organised as limited-liability companies, were erected in Ghent. They were among the biggest linen mills in Europe.[27] Thus the linen industries of Ghent and its surroundings began to modernise, generally at the expense of the rural linen industry in eastern and western Flanders, which, with good reason, became known as 'Poor Flanders'. It was not to wait until the second half of the nineteenth century that a slow but steady mechanisation of rural production occured in Flanders.[28]

There were other structural shortcomings in the industrialisation process of Ghent. Firstly, it failed to set off a chain reaction through which industrialisation could develop a dynamic of its own. Hence, it failed as a leading sector or 'growth pole'. Although a machine construction industry emerged in the 1820s, in factories like the Phoenix built by Jacques Huyttens-Kerremans in 1821 or that of Carels, these companies could not meet even local demand.[29] In addition, the industrial mechanisation of Ghent was an exception, not the rule. It was located in the middle of a rural and poor region, where abundant cheap labour discouraged entrepreneurs from investing in cost-saving improvements. Moreover, the domestic market of Ghent was too small and the purchasing power of its population insufficient to support its industrial development.[30] A similar pattern can be recognised in Lier, where the cheap labour force, depending wholly or partly on the factory of De Heyder & Co. for its income, did not provide real incentives for cost-saving capital investments, such as the installation of power looms or steam engines. Shortly after the Belgian revolution, the factory moved to Leiden in the Northern Netherlands (1834), attracted by the financial support of the Dutch government and the Nederlandse Handel-Maatschappij. An army of unskilled labourers was left without alternative employment.[31] However heroic and pioneering the achievements of Lieven Bauwens may seem, the textile industry in this region cannot be viewed as a leading sector in the industrial revolution of Belgium. True, there are some superficial parallels between the Flanders-Brabant region and the east Midlands, with the important role in both areas of established towns as the foci of industrial development. But there were also substantial differences which help to explain the different growth trajectories of the two areas. Unlike the east Midlands, Flanders and Brabant were dependent upon imported technology, whilst low wage levels discouraged the introduction of successive cost-cutting innovations and, through weak domestic demand, created an over-dependence on foreign markets. Together these made the region's industrial development fragmented, fragile and difficult to sustain: a stark contrast with the innovative, integrated and dynamic urban-industrial network in the east Midlands.

Verviers-Liège: chains of innovation in textiles, machine building, coal and iron

A second important growth pole was the Maas-Vesder region, where the English technician William Cockerill acted as a pioneer. The town of Verviers already had a long tradition of wool dressing going back to the seventeenth century, and mechanisation concentrated dozens of labourers into a single factory.[32] For this small town, located far away from the port cities that supplied the raw material (wool), the arrival of the Cockerill in 1799 was of crucial importance. He constructed the first mechanised wool-spinning mill contracted by the firm Simonis & Biolley, an important local manufacturer.[33] This innovation provided a powerful example to the biggest manufacturers in the region. In 1810 scarcely six firms out of a total of 144 were mechanised, but they already controlled more than 50 per cent of total output. With the abundant supply of water power, however, the first steam machine did not appear until 1816. Moreover, entrepreneurs in the region generally tended to concentrate on the finishing process and the diversification of production, showing little interest in intensified mechanisation. Weaving in fact was modernised only after 1845.[34] Yet Verviers was a dynamic single-industry town that succeeded in competing with Britain for export markets across Europe, in South and North America and in Asia. In 1808 the town was already being depicted by a German traveller as the 'Tuchdistrikt'. Forty years later, it dominated the Belgian woollen industry, housing 42 per cent of businesses and 63 per cent of labourers in the sector.[35] Not surprisingly, the population of the town grew between 1806 and 1846 by 138 per cent. However impressive this may look at first sight, by nineteenth-century industrial standards it was a rather modest population gain which has to be seen in the context of spectacular labour productivity gains achieved in the woollen industry. Verviers remained a relatively small town, with approximately 22,000 inhabitants in 1846. It also grew at the expense of the surrounding settlements. Indeed, the mechanisation of the spinning process deprived inhabitants of these surrounding villages of their income and pulled them into town. Hence the mechanisation of spinning contributed to the concentration of wage-earners in the town – a process which parallels the experience of framework-knitting in the east Midlands as well as that of spinners and weavers in the Yorkshire woollen industry.

Verviers was not typical in the region. Elsewhere the growth of the Walloon iron and coal industries led to the genesis of a very different industrial region which after 1814 had its centre in the nearby town of Liège. At the end of the eighteenth century the coal and iron industry in Liège urgently needed new men and products as well as fresh financial resources.[36] The move of the Cockerill family to Liège in 1807 marked the beginning of the development of factory production of textile machinery and the origin of a new era for *la ville ardente*. In 1817 the Cockerill enterprise, managed by John, son of William, moved to the former ecclesiastical residence in the castle in Seraing. Soon thereafter it developed into a vertically integrated industrial enterprise, including the exploitation of coal and the extraction of minerals, the manufacturing, purging and melting of iron ore, the processing of pig-iron and the forging and rolling of metal. In the Cockerill factory the puddling process was introduced in 1822; the first modern blast furnace was installed in 1824, and steam engines were employed as early as 1819. These were used in the extraction of coal and in the textile industry, but also for shipbuilding and in railway locomotives.[37] The Cockerill concern was of incalculable value for the industrial progress in the region. However, it also acts as a classic example of the financial difficulties with which industrial capitalists had to reckon. The rapid growth of his industrial empire was financed through external loans. In the 1830s Cockerill was repeatedly facing severe difficulties. Around 1840 the Banque de Belgique and the Belgian government saved the company, employing about 30,000 industrial workers, from bankruptcy. Notwithstanding this, Cockerill's lead was followed by other entrepreneurs such as the Orbans (a merchant family who invested in the mining of coal and iron ore) and the merchant Gilles-Antoine Lamarche (who founded the factory of Ougrée in 1829). This generation of entrepreneurs strove to establish fully integrated enterprises, from the exploitation of raw materials (minerals and coal) to the setting up of plants for machine building and metal-working. In addition, they proved eager to introduce technological innovations,[38] and contributed to the establishment of new coalmines in the region.

In less than two decades the whole Maas-Vesder valley became one of the most dynamic industrial regions in Europe, specialised in the production of machines and tools necessary for the expansion of other sectors, and exporting its products across the continent. Soon after the arrival of the British pioneers, a whole generation of technicians was trained in Liège.[39] As a result, the town grew impressively between 1806 and 1846: from about 46,000 inhabitants to nearly 76,000. Yet the industrialising process did not foster urban growth very widely. In order to minimise transport costs, the iron industry, for instance, tended to be primarily located in close proximity to coalmines, which often meant in the 'countryside'. A whole series of rapidly expanding settlements such as Seraing, Tilleur and d'Ougrée testify of the genesis of a dispersed industrial basin, deprived largely of urban central place functions. If the Flemish-Brabant region centred on Ghent showed some outline similarity with the east Midlands, the Verviers-Liège district had some resemblance to the area around Birmingham and the Black Country. In both cases we find the key role of dynamic established centres (Liège and Birmingham), irrigating their hinterlands with innovation and investment and serving as both marketing and production centres. In both districts we find older secondary centres, like Verviers or Bromsgrove, which were expanding rapidly, and the emergence of embryonic new towns like West Bromwich or Seraing. However, once again the parallels are incomplete. Large entrepreneurs like Cockerill, creating integrated manufactures, seem to have been more crucial in the Belgian region than in the west Midlands, where production continued to be dominated by small firms and workshops (though see Chapter 7).

Mons-Charleroi: the Midlands of Belgium?

The third industrial growth pole was the Mons-Charleroi region. This area was fortunate in possessing important coal basins: the Borinage or Couchant de Mons, Le Centre near the town of Louvière and the basin of Charleroi. In some ways, its development too echoed that seen in the Black Country. Already in the eighteenth century coalmining had expanded rapidly and substantially contributed to economic growth in this region.[40] The French law of 1791 on the exploitation of coalmines stimulated capital concentration in the area. Under this law, the state became owner of the subsoil, supervised mining and granted licenses to entrepreneurs.[41] In the Borinage, near the town of Mons, the Newcomen pump was already widespread in the eighteenth century.[42] Growing demand for coal and the improvement of transport facilities encouraged export-led growth, with sales on the markets of Flanders and the northern parts of France. Local commercial and financial elites co-operated in order to establish mining firms. After 1835, during a period of economic and financial uncertainty, these firms were transformed into limited-liability companies, in which the Brussels banks acquired major shares (40 per cent by 1838).[43] Although the production capacity of the coalmining industry mushroomed from the French period onwards, few direct linkages to other industries developed. Along the northern part of the river Samber, in the neighbourhood of Charleroi, a rural nail industry, strongly dependent on the mercantilist policies of the Austrian government for the import of iron, stimulated some minor iron manufacturing and glass production in the eighteenth century.[44] However, strong competition from the expanding Liège region forced local entrepreneurs to develop a completely different strategy. Heavy industry, based on iron smelting and processing according to the latest English innovations, arrived in the Charleroi region during the 1820s and 1830s, giving a strong impetus to the modernisation of coalmining in the region. Charleroi became the centre of an industrial basin, divided into two parts: coalmining and handicraft glass production took place in the northern part, and new metalworking industries were concentrated in villages such as Monceau-sur-Sambre, Marchienne au Pont to the west and Marcinelle, Montignies and Châtilineau to the east.[45]

The major take-off in the region occurred later than in the Black Country where expansion from the late eighteenth century was propelled by major advances in communication, in particular road and canal networking (see Chapters 5 and 7). The railway 'mania' in Belgium in the 1830s and 1840s opened up connections between the rivers Scheldt, Meuse and Rhine. It also generated considerable backward linkages, such as a fast-growing demand for wood, iron, glass and modern machinery, which in turn stimulated industrial development in the southern areas of Belgium.[46] The railway boom also served to ameliorate the devastating effects of the economic crisis of the 1830s. Between 1834 and 1843 around 560 kilometres of railways were constructed along two main axes, connecting service or trading centres such as Antwerp, Brussels and Ostend with the industrial growth poles in the Walloon part of the country. Cheaper and faster transport of materials and labour was now possible within and between Belgium and its neighbouring countries.[47] In addition, the railway connection between the Walloon region and the emerging German Ruhr area was of decisive importance for the harbour of Antwerp, facilitating the growth of transit trade, which had been obstructed by Dutch policies after 1830. It also transformed Antwerp into a commercial platform for the industrial production in the Walloon part of the country.

The service sector: trade and finance in Antwerp and Brussels

Antwerp became one of the most important centres servicing these three industrial growth poles. The city reaped the benefits of the re-opening of the river Scheldt in 1795 after a so-called closure for international maritime transport lasting two centuries.[48] The city rapidly evolved into an international port, despite political instability which threatened the freedom of navigation and repeatedly forced the commercial elite of the city to adapt to changing circumstances.[49] In 1800 Antwerp was virtually non-existent as a port city, but by 1840, measured by the total tonnage of ships entering the port, it was one of the top twenty harbours in the world. In 1875 the city had risen to fourth place, after London, New York and Liverpool.[50] This huge growth in trade activity gave a strong impulse to the development of a better maritime infrastructure and trade organisation. Antwerp also exerted a strong attraction on foreign mercantile houses, especially German ones, which through their commercial experience and networks abroad acquired a big share of Antwerp's sea-borne trade.[51] In step with its commercial expansion, the city also became an important service centre, with the formation of insurance companies specialising in maritime business (after 1819) and new banking companies (after 1824), organised on a limited-liability basis.[52]

The industrialisation of Belgium was vital for the development of the port. It stimulated the import of raw materials such as cotton and wool, and it generated a multitude of export possibilities. And yet the export position of Antwerp remained rather weak until 1840. It was only in the second half of the nineteenth century, when Belgian industrial development reached a more mature level, that traffic in the port steadily grew, thanks mainly to its gateway function for the Walloon and German industrial districts.[53] Unlike other great port cities during the first half of the nineteenth century, such as Liverpool and Bristol, which served as the principal ports for the west Midlands and which acquired a wide range of industrial and processing activities, Antwerp failed to develop a strong manufacturing industry of its own. The local cotton industry was in decline after the re-opening of the Scheldt. One cannot argue that there was a lack of technological knowledge, since the local French prefect offered several opportunities for Antwerp firms to contract English engineers. However, the big merchant-entrepreneurs, who had invested capital in large cotton-printing works from the second half of the eighteenth century onwards, were now more attracted by profits in international trade, finance and insurance.[54] They were willing to invest only in port-related industrial activities, such as the processing of colonial products like sugar. Even in these branches small-scale and handicraft production dominated until 1850.[55]

The other service centre vital to Belgian industrialisation was Brussels. During the second half of the eighteenth century, the town had already considerably reinforced its relative position within the Brabantine economy.[56] The town functioned as the administrative and political capital of the country, greatly profited from a flourishing hinterland, and fulfilled a key role as a central place and a trading centre for the southern part of the Duchy of Brabant. In 1830 it became the capital city of the independent kingdom. It also reinforced its central position through its role as a major supplier of capital for the industrial revolution.[57] In 1822 the Dutch King William I had established the Société Générale des Pays-Bas pour Favoriser l'Industrie Nationale, following the model of the Nederlandse Bank and the Bank of England.

According to its statutes, this institution embodied all the functions of a major financial institution, though it essentially acted as the Bank of the Crown Lands during the years under Dutch rule. After the revolution of 1830 the bank retained its position, sold a lot of its estates and developed a well-considered strategy to support industrialisation in the country. It did so by granting long-term credit to industrial firms in the southern part of the country.[58] Because of high investment costs, the majority of the firms in these basic and capital goods industries lacked adequate financial reserves, hence the need to attract external funds. The Société soon became of pivotal importance for a group of enterprises through the creation of branches, the participation in the formation of new enterprises, the acquisition of shares in existing companies and the transformation of family firms into public limited companies, in which the bank became a major shareholder.[59] From the beginning, investments were directed towards a variety of sectors, with a special interest in mining. They also were regionally diversified, albeit with a preference for the Hainault area. After 1835 the dominant position of the Société was challenged by the establishment of the Banque de Belgique, which used the same techniques as the Société, although it never gained the same importance. It built up a network of enterprises especially in the metal and machinery sectors in the region of Liège.[60] In contrast to the classic English banking system, both banks acted after 1834–35 as mixed banks (combining commercial banking with long-term investment). After the crisis of 1848 and the monetary reform that gave birth to the Nationale Bank (1850), the Société Générale lost its position as cashier of the state bank, and concentrated on functioning as a private industrial credit institution.[61] The entwining of financial, industrial and political interests in the city of Brussels made it the undisputed centre of business in the country, although investments were directed almost exclusively to the southern or Walloon part of the country, where heavy industry was located. In the Midlands, we have seen in Parts I and II of this book, the picture was much more complicated, with London banking investment only one of the players in the financial and industrial development of the region, alongside regional and local investment networks.

Industrialisation and the Belgian urban network

Given the geographical pattern of Belgian industrialisation, with thousands of industrial and mineworkers dispersed in so-called industrial basins, it is not easy to make use of population totals to measure the impact of the industrial changes on the Belgian urban network.[62] Charleroi, for instance, does not figure in the list of the ten most important nineteenth-century urban centres, listed in Table 13.1. In any case, population numbers by themselves fail to

illuminate the centrality and economic importance of urban and rural settlements. For example, recent research on the urban network of
eighteenth-century Brabant demonstrates how little urban growth was generated by the then fast-growing textile industries.[63] Furthermore, evidence for
Verviers and Mons underscores how little urban wealth was created by early-
nineteenth-century industrial development.[64] By contrast, town–countryside
relationships, service functions, transport and commerce often generated
important gains in urban centrality. Even eighteenth-century Ghent probably
benefited more from the influx of revenue from rising rents in the Flemish
countryside than it did from its textile industry.[65]

Table 13.1 *The populations of the ten most important urban centres
in Belgium, 1784–1900*

Rank	1784	1829	1846	1866	1900
1	Brussels (74,427)	Brussels (98,279)	Brussels (123,874)	Brussels (163,434)	Antwerp (302,058)
2	Antwerp (50,973)	Ghent (83,783)	Ghent (102,977)	Antwerp (123,571)	Brussels (183,686)
3	Ghent (50,963)	Antwerp (77,199)	Antwerp (88,487)	Ghent (116,693)	Ghent (160,133)
4	Liège (50,000)	Liège (58,087)	Liège (75,961)	Liège (101,594)	Liège (157,760)
5	Brugge (30,846)	Brugge (42,198)	Brugge (49,308)	Brugge (47,205)	Schaarbeek (63,508)
6	Tournai (26,000)	Tournai (28,737)	Leuven (30,278)	Mechelen (35,529)	Elsene (48,615)
7	Leuven (20,831)	Leuven (25,643)	Tournai (30,125)	Leuven (32,976)	Molenbeek (58,445)
8	Mechelen (20,273)	Mechelen (24,436)	Mechelen (29,693)	Verviers (32,381)	Mechelen (55,705)
9	Mons (20,000)	Mons (23,010)	Mons (24,442)	Tournai (31,531)	Sint-Gillis (51,763)
10	Kortrijk (15,000)	Namur (21,571)	Verviers (23,363)	Molenbeek (24,032)	Brugge (51,657)

Source: Deprez and Vandenbroeke, 'Population', p. 226.

To a certain extent, and in stark contrast with the general experience in the
English Midlands, industrialisation and urbanisation in Belgium moved inde-
pendently. Unsurprisingly, then, the Belgian urban hierarchy was not
fundamentally affected by early-nineteenth-century industrialisation. Up to

1846, for instance, the position of several of the most important Belgian towns was firmly rooted in their traditional roles within the urban network. Whereas Ghent ranked quite high in the early nineteenth century, owing in part (but not completely) to its industrial development, it was the two Brabant service cities, Antwerp and Brussels, that benefited most from economic modernisation. At the end of our period (in 1846), industrialising Verviers, for instance, held only a modest tenth position in the urban rank-order. With the appearance in 1866 of Molenbeek, a growing industrial suburb of Brussels, the urbanisation process had reached a new stage. Though Brussels ranked only second in 1900, the process of suburbanisation around the city was widespread by that time (see Table 13.1 under Schaarbeek, Elsene, Molenbeek and Sint-Gillis). The 'vulnerability' of the urban industrialisation process of the nineteenth century has been confirmed by the severe urban difficulties of present-day Walloon cities after de-industrialisation in the twentieth century.

Conclusions

Our discussion of Belgian regional developments has highlighted some of the key dynamics of industrial growth which were equally important in the English Midlands: technological innovation (often imported from England), entrepreneurial leadership (including British immigrants such as William Cockerill), transport improvements and financial investment structures. The Belgian pattern of regional industrialisation also parallels that of the Midlands in other ways. One sees the significant role of older smaller towns like Verviers as centres of new industry (not unlike that of Wolverhampton or Loughborough – see Chapters 8 and 10), the limited number of new industrial urban centres like Seraing (comparable to West Bromwich or Burslem – see Chapter 7) and also the continuing role of long-established towns, with Ghent in Flanders having a position akin to that of the old east Midlands textile centres of Leicester and Nottingham (see Chapter 9). At the same time, Belgian trends were no clone of Midlands developments. Belgian industrialisation and modernisation came later; it was more geographically uneven, and in Flanders clearly less successful in maintaining economic and urban growth. No less crucial, in Belgium (as in the Midlands, but with different spatial outcomes) we see the highly localised and differentiated pattern of urban-industrial development

The Belgian experience, taken in conjunction with research on other areas, is also helpful in understanding those factors which could serve to check the self-sustaining expansion of urban manufacturing regions. Various factors seem particularly significant from an urban perspective. Some were broadly institutional ones. In continental towns civic magistracies were often relatively closed with conservative economic agendas.[66] Energetic, innovative newcomers could appear and have a dramatic impact (as was the case in Liège), but in general entrepreneurial networks seem to have been somewhat less dynamic or ambitious than in British towns. Though urban guilds, widespread in continental cities (unlike in Britain) until the early nineteenth century, are no longer considered to have been a fundamental obstacle to modernisation, it may be significant that Verviers developed outside the constraints of the guild model. For obvious reasons, commerce and agriculture remained strong priorities for continental urban elites. Even in the dynamic smaller towns, manufacturers were often too small to maintain the momentum of expansion on their own. Certainly there was a strong and continuing sense of competition and rivalry with the countryside and other urban communities in many continental countries which was much less important in Britain by 1800. Again unlike in Britain, the state clearly played a much larger role in Belgium – and other European countries – in promoting transport improvements, reforming corporate structures, supervising mining activities and opening up markets. But, as we have seen, government action could also have a disruptive effect on urban expansion (as with the exclusion of Belgian manufactures from Dutch colonial markets after 1830), and this problem might be aggravated by political instability, notably during the French Revolution and its aftermath. In Britain long-standing political stability at home was an important precondition for the mounting regional specialisation which counter-balanced national economic integration.

The state of the wider regional economy could be crucial. Agricultural problems and rural poverty, though promoting cheap rural manufactures, could seriously limit regional demand and reinforce economic instability.[67] In consequence, the evolution of urban networks – with the growth of complementary and mutually supportive networks of industrial, commercial, administrative and other centres – might be retarded, as might the development of new urban centres. In this context the adoption of technological innovation cannot be seen as necessarily natural or inevitable. What slowed the process of reception in some regions was not just urban conservatism, but the very real counter-attractions of cheap rural labour and traditional energy sources. In general then, many Belgian (and other European) towns, together with their entrepreneurs and elites, moved cautiously, crab-like, into the new universe of large-scale manufacturing on a regional basis. And who can blame them? In Britain, the expansive development by the 1830s of urban industrial regions like the Midlands had been in gestation for over a century and still had significant traditional dimensions: most manufacturing remained workshop- rather than factory-based; there were few genuinely new industrial towns; rural industry retained a significant, albeit declining role; and most specialist industrial centres diversified into service sectors in order to ensure economic stability. Even today modern capitalists in their global cities often show an abiding appetite for conservative business practices rather than for real innovation.

Notes

1 For more detailed discussion and an attempt to categorise these areas see Chapter 14; van der Wee, *Urban Industries*; Berg, *Markets and Manufacture*, chapters 2–3; Mokyr, *Industrialization*; Neufeld, *Skilled Metalworkers*; Ogilvie and Cerman, *Proto-industrialization*.

2 Reddy, *Market Culture*; Terrier, *Les deux âges*; Hanagan, *Nascent Proletarians*.

3 Schultz, 'The metropolis'; Schwarz, *London*.

4 Landes, *Unbound Prometheus*, pp. 125–33; Bairoch, *La Belgique*, pp. 627–8; O'Brien, 'European industrialization', p. 296.

5 Tilly, 'German industrialization', pp. 98–102; Tilly, 'Capital formation', pp. 386 ff.

6 Pluymers, 'Het kleine België', p. 37.

7 In 1846 55 per cent of the active population still worked in the agrarian sector, against c. 30 per cent in industry and 15 per cent in the tertiary sector. In 1896 the tertiary sector accounted for c. 30 per cent of employment, industry for c. 38 per cent and the agrarian sector for c. 31 per cent: De Brabander, *De regionaal*, pp. 131–2.

8 Van Neck, *Les débuts*, pp. 878–9.

9 Van der Wee, 'Industrial revolution in Belgium', p. 71.

10 Bruwier, 'L'industrie', pp. 25–35.

11 Hasquin, 'Déjà puissance', pp. 343–5.

12 Cameron, 'New view'.

13 Pollard, 'Industrialization', pp. 165–8.

14 Van der Wee, 'Industrial revolution in Belgium', p. 307–81.

15 Blondé and Greefs, 'Werk', pp. 222–3.

16 Lis and Soly, 'Restructuring', pp. 106–7.

17 In January 1749 import duties on a large number of cheap textile products were raised. The measure was the first in a large series that were taken by the central Austrian government to protect its own textile producers: Lis and Soly, 'Entrepreneurs'.

18 Leleux, *A l'aube*, pp. 29–44.

19 Dhondt, 'La région', pp. 113–18.

20 Scholliers, 'Van de proto-industrie', p. 61.

21 Dhondt, 'Cotton industry at Ghent', pp. 21–37.

22 Lis and Soly, *Een groot*, pp. 46–51, 57–62.

23 Scholliers, *Wages*, pp. 52–4.

24 Coppejans-Desmedt, 'Koning Willem I', pp. 48–9, 53–7; Demoulin, *Guillaume Ier*, pp. 150–2; Scholliers, *Bedrijfsgeschiedenis*, pp. 16–17.

25 For example, the low-wage strategy was a key element in keeping down wage costs in the factory of Voortman, although huge wage differentials existed within the factory. From 1835 to 1845, this implied a considerable loss of purchasing power for the Voortman's workers. See Scholliers, *Wages*, pp. 143, 163, 213–14.

26 Goossens, *Belgian Agriculture*, pp. 317–19.
27 Solar, 'Die belgische', p. 95.
28 Scholliers, 'Van de proto-industrie', pp. 71 ff.
29 Scholliers, *Wages*, p. 12.
30 Hannes, 'Industrialization', pp. 11–12.
31 Lis and Soly, *Een groot bedrijf*, pp. 69–70, 101–11.
32 Hansotte, 'La région', pp. 166–8, 177.
33 Pasleau, *John Cockerill*, pp. 16–19.
34 Desama and Bauwens, *Een kleine*, p. 91.
35 Hélin, 'Genèse', p. 484.
36 Hansotte, *La métallurgie*, pp. 341–4.
37 Iron rails were also produced: see Hasquin, 'Déjà puissance', pp. 328–30.
38 Hansotte, 'La région', pp. 277–81.
39 Caulier-Mathy, 'Le patronat', pp. 49–55.
40 Caulier-Mathy, 'De wording', p. 205.
41 This was not the case in Liège before. By the law of 21 April 1810 entrepreneurs were no longer restricted in time; they also enjoyed more organisational liberty henceforth: Caulier-Mathy, 'De wording', pp. 181–5.
42 Bruwier, 'Le charbon', pp. 345 ff.
43 Puissant, 'A propos', pp. 63–92.
44 Delaet, 'La mécanisation', pp. 121–4.
45 Delaet, 'Genèse', p. 425.
46 Laffut, *Les chemins*, pp. 165–6, 187–94.
47 Laffut, *Les chemins*, pp. 373–9, 471.
48 A complete liberalisation of the traffic did not occur until 1863, when the toll on the Scheldt estuary imposed by the Northern Netherlands was abolished.
49 For a good overview of the fast expansion of port activity, see Lis, *Social Change*, pp. 27–38; Veraghtert, 'From inland port', p. 274–422.
50 Bairoch, 'La Belgique', pp. 648–9.
51 Greefs, 'Foreign', pp. 101–17.
52 Veraghtert, 'De Antwerpse'.
53 Veraghtert, 'From inland port', pp. 364–6.
54 Lis, *Social Change*, pp. 20–3.
55 Thijs, 'De geschiedenis'.
56 Blondé, *Een economie*.
57 Van Uytven, 'Brabantse', pp. 29–79.
58 Houtman-De Smedt, 'Société Générale', pp. 48–9.
59 Laureyssens, 'The Société', p. 93.
60 The two banks were engaged in cut-throat competition with each other until 1841, when the financial crisis obliged the Banque de Belgique to grant only short-run commercial credit from then onwards. For the importance of its investment policy, see Lebrun *et al.*, *Essai*, pp. 538–9, 561.
61 Kurgan-Van Hentenryk, 'The Société', pp. 69 ff.
62 For parallel analysis of the English Midlands, see Langton, 'Town growth'.
63 Blondé, 'Disparities', pp. 41–52.
64 Bruwier, 'Etudes', pp. 251–316.
65 Kint, *Prometheus*.

66 For the slow adaptation of a conservative elite at Cologne see Aycoberry, *Cologne*.

67 For lack of demand caused by rural poverty in the Liège region see Haesenne-Peremans, *La pauvreté*.

14

Towns, industries and regions: a European perspective on theoretical and practical relationships[1]

Steve King

Introduction

The contributions to this volume have seen an intricate connection between urban development on different levels and regional industrial development, using a broadly defined Midlands as a vehicle for exploration. They draw on a rich, particularly English, tradition of urban history that has predisposed historians to privilege capital cities, traditional provincial towns and vibrant new industrial towns as motors of the industrial revolution.[2] Some of the problems with drawing this sort of empirical and theoretical link are readily apparent from previous chapters. Much depends upon how we define towns. As Stobart and Raven, and Ellis suggest, towns require effective transport and business networks if they are to energise regional development (see Chapter 5 and 9). And where old and new towns were present in the same industrial region, competing urban spheres could actually retard industrial development. There are also related problems centring on how we define the existence of a 'region' and in particular how we draw regional boundaries when, as Ellis has shown, there could be multi-level inter-connections between urban and industrial centres across a fairly wide area. Such inter-connections partly explain why there is often a tension in studies of industrialisation between regarding a spatial area as a single economic region and regarding the area as five or six distinct economies. Such problems are exacerbated by the fact that, as Wanklyn demonstrates, eighteenth- and nineteenth-century industrial areas were notionally part of a domestic region at the same time as they were tightly locked into the continental, Atlantic or imperial economies (see Chapter 12). In the same way that Welsh historians have asked, 'When and where was

Wales?', we should probably be asking ourselves, 'When and where were the Midlands?' More widely, in trying to draw even crude regional boundaries, the process of disentangling the influences of capital cities, large traditional towns (both expanding and stagnating) and new industrial towns – each, as Stobart and Raven point out in Chapter 1, with their own networks extending out into the countryside – is both difficult and uncertain.

However, in this chapter I do not want to get into the complex literature on how we draw lines on the historical landscape.[3] As Stobart and Raven argue, the fact that geography is as much a cause of change as an effect of it makes this exercise tortuous. Rather, I want to draw upon and extend some of the lessons of the preceding chapters and to make two broad points. First, English historians have been largely cut off from the rich traditions of regional history on the continent, and this literature offers us many competing models of the key variables which underpinned different forms and intensities of regional industrial development. Second, when we examine the European literature, particularly with regard to the development of regional textile industries, we find that urbanisation often plays an ambiguous role in regional economic development. As Wanklyn has shown us, the Midlands in general and some of its towns in particular were tied into wide international markets. This observation carries more general resonance, highlighting the fact that it was quite possible for communities that were notionally part of one narrowly defined 'region' or industrial district to be tied into several alternative 'regional' realities – national and international markets, cross-border merchant networks or widespread capital markets – and that it was the existence of these wider links which fostered development of economic and urban infrastructures. In other words, urban areas might be dependent rather than independent variables in the foundation and development of regional economies. Ranging widely across the European literature, I will suggest that it is possible to draw broad regional development typologies which can more precisely locate the role of urbanisation in the development process vis-à-vis other potential influences on regional development. The chapter will close with a brief review of what the European research and methodological agenda can tell us about the Midlands industrial region that lies at the heart of this volume.

Models of regional development

What made a regional industrial system grow? What factors determined the boundaries of the regional production system at any point in time and over the life cycle of the region? Why did certain regions and sub-regions industrialise faster than others? Why did some regions go through a 'classic' development path of domestic industry–proto-industry–factory/workshop industry, as was often the case in the Midlands, whilst others just exploded on the scene when factories became the normal structures through which production was organised? Why did some industrial regions flourish for many hundreds of years, generating and regenerating technical, institutional and product structures favourable to industrialisation, while other industrial regions flared relatively briefly and then declined/re-ruralised?

Answering questions such as these has proved problematic in a European historiography of industrialisation where contributors from different countries have radically different traditions of 'regional' history[4] and in which attempts to borrow the theoretical clothes of other disciplines have usually proved awkward and inconclusive.[5] As we have seen throughout this volume, the nature and scale of urban development had a part to play in English regional development. Indeed, for the Midlands, Ellis suggests that urbanisation was the crucial driver of economic development (see Chapter 9). Urban historians on the continent have drawn similar conclusions. Adapting the urban-industrial development models originally developed by Christaller,[6] urban historians such as Hohenberg, van der Wee, Lepetit, Birke and Kettenacker, and Freudenberger have shown that the character of capital cities, new industrial towns, market towns and traditional manufacturing centres could significantly shape the pace, scale and longevity of regional industrialisation, both directly in terms of their role in the manufacturing process and indirectly through their role as a focus of innovative consumer demand.[7] In Chapter 1, Stobart and Raven suggest that urban areas offered an even greater range of stimuli to regional economies and that in places like the Midlands we witness the emergence of 'dynamic networks' of towns and individuals that drove development forward. German historians, meanwhile, have been particularly active in teasing out the links between regional industrialisation and urban development, employing econometrics and complex geographical information systems to map regional boundaries and urban spheres of influence.[8] They have also made the key theoretical distinction between the (limited) role of urban areas in the foundation of industrial regions and the (potentially more extensive) role of urban areas in fostering long-term success.[9] For many commentators, then, urbanisation was one of the key features of industrialisation and vice versa.

This said, the European historiography of industrialisation has frequently afforded a much less central role to urbanisation in the regional development process than has been the case in the English literature. Urban development might be just one, and by no means the most important, of a range of influences on industrialisation. As Mager, Lis and Soly remind us, capital flows, movement of entrepreneurs, state intervention, labour market architecture and the exact product type could all influence where industry developed and where it flourished, irrespective of the levels of regional urban development.[10] Moreover, urban development might actually be a direct impediment to regional industrial development, as was the case in Sweden, where regional industrialisation took place in spite of, rather than because of, the presence of Stockholm.[11] In some of the French textile regions too the presence and structure of urban areas served to retard industrial growth.[12] And town development might be the dependent variable in the regional development process. In Germany, the fortunes of the ancient town of Aachen were revived only because of largely independent industrialisation in the surrounding countryside, as was the case in some important German metalworking areas and some of the Midland towns reviewed in this volume.[13] Indeed, for France, Luxembourg, Germany, Scandinavia, Hungary and much of eastern Europe the surprising thing about the historiography of industrialisation is not how much urbanisation features, but how little.

Against this backdrop, it is unsurprising that European historians have adopted a much wider range of macro-models to conceptualise the problem of regional industrialisation and to respond to Franklin Mendels's perceptive early observation that 'the region, if defined with care, is where the primary ingredients for industrialisation were most readily mixed in the past'.[14] Thus, the theory of proto-industrialisation – Franklin Mendels's simple model of why commercialised industry in the countryside emerged during the eighteenth century, and why certain industrial regions went on to experience enduring but organic industrial organisation – has more often (and more successfully) been used as a framework for regional analysis on the continent than in England. In a series of articles, Mendels suggested that a proto-industrial region would have several key attributes: a close inter-connection between itself and a proximate region of commercialised agriculture; a structural labour surplus underpinned by demographic growth and the nature of the land market; towns as centres of distribution rather than production; a long history of rural handicraft production; and increasingly strong linkages to national and international markets.[15] Towns in the original sketch of the model were largely passive parts of the regional industrialisation process.[16] In turn, Mendels believed that a rural industrial tradition was likely to have been a key predictive indicator of which regions might go on to the second phase of the industrialisation process with centralised and urbanised production.

Early commentators, such as Kriedte, Medick and Schlumbohm, drawing on the work of Sombart and others in the German Historical School of Economics,[17] modified and extended this basic theory, drawing a connection between upland communities and proto-industry, for instance, and laying more emphasis on the flexibility of institutional structures in generating successful and enduring rural industrial structures. They also saw proto-industrialisation as an intervening stage between feudalism and capital-ism.[18] Most subsequent empirical and historiographical commentary has been critical. The high-pressure demography of rural industrial areas has been questioned, increasing stress has been laid on the function of the entrepreneurs who controlled the development process (and about whom the original theory said little), and it has frequently been observed that rural industrial and modern factory structures developed alongside each other.[19] Urban historians too have been active in pointing to vibrant production structures in early modern European towns which could rival or complement those developing in the countryside.[20] Ellis and Clark in this volume have skilfully drawn similar conclusions about both large urban centres and small market towns in the English Midlands (Chapter 9 and 10), implicitly questioning the work of Levine which portrayed the Midlands hosiery region as fitting closely to proto-industrial theory.[21] As Sabel and Zeitlin point out, 'what began as an elegant theory connecting property relations, markets and technological change ends as a collection of irreducibly diverse factors contributing to economic development'.[22] The key point, however, is that there are at least 100 local and regional studies of continental Europe which use the macro-theory as an initial organising framework, compared with just a handful in England. Not until we have more by way of systematic British local studies can we begin to discern whether proto-industrialisation remains a useful theoretical perspective, and in this sense the current volume offers a model for future studies.

An alternative organising framework has been the core-periphery model advanced by historical geographers. Berend and Ranki laid a core-periphery model at the heart of their 1982 study of industrialisation in Hungary. They noted that 'We thus understand by "periphery" an area dependent upon the core ... the economy, foreign trade, balance of payments, and production develop tied to, influenced and subordinated to the core countries. The relationship ... is often destructive of the periphery; but it can also be an inducement to development, serving – under appropriate conditions – to lift the area from its peripheral position'[23] and suggested that the proximity of countries or regions to trade routes and the particular institutional structures of those places were two of the key variables that parcelled areas into the core or periphery categories.[24] In terms of whole countries, they assigned all of southern and eastern Europe and much of Scandinavia to the periphery, noting that even as late as 1860 the gross domestic product of these areas was less than 50 per cent of that of Britain. Some of the most exciting work on European industrialisation has involved the application of a core-periphery model to the development of industrial regions within states. As early as 1976, Lieberman was using this sort of model to show how the dismantling of urban monopolies on trade and industry in Norway created a pattern of regional core and periphery that was to shape a century of industrial development in the country.[25] More recently, Langton and Hoppe have employed a subtle core-periphery model in their analysis of the Swedish iron industry.[26] Moreover, the model has proved particularly popular in shaping our understanding of the development of eastern European economies. Poztsgai, for instance, has shown that feudal landlords and the state actively colluded to create a core-periphery structure in the textile industry to facilitate regional economic development.[27] And in this volume, both Schwarz (Chapter 11) and, to a lesser extent, Clark (Chapter 10) draw on a core-periphery model to explain the development of small towns in the Midlands. We should appreciate, however, that the European literature that uses this model frequently sees little role for towns and their inhabitants in the industrialisation process. It is not hard to see why this should be the case if we look at the example of Sweden. Between 1870 and 1920 regional industrial development generated rapid productivity growth but without a dense network of urban centres; indeed, industrial productivity in Sweden grew by over seven times that in Italy, which did have significant urban networks.[28]

A related, but nonetheless discrete, organising model – the theory of regional comparative advantage – has little more to say about the role of urban areas when applied by continental historians. Pollard drew together a substantial European literature on the location of rural industry and offered a 'shopping list' of variables which might shape regional industrial structures – a list implicitly drawn on by many of the contributions to this volume. Pollard suggested that a vigorous and evolutionary set of industrial structures would be found in those regions that could demonstrate strong physical cohesion (good transport infrastructure, access to trade routes, unity as a financial region through mechanisms of credit); had access to a skilled and flexible labour force; were open to entrepreneurial activity and the development of entrepreneurial networks through marriage or association; gave entrepreneurs access to local political power, allowing them to shape the creation of a basic regional social infrastructure; had strong links to regions of commercial agriculture for food and raw materials; possessed plentiful natural resources and the peculiar regional ability to make use of them; had an industrial tradition; were tied into a system of responsive (not necessarily open) national and regional government; and fostered flexible connections with markets.[29] Urbanisation, or at least access to domestic urban markets, was a further important variable, though not in itself sufficient to underpin regional industrialisation: an observation that is also implicit in the analysis of Trinder and Stobart (Chapter 7).

This is less a theory of regional industrialisation than a call to arms for local and regional historians. In practice, however, scholars have tended to concentrate their empirical analysis on just a few of these variables rather than asking wider questions about the nature of regional industrialisation, conforming to a European historiographical tendency at the end of the twentieth century to think small rather than big.[30] Micro-studies have increasingly suggested that comparative advantage in factors of production is not sufficient to explain why some regions industrialise and others not, or why some regions industrialise a lot and others a little.[31] This said, the relative distribution of factors of production and production advantages retains a hold on the psyche of many industrial historians. In this volume too we can see much by way of the balancing of comparative advantages, with Stobart and Raven pointing persuasively to 'layers' of previous investment in the physical, cultural, social and economic infrastructure of the Midlands (see Chapter 1). This investment paid off, they argue, and placed towns at the hub of the comparative advantages enjoyed by Midlands industries. In turn, this concept of layered investment may provide a vehicle for refining the notion of comparative advantage to realise the systematic regional studies that lay at the heart of Pollard's wish list.

Pollard's wider conclusion, that the most vibrant European industrial regions were locked together in complex relationships of competition and complementarity, has also underpinned subtler continental model-building on the causes, location and character of regional industrialisation. In particular, Pfister has used transaction-cost theory to construct a simplified model of the criteria for industrial growth, arguing that regions with low internal transaction costs and those (often the same places) whose transaction costs were lowered by wider European industrialisation were most likely to experience consistent industrialisation.[32] He suggests that proto-industrial regions contained the seeds of stagnation and decline in their very fabric, and that the degree to which the germination of these seeds could be retarded or compensated for shaped the nature of the proto-industrial growth process and determined which if any regions moved forward from a proto-industrial base. Thus if we assume constant factor productivity, one of the key influences on the viability of the regional industrialisation process is likely to have been the supply of labour and the way in which that labour was configured in a labour market. The key, according to Pfister, was to have a flexible labour market in which the transaction costs of employing and supervising the right type of labour were minimised. It thus does not matter in this model whether guilds, manorial regulation or bodies intervening between entrepreneur and labour were present, merely whether they actively facilitated the development of a local industrial system. The size of the labour force was a central variable, and this might be expanded either by using population growth within a region and fostering greater industrial involvement at household level, or by seeking to expand the labour market geographically. Alternatively, and implicitly in the Pfister model, entrepreneurs could locate industrial establishments in towns, using the traditional 'honey-pot' effect on migrant labour to facilitate regional industrial expansion.[33] The nature of the transport network was also an important variable in determining the extent and durability of growth. Rapid transport facilities and multi-level interconnection of proto-industrial regions with railways, canals and roads kept down the marginal costs of employment and marketing and in the best cases could facilitate the development of near-perfect information markets. In a similar fashion, good transport infrastructure within proto-industrial regions could minimise the opportunity costs of merchants and sub-contractors. The role of the state in protecting or subsidising industries (and thus influencing transaction costs) was also, Pfister suggests, a key variable in shaping the nature of European regional industrial growth, something which English historians tend to forget.[34] Moreover, Pfister takes up earlier work from Hudson and other European financial historians to emphasise the importance of a developed credit and financial network as a way of containing the inherent destructive tendencies of the proto-industrial system, suggesting that transaction and unit costs could be contained for much longer in proto-industrial communities such as Lancashire, Yorkshire and Zurich than was the case in the European metalworking areas simply because of the nature of credit mechanisms.

Ultimately, however, Pfister argues that overhead costs per unit of output inevitably increased with the maturity of the proto-industrial regions and their level of output, making industrial production in these centres vulnerable to undercutting by younger regions where labour and other externalities could be accumulated anew. Since marginal profit rates tended to fall in the established industrial regions – because of these labour market conditions, because the amount of circulating capital needed to run a proto-industrial concern rose while its velocity fell and because systems of inspection became more expensive – entrepreneurs also tended to starve existing proto-industrial regions of new investment, increasing the likelihood of stagnation. This is essentially a negative model, but its implication is that there would have been considerable pressure to both mechanise and centralise (usually in urban areas) as a way of reducing marginal overhead costs. Pfister also argues that putting these strategies into practice and thus creating a new phase of industrialisation in proto-industrial regions was most likely to occur where such regions were 'mature' and had already experienced organisational complexity, and in those regions where a distant state and weak manorial structures combined to foster an acceptance of the need for organic development, as was the case for instance in much of English proto-industry. Interestingly, many of the contributions to this volume use basic transaction-cost analysis as a way of understanding the industrialisation of parts of the Midlands, stressing the importance of transport improvement, the spatial concentration of certain industrial functions (such as pottery, for instance) or the foundation of a banking structure (in Nottingham, for instance) for the industrialisation process. These are precisely the sorts of things that Pfister saw as capping inherent tendencies for transaction costs to spiral in maturing industrial regions.

Of course, all models are based upon simplifying assumptions, and Pfister's framework is no different. Thus while there is considerable evidence that overhead costs *could* increase as industrial regions expanded and aged, this is not to say that they inevitably *did* increase. Moreover, where industrial regions changed the exact mix of production processes that they hosted, it is possible – as Ellis suggests for the industrial region centred upon Nottingham (Chapter 9) – that marginal overhead costs may have fallen in the more advanced stages of regional industrial development. This was also the case where the exact path of regional development led to an increase in the speed of the circulation of capital, which could outweigh the rising costs associated with a geographic expansion in the labour force needed to underpin increased early industrial production. Nor is transaction-cost theory a logical model for all situations. Urban areas pose a particular problem. Under certain conditions, older European manufacturing towns remained an important focus of production rather than simply finishing and marketing. Nottingham is a classic example. The marginal costs of labour and power in these places tended to be higher than in rural areas or new manufacturing towns. Such costs were only partly compensated by easier and cheaper access to capital, access to the cultural and social facilities of urban areas for entrepreneurs (something that Hann deals with in Chapter 3) and the development of new and cheaper ways of identifying and retaining the most productive and honest workers. In other words, regional industrialisation could take place within a framework of rising transaction costs, particularly where the need for specialised labour was important or where there was a long-term technological imperative. The need to access market information speedily, or to take advantage of the labour and quality systems established by guilds, might also lead entrepreneurs to act in ways alien to the logic of transaction-cost theory.[35] Yet it is clear that Pfister's attempt to theorise regional industrial development provides a powerful tool that will be used extensively to guide local and regional empirical research in the future. In particular it would be useful to apply a more carefully defined transaction-cost model to the Midlands experience to find out if some of the contradictions identified by contributors to this volume – the marginal role of Lichfield versus the fuller industrialisation of Loughborough, for instance – can be explained by differing level of transaction costs or different cost trajectories.

Other European scholars have employed alternative organising frameworks. Lis and Soly, and more recently Gorissen, have suggested that the key factor in understanding regional industrialisation across Europe is not the relative balance of comparative advantage or the role of towns on the supply and demand side, but the presence and relative capacities of entrepreneurs.[36] Such conclusions chime with many of the contributions to this volume. Meanwhile, Ogilvie has placed the flexibility of institutional structures at the heart of her study of the development of the Württemberg woollen industry, as have Hudson and King in their analysis of the Yorkshire woollen industry.[37] De Vries offers a further model of regional industrialisation, suggesting that such development was powered by rising consumption standards on the demand side and the industrious revolution on the supply side.[38] This model also resonates through several of the chapters in this volume. Whilst much more could be said on these and other organising frameworks, the key point is that these competing theoretical frameworks – allied with a recent tendency for the 'grand theory' as an analytical framework for regional analysis to be displaced by micro-research and the econometric analysis of national economic numbers – mean that we can only begin to map out the most sketchy of answers to questions such as why some industrial regions develop rapidly and others slowly, or why some demonstrate considerable longevity and others flare brilliantly but briefly. Even sketchy answers, however, highlight the fact that the role of towns in the industrialisation process in general and regional industrialisation in particular is by no means clear on the European stage. Towns might be important drivers of regional economic change, acting, as they often seem to have done in England and certainly in the Midlands, as vibrant sources of production and consumption. On the other hand, they might be dependent variables, developing in response to wider regional trends, and at best sustaining industrial development rather than providing initial momentum. Or towns might, as is the case with the framework offered by proto-industrial historians, be a positive hindrance to regional economic development. Local empirical studies across Europe could sustain all three arguments.

Urbanisation and regional development: some typologies

To make sense of the plethora of regional and local studies, we must come back again to some of the basic observations of Pollard. He argued that the yardsticks by which we should measure what made a successful industrial region were clear: urbanisation or access to domestic urban markets, capitalised entrepreneurs, mobile and previously skilled workforce, access to favourable natural resources, the absence of obstruction in the product and factor markets and a transport system that was sufficiently fast, reliable and extensive to allow the creation of outward-looking regions within which significant externalities could be created. Pollard also argued that in the macro-sense there were many similarities between the basic infrastructures of European industrial regions. The latter observation in particular should not surprise us. It becomes ever clearer that technology, capital, skilled labour, product design and market information flowed around the European economic system with much more velocity and effect than historians have ever realised.[39] European exporters, whether based in Birmingham, Nottingham, Zurich or Ravensberg, competed for market share based upon price, quality and product and faced similar pressures for innovation, product development and cost-cutting.[40]

Micro-studies of European textile regions provide support for the idea of macro-similarities in basic infrastructure. Thus the artisans of the west Yorkshire woollen cloth industry produced similar products to their counterparts in the Pays de Mauges or the Cambresis. They faced the same struggle to maintain their artisan traditions against technological and entrepreneurial incursion, deployed similar coping mechanisms, used exactly the same language in describing their struggle and lived in similar economic regions.[41] Manchester looked, in terms of economic structure, economic function, relation to its hinterland and even its basic industrial archaeology, much like Aachen or Brno. The towns also had a similar entrepreneurial structure.[42] In terms of products, production structures and trajectories of growth and decline, the west Yorkshire worsted industry centred on Halifax looked very similar to the new drapery industries of the Sedan. Nor were the macro-similarities between industrial regions confined simply to textile areas. In terms of the nature of their products, the structure of the labour force, the relationship between land and industry and the nature of entrepreneurship, Birmingham and its hinterland (including places such as West Bromwich, analysed earlier in this volume) looked much like Ravensberg or Solingen.

These and other themes – particularly the similarities in the institutional and agrarian starting points of several European industrial regions – were brought together by Berg, Hudson and Sonenscher in 1983 in an initial attempt to theorise the construction and deconstruction of the industrial region.[43] But we have moved little further since then. Whilst it is possible to identify common influences on, and characteristics of, the European regional industrialisation process by reading micro-studies side by side, differences in sources, methods, key questions and philosophies make systematic synthesis difficult. The potentially complex relationship between urbanisation and economic development has been a particular casualty of the lack of historiographical synthesis. It would be much easier, for example, to understand the role of towns in the industrialisation of the Midlands were we able to locate the process firmly in the European literature, but this is still not possible, despite the presence in this volume of the comparative analysis of Belgian industrialisation. Yet there is a bigger theoretical picture to be drawn, and one that must be drawn if we accept Pollard's conclusion that the mechanism that shaped the regional distribution of industries 'lies at the heart of the mechanism of industrialisation itself '.[44] One way forward is to draw on Pollard's shopping list and the similarities and differences in the regional industrialisation process that increasingly emerge out of European micro-studies to produce several regional industrial development typologies. Of course, such an exercise would be beset with exceptions, would be overly static whereas most regional structures tend to be relatively dynamic, and would smack of subjectivity. However, in the final part of this chapter I will suggest that – using the criteria devised by Pollard – it is possible to begin parcelling the results of European micro-studies, as well as those contained in this volume, into five typologies.

Firstly, we might think in terms of opportunistic/fragile industrial regions. In this typology we might include some of the hosiery districts of the east Midlands, the Alps, most of the Swiss Cantons and the German Westerwald.[45] Such regions, sometimes extensions of more fully developed industrial regions, had strict limits to growth with inevitable increases in marginal costs as production expanded. Relatively poor intra- and inter-regional transport systems, unsegmented labour markets and the fact that the capital and entrepreneurship needed to underpin the organisation of production were usually drawn from outside the region created a fragile equilibrium between rising profits and rising transaction costs, and these were the peripheral regions that suffered first and most in the face of international competition. Such regions were relatively weakly urbanised, with a disproportionate number of large industrial villages (a contention supported by Hann's analysis of urban service provision in Chapter 3), and demonstrated little entrepreneurial connection with markets and limited responsiveness to changing fashions. Natural resources tended to be relatively poor, and these fragile industrial regions generally failed (even if some individual urban areas such as Loughborough bucked the trend) to generate the strong growth of middling classes which helped to underpin longer-term development in some of the other typologies suggested here.

Secondly, many micro-studies have been concerned with mono-industrial/simple-product regions. In this typology we might include the textile industries of the French Cambresis, the German metalworking areas of Spenge and Ravensberg, the German linen areas of Belm and Osnabrück, the Swedish linen regions of Hälsningland and Angermansland and the Württemberg worsted industry.[46] Such regions could also be characterised by strict limits to growth and were particularly vulnerable to external market conditions. However, they often had relatively good intra- and inter-regional transport systems and good access to food supplies, and, while production was based upon the capacities of a largely unsegmented labour force, the fact that economic development rarely broke completely the strong connection between industrial and agrarian systems helped to contain transaction costs. These basic infrastructural aspects allowed some of these regions to develop from a proto-industrial base, though in other cases rising transaction costs merely brought industrial involution. The capital input to such regional industrial structures was drawn from both inside and outside the region. In similar fashion, the entrepreneurial talent for regional industrialisation was a mixture of native regional and non-native, with farmers often figuring prominently in the entrepreneurial class. As a consequence, at least some of the profits from industrialisation were kept inside the region, helping to foster the development of a middling class, which could help to underpin the development of consumer markets. Large-scale urban development in such regions was often sparse, but the key point is that urbanisation, where it did occur, was a dependent variable.

Thirdly, we might identify diversified industrial/complex-product regions. In this typology we might include the Black Country, west Yorkshire and Lancashire, the Aachen textile region, the Pays de Mauges and much of the Hungarian industrial belt.[47] We might also include Nottingham and the other two county capitals of the east Midlands analysed by Ellis (see Chapter 9), for despite the discrete nature of economic activity in some of these towns it is nonetheless clear that collectively they formed one overarching diversified product region. Such regions benefited from extensive externalities and the rise of complementary industries, and together these influences slowed the rise of transaction costs. Limits to growth were thus frequently pushed backwards in a classic economic growth scenario, allowing rapid development from a proto-industrial base. When marginal costs rose, the fact that both capital and entrepreneurship were usually drawn from inside the region meant that there were both the resources and the drive to move regional industrial structures onto a new plane. Organic diversified regions of this sort usually had strong transport systems and multi-segmented labour markets (in turn underpinned by a high-pressure migratory system), which allowed entrepreneurs greater manoeuvrability when it came to creating production chains. Such entrepreneurs had good connections with product markets, and regional industrial development coincided with strong intra-regional consumption markets and the rise of a substantial and wealthy middling class, as was the case for instance in West Bromwich. Where the development of this sort of region coincided with urban growth (and it did not always do so) the relationship was usually one in which urban growth was initially the dependent variable.

Moreover, even when such industrial regions matured, there was often an ambiguous relationship between urbanisation and industrialisation, particularly where the older towns of the region were concerned. Raven and Hooley, and Stobart and Raven confirm that this is the case in their contributions to this volume.

Fourthly, we might think in terms of specialist industrial regions. In this typology we might include the lace-making industries of south-west England and northern France, the Danish and Swiss watchmaking region, the cutlery-making industries of Germany and England, the silk industry of Krefeld, the fine woollen industry in Brno and Moravia and the pottery districts of Staffordshire (see Chapter 7) and Jutland.[48] Such regions were often mono-industrial, relied on raw materials from outside the region, and were tied very closely to fashions in national and international markets. Production was largely workshop-based and centred on urban areas, thereby limiting the potential for rising transaction costs to disrupt regional production systems. In any case, given that such regions often displayed a very diversified product base, continually shifting what was produced and its style or quality, trends in marginal costs would rarely have been clear. Entrepreneurial drive for the region was substantially drawn from the ranks of native workshop owners, and these entrepreneurs could usually draw on an experienced handicraft workforce with long traditions of education and skill development. Labour markets were generally unsegmented, and this, together with high-quality inter-regional transport links and early technical innovation, was a major factor in extraordinary responsiveness to new threads of market information. The boundaries of these specialist regions tended to be very clear and stable, in contrast to those of all the other regional typologies, as was the case certainly in the Staffordshire pottery industry.

Finally, the European literature, in contrast to that in England, is full of instances of planned industrial regions. In this typology we might include the Italian entrepôts, the French fine wool regions, most of the Dutch textile regions and the heavy industrial regions of Luxembourg and Scandinavia.[49] Such regions inevitably witnessed a strong overlap between political and industrial systems, and the involvement of the state at national or regional level frustrates the logic of transaction-cost models. A combination of subsidy, protection and other perks (in most planned regions there was a strong connection to military supply) meant that marginal costs were not important to the entrepreneurs who founded and grew such regions. Entrepreneurs were usually outsiders, and they employed capital that was jointly from inside and outside the regional industrial system. Labour markets in such areas tended to be highly segmented, and some labour was always external to the region itself. Comparative advantage in terms of power or raw materials was usually missing from planned regions, and transport links were often only moderate. The development of planned regional systems was often connected with the foundation or expansion of urban settlements, and even where it was not urban areas in planned systems had important production and marketing functions.

Conclusion

As we know from the case of the Midlands, it was possible for the characteristics of regional economies to change rapidly over time, and even for regions to switch between the sorts of typology suggested here. The development of the east Midlands, which saw industrial involution at its periphery but developed into a diversified product region at its core in the nineteenth century, is a classic example. Were we to compile an exhaustive list of the continental micro-studies of industrial communities and regions, more, and more complex, typologies might become necessary to cope with the vagaries of regional dynamism or decline. However, it is possible to contemplate the creation of regional typologies of the sort suggested by Pollard, even if the models advanced here do not exactly hit the mark. If we are ever to pin down the theoretical and practical role of towns in the industrialisation process in general and the regional industrialisation process in particular, we must bring together the lessons of several hundred continental as well as English micro-studies and come up with new models of regional economic development. For the purposes of this chapter, what these admittedly crude typologies show is that, when we take account of the continental literature, there was no inevitable or necessarily strong relationship between towns, industry and regional economic development: a conclusion which echoes the findings of Greefs, Blondé and Clark (Chapter 13). Urbanisation could be a dependent or an independent variable in different regions, and it could be both in the same region at different times. In the most complex industrial regions, it is perfectly feasible for one town to have been stimulating economic development at the same time as another, because of peculiar institutional or socioeconomic factors, was holding it back. This difference of emphasis between the English and continental historiography may, as Stobart and Raven suggest in Chapter 1, reflect the fact that England had a very different, urban-based, industrial revolution from the continent. The jury must remain out on this idea for two reasons. First detailed regional pictures are rare. Indeed, judged as a whole, this volume provides a model for the systematic regional case studies that are necessary across Europe if we are to reconstruct the nature of the regional industrialisation process. Second, we lack the conceptual framework to generalise from the numerous micro-studies available to us. Thus, while this volume takes the English literature forward, it also demonstrates the difficulty of making wider claims. A distinction has been drawn between textile, pottery and metalworking areas within the Midlands, between industrial areas centred on coalfields and those not, and between areas tied into the international economy and those more loosely integrated. As Stobart and Raven observe, there was a significant difference of economic emphasis between east and west Midlands, with the Birmingham area at the core of the industrial identity of the Midlands. Nonetheless, they suggest, personal and business networks, transport networks and retailing patterns tied together different economic parts of the Midlands sufficiently to give some industrial and spatial coherence. Many continental historians looking at England or faced with exactly similar circumstances in their own country might disagree. They might, instead, regard the Midlands as several discrete industrial districts, concentrating less on networks of linkage than on the clear space between the spheres of influence of different towns and villages, and the significant differences of experience and structure between core and periphery. This much is clear from the existing literature. To go further and to see if England really was different would require a subtler conceptual framework. The typologies suggested here might be a starting point and, in a process of reconstructing *European regional* industrialisation, their use would probably link the experiences of Birmingham more forcefully with those of Solingen or Ravensberg than with Nottingham. Alternatively we might employ a transaction-cost framework; if so, the contributors to this volume have made a powerful implicit case for regarding the Midlands as one economic region. Or we might, as Stobart and Raven suggested right at the start of the volume, employ geographical and network analysis models to the experiences of individual towns. Whatever future agenda we employ, this volume on the industrialisation of the English Midlands can surely make wider claims to be a template for that agenda.

Notes

1 This chapter arises out of work on comparisons between English and German industrial regions with Professor Dr Dietrich Ebeling of the University of Trier. We are grateful to the British Academy and the Deutchsforschungsgemeinschaft for financial support.

2 Much of the literature is summarised elsewhere in this volume, but for a few examples that are pertinent to this chapter, see Wrigley, 'Simple model'; Corfield, 'Provincial capital'; Schwarz, *London*. However, see More, *Industrial Revolution*, pp. 132–5 for a recent contribution that makes little reference to towns as growth generators.

3 This is explored extensively in the contributions to the excellent Brakensiek and Flugel, *Regionalgeschichte*.

4 Witness, for instance, the peculiarly German debate over 'greater' and 'lesser' industrial regions reviewed in Ebeling and Mager, *Protoindustrie*.

5 For a more general discussion of theory, see North, *Theorie*. For a stimulating theoretical discussion of the role of 'second cities' see Belchem, *Merseypride*.

6 Christaller, *Central Places*.

7 See van der Wee, *Rise and Decline*; Hohenberg, 'Urban manufactures'; Lepetit, *Urban System*; Birke and Kettenacker, *Wettlauf*; Freudenberger, *Industrialisation*. On the particular importance of urban demand see Chapters 3 and 6 of this volume.

8 Ebeling, *Historisch-thematische*.

9 This is a very old distinction in the German literature, but has much more rarely been made in the study of English industrial regions. See Barkhausen, *Die Tuchindustrie*; Baar, *Die Berliner*.

10 See Lis and Soly, 'Entrepreneurs'; Lis and Soly, 'Stadtische Industrialisierungswege'.

11 Soderberg, *A Stagnating*.

12 See Chassagne, *Le coton*; Reddy, *Market Culture*; Vardi, *Land and the Loom*.

13 Ebeling and Schmidt, 'Zunftige'; Gorissen, 'Vorindustrielle'.

14 Mendels, 'Des industries', p. 984.

15 Mendels, 'Proto-industrialisation'; Mendels, 'Agriculture and peasant industry'.

16 Mendels, 'Industrialization and population pressure'.

17 Sombart, *Der moderne*.

18 Kriedte, Medick and Schlumbohm, *Industry*. For more detailed individual work, see Kriedte, *Eine Stadt*; Medick, *Weben*; Schlumbohm, *Lebenslaufe*.

19 For synthesis see Cerman and Ogilvie, *Proto-Industrialisation*. The most perceptive commentary is perhaps Flugel, 'Region und Gewerbe'.

20 See Berg, Hudson and Sonenscher, *Manufacture*; Lewis, 'Proto-industrialization'; Ditt and Pollard, *Von der Heimarbeit*.

21 Levine, *Family Formation*.

22 Sabel and Zeitlin, 'Historical alternatives', p. 140.

23 Berend and Ranki, *European Periphery*, p. 9.

24 Berend and Ranki, *European Periphery*, pp. 10–11. In particular they claimed that 'centuries of changelessness, centralisation, state serfdom and the particular tenacity of communal landholding' were the institutional factors marking out the periphery.

25 Lieberman, *Industrialisation of Norway*.

26 Hoppe and Langton, *Peasantry to Capitalism*.

27 Poztsgai, *Industrialisation of Hungary*.

28 Landes, *Unbound Prometheus*; Kemp, *Industrialisation*; Isacson and Magnusson, *Proto-Industrialisation*.

29 Pollard also made the key point that many regions contained the seeds of their own destruction: Pollard, 'Regional markets'.

30 See Komlos, 'Ein Überblick'.

31 See for instance Ebeling and Schmidt, 'Zunftige' and also Chapter 7 in this volume.

32 For different stages of the formulation of this theory, see Pfister, *Die Zürcher*; Pfister, 'A general model'; Pfister, 'Proto-industrial household'.

33 Ellis, in Chapter 9 of this volume, portrays Nottingham as just such a honey-pot

in her attempt to locate the town at the centre of industrialisation in the east Midlands.

34 There is a rich literature on state-sponsored industrialisation. For one of the best early studies see Fischer, *Government Activity*; more recent is Kriedte, 'Die Stadt'.

35 A logical extension of the argument of Wanklyn in Chapter 12 of this volume. See Hickson and Thompson, 'A new theory'.

36 Lis and Soly, 'Entrepreneurs'; Gorissen, *Vom Handelshaus*.

37 Ogilvie, *State*; Hudson and King, 'Industrialising townships'.

38 De Vries, 'Industrial revolution'. See also Chapter 3 of this volume.

39 See Berg and Bruland, *Technological Revolutions*.

40 Chaudhury and Morineau, *Merchants*.

41 See Heaton, *Yorkshire Woollen*; Vardi, *Land and the Loom*; Liu, *Weaver's Knot*.

42 Lloyd Jones and Lewis, *Manchester*; Freudenberger, *Industrialisation*.

43 Berg, Hudson and Sonenscher, *Manufacture*.

44 Pollard, *Peaceful Conquest*, p. 23. He also warned that 'We are very far from a full understanding of that mechanism', something which remains true despite a burgeoning list of micro-studies.

45 Although Clark in Chapter 10 shows that Loughborough had a broad-based economy, it was located in a region where industrial development was built upon relatively weak foundations. See Levine, *Family Formation*.

46 Vardi, *Land and the Loom*; Mager, 'Spenge'; Flugel, 'Region und Gewerbe'; Schlumbohm, *Lebenslaufe;* Magnusson, 'Proto-industrialisation'; Ogilvie, 'Soziale Institutionen'.

47 Timmins, *Made in Lancashire;* Liu, *Weaver's Knot*; Poztsgai, *Industrialisation of Hungary*.

48 Guldberg, *Domestic Industry;* King and Timmins, *Making Sense*; Kriedte, *Peasants*; Freudenberger, *Industrialisation*.

49 Ciriacono, 'Mass consumption'; van der Wee, *Rise and Decline*.

Bibliography

Aikin, J., *A Description of the Country from Thirty to Forty Miles round Manchester* (London, 1795).

Albert, W., *The Turnpike Road System in England 1663–1840* (Cambridge, 1972).

Aldcroft, D. and Freeman, M. (eds), *Transport in the Industrial Revolution* (Manchester, 1983).

Alderton, D. and Booker, J., *Guide to the Industrial Archaeology of East Anglia* (London, 1980).

Alexander, D., *Retailing in England during the Industrial Revolution* (London, 1970).

Angerstein, R., *Industry in England and Wales from a Swedish Perspective* (London, 2001).

Armstrong, W. A., 'The use of information about occupation', in E. A. Wrigley (ed.), *Nineteenth-Century Society* (Cambridge, 1972).

Arnade, P., Howell, M. and Simons, W., 'Fertile spaces: the productivity of urban space in northern Europe', *Journal of Interdisciplinary History*, 32 (2002), 515–48.

Arthur, W. B.,'Competing technologies, increasing returns and lock-in by historical events', *Economic Journal*, 99 (1989), 116–31.

Aspin, C., 'New evidence on James Hargreaves and the spinning industry', *Textile History*, 1 (1968), pp. 119–21.

Aycoberry, P., *Cologne entre Napoleon et Bismarck* (Paris, 1981).

Baar, L., *Die Berliner Industrie in der industriellen Revolution* (Berlin, 1966).

Bairoch, P., 'La Belgique dans le commerce international, 1830–1990', in P. Klep and E. Van Cauwenberghe (eds), *Entrepreneurship and the Transformation of the Economy* (Leuven, 1994).

Barker, H., 'Women, work and the industrial revolution', in H. Barker and E. Chalus (eds), *Gender in Eighteenth-Century England: Roles, Representations and Responsibilities* (Harlow, 1997).

Barker, H. and Chalus, E., 'Introduction', in H. Barker and E. Chalus (eds), *Gender in Eighteenth-Century England: Roles, Representations and Responsibilities* (Harlow, 1997).

Barker, T. and Gerhold, D., *The Rise and Rise of Road Transport, 1700–1990* (Basingstoke, 1993).

Barkhausen, E., *Die Tuchindustrie in Montjoie: Aufstieg und Niedergang* (Aachen, 1925).

Barnsby, G. J., 'The standard of living in the Black Country during the nineteenth century', *Economic History Review*, 24 (1971), 220–39.

Barnsby, G. J., *The Working Class Movement in the Black Country 1750–1867* (Wolverhampton, 1977).

Barnsby, G. J., *A History of Housing in Wolverhampton, 1750–1975* (Wolverhampton, no date).

Barry, J., 'Cultural patronage and the Anglican crisis: Bristol c. 1689–1775', in J. Walsh, C. Haydon and S. Taylor (eds), *The Church of England c. 1689–1833* (Cambridge, 1993).

Bartlett, J., *Carpeting the Millions* (Edinburgh, 1978).

Bartley, P., 'Moral regeneration: women and the civic gospel in Birmingham, 1870–1914', *Midland History*, 25 (2000), 143–61.

Beckett, J. V., *The East Midlands from AD 1000* (London, 1988).

Beckett, J. V. (ed.), *A Centenary History of Nottingham* (Manchester, 1997).

Beckett, J. V. and Smith, C. 'Urban renaissance and consumer revolution in Nottingham, 1688–1750', *Urban History*, 27 (2000), 31–50.

Beckwith, I., 'The river trade of Gainsborough, 1500–1850', *Lincolnshire History and Archaeology*, 2 (1967), 3–20.

Behagg, C., *Politics and Production in the Early Nineteenth Century* (London, 1990).

Belchem, J., *Merseypride: Essays in Liverpool Exceptionalism* (Liverpool, 2000).

Bennett, J., 'History that stands still: women's work in the European past', *Feminist Studies*, 14 (1988), 269–83.

Benson, J., *et al.*, 'Sources for the study of urban retailing', *Local Historian*, 29 (1999), 167–82.

Berend, I. and Ranki, G., *The European Periphery and Industrialisation, 1780–1914* (Cambridge, 1982).

Berg, M., 'Women's work, mechanisation and the early phases of industrialisation in England', in P. Joyce (ed.) *The Historical Meanings of Work* (Cambridge, 1987).

Berg, M., 'Commerce and creativity in eighteenth-century Birmingham', in M. Berg (ed.), *Markets and Manufactures in Early Industrial Europe* (London, 1991).

Berg, M. (ed.), *Markets and Manufacture in Early Industrial Europe* (London, 1991).

Berg, M., 'What difference did women's work make to the industrial revolution?', *History Workshop Journal*, 35 (1993), 22–44.

Berg, M., 'Women's property and the industrial revolution', *Journal of Interdisciplinary History*, 24 (1993), 233–50.

Berg, M., *The Age of Manufactures, 1700–1820: Industry, Innovation and Work in Britain* (London, second edition, 1994).

Berg, M., 'Women's consumption and the industrial classes of eighteenth-century England', *Journal of Social History*, 30 (1996), 415–34.

Berg, M., 'New commodities, luxuries and their consumers in eighteenth-century England', in M. Berg and H. Clifford (eds), *Consumers and Luxury: Consumer Culture in Europe 1650–1850* (Manchester, 1999).

Berg, M. and Bruland, K., *Technological Revolutions in Europe: Historical Perspectives* (Cheltenham, 1998).

Berg, M. and Hudson, P., 'Rehabilitating the industrial revolution', *Economic History Review*, 45 (1992), 4–50.

Berg, M., Hudson, P. and Sonenscher, M, *Manufacture in Town and Country before the Factory* (Cambridge, 1983).

Birke, A. and Kettenacker, L., *Wettlauf in die Moderne: England und Deutschland seit der industriellen Revolution* (Göttingen, 1988).

Black, I., 'Geography, political economy and the circulation of finance capital in early industrial England', *Journal of Historical Geography*, 15 (1989), 366–84.

Black, I., 'Money, information and space: banking in early nineteenth century England and Wales', *Journal of Historical Geography*, 21 (1995), 398–412.

Blackner, J., *The History of Nottingham* (Nottingham, 1815).

Blalock, H. M., *Social Statistics* (London, 1981).

Blome, R., *Britannia* (London, 1673).

Blondé, B., 'Disparities in the development of the Brabantine urban network: urban centrality, town-countryside relationships, and transportation development', in C.-E. Núñez (ed.), *Recent Doctoral Research in Economic History* (Madrid, 1998).

Blondé, B., *Een economie met verschillende snelheden: ongelijkheden in de opbouw en de ontwikkeling van het Brabantse stedelijke netwerk* (Brussels, 1999).

Blondé, B. and Greefs, H., 'Werk aan de winkel: de Antwerpse meerseniers: aspecten van de kleinhandel en het verbruik', *Bijdragen tot de geschiedenis*, 84 (2001), 207–29.

Borsay, P., *The English Urban Renaissance: Culture and Society in the Provincial Town 1660–1770* (Oxford, 1989).

Borsay, P., 'Health and leisure resorts 1700–1840', in P. Clark (ed.), *The Cambridge Urban History of Britain*, vol. 2: *1540–1840* (Cambridge, 2000).

Botham, F. and Hunt, E., 'Wages in Britain during the industrial revolution', *Economic History Review*, 40 (1987), 380–99.

Brakensiek, S. and Flugel, A. (eds), *Regionalgeschichte in Europa: Methoden und Ertrage der Forschung* (Paderborn, 2000).

Brewer, J., *The Pleasures of the Imagination: English Culture in the Eighteenth Century* (London, 1997).

Brown, A. (ed.), *The Growth of Leicester* (Leicester, 1972).

Bruwier, M., 'Le charbon dans le Borinage et le centre', in P. Lebrun, M. Bruwier, J. Dhondt and G. Hansotte, *Essai sur la révolution industrielle en Belgique, 1770–1847* (Brussels, 1979).

Bruwier, M., 'Etudes sur le réseau urbain en Hainaut de 1350 à 1850', in M. Bruwier, *Le réseau urbain en Belgique dans une perspective historique (1350–1850)* (Brussels, 1992).

Bruwier, M., 'L'industrie avant la révolution industrielle: une proto-industrialisation?', in M. Bruwier, *Industrie et société en Hainaut et en Wallonie du XVIIIe au Xxe siècle* (Brussels, 1996).

Burritt, E., *Walks in the Black Country and its Green Borderland* (London, 1863).

Burt, R., 'The network entrepreneur', in R. Swedberg (ed.), *Entrepreneurship: The Social Science View* (Oxford, 2000).

Byng, J., *The Torrington Diaries*, ed. C. Bruyn Andrews, 4 vols (London, 1934).

Cameron, R., 'A new view of European industrialization', *Economic History Review*, 38 (1985), 1–23.

Campion, G., 'People, process, power and place: an archaeology of control in east Midlands outworking, 1820–1900', in M. Palmer and P. Neaverson (eds), *From Industrial Revolution to Consumer Revolution* (Telford, 2001).

Cannadine, D., 'British history: past, present and future?', *Past and Present*, 116 (1987), 169–91.

Carter, H., *The Study of Urban Geography* (London, fourth edition, 1995).

Carus-Wilson, E. M., 'An industrial revolution in the thirteenth century', *Economic History Review*, 2 (1940–41), 39–60.

Casson, M. and Rose, M. B., 'Institutions and the evolution of modern business', *Business History*, 39 (1997), 1–8.

Caulier-Mathy, N., 'Le patronat et le progrès technique dans les charbonnages liégeois, 1800–1914', in G. Kurgan-Van Hentenryk and J. Stengers (eds), *L'innovation technologique: facteur de changement* (Brussels, 1986).

Caulier-Mathy, N., 'De wording van de steenkoolindustrie', in B. Van der Herten, M. Oris and J. Roegiers (eds), *Nijver België: het industriële landschap omstreeks 1850* (Deurne, 1995).

Cerman, M. and Ogilvie, S. (eds), *Proto-Industrialization in Europe* (Cambridge, 1996).

Chaloner, W. H. and Marshall, J. D., 'Major Cartwright and the revolution mill', in N. B. Harte and K. G. Ponting (eds), *Textile History and Economic History* (Manchester, 1973).

Chalus, E., '"That epidemical madness": women and electoral politics in the late eighteenth century', in H. Barker and E. Chalus (eds), *Gender in Eighteenth-Century England: Roles, Representations and Responsibilities* (Harlow, 1997).

Chambers, J., *A General History of Worcester* (Worcester, 1820).

Chambers, J. and Mingay, G., *The Agricultural Revolution 1750–1880* (London, 1966).

Champion, W., 'John Ashby and the history and environs of the Lion Inn, Shrewsbury', *Shropshire History and Archaeology*, 75 (2000), 49–58.

Chapman, S. and Sharpe, P., 'Women's employment and industrial organisation: commercial lace embroidery in early nineteenth-century Ireland and England', *Women's History Review*, 5 (1996), 325–50.

Chapman, S. D., *The Early Factory Masters: The Transition to the Factory System in the Midlands Textile Industry* (Newton Abbot, 1967).

Chapman, S. D., 'Memoirs of two eighteenth-century framework knitters', *Textile History*, 1 (1968), 91–114.

Chapman, S. D., 'Working-class housing in Nottingham during the industrial revolution', in S. D. Chapman (ed.), *The History of Working-Class Housing* (Newton Abbot, 1971).

Chapman, S. D., 'Enterprise and innovation in the British hosiery industry, 1750–1850', *Textile History*, 5 (1974), 14–37.

Chartres, J., 'Country trades, crafts and professions', in J. Thirsk (ed.), *The Agrarian History of England and Wales*, vol. 6 (Cambridge, 1989).

Chartres, J. and Turnbull, G., 'Road transport', in D. Aldcroft and M. Freeman (eds), *Transport in the Industrial Revolution* (Manchester, 1988).

Chassagne, S., *Le coton et ses patrons: France 1760–1840* (Paris, 1991).

Chaudhury, S. and Morineau, M. (eds), *Merchants, Companies and Trade: Europe and Asia in the Early Modern World* (Cambridge, 1999).

Chilton, C. W., 'The Universal British Directory – a warning', *Local Historian*, 15 (1982), 144–6.

Christaller, W., *Central Places in Southern Germany* (Englewood Cliffs, New Jersey, 1966).

Church, R. A., *Economic and Social Change in a Midland Town: Victorian Nottingham 1815–1900* (London, 1966).

Church, R. A., *Kenricks in Hardware* (Newton Abbot, 1969).

Churches, C., 'Women and property in early modern England: a case study', *Social History*, 23 (1998), 165–80.

Ciriacono, S., 'Mass consumption goods and luxury goods: the de-industrialisation of the Republic of Venice', in H. van der Wee (ed.), *The Rise and Decline of Urban Industries in Italy and the Low Countries* (Leuven, 1988).

Clapham, J. H. *An Economic History of Modern Britain* (Cambridge, 1930).

Clark, C., *The British Malting Industry since 1830* (London, 1998).

Clark, G., Huberman, M. and Lindert P., 'The British food puzzle 1770–1850', *Economic History Review*, 48 (1995), 215–37.

Clark, P., *The English Alehouse: A Social History* (London, 1983).

Clark, P., 'Introduction', in P. Clark (ed.), *The Transformation of English Provincial Towns 1600–1800* (London, 1984).

Clark, P., 'Small towns, 1700–1840', in P. Clark (ed.), *The Cambridge Urban History of Britain*, vol. 2: *1540–1840* (Cambridge, 2000).

Clark, P., *British Clubs and Societies 1580–1800: The Origins of an Associational World* (Oxford, 2000).

Clark, P. and Corfield, P. (eds), *Industry and Urbanisation in Eighteenth Century England* (Leicester, 1994).

Clark, P. and Hosking, J., *Population Estimates of English Small Towns, 1550–1851* (Leicester, 1993).

Clark, P. and Houston, R. A., 'Culture and leisure 1700–1840', in P. Clark (ed.), *The Cambridge Urban History of Britain*, vol. 2: *1540–1840* (Cambridge, 2000).

Clinker, C., 'The Leicester and Swannington railway', *Transactions of the Leicestershire Archaeological Society*, 30 (1954), 59–78.

Clowes, W. B., *Family Business 1803–1953* (London, 1953)

Cole, W., 'Factors in demand 1700–1800', in R. Floud and D. McCloskey (eds), *The Economic History of Britain since 1700*, vol. 1 (Cambridge, second edition, 1994).

Coleman, D., 'Proto-industrialization: a concept too many', *Economic History Review*, 36 (1983), 435–48.

Collins, D., 'Primitive or not? Fixed shop retailing before the industrial revolution', *Journal of Regional and Local Studies*, 13 (1993), 23–38.

Coppejans-Desmedt, H., 'Koning Willem I: promotor van de Gentse katoenindustrie', in H. Coppejans-Desmedt, *Album aangeboden aan Charles Verlinden ter gelegenheid van zijn dertig jaar professoraat* (Gent, 1975).

Corfield, M. C., *A Guide to the Industrial Archaeology of Wiltshire* (Trowbridge, 1978).

Corfield, P. J., 'A provincial capital in the late seventeenth century: the case of Norwich', in P. Clark and P. Slack (eds), *Crisis and Order in English Towns, 1500–1700* (London: 1975).

Corfield, P. J., *The Impact of English Towns 1700–1800* (Oxford, 1982).

Corfield, P. J., *Power and the Professions in Britain 1700–1850* (London, 1995).

Corfield, P. J. and Kelly, S., 'Giving directions to the town: the early town directories', *Urban History Yearbook* (1984), 22–35.

Court, W. H. B., *The Rise of the Midlands Industries 1650–1838* (Oxford, 1953).

Cox, N., 'The distribution of retailing tradesmen in north Shropshire, 1660–1750', *Journal of Regional and Local Studies*, 13 (1993), 4–22.

Cox, N., *The Complete Tradesman: A Study of Retailing, 1550–1820* (Aldershot, 2000).

Crafts, N. G. R., *British Economic Growth during the Industrial Revolution* (Oxford, 1985).

Crafts, N. G. R., 'British industrialisation in an international context', *Journal of Interdisciplinary History*, 19 (1989), 415–28.

Crafts, N. G. R. and Mills, T. C., 'Trends in real wages in Britain, 1750–1913', *Explorations in Economic History*, 31 (1994), 176–94.

Daunton, M., 'Towns and economic growth in eighteenth-century England', in P. Adams and E. A. Wrigley (eds), *Towns in Societies* (Cambridge, 1978).

Davidoff, L. and Hall, C., *Family Fortunes: Men and Women of the English Middle Class 1780–1850* (London, 1992).

Davis, D., *A History of Shopping* (London, 1966).

Davis, R., *The Industrial Revolution and British Overseas Trade* (Leicester, 1979).

Dawes, M. and Ward-Perkins, C. N., *Country Banks*, 2 vols (Canterbury, 2000).

De Brabander, G., *De regionaal sectoriële verdeling van de economische activiteit in België, 1846–1979* (Leuven, 1984).

De Vries, J., *European Urbanization 1500–1800* (London, 1984).

De Vries, J., 'The industrial revolution and the industrious revolution', *Journal of Economic History*, 54 (1994), 249–71.

Deakin, J., *Loughborough in the Nineteenth-Century* (Loughborough, 1927).

Deering, C., *Nottinghamia vetus et nova, or An Historical Account of the Ancient and Present State of the Town of Nottingham* (Nottingham, 1751).

Defoe, D., *Tour through the Whole Island of Great Britain*, 2 vols (1724–26, reprinted London, 1962).

Delaet, J.-L., 'La mécanisation de la verrerie à vitres à Charleroi dans la première moitié du Xxe siècle', in G. Kurgan-Van Hentenryk and J. Stengers (eds), *L'innovation technologique: facteur de changement* (Brussels, 1986).

Delaet, J.-L., 'Genèse d'un réseau urbain: Charleroi, 1750–1850', in J.-L. Delaet, *Le réseau urbain en Belgique dans une perspective historique (1350–1850)* (Brussels, 1992).

Demoulin, R., *Guillaume Ier et la transformation économique des provinces belges (1815–1830)* (Luik and Paris, 1938).

Deprez, P. and Vandenbroeke, C., 'Population growth and distribution, and urbanization in Belgium', in R. Lawton and R. Lee (eds), *Urban Population Development in Western Europe* (Liverpool, 1989).

Desama, G. and Bauwens, G., 'Een kleine stad in het hart van de industriële revolutie', in B. Van der Herten, M. Oris and J. Roegiers (eds), *Nijver België: het industriële landschap omstreeks 1850* (Deurne, 1995).

Dhondt, J., 'The cotton industry at Ghent during the French régime', in F. Crouzet, W. H. Chaloner and W. M. Stern (eds), *Essays in European Economic History, 1789–1914* (London, 1969).

Dhondt, J., 'La région gantoise: l'industrie cotonnière', in P. Lebrun, M. Bruwier, J. Dhondt and G. Hansotte, *Essai sur la révolution industrielle en Belgique, 1770–1847* (Brussels, 1979).

Dicken, P. and Lloyd, P., *Location in Space: Theoretical Perspectives in Economic Geography* (New York, third edition, 1990).

Ditt, K. and Pollard, P. (eds), *Von der Heimarbeit in die Fabrik: Industrialisierung und Arbeiterschaft in Leinen- und Baumwollregionen West Europas* (Paderborn, 1992).

Dowell, S., *A History of Taxation and Taxes in England*, vol. 3 (London, 1888).

Driver, F., *Power and Paupers: The Workhouse System 1834–84* (Cambridge, 1993).

Duggan, E. P., 'Industrialisation and the development of urban business communities: research problems, sources and techniques', *Local Historian*, 8 (1975), 457–65.

Dyer, A., 'The Midlands', in P. Clark (ed.), *The Cambridge Urban History of Britain*, vol. 2: *1540–1840* (Cambridge, 2000).

Dyos, H. J. and Aldcroft, D. *British Transport: An Economic Survey* (Leicester, 1969).

Earle, P., 'The female labour market in London in the late seventeenth and early eighteenth centuries', *Economic History Review*, 42 (1989), 328–53.

Ebeling, D. (ed.), *Historisch-thematische Kartographie* (Bielefeld, 1999).

Ebeling, D. and Mager, W. (eds), *Protoindustrie in der Region* (Bielefeld, 1997).

Ebeling, D. and Schmidt, M., 'Zunftige Handwerkswirtschaft und protoindustrieller Arbeitsmarkt', in D. Ebeling and W. Mager (eds), *Protoindustrie in der Region* (Bielefeld, 1997).

Eden, F. M., *The State of the Poor* (London, 1797).

Ellis, J., 'Regional and county centres 1700–1840' in P. Clark (ed.), *The Cambridge Urban History of Britain*, vol. 2: *1540–1840* (Cambridge, 2000).

Ellis, J., *The Georgian Town* (Basingstoke, 2001).

Estabrook, C., *Urbane and Rustic England: Cultural Ties and Social Spheres in the Provinces, 1660–1780* (Manchester, 1998).

Everitt, A., 'The English urban inn 1560–1760', in A. Everitt (ed.), *Perspectives in English Urban History* (Leicester, 1973).

Everitt, A., 'The Banburys of England', *Urban History Yearbook* (1974), 179–202.

Everitt, A., 'Country carriers in the nineteenth century', *Journal of Transport History*, 3 (1976), 179–202.

Everitt, A., 'Country, county and town: patterns of regional evolution in England', in A. Everitt, *Landscape and Community in England* (London, 1985).

Eversley, D., 'The home market and economic growth in England 1750 to 1780', in E. L. Jones and G. Mingay (eds), *Land, Labour and Population in the Industrial Revolution* (London, 1967).

Feinstein, C. H., 'Pessimism perpetuated: real wages and the standard of living in Britain', *Journal of Economic History*, 58 (1998), 625–58.

Felkin, W., *A History of the Machine-Wrought Hosiery and Lace Manufactures* (1867, reprinted Newton Abbott, 1967).

Finn, M., 'Women, consumption and coverture in England, c. 1760–1860', *Historical Journal*, 39 (1996), 703–22.

Finn, M., 'Men's things: masculine possessions in the consumer revolution', *Social History*, 25 (2000), 133–55.

Fischer, W., *Government Activity and Industrialisation in Germany* (Cologne, 1965).

Fitton, R. S. and Wadsworth, A. P., *The Strutts and the Arkwrights, 1758–1830* (Manchester, 1958).

Flugel, A., 'Region und Gewerbe: Protoindustrie in Ravensberg', in D. Ebeling and W. Mager (eds), *Protoindustrie in der Region* (Bielefeld, 1997).

Fowler, C., 'Changes in provincial retailing practice during the eighteenth century', in N. Alexander and G. Akehurst (eds), *The Emergence of Modern Retailing, 1750–1950* (London, 1999).

Freeman, M., 'The carrier system of south Hampshire, 1771–1851', *Journal of Transport History*, 2 (1977), 61–85.

Freudenberger, H., *The Industrialisation of a Central European City: Brno and the Fine Woollen Industry in the 18th Century* (Edington, 1977).

Gaskell, E., *Cranford* (London, 1851).

Gaskell, P., *Artisans and Machinery: The Moral and Physical Condition of the Manufacturing Population* (London, 1836).

Gleadle, K., *British Women in the Nineteenth Century* (Basingstoke, 2001).

Glennie, P. and Thrift, N., 'Consumers, identities and consumption spaces in early-modern England', *Environment and Planning A*, 28 (1996), 25–45.

Glover, S., *History, Gazetteer, and Directory of the County of Derby*, vol. 2 (Derby, 1829).

Glover, S., *The History of Ilkeston and Shipley* (Ilkeston, 1831).

Gomersall, H. M., 'Departed glory: the archaeology of the Leeds tanning industry 1780 to 1914', *Industrial Archaeology Review*, 22 (2000), 133–44.

Goossens, M., *The Economic Development of Belgian Agriculture: A Regional Perspective, 1812–1846* (Brussels, 1992).

Gorissen, S., 'Vorindustrielle Gewerberegionen im Vergleich: die eisenverarbeitenden Gewerbe des bergischen Landes und Sheffields', *Zeitschrift des bergischen Geschichtsvereins*, 95 (1991–92), 235–74.

Gorissen, S., *Vom Handelshaus zum Unternehmen: Sozialgeschichte der Harkort im Zeitalter der Protoindustrie* (Göttingen, 2001).

Gorton, J., *A Topographical Dictionary*, 3 vols (London, 1833).

Gourvish, T. R. and Wilson, R. G., *The British Brewing Industry 1830–1980* (Cambridge, 1994).

Gräf, H. T., 'Leicestershire small towns and pre-industrial urbanisation', *Transactions of the Leicestershire Archaeological Society*, 68 (1994), 98–120.

Granville, A., *The Spas of England*, 2 vols (London, 1835).

Greefs, H., 'Foreign Entrepreneurs in Early Nineteenth-Century Antwerp', in C. Lesger and L. Noordegraaf (eds), *Entrepreneurs and Entrepreneurship in Early Modern Times: Merchants and Industrialists within the Orbit of the Dutch Staple Market* (Den Haag, 1995).

Gregory, D., *Regional Transformation and Industrial Revolution* (Basingstoke, 1982).

Gregory, D., 'The production of regions in England's industrial revolution', *Journal of Historical Geography*, 14 (1988), 50–8.

Gregory, J., 'Anglicanism and the arts', in J. Black and J. Gregory (eds), *Culture, Politics and Society in Britain 1660–1800* (Manchester, 1991).

Guldberg, M., *Domestic Industry and the Concept of Proto-industrialisation* (Fiskeri, 1992).

Hadfield, C., *The Canals of the East Midlands* (Newton Abbot, 1966).

Hadfield, C., *The Canals of the West Midlands* (Newton Abbot, 1966).

Haesenne-Peremans, N., *La pauvreté dans la région liégeoise à l'aube de la révolution industrielle* (Paris, 1981).

Hamilton, H., *The History of the British Copper and Brass Industries to 1800* (Newton Abbot, 1967).

Hanagan, M. P., *Nascent Proletarians: Class Formation in Post-Revolutionary France* (Oxford, 1989).

Hanford, M., *The Stroudwater Canal* (Bradford-on-Avon, 1976).

Hannes, J., 'Industrialization without development: some aspects of the history of Ghent', in P. Kooij and P. Pellenbarg (eds), *Regional Capitals: Past, Present, Prospects* (Assen, 1994).

Hansotte, G., 'La région Verviers-Liège: l'industrie lainière', in P. Lebrun, M. Bruwier, J. Dhondt and G. Hansotte, *Essai sur la révolution industrielle en Belgique, 1770–1847* (Brussels, 1979).

Hansotte, G., *La métallurgie et le commerce international du fer dans les Pays-Bas autrichiens et la principauté de Liège* (Brussels, 1980).

Hardcastle, J. B., *Old Wolverhampton: Sixty Years Ago* (Wolverhampton, 1888).

Harper, C. G., *The Manchester and Glasgow Road: London–Manchester* (London, 1907).

Hasquin, H., 'Déjà puissance industrielle (1740–1830)', in H. Hasquin (ed.), *La Wallonie: le pays et les hommes: histoire, économies, sociétés*, vol. 1 (Brussels, 1975).

Hayter, R., *The Dynamics of Industrial Location: The Factory, the Firm and the Production System* (Chichester, 1998).

Heaton, H., *The Yorkshire Woollen and Worsted Industries* (Oxford, 1920).

Hélin, E., 'Genèse et éclatement d'une région industrielle', in E. Hélin, *Le réseau urbain en Belgique dans une perspective historique* (Brussels, 1992).

Henson, G., *The Civil, Political and Mechanical History of the Framework-Knitters in Europe and America* (Nottingham, 1831).

Henstock, A. (ed.), *The Diary of Abigail Gawthern of Nottingham 1751–1810* (Nottingham, 1980).

Herbert, G., *Shoemaker's Window* (Banbury, 1979).

Hey, D., *The Rural Metalworkers of the Sheffield Region*, Leicester University Department of Local History Occasional Papers, 5 (1972).

Hickman, T., *The History of the Melton Mowbray Pork Pie* (Stroud, 1997).

Hickson, C. R. and Thompson, E. R., 'A new theory of guilds and European economic development', *Explorations in Economic History*, 28 (1991), 127–68.

Hohenberg, P., 'Urban manufactures in the proto-industrial economy: culture versus commerce?', in M. Berg (ed.), *Markets and Manufacture in Early Industrial Europe* (London, 1991).

Honeyman K., *Women, Gender and Industrialisation in England, 1700–1870* (Basingstoke, 2000).

Hopkins, E., 'The trading and service sectors of the Birmingham economy 1750–1800', *Business History*, 28 (1986), 76–97.

Hopkins, E., *The Rise of the Manufacturing Town: Birmingham and Industrial Revolution* (Stroud, second edition, 1998).

Hopkins, M. A., *Dr Johnson's Lichfield* (New York, 1952).

Hoppe, G. and Langton, J., *Peasantry to Capitalism: Western Ostergotland in the Nineteenth Century* (Cambridge, 1994).

Horrell, S., 'Home demand and British industrialisation', *Journal of Economic History*, 56 (1996), 564–82.

Horrell, S. and Humphries, J., 'Old questions, new data and alternative perspectives: families' living standards 1787–1865', *Journal of Economic History*, 52 (1992), 849–80.

Horsfall, J., *The Iron Masters of Penns 1720–1970* (Kineton, 1971).

Houtman-De Smedt, H., 'Société Générale from 1822 to 1848: from "Bank of the Crown Lands" to "mixed-type bank"', in E. Buyst (ed.), *The Generale Bank, 1822–1997* (Tielt, 1997).

How Shall the Town be Governed? Addressed to the Ratepayers of Wolverhampton by One of Themselves (Wolverhampton, 1847).

Hudson, P., *The Genesis of Industrial Capital: A study of the West Riding Wool Textiles Industry* (Cambridge, 1982).

Hudson, P. (ed.), *Regions and Industries: A Perspective on the Industrial Revolution in Britain* (Cambridge, 1989).

Hudson, P., *The Industrial Revolution* (London, 1992).

Hudson, P., 'Proto-industrialization in England', in S. Ogilvie and M. Cerman (eds), *European Proto-Industrialization* (Cambridge, 1996).

Hudson, P., 'Regional and local history', *Journal of Regional and Local Studies*, 20 (1999), 5–24.

Hudson, P. and King, S., 'Industrialising townships and urban links in eighteenth century Yorkshire', in P. Clark and P. Corfield (eds), *Industry and Urbanisation in Eighteenth Century England* (Leicester, 1994).

Hudson, S., 'Attitudes to investment risk amongst west Midland canal and railway company investors 1700–1850', unpublished PhD thesis, University of Warwick, 2002.

Huffer, D. B. M., 'The growth of the township of Wolverhampton to 1850', *West Midlands Studies*, 7 (1974), 5–17.

Hussey, D., *Coastal and River Trade in Pre-Industrial England: Maritime Economies of the Bristol Region* (Exeter, 2000).

Hussey, D., Milne, G., Wakelin, P. and Wanklyn, M., *The Gloucester Port Books 1576–1765: A Summary* (Wolverhampton, 1995).

Hutton, W., *A History of Birmingham* (Birmingham, 1783).

Hutton, W., *The Life of William Hutton* (Birmingham, 1817).

Hyde, F., *Liverpool and the Mersey* (Newton Abbot, 1971).

Ingamells, J., *Directory of Newcastle-under-Lyme* (Newcastle under Lyme, 1871).

Innes, J. and Rogers, N., 'Politics and government 1700–1840', in P. Clark (ed.), *The Cambridge Urban History of Britain*, vol. 2: *1540–1840* (Cambridge, 2000).

Isacson, M. and Magnusson, L., *Proto-Industrialisation in Scandinavia: Craft Skills in the Industrial Revolution* (Leamington Spa, 1987).

Jackson, G., *Hull in the Eighteenth Century* (Hull, 1971).

Jefferey, R. W. (ed.), *Dyott's Diary*, 2 vols (1907).

Jefferies, R., *Hodge and his Masters* (London, 1966).

Jefferys, J. B., *Retail Trading in Britain, 1850–1950* (Cambridge, 1954).

Jenning, T., *Master of my Art: The Taylor Bellfoundries, 1784–1987* (Loughborough, 1987).

Jephcott, W. E., *The House of Izons* (1948).

Jones, G. W., *Borough Politics: A Study of Wolverhampton Borough Council 1888–1964* (London, 1969).

Jones, S., 'The country trade and the marketing and distribution of Birmingham hardware', *Business History*, 26 (1984), 24–42.

Jones, W. H., *The Story of the Municipal Life of Wolverhampton* (London, 1903).

Keaveny, B. A., 'Urban expansion: the role of banks in eight small Leicestershire towns', Certificate dissertation, University of Leicester, 1993.

Kemp, T., *Industrialisation in Nineteenth Century Europe* (London, 1985).

Kerridge, E., *Textile Manufacture in Early Modern England* (Manchester, 1985).

King, S. and Timmins, J. G., *Making Sense of the Industrial Revolution* (Manchester, 2001).

Kint, P., *Prometheus aangevuurd door Demeter: de economische ontwikkeling van de landbouw in Oost-Vlaanderen, 1815–1850* (Amsterdam, 1989).

Klein, L., 'Politeness for plebes: consumption and social identity in early eighteenth-century England', in J. Brewer and A. Bermingham (eds), *The Culture of Consumption* (London, 1995).

Komlos, J., 'Ein Überblick über die Konzeptionen der industriellen Revolution', *Vierteljahrsschrift für Wirtschafts- und Sozialgeschichte*, 84 (1997), 23–57.

Kriedte, P., 'Die Stadt im Prozess der europaischen Protoindustrialisierung', *Die alte Stadt*, 9 (1982), 19–51.

Kriedte, P., *Peasants, Landlords and Merchant Capitalists: Europe and the World Economy* (Providence, 1983).

Kriedte, P., *Eine Stadt am seidenen Faden: Haushalt, Hausindustrie und soziale Bewegung in Krefeld in der Mitte des 19. Jahrhunderts* (Göttingen, 1991).

Kriedte, P., Medick, H. and Schlumbohm, J., *Industry before Industrialization* (Cambridge, 1981).

Krugman, P., *Geography and Trade* (Cambridge, MA, 1991).

Kurgan-Van Hentenryk, G., 'The Société Générale, 1850–1934', in E. Buyst (ed.), *The Generale Bank, 1822–1997* (Tielt, 1997).

Kurgan-Van Hentenrijk, G., Jaumain, S. and Montens V. (eds), *Dictionnaire des patrons en Belgique: les hommes, les entreprises, les réseaux* (Louvain-La-Neuve, 1996).

Laffut, M., *Les chemins de fer belges (1830–1913): genèse du réseau et présentation critique des données statistiques* (Brussels, 1998).

Laffut, M., 'De uitbouw van het dichtste spoorwegnet ter wereld', in M. Laffut, *Sporen in België: 175 jaar spoorwegen, 75 jaar NMBS* (Leuven, 2001).

Laird, F. C., *The Beauties of England and Wales*, vol. 3 (London, 1802).

Laithwaite, P., *The History of the Lichfield Conduit Lands Trust, 1546 to 1946* (Lichfield, 1947).

Landes, D. S., *The Unbound Prometheus: Technological Change and Industrial Development in Western Europe from 1750 to Present* (Cambridge, 1969).

Lane, P., 'Work on the margins: poor women and the informal economy of eighteenth- and nineteenth-century Leicestershire', *Midland History*, 22 (1997), 85–99.

Lane, P., 'Women in the regional economy: the east Midlands 1700–1830', unpublished PhD thesis, University of Warwick, 1999.

Lane, P., 'An industrialising town: social and business networks in Hinckley', in J. Stobart and P. Lane (eds), *Urban and Industrial Change in the Midlands, 1700–1840* (Leicester, 2000).

Lane, P., 'Women, property and inheritance: wealth creation and income generation in small English towns, 1750–1835', in J. Stobart and A. Owens (eds), *Urban Fortunes: Property and Inheritance in the Town 1700–1900* (Aldershot, 2000).

Langford, P., *A Polite and Commerical People: England 1727–1783* (Oxford, 1989).

Langton, J., 'The industrial revolution and the regional geography of England', *Transactions of the Institute of British Geographers*, 9 (1984), 145–67.

Langton, J., 'Town growth and urbanisation in the Midlands from the 1660s to 1841', in J. Stobart and P. Lane (eds), *Urban and Industrial Change in the Midlands 1700–1840* (Leicester, 2000).

Langton, J., 'Urban growth and economic change c. 1688–1841', in P. Clark (ed.), *The Cambridge Urban History of Britain*, vol. 2: *1540–1840* (Cambridge, 2000).

Large, P., 'Urban growth and agricultural change in the west Midlands', in P. Clark (ed.), *The Transformation of English Provincial Towns 1600–1800* (London, 1984).

Laureyssens, J., 'The Société Générale and the origin of industrial investment banking', *Belgisch tijdschrift voor nieuwste geschedenis*, 6 (1975), 93–115.

Leboutte, R. (ed.), *Proto-Industrialisation: Recent Research and New Perspectives* (Geneva, 1996).

Lebrun, P., Bruwier, M., Dhondt, J. and Hansotte, G., *Essai sur la révolution indus-trielle en Belgique, 1770–1847* (Brussels, 1979).

Lee, J. 'The rise and fall of a market town: Castle Donington in the 19th century', *Transactions of the Leicestershire Archaeological Society*, 32 (1956), 53–80.

Lee, R., 'Making Europe: towards a geography of European integration', in M. Chisholm and D. Smith (eds), *Shared Space: Divided Space* (London, 1990).

The Leicester Directory (Leicester, 1815).

Leleux, F., *A l'aube du Capitalisme et de la Révolution Industrielle: Liévin Bauwens, industriel gantois* (Paris, 1969).

Lemire, B., 'The theft of clothes and popular consumerism in early modern England', *Journal of Social History*, 24 (1990), 255–76.

Lepetit, B., *The Pre-Industrial Urban System: France, 1740–1840* (Cambridge, 1994).

Levine, D. *Family Formation in an Age of Nascent Capitalism* (London, 1977).

Lewis, G., 'Proto-industrialization in France', *Economic History Review*, 47 (1994), 150–64.

Lieberman, S., *The Industrialisation of Norway, 1800–1970* (Oslo, 1976).

Lindert, P. and Williamson, J., 'English workers' living standards during the industrial revolution: a new look', *Economic History Review*, 36 (1983), 1–25.

Lis, C., *Social Change and the Labouring Poor: Antwerp, 1770–1860* (New Haven and London, 1986).

Lis, C. and Soly, H., *Een groot bedrijf in een kleine stad: de firma De Heyder en Co. te Lier, 1757–1834* (Lier, 1987).

Lis, C. and Soly, H., 'Restructuring the urban textile industries in Brabant and Flan-ders', in E. Aerts and J. H. Munro (eds), *Textiles of the Low Countries in European Economic History* (Leuven, 1990).

Lis, C. and Soly, H., 'Entrepreneurs, corporations et autorités publiques au Brabant et en Flandre à la fin de l'Ancien Régime', *Revue du nord*, 76 (1994), 725–44.

Lis, C. and Soly, H., 'Stadtische Industrialisierungswege in Brabant und Flandern: De Heyder and Co. in Lier (1750 bis. 1815)', in D. Ebeling and W. Mager (eds), *Pro-toindustrie in der Region* (Bielefeld, 1997).

Liu, T., *The Weaver's Knot: The Contradictions of Class Struggle and Family Soli-darity in Western France, 1750–1914* (New York, 1994).

Lloyd Jones, R. and Lewis, M., *Manchester in the Age of the Factory* (London, 1988).

MacRitchie, W., *Diary of a Tour through Great Britain in 1795* (London, 1897).

Mager, W. (ed.), *Geschichte der Stadt Spenge* (Spenge, 1984).

Mager, W., 'Spenge vom frühen 18. Jahrhunderts bis zur Mitte des 19. Jahrhunderts', in W. Mager (ed.), *Geschichte der Stadt Spenge* (Spenge, 1984).

Magnusson, L., 'Proto-industrialisation in Sweden', in M. Cerman and S. Ogilvie (eds), *Proto-Industrialisation in Europe* (Cambridge, 1996).

Mander, G. P. and Tildesley, N., *A History of Wolverhampton to the Early Nineteenth Century* (Wolverhampton, 1960).

Mander, G. P., *The Wolverhampton Antiquary*, 2 vols (Wolverhampton, no date).

Mann, J. de Lacy, *The Clothing Industry of the West of England from 1640 to 1880* (Stroud, 1987).

Marshall, J. D., 'The rise and transformation of the Cumbrian market town, 1660–1900', *Northern History*, 19 (1983), 128–209.

Mason, A., 'The impact of the railway on Leicestershire', Certificate dissertation, University of Leicester, 1992.

Mason, F., *Wolverhampton Town Commissioners, 1778–1848* (Wolverhampton, 1976).

Mason, F., *The Book of Wolverhampton* (Wolverhampton, 1979).

Massey, D., *Spatial Divisions of Labour: Social Structures and the Geography of Production* (Basingstoke, second edition, 1995).

Matthias, P., *The Brewing Industry in England 1700–1830* (Cambridge, 1959).

Mayes, L. J., *The History of Chairmaking in High Wycombe* (London, 1969).

McInnes, A., 'The emergence of a leisure town: Shrewsbury 1660–1760' *Past and Present*, 120 (1988), 53–87.

McKendrick, N., 'Home demand and economic growth: a new view of the role of women and children in the industrial revolution', in N. McKendrick (ed.), *Historical Perspectives in English Thought and Society* (London, 1974).

McKendrick, N., Brewer, J. and Plumb, J. H., *The Birth of a Consumer Society: The Commercialization of Eighteenth-Century England* (London, 1982).

Medick, H., *Weben und Überleben in Laichingen 1650–1900* (Göttingen, 1996).

Mendels, F., 'Industrialization and population pressure in eighteenth century Flanders', unpublished PhD thesis, University of Wisconsin, 1969.

Mendels, F., 'Proto-industrialisation: the first phase of the process of industrialisation', *Journal of Economic History*, 32 (1972), 241–61.

Mendels, F., 'Agriculture and peasant industry in eighteenth century Flanders', in W. N. Parker and E. L. Jones (eds), *European Peasants and their Markets* (Princeton, 1975).

Mendels, F., 'Des industries rurales à la protoindustrialisation: historique d'un changement de perspective', *Annales ESC*, 39 (1984), 977–1,008.

Mills, D. R., *Rural Community History from Trade Directories* (Aldenham, 2001).

Mills, T. C. and Crafts, N. F. R., 'Trend growth in British industrial output, 1700–1913: a reappraisal', *Explorations in Economic History*, 33 (1996), 277–95.

Millward, R. and Robinson, A., *Landscapes of Britain: The West Midlands* (London, 1971).

Mitchell, B. and Deane, P., *Abstract of British Historical Statistics* (Cambridge, 1962).

Mitchell, S. I., 'Urban markets and retail distribution 1730–1815 with particular reference to Macclesfield, Stockport and Chester', unpublished DPhil thesis, University of Oxford, 1974.

Mitchell, S. I., 'Retailing in eighteenth and early nineteenth-century Cheshire', *Transactions of the Historic Society of Lancashire and Cheshire*, 130 (1981), 37–60.

Mokyr, J., *Industrialization in the Low Countries, 1795–1850* (New Haven, 1976).

Mokyr, J., *The Economics of the Industrial Revolution* (London, 1985).

More, C., *Understanding the Industrial Revolution* (London, 2000).

Morgan, K., *Bristol and the Atlantic Trade in the Eighteenth Century* (Cambridge, 1993).

Moritz, K. P., *Journeys of a German in England: A Walking Tour of England in 1782* (1783, paperback edition, London, 1983).

Mountford, A. R., 'Thomas Wedgwood, John Wedgwood and Jonah Malkin, Potters of Burlsem', unpublished MA thesis, University of Keele, 1972.

Moxon, C. J., 'Ashby-de-la-Zouch: a social and economic survey of a market town', unpublished DPhil thesis, University of Oxford, 1971.

Mui, H. and Mui, L. H., *Shops and Shopkeeping in Eighteenth-Century England* (London, 1989).

Muldrew, C., *The Economy of Obligation: The Culture of Credit and Social Relations in Early-Modern England* (Basingstoke, 1998).

Musson, A., *The Growth of British Industry* (London, 1978).

Nef, J., 'The Industrial revolution reconsidered', *Journal of Economic History*, 3 (1943), 1–31.

Nenadic, S., 'Middle rank consumers and domestic culture in Edinburgh and Glasgow, 1720–1840', *Past and Present*, 145 (1994), 122–56.

Neufeld, M. J., *The Skilled Metalworkers of Nuremberg: Craft and Class in the Industrial Revolution* (London, 1989).

Nichols, J., *The History and Antiquities of the County of Leicestershire* (1795–1811, reprinted East Yardsley, Yorkshire, 1971).

Noble, M., 'Growth and development in a regional urban system: the county towns of east Yorkshire 1700–1880', *Urban History Yearbook* (1987), 1–19.

North, D., *Theorie des institutionellen Wandels* (Tübingen, 1988).

Norton, J. E., *Guide to National and Provincial Directories of England and Wales, Excluding London, Published before 1856* (London, 1950).

O'Brien, P., 'Agriculture and the home market for English industry 1660–1820', *English Historical Review*, 100 (1985), 773–800.

O'Brien, P., 'Do we have a typology for the study of European industrialization in the XIXth century?', *Journal of European Economic History*, 15 (1986), 291–333.

O'Brien, P. and Engerman, S., 'Changes in income and its distribution during the industrial revolution', in R. Floud and D. McCloskey (eds), *The Economic History of Britain since 1700*, vol. 1 (Cambridge, second edition, 1994).

Ogilvie, S., 'Social institutions and proto-industrialisation', in S. Ogilvie and M. Cerman (eds), *European Proto-Industrialisation* (Cambridge, 1996).

Ogilvie, S., 'Soziale Institutionen, Korporatismus und Protoindustrie: die Wurtermbergische Zeugmarcherei', in D. Ebeling and W. Mager (eds), *Protoindustrie in der Region* (Bielefeld, 1997).

Ogilvie, S., *State, Corporatism and Proto-Industry* (Cambridge, 1997).

Ogilvie, S. and Cerman, M. (eds), *European Proto-Industrialization* (Cambridge, 1996).

Osterud, N., 'Gender divisions and the organization of work in the Leicester hosiery industry', in A. John (ed.), *Unequal Opportunities: Women's Employment in England 1800–1918* (Oxford, 1986).

Owen, C., *Burton-on-Trent* (Chichester, 1978).

Palmer, M. (ed.), *The Aristocratic Estate: The Hastings Family in Leicestershire and South Derbyshire* (Loughborough, 1982).

Parsons, W. and Bradshaw, T., *The New General and Commercial Directory of Staffordshire* (Manchester, 1818).

Pasleau, S., *John Cockerill: itinéraire d'un géant industriel* (Liège, 1992).

Patten, J., 'Village and town: an occupational study', *Agricultural History Review*, 20 (1972), 1–16.

Patterson, A., *Radical Leicester* (Leicester, 1954).

Pawson, E., *Transport and Economy: The Turnpike Roads of Eighteenth-Century Britain* (London, 1977).

Pearson, R. and Richardson, D., 'Business networking in the industrial revolution', *Economic History Review*, 54 (2001), 657–79.

Peet, R., 'The cultural production of economic forms', in R. Lee and J. Wills (eds), *Geographies of Economies* (London, 1997).

Pennell, P., 'The economy of Bewdley 1770–1860', unpublished MPhil thesis, University of Wolverhampton, 2001.

Pfister, U., *Die Zürcher Fabriques: proto-industrielles Wachstum vom 16. zum 18. Jahrhundert* (Zurich, 1992).

Pfister, U., 'The proto-industrial household economy: towards a formal analysis', *Journal of Family History*, 17 (1992), 201–32.

Pfister, U., 'A general model of proto-industrial growth', in R. Leboutte (ed.), *Proto-Industrialisation: Recent Research and New Perspectives* (Geneva, 1996).

Phillips, A. D. M. and Turton, B. J., 'Staffordshire turnpike trusts and traffic in the early nineteenth century', *Journal of Transport History*, 8 (1987), 126–46.

Phillips, A. D. M. and Turton, B. J., 'The turnpike network of Staffordshire, 1700–1840', *Collections for a History of Staffordshire*, 13 (1988), 61–118.

Picturesque Views and Descriptions of Cities and Towns, Castles, Mansions in Staffordshire and Shropshire (Birmingham, 1830).

Pigot, J. & Co., *National and Commercial Directory* (London, 1835, 1841, 1842).

Pilkington, J., *A View of the Present State of Derbyshire*, vol. 2 (Derby, 1789).

Pinchbeck, I., *Women Workers and the Industrial Revolution 1750–1850* (London, 1930).

Pluymers, P. and Pasleau, S., 'Het kleine België: een grote industriële mogendheid', in B. Van der Herten, M. Oris and J. Roegiers (eds), *Nijver België: het industriële landschap omstreeks 1850* (Deurne, 1995).

Pochin, T., *Loughborough in 1770*, ed. J. D. Bennett (Loughborough, 1970).

Pollard, S., *Peaceful Conquest: The Industrialisation of Europe, 1760–1970* (Oxford, 1981).

Pollard, S., 'Industrialization and the European economy', in J. Mokyr (ed.), *The Economics of the Industrial Revolution* (London, 1985).

Pollard, S., 'Regional markets and national development', in M. Berg (ed.), *Markets and Manufacture in Early Industrial Europe* (London, 1991).

Porteous, J. D., *Canal Ports: The Urban Achievement of the Canal Age* (London, 1977).

Postles, D., 'An English small town in the later Middle Ages: Loughborough', *Urban History*, 20 (1993), 7–29.

Poztsgai, P., *The Industrialisation of Hungary* (Budapest, 2002).

Pressnell, L. S., *Country Banking in the Industrial Revolution* (Oxford, 1956).

Puissant, J., 'A propos de l'innovation technologique dans les mines du Hainaut', in G. Kurgan-Van Hentenrijk and J. Stengers (eds), *L'innovation technologique: facteur de changement* (Brussels, 1986).

Putnam, R., *Making Democracy Work* (Princeton, 1993).

Raistrick, A., *Dynasty of Iron Founders: The Darbys and Coalbrookedale* (London, 1953).

Rath, T., 'The Tewkesbury hosiery industry', *Textile History*, 7 (1976), 140–53.

Raven, N., 'De-industrialisation and the urban response: the small towns of the North Riding of Yorkshire, c. 1790–1850', in R. Weedon and A. Milne (eds), *Aspects of English Small Towns in the 18th and 19th Centuries* (Leicester, 1993).

Raven, N., 'The trade directory: a source for the study of early nineteenth century urban economies', *Business Archives Sources and History*, 74 (1997), 13–30.

Raven, N., 'Manufacturing and trades: the urban economies of the north Essex cloth towns, 1770–1851', unpublished PhD thesis, University of Leicester, 1999.

Raven, N., 'Industry and the small towns of Derbyshire: evidence from trade directories

c. 1790–1850', in J. Stobart and P. Lane (eds), *Urban and Industrial Change in the Midlands 1700–1840* (Leicester, 2000).

Reddy, W. M., *The Rise of Market Culture: The Textile Trade and French Society, 1750–1900* (Cambridge, 1984).

Reed, M., 'The cultural role of small towns in England 1600–1800', in P. Clark (ed.), *Small Towns in Early Modern Europe* (Cambridge, 1995).

Reeder, D., 'H. J. Dyos and the urban process', in D. Cannadine and D. Reeder (eds), *Exploring the Urban Past* (Cambridge, 1982).

Reeder, D., and Rodger, R., 'Industrialisation and the city economy', in M. Daunton (ed.), *The Cambridge Urban History of Britain*, vol. 3: *1840–1950* (Cambridge, 2000).

Reeves, J., *The History and Topography of West Bromwich* (London, 1836).

Reilly, R., *Josiah Wedgwood* (London, 1992).

Richards, E., 'Margins of the industrial revolution', in P. O'Brien and R. Quinault (eds), *Industrial Revolution and British Society* (Cambridge, 1993).

Richardson, H. W., *Regional Growth Theory* (London, 1973).

Robinson, E., 'Boulton and Fothergill, 1762–1782, and the Birmingham export of hardware', *University of Birmingham Historical Journal*, 7 (1959–60), 60–79.

Robson, B., *Urban Growth: An Approach* (London, 1973).

Rodger, R., *Housing in Urban Britain 1780–1914: Class, Capitalism and Construction* (Basingstoke, 1989).

Rogers, H., *Women and the People: Authority, Authorship and the Radical Tradition in Nineteenth-Century England* (Aldershot, 2000).

Roper, J. S., *A List of Trades and Occupations from the Town Rate Book, 1792* (Wolverhampton, 1964).

Roper, J. S., *Wolverhampton: The Early Town and its History* (Wolverhampton, 1966).

Rowlands, M. B., *Masters and Men in the West Midlands Metalware Trades before the Industrial Revolution* (Manchester, 1975).

Rowlands, M. B., *The West Midlands from AD 1000* (London, 1987).

Rowlands, M. B., 'Continuity and change in an industrialising society: the case of the west Midlands industries', in P. Hudson (ed.), *Regions and Industries* (Cambridge, 1989).

The Royal Visit to Wolverhampton (Wolverhampton, 1867).

Rutherford, M., *The Revolution in Tanner's Lane* (London, 1887).

Rutherford, M., *Catherine Furze* (Oxford, 1936).

Sabel, C. and Zeitlin, J., 'Historical alternatives to mass production: politics, markets and technology in nineteenth century industrialization', *Past and Present*, 108 (1985), 133–76.

Schlumbohm, J., *Lebenslaufe, Familien, Hofe: die Bauern und Heuerleute des Osnabrückischen Kirchspiels Belm in proto-industrieller Zeit, 1650–1880* (Göttingen, 1994).

Scholliers, P., *Bedrijfsgeschiedenis van de firma A. Voortman–N.V. Texas* (Brussels, 1976).

Scholliers, P., 'Van de proto-industrie tot de industriële revolutie: de katoen- en linnennijverheid', in B. Van der Herten, M. Oris and J. Roegiers (eds), *Nijver België: het industriële landschap omstreeks 1850* (Deurne, 1995).

Scholliers, P., *Wages, Manufacturers and Workers in the Nineteenth-Century Factory: The Voortman Cotton Mill in Ghent* (Oxford, 1996).

Schultz, H., 'The metropolis in the sandpit – Berlin and Brandenburg', in P. Clark and B. Lepetit (eds), *Capital Cities and their Hinterlands in Early Modern Europe* (Aldershot, 1996).

Schumpeter, E., *English Overseas Trade Statistics 1698–1808* (Oxford, 1960).

Schwarz, L., *London in the Age of Industrialisation* (Cambridge, 1992).

Schwarz, L., 'Residential leisure towns in England towards the end of the eighteenth century', *Urban History*, 27 (2000), 51–61.

Scola, R., *Feeding the Victorian City: The Food Supply of Manchester 1770–1870* (Manchester, 1992).

Seward, A., *Memoirs of the Life of Dr Darwin: Chiefly during his Residence at Lichfield* (London, 1804).

Shammas, C., *The Pre-Industrial Consumer in England and America* (Oxford, 1990).

Sharpe, P., 'De-industrialization and re-industrialization: women's employment and the changing character of Colchester 1700–1850', *Urban History*, 21 (1994), 76–96.

Shaw, G., 'The content and reliability of nineteenth century trade directories', *Local Historian*, 13 (1978), 205–9.

Shaw, G. and Alexander, A., 'Directories and the local historian III: directories as sources in local history', *Local History*, 46 (1994), 12–17.

Short, B., 'The de-industrialisation process: a case study of the Weald, 1600–1850', in P. Hudson (ed.), *Regions and Industries* (Cambridge, 1989).

Simmons, J., *Leicester Past and Present*, vol. 1: *Ancient Borough to 1860* (London, 1974).

Simmons, J. W., 'The organization of the urban system', in L. S. Bourne and J. W. Simmons (eds), *Systems of Cities* (New York, 1978).

Skedd, S., 'Women teachers and the expansion of girls', in H. Barker and E. Chalus (eds), *Gender in Eighteenth-Century England: Roles, Representations and Responsibilities* (Harlow, 1997).

Smith, C., 'The renaissance of the English market town: a study of six Nottinghamshire market towns, 1680–1840', unpublished PhD thesis, University of Nottingham, 1997.

Smith, C., 'Urban improvement in the Nottingham market town, 1770–1840', *Midland History*, 25 (2000), 98–114.

Smith, D., *Conflict and Compromise: Class Formation in English Society 1830–1914: A Comparative Study of Birmingham and Sheffield* (London, 1982).

Smith, J. B., 'The governance of Wolverhampton, 1848–1888', unpublished PhD thesis, University of Leicester, 2001.

Smith, L., *Carpet Weavers and Carpet Masters* (Kidderminster, 1986).

Smith, L. T. (ed.), *The Itinerary of John Leland*, 5 vols (London, new edition, 1964).

Smith, R., 'Population movements and the development of working-class suburbs 1801–1851: the case of Nottingham', *Local Population Studies*, 47 (1991), 56–64.

Smith, S., 'The market for manufactures in the thirteen continental colonies, 1698–1776', *Economic History Review*, 51 (1998), 676–708.

Smith, W. A., 'The town commissioners in Wolverhampton, 1777–1848', *West Midlands Studies*, 1 (1967), 26–47.

Smith, W. A., 'The Wolverhampton Old Bank', *West Midlands Studies*, 7 (1975), 1–5.

Smith, W. D., *Consumption and the Making of Respectability, 1600–1800* (London, 2002).

Snooks, G. D. (ed.), *Was the Industrial Revolution Necessary?* (London, 1994).

Soderberg, J., *A Stagnating Metropolis: the Economy and Demography of Stockholm, 1750–1850* (Cambridge, 1991).

Solar, p., 'Die belgische Leinenindustrie in 19. Jahrhundert', in K. Ditt and S. Pollard (eds), *Von der Heinarbeit in die Fabrik* (Paderborn, 1992).

Sombart, W., *Der moderne Kapitalismus*, 2 vols (Leipzig, 1902).

Stobart, J., 'The spatial organisation of a regional economy: central places in NW England in the early eighteenth century', *Journal of Historical Geography*, 22 (1996), 147–59.

Stobart, 'Geography and industrialization: the space economy of northwest England, 1701–1760', *Transactions of the Institute of British Geographers*, 21 (1996), 681–96.

Stobart, J., 'Burslem as a town: the industrial and the urban', in J. Stobart and P. Lane (eds), *Urban and Industrial Change in the Midlands 1700–1840* (Leicester, 2000).

Stobart, J., 'In search of a leisure hierarchy: English spa towns in the urban system', in P. Borsay, G. Hirschfelder and R. Mohrmann (eds), *New Directions in Urban History* (Munster, 2000).

Stobart, J., 'In search of causality: a regional approach to urban growth in eighteenth-century England', *Geografiska Annaler B*, 82 (2000), 149–63.

Stobart, J., 'Regions, localities and industrialisation: evidence from the east Midlands circa 1780–1840', *Environment and Planning A*, 33 (2001), 1,305–25.

Stobart, J., 'Culture versus commerce: societies and spaces for elites in eighteenth-century Liverpool', *Journal of Historical Geography*, 28:4 (2002), 471–85.

Stobart, J., *The First Industrial Region: North-West England 1700–1760* (Manchester, 2004).

Stobart, J., 'Building an urban identity: cultural space and civic boosterism in an English "new town", 1761–1911', *Social History* (forthcoming, 2004).

Stobart, J., 'Leisure and shopping in the small towns of Georgian England', *Journal of Urban History* (forthcoming, 2005).

Stobart, J. and Hann, A., 'Retailing revolution in the eighteenth century', *Business History* 46:2 (2004), 171–94.

Stratton, M. *The Terracotta Revival* (London, 1993).

Stratton, M. and Trinder, B., *Long's Building, Devizes: A Report for English Heritage* (Telford, 1993).

Stratton, M. and Trinder, B., *Industrial England* (London, 1997).

Sweet, R., *The English Town: 1680–1840* (Harlow, 1999).

Sweet, R., 'Topographies of politeness', *Transactions of the Royal Historical Society*, 12 (2002), 355–74.

Temple-Patterson, A., 'The making of the Leicestershire canals, 1768–1814', *Transactions of the Leicestershire Archaeological Society*, 27 (1951), 65–99.

Terrier, D., *Les deux âges de la proto-industrie: les tisserands du Cambresis et du St-Quintinois 1730–1880* (Paris, 1996).

Thijs, A. K. L., 'De geschiedenis van de suikernijverheid te Antwerpen (16de–19de eeuw)', *Bijdragen tot de Geschiedenis*, 62 (1979), 23–50.

Thomas, J., *The Rise of the Staffordshire Potteries* (Bath, 1971).

Thoroton, R., *Antiquities of Nottinghamshire* (Nottingham, 1677).

Thorpe, H., 'Lichfield: a study of its growth and function', *Staffordshire Record Society* (1954), 139–211.

Thrift, N., 'Transport and communication, 1730–1914', in R. A. Dodgshon and R. A. Butlin (eds), *An Historical Geography of England and Wales* (London, second edition, 1990).

Throsby, J. *The Supplementary Volume to Leicestershire Views* (London, 1790).

Throsby, J., *Thoroton's History of Nottinghamshire*, 3 vols (Nottingham, 1790).

Tilly, R., 'Capital formation in Germany in the nineteenth century', in P. Mathias and M. M. Postan (eds), *The Cambridge Economic History of Europe*, vol. 7 (Cambridge, 1978).

Tilly, R., 'German industrialization', in M. Teich and R. Porter (eds), *The Industrial Revolution in National Context: Europe and the USA* (Cambridge, 1996).

Timmins, J. G., *Made in Lancashire. A History of Regional Industrialisation* (Manchester, 1998).

Towner, J., *An Historical Geography of Recreation and Tourism in the Western World, 1540–1940* (Chichester, 1996).

Toynbee, A., *The Industrial Revolution* (London, 1884).

Trainor, R. H., *Black Country Elites: The Exercise of Authority in an Industrialized Area 1830–1900* (Oxford, 1993).

Trinder, B., 'The Holyhead Road: an engineering project in its social context', in A. Penfold (ed.), *Thomas Telford: Engineer* (London, 1980).

Trinder, B., *Industrial Revolution in Shropshire* (Chichester, second edition, 1981).

Trinder, B., *Victorian Banbury* (Chichester, 1982).

Trinder, B. (ed.), *Victorian Shrewsbury* (Shrewsbury, 1984).

Trinder, B., 'The archaeology of the British food industry 1660–1960: a preliminary survey', *Industrial Archaeology Review*, 15 (1993), 129–31.

Trinder, B., 'Industrial Archaeology in Northamptonshire', unpublished report for Northamptonshire Heritage, 1998, Northampton.

Trinder, B., *The Industrial Archaeology of Shropshire* (Chichester, third edition, 1998).

Trinder, B., 'Industrialising towns, 1700–1840', in P. Clark (ed.), *The Cambridge Urban History of Britain*, vol. 2: *1540–1840* (Cambridge, 2000).

Trinder, B. and Cox, J. (eds), *Yeomen and Colliers in Telford* (Chichester, 1980).

Turnbull, G., 'Canals, coal and regional growth during the industrial revolution', *Economic History Review*, 40 (1987), 537–60.

Turnbull, G., *Traffic and Transport: An Economic History of Pickfords* (London, 1979).

Universal British Directory of Trade, Commerce and Manufacture, vols 2–5 (London, 1794–98).

Unwin, G., *Industrial Organisation in the Sixteenth and Seventeenth Centuries* (Oxford, 1904).

Upton, C., *A History of Wolverhampton* (Chichester, 1998).

Ure, A., *The Philosophy of Manufactures* (1835, reprinted London, 1967).

Van der Wee, H., 'Industrial dynamics and the process of urbanization and de-urbanization in the Low Countries', in H. van der Wee (ed.), *The Rise and Decline of Urban Industries in Italy and in the Low Countries* (Leuven, 1988).

Van der Wee, H. (ed.), *The Rise and Decline of Urban Industries in Italy and in the Low Coutries* (Leuven, 1988).

Van der Wee, H., 'The industrial revolution in Belgium', in M. Teich and R. Porter (eds), *The Industrial Revolution in National Context: Europe and the USA* (Cambridge, 1996).

Van der Wee, H., 'The west European woollen industries 1500–1750', in D. Jenkins (ed.) *The Cambridge History of Western Textiles* (Cambridge, 2004).

Van Neck, A., *Les débuts de la machine à vapeur dans l'industrie belge, 1800–1850* (Brussels, 1979).

Van Uytven, R., 'Brabantse en Antwerpse centrale plaatsen (14de–19de eeuw)', in R. Van Uytven, *Het stedelijk netwerk in België in historisch perspectief* (Brussels, 1992).

Vardi, L., *The Land and the Loom: Peasants and Profits in Northern France, 1680–1800* (Durham, 1993).

Varley, D. E., 'John Heathcoat (1783–1861): founder of the machine-made lace industry', *Textile History*, 1 (1968), 2–45.

Veraghtert, K., 'De Antwerpse bankwereld en de expansie van de haven, 1820–1850', in *Bank en Financiewezen*, 8(9) (1980), 191–203.

Veraghtert, K., 'From inland port to international port, 1790–1914', in F. Suyckens and G. Asaert (eds), *Antwerp: A Port for All Seasons* (Antwerp, 1986).

Vickery, A., 'Golden age of separate spheres? A review of the categories and chronology of English women's history', *Historical Journal*, 36(2) (1993), 383–414.

Vickery, A., *The Gentleman's Daughter: Women's Lives in Georgian England* (London, 1998).

Victoria County History of Worcestershire, 4 vols (London, 1901–26).

Victoria County History of Warwickshire, 12 vols (London, 1904–69).

Victoria County History of Leicestershire, 5 vols (London, 1907–64)

Victoria County History of Staffordshire, 14 vols (London, 1908–96).

Victoria County History of Shropshire, 7 vols (London, 1909–89).

Walsh, C., 'The newness of the department store: a view from the eighteenth century', in G. Crossick and S. Jaumain (eds), *Cathedrals of Consumption: The European Department Store, 1850–1939* (Aldershot, 1999).

Walters, J. D., 'The evangelical embrace: relations between Anglicans and Dissenters in the period 1830–1870', *West Midlands Studies*, 14 (1981), 32–8.

Walton, J. R., 'Trades and professions in late eighteenth-century England: assessing the evidence of directories', *Local Historian*, 17 (1987), 343–50.

Wanklyn, M., 'The impact of water transport facilities in the economies of English river ports, c. 1660–c. 1760', *Economic History Review*, 49 (1996), 20–34.

Wanklyn, M., 'Urban and industrial change', in J. Stobart and P. Lane (eds), *Urban and Industrial Change in the Midlands 1700–1840* (Leicester, 2000).

Ward, J., *The Borough of Stoke-upon-Trent* (London, 1843).

Weatherill, L., *Pottery Trade in North Staffordshire, 1660–1760* (Manchester, 1971).

Weatherill, L., 'The growth of the pottery industry in England 1660–1815', *Post-Medieval Archaeology*, 17 (1983), 15–46.

Weatherill, L., 'The business of middlemen in the English pottery trade before 1780', in R. Davenport-Hines and J. Liebenau (eds), *Business in the Age of Reason* (London, 1987).

Weatherill, L., *Consumer Behaviour and Material Culture in Britain 1660–1760* (London, second edition, 1996).

Weber, A. F., *The Growth of Cities in the Nineteenth Century: A Study in Statistics* (1899, reprinted New York, 1963).

Wells, F. A., *The British Hosiery and Knitwear Industry: Its History and Organisation* (Newton Abbot, second edition, 1972).

West, W., *Picturesque Views and Descriptions of Cities, Towers, Castles, Mansions in Staffordshire and Shropshire* (Birmingham, 1830).

Whatley, S., *England's Gazetteer* (London, 1751).

Whipt, R., *Patterns of Labour: Work and Social Change* (London, 1990).

White, A., *A History of Loughborough Endowed Schools* (Loughborough, 1969).

White, A. (ed.), *A History of Lancaster 1193–1993* (Keele, 1993).

White, W., *History, Gazetteer and Directory of Staffordshire* (Sheffield, 1832, 1834, 1851).

White, W., *Directory of Leicester and Rutland* (Sheffield, 1846).

White, W., *Directory of Nottinghamshire* (Sheffield, 1853).

White, W., *All Round the Wrekin* (London, 1860).

Whitehead, R., *Buckles: 1250–1800* (Chelmsford, 1996).

Wilde, P., 'The use of business directories in comparing the industrial structure of towns: an example of the south-west Pennines', *Local Historian*, 12 (1976), 152–6.

Willan, T. S., *The Inland Trade: Studies in English Internal Trade in the Sixteenth and Seventeenth Centuries* (Manchester, 1976).

Wilson, R., *Gentlemen Merchants: The Merchant Community in Leeds, 1700–1830* (Manchester, 1971).

Wiskin, C., 'Women, finance and credit in England, c. 1780–1826', unpublished PhD thesis, University of Warwick, 2000.

Wiskin, C., 'Urban businesswomen in eighteenth-century England', in R. Sweet and P. Lane (eds), *Women and Urban Life in Eighteenth-Century England* (Aldershot, 2003).

Worpell, J. G., 'The iron and coal trades of the south Staffordshire area 1843–1853', *West Midlands Studies*, 9 (1977), 34–48.

Wright, G. H., *Chronicles of the Birmingham Chamber of Commerce 1813–1913* (Birmingham, 1913).

Wright, N. R., *Lincolnshire Towns and Industry 1700–1914* (Lincoln, 1982).

Wrigley, E. A., 'The supply of raw materials in the industrial revolution', *Economic History Review*, 15 (1962), 1–16.

Wrigley, E. A., 'A simple model of London's importance in changing English society and economy, 1650–1750', *Past and Present*, 37 (1967), 44–70.

Wrigley, E. A., 'Parasite or stimulus: the town in a pre-industrial economy', in P. Adams and E. A. Wrigley (eds), *Towns in Societies* (Cambridge, 1978).

Wrigley, E. A., *Continuity, Chance and Change* (Cambridge, 1987).

Wrigley, E. A., 'Urban growth and agricultural change', in P. Borsay (ed.), *The Eighteenth-Century Town, 1688–1820* (London, 1990).

Young, A., *A Six Months Tour through the North of England*, 3 vols (London, 1771).

Young, A., *Tours in England and Wales* (1784–98, reprinted London, 1996).

Index

ab initio (new) towns 5, 12, 34, 121–33,
 147, 230
agriculture 82, 163, 188, 193
 link with industrialisation 23, 38, 165,
  166, 188, 195–6, 212, 231
Alfreton 153
Alt, Mary (post mistress) 75, 82
Alcester 50–1, 53
Antwerp 212, 213, 214, 219–21, 223
Arkwright, Richard 149, 150
Ashby de la Zouch 31, 75, 84–5, 91, 163
Atherstone 84–5, 90

Banbury 104, 106, 107–8
banks 75, 105–6, 126, 138, 165, 183, 217,
 218, 220–1
Basford 156–7, 198
Belper 24, 152, 153, 155–8
Bewdley 50–1, 83, 195
Bilston 30, 32, 34–7 passim, 85–6, 201
Birmingham 4, 16, 66, 68, 75, 124, 127,
 132, 135–6, 218, 238, 243
 metal working industries 30, 32, 37–8,
  72, 116, 129, 195, 199–200
 population growth 199, 201
 retail trades 45, 49, 72, 73, 74
 transport services 82, 83–7, 89–91, 93,
  95, 99, 129
 women 64, 70, 73, 74
Birmingham Canal 82, 87, 111, 123, 129
Black Country 44, 132, 134, 136, 218,
 240
 coal mining 87, 103
 metal working industries 36, 37, 87,
  199, 201
 population growth 125, 199, 201
 transport services 82, 85, 87, 95

Bolsover 35, 36
booksellers 53, 55, 72, 94, 125
Borsay, P. 5–6, 42
Boulton, Matthew 72, 75, 194
Brabant 213–16, 222
brewing industry 32, 33, 108, 109–10,
 198–9
Bridgnorth 94, 104, 107, 130, 203
Bristol 86, 91–2, 194, 198, 203, 220
Brussels 212, 213, 218, 219–21, 223
buckle making 32, 35
Burslem 64–5, 223
 civic institutions 127, 129, 131–2
 elites 17, 126, 128–9, 131
 population growth 33, 124
 pottery and china production 33, 38,
  96–8, 122–3
 retail trades 45, 52, 125–7
 transport services 90–1, 95, 129–31
Burton-upon-Trent 32, 33, 94, 108,
 198–9
Buxton 46–7, 90

canals 75, 80, 96, 137, 197, 212
 industrial location 111, 123, 129–30,
  199, 219
 see also named canals
capital and credit 75–6, 99, 212, 213,
  217, 219–21, 230, 233, 235, 239–42
  passim
 see also banks
carpets 194–5, 203
carrier services 83–9, 106
central place hierarchy 7, 43, 58, 116,
  161, 164
ceramics see pottery and china industries
Charleroi 218–19, 221

Chester 130, 195
Chesterfield 84–5, 93, 98
Christaller, W. 7, 43, 58, 116, 161, 164, 230
clergy 105, 177–8
clothing industries 66, 68, 112–13, 116
  see also individual industries
coach services 89–94, 130
coal mining 103, 123, 193, 199, 210, 217–19
  see also mineral-based economy
comparative advantage 233–4, 237
consumer goods 72, 112–15, 116
  see also luxury and semi-luxury goods
consumption 6, 63, 72–7, 237
core and periphery 2, 16, 151, 239, 243
model of regional development 154, 232–3
Corfield, P. 23, 24
cotton industry 28, 29–30, 32, 33, 35, 203, 210, 214–15, 220
county towns 35, 45, 52, 55, 96, 147, 158
transport services 82, 89, 91, 94–5
  see also individual towns
Coventry 30, 32, 33, 34
  retail trades 49, 55, 70, 72, 74–5
  transport services 82, 90–1, 93
  women 64–5, 70
craft industries 26, 65, 103–4, 107–9, 211–12
Cresswell, Ann (bookseller) 13, 73–4
Cromford Canal 83

de-industrialisation 27, 35, 181, 182, 230, 234
demand 193–9, 215–16, 224
Derby 107, 109
  silk industry 30, 32, 33, 35, 112
  transport services 84–5, 87, 89–91, 93
Derby Canal 83, 112
divisions of labour
  gender 66–72
  spatial 80, 99, 103, 214–15
  see also urban system
domestic manufacturing 99, 112–15, 123, 131, 214–15, 219
  see also proto-industrialisation
drapers 53, 94, 105, 125, 126

dress making 28, 29, 66, 68, 107
Droitwich 50–1, 83, 198
Dudley 195, 201
  iron production/working 30, 32, 37, 123
  retail trades 49–50, 56, 85, 90–1

earthenware see pottery and china industries
East Retford 85, 90, 93–4, 152
elites 126–7, 140, 141, 142, 143, 239, 240
  role in industrialisation 16–17, 122, 128–9, 131, 161, 218, 223–4
  see also clergy; professional services
engineering 103, 109–11, 114, 115
entrepreneurial activity 75–6, 94, 149, 150, 173, 213, 218, 220, 223–4, 230, 232, 235, 240–1
Erewash Canal 83, 162, 165

factories 72, 112–15, 196–9, 211, 224, 230
  see also technological innovation
Felkin, William (framework knitter) 153, 154
Flanders 212, 213–16, 223
food and drink industries 28, 29, 65, 114–15
  see also individual trades
framework knitting see hosiery industry 30, 33, 148–53, 167–170
France 210, 212, 214, 231, 239, 241

Gainsborough 91–2
gentry see elites
Germany 210, 219, 222, 231, 239, 241
Ghent 213, 214–15, 218, 222, 223
glass making 124, 198, 218
Gloucester 87, 89
glove making 31, 32, 96, 197, 203
Grand Junction Canal 193
grocers 57, 105, 125, 126

Hanley 34, 124, 130
  pottery and china production 38
  retail trades 44, 45, 52, 127
hat making 35, 38

Hearth Tax 148
Heathcote, John 37, 149, 154, 166, 167
Hinckley 163
    hosiery industry 31, 32, 33, 163
hinterlands *see under* urban system
Holyhead Road 82, 127, 130
horse racing 148, 185
hosiery industry 30, 33, 37, 148–53, 158,
    167–70, 194, 217
    exports 204–6
    geography 31, 33, 37, 151, 204–6
    organisation of production 96, 112,
        151, 197, 232, 239
    see also individual towns
Hull 91–2, 98
    trade with Midlands 86, 89, 194, 198,
        203, 204

Ilkeston 154
improvement commissions 128, 135,
    140–2
    see also elites
industrial villages 153–8, 239
    see also individual villages
inns and hotels 69, 105, 128, 183
    links with carriers services 94, 130, 165
iron making 28, 29, 30, 32, 34–5, 37,
    103, 109–10, 136, 137, 199–200, 210,
    217–19, 233
ironmongers 107, 109, 110, 123
ironworking 28, 30, 32, 37–8, 70, 72,
    116, 123, 129, 134, 136–7, 195,
    199–201, 210, 217, 219
    see also under individual trades
Izon, John (iron founder) 123, 129

Kenrick, Archibald (iron founder) 123,
    129
Kettering 113–14
Kidderminster 31, 33, 49–51, 83, 109,
    194–5, 199, 203

labour supply 212, 215, 224, 230, 231,
    234, 236–42 *passim*
lace making 37, 38, 149, 150, 151, 203–6,
    241
    geography 37, 38
    organisation of production 38, 68, 112

Lancashire 2, 235, 240
Langton, J. 5, 10, 23, 102, 115, 233
layers of investment 2, 104, 234
Leamington Spa 87, 90–1, 105, 110
leather industries 66, 94, 181–3
Leeds 4, 8, 86, 91–2, 98, 104
Leek 30, 32, 203
Leicester 115, 223
    hosiery industry 31, 33, 35, 72, 96,
        167, 204
    retail trades 45
    transport services 83–5, 87, 89–91,
        93
    leisure 5, 17, 73, 177, 185
Lepetit, B. 4, 230
libraries 6, 73, 74, 127
Lichfield 109, 236
    civic institutions 177, 178, 185, 186
    elites 177–8, 185–6
    de-industrialisation 180–3
    hinterland 6, 186–7
    population growth 176, 185–6
    retail trades 183
    transport services 86, 176, 178–80,
        183, 187
    women 64–5, 68, 75, 184–5
Liège 216–18
linen industry 112, 203, 215
Liverpool 4, 8, 36, 92, 129, 220
    trade with Midlands 86–9 *passim*, 98,
        198
London 65, 82–3, 91–3, 130
    trade with Midlands 73, 86, 87–9, 98,
        113, 122, 198, 199, 203
Loughborough 8, 104, 223, 236, 239
    civic institutions 17, 172
    elites 17, 162, 165, 169, 170–1
    hinterland 163–4
    hosiery industry 31, 37, 162, 165–7
    population growth 162
    transport services 84–5, 92–3, 95,
        163–4, 165, 168–70
    women 64–5
luddites 167
Ludlow 31, 35, 49, 83, 104, 106, 107,
    198
luxury and semi-luxury goods 73–4, 77,
    94, 95, 123

malting 104, 108, 164
Manchester 4, 83, 86, 90, 92, 98, 110, 126, 139, 238
Mansfield 30, 32, 33, 84–5, 90, 104, 154
manufacturing – definition 26, 29, 30, 104
Market Harborough 38, 52, 84–5, 93, 113, 116
Melton Mowbray 47, 83–5, 115
Mendels, F. 231–2
metalworking *see* ironworking
micro-history 2, 234, 238–9
mineral-based economy 4, 82, 96
Much Wenlock 27, 28

nail making 123, 198, 200, 201, 218
new institutionalist economics 8, 98
Newark 83–5, 90–4 *passim*, 104, 108, 152
Newcastle-under-Lyme 31, 34, 35, 38, 45, 46, 83, 90, 92–5, 124, 127, 130
Noble, M. 10, 16
North America *see* United States
Northampton 113–14
Nottingham 148, 223, 240, 243
    hinterland 151–5
    hosiery industry 30, 72, 96, 148–51, 167, 205, 236
    lace industry 33, 37, 38, 68, 72, 149–51
    industrial suburbs 155–8
    population growth 148, 157
    retail trades 45, 49, 98
    transport services 84–5, 87, 89–91, 93
    women 64–5, 70, 72
Nuneaton 30

Oakham 85, 89
occupational classification 26, 180
organic economy 4, 69, 240
Oxford Canal 103, 106, 193

personal and social networks 7–8, 16–17, 63, 98, 164–71 *passim* 243
Pfister, U. 234–6
Pollard, S. 36, 213, 233–4, 237–8, 239, 242
Poor Law Unions 130–1

population growth
    and industrialisation 102–3, 114, 124–5, 194, 198–9, 201, 205–6, 216, 217, 221–3
    see also individual towns
Potteries 33, 34, 37, 38, 44, 83, 87, 103, 130, 195, 203
    see also individual towns
pottery and china industries 72, 96–8, 122–3, 194, 197, 202–3, 241
    see also individual towns
professional services 46, 105–6, 125–6
    see also elites
proto-industrialisation 1, 2, 3, 131,155, 215, 230–2, 234–5, 237, 240
    see also domestic manufacturing

Radford 155–7, 198
railways 132, 137, 168, 169, 179, 180, 195, 217, 219
regions 2, 8–11, 102–3, 193, 228–9, 238
    development models 36, 229–37
    industrial typologies 239–42
religion 105, 127, 142, 143
retailing 164
    growth 48–58, 72–4, 125–6
    hierarchies 46, 51–2
    and industrialisation 43–5, 52, 55–8, 243
    see also individual trades
roads *see* turnpikes
Rollason, Mary (china seller) 73, 74
Rugby 93, 107
Rugeley 31, 35
rural industrialisation *see* proto-industrialisation

schools 68, 107
Severn (river) 87, 94, 98, 193, 194, 199–200
Seward, Anna 75, 186
Sheffield 92, 98, 116, 198, 200
shoemaking 48, 96, 107, 113–14, 116
Shop Tax 49–50, 164, 183, 184
shops
    geography 49–52, 107, 132
    specialisation 48, 53–4, 56, 105, 113
    see also individual trades; retailing

Shrewsbury 94, 104, 198
  manufacturing 103, 109, 111, 115, 203
  services 105, 107
  transport services 82, 83–5, 89–91, 130
silk industry 28, 29, 30, 32, 34, 35, 37,
  203
Simmons, J. 7, 81, 86–7, 95
Snooks, D. 23, 28, 36
Soar Navigation 162–5, 168
Southwell 46–7, 85, 93
Stafford 89, 96, 104, 114
stage coaches see coach services
stocking knitting see hosiery industry
Stourbridge 30, 32, 37, 50–1, 55, 83, 87,
  90, 123, 194
Stourport 130, 195
Stratford upon Avon 27, 28, 47, 50–1
Strutt, Jedediah 149, 158, 203

technological innovation 71–2, 112, 218,
  223–4, 238, 241
  and factories 212, 214–15, 216
  role in industrialisation 196–7, 199,
    216–17
Tenbury 50–1, 83
theatres 6, 42, 47, 105
thoroughfare towns 91–4
town halls 126, 127, 129
toy making 72, 200
trade directories (as a source) 23–6, 43,
  63, 102, 104
transaction costs 234–5, 240, 241
transport 147, 162, 168, 169, 176, 178,
  179, 180, 187
  and industrial development 4, 16,
    80–3, 87–8, 94–8, 134, 137, 195,
    233, 235–6, 240
  and spatial integration 16, 81–3, 91,
    95–7, 223, 243
  see also individual modes
Trent and Mersey Canal 82, 122, 129,
  193
Trent (river) 83, 87, 98, 194, 199
Tunstall 34, 124, 127
turnpikes 80, 106, 179, 187
  geography 81–3, 86,
  and industrial development 122–3,
    130

United States 114–15, 116, 199, 200, 202,
  205
Uppingham 27, 28, 84–5, 107
urban identity 143, 144
urban hierarchy 4, 47, 38, 222–3
urban institutions 105, 106, 127–8, 129,
  131–2
urban system 7, 9–10, 147, 224, 230
  hinterlands 46, 58, 81, 95, 130–1, 134,
    147, 168, 186, 187, 220
  industrial specialisation model 7, 81,
    86–7, 95, 99
  staple export model 81, 86, 95, 99

Verviers 216–18, 222, 223, 224

Walsall 34, 201
  metal working industries 30, 32,
    37
  transport services 85–6, 90, 130
war – impact on trade and industry
    137, 201, 202, 213
Warwick 49, 64–5, 84–5, 89–91, 93
watch and clock making 29, 30, 32
Weaver (river) 122, 194
Wedgwood, John (pottery manufacturer)
    8, 82, 96–8, 122, 128, 129
Wedgwood, Josiah 36, 72, 82, 194, 196,
    202
Wednesbury 32, 37, 45, 52, 55, 85–6, 90,
    201
West Bromwich 103, 218, 223, 238
  civic institutions 106, 127–8, 131–2
  elites 128–9, 131, 240
  metal working 111, 123–4
  population growth 124–5
  transport services 85–6, 95, 129–30
Wolverhampton 5, 8, 34, 64–5, 223
  civic institutions 142–3
  elites 17, 135, 140–3
  iron production 30, 32
  metal working 30, 32, 35, 37, 38, 134,
    136–7
  population growth 134, 135, 138–40,
    201
  retail trades 45, 55, 56, 72, 73
  transport services 82, 84–7, 89–91, 93,
    95, 99, 137

wool and worsted industry 30, 31, 33, 38, 216
Worcester 47
  manufacturing 32, 35, 96, 112, 115–16, 197, 203
  retail trades 49–51
  transport services 82, 84–5, 87–9, 90–1, 93
  women 64–5, 66

women
  consumers 72–7
  and the domestic sphere 66–9, 70–1, 73
  employment 64–6, 71–2, 116
workshops 116, 224, 230, 241
Wrigley, E. A. 3–5, 96

Yorkshire 2, 217, 235, 237, 238, 240